CROWNS

AND

TRENCHCOATS

A RUSSIAN PRINCE IN THE CIA

An Autobiography

DAVID CHAVCHAVADZE

ATLANTIC INTERNATIONAL PUBLICATIONS

ISBN 0-938311-10-7
Library of Congress # 89-080694

Editor: G. Nicholas Tantzos

For Information:

Atlantic International Publications
701 Seventh Avenue, Suite 9W
New York, New York 10036
Tel. (212) 757-6300

Published in the United States of America

THE CHAVCHAVADZES OF TSINANDALI
(simplified)

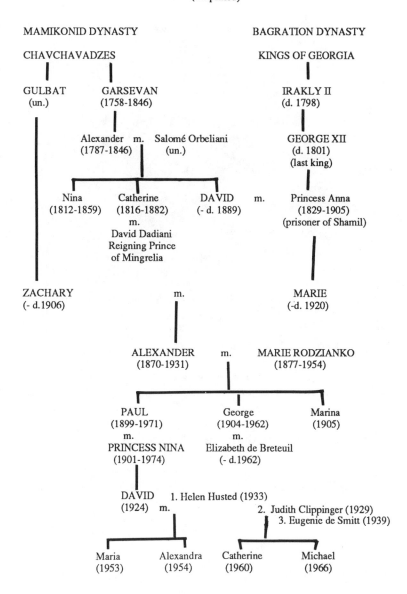

MAMIKONID DYNASTY

CHAVCHAVADZES

GULBAT (un.)   GARSEVAN (1758-1846)

Alexander m. Salomé Orbeliani
(1787-1846)   (un.)

Nina   Catherine   DAVID   m.
(1812-1859)   (1816-1882)   (- d. 1889)
                m.
                David Dadiani
                Reigning Prince
                of Mingrelia

ZACHARY   m.
(- d.1906)

ALEXANDER   m.
(1870-1931)

PAUL   George   Marina
(1899-1971)   (1904-1962)   (1905)
m.   m.
PRINCESS NINA   Elizabeth de Breteuil
(1901-1974)   (- d.1962)

DAVID   1. Helen Husted (1933)
(1924)   m.
                       2. Judith Clippinger (1929)
                       3. Eugenie de Smitt (1939)

Maria   Alexandra   Catherine   Michael
(1953)   (1954)   (1960)   (1966)

BAGRATION DYNASTY

KINGS OF GEORGIA

IRAKLY II
(d. 1798)

GEORGE XII
(d. 1801)
(last king)

Princess Anna
(1829-1905)
(prisoner of Shamil)

MARIE
(-d. 1920)

MARIE RODZIANKO
(1877-1954)

SHAMIL
Drawing by Princess Anna

CHAPTER I

Most of my adult life has been spent in the service of the government of the United States. First in the army during World War II, then for twenty-five years as a Central Intelligence Agency officer.

My decision to move my life in this direction was partially come about accidentally, the force of chance and fate; it was also a deep desire to serve my adoptive country, and to 'do something' about the dangers of international communism. Some may speculate that my unique background, a Georgian Prince, and Romanov relation, may have influenced my choice of a career. Perhaps it did. Perhaps the few blows I have been able to strike against communism was getting a little back for what was done to my family. . . . and to the peoples of Russia. Perhaps—but the reader can judge that for himself.

Who am I? Prince David Chavchavadze. Chavchavadze is a Georgian name, which first came into use around 1500, with other names used earlier. On my mother's side, Princess Nina of Russia, I am descended from Emperor Nicholas I and Catherine the Great of Russia, Kings George II of England, Christian IX of Denmark and George I of Greece. On my father's side, Prince Paul, I am a direct descendant of the last King of Georgia, George XII.

So many times in my life Americans have drawn a complete blank over the pronunciation of my name, even the thinning ranks of those who have been taught to read by individual letters instead of by sight. "What kind of name is that?" they ask.

My father occasionally solved this problem by answering, "American Indian," which usually made the name easier to pronounce for Americans. When I use this ploy, I add that I am a Cherokee from Georgia, employed by the Bureau of Indian Affairs!

But when I am not feeling that puckish, I will say it is a Georgian name. Brows furrow, and people will say, "No, I mean what country is it from?" Then I have to explain that it is not the Georgia next to Alabama, but the one next to Armenia. It used to be easier when people still actively remembered Stalin. "Ah, yes, Stalin was a Georgian, wasn't he?" I always had to fight down a stab of gratitude toward the old tyrant. But even for the few Americans who know about it at all, Georgia is merely a 'state' in the USSR. Once even a colonel belonging to the elite operations group in the Pentagon refused to believe that the Georgians are not Slavs.

Even the name *Georgia* causes confusion. It was probably invented by a foreigner who noticed the large number of icons of St. George in the country. The Russians call it *Gruzia*, the Turks *Gurdjestan*, and the Georgians themselves say *Sakartvelo*. They also say *mama* for father, and *deda* for mother. Their language is totally unrelated to Russian, Slavic, Indo-European, Finno-Ugric, Semitic or Turkic languages. It is a language pocket all by itself, like Basque in Spain and France. In fact, there is a theory that these two peoples were related in ancient times, in a migration from the Caucasus westward. Legends to this effect exist among both peoples, and ancient Georgia was called Iberia, as was ancient Spain.

Recorded Georgian history is far older than that of Russia, going back to Roman times. It was the place to which Jason and his Argonauts went in quest of the golden fleece, and it was to a Caucasian mountainside that Prometheus was chained. Its royal dynasty of Bagration ruled longer than any other on record, except that of Japan. Georgia became Christian in the 4th century, 500 years before any Russian state came into being, and 600 years before Kiev's Grand Prince Vladimir (980-1015), decreed that his people would enter the Dnieper River and be baptized into the Orthodox Christian faith; it stayed a Christian island in a Moslem sea and kept its language in spite of frequent invasions by Arabs, Mongols, Persians and Turks.

Georgia had its last moments of greatness in the 12th century under King David II and his daughter, Tamara. Ghengis Khan's 20,000 horsemen, on their way to Russia, put an end to this glory. Eventually, Georgia began to look to its fellow Orthodox Tsar in Moscow for protection, beginning in the reign of Boris Godunov, but it was almost 200 years before Russia was able to offer protection, which was followed by annexation.

This embattled land was the home of the princely family of Chavchavadze, a branch of the Mamikonid Dynasty, traceable in the male line to the 4th century A.D., and by tradition to an ancestor called Manceus, who defended an Armenian fortress against the Romans in 69 B.C.

Snide remarks have often been made to the effect that anybody with a few goats could be a prince in Georgia. While some princes may have been down to a few goats, or no goats at all, they were not considered less princely for that. My father's family had a coachman who was a real prince whose family had become impoverished. Blood, not wealth, counted. All Georgian princes (and all Russian princes before Peter the Great) were descended from some dynasty or other. There were a lot of Georgian princely families, because one of the many tragedies in Georgian history was the fact that the Georgian kings were seldom able to control the feudal dynasts who ruled in various parts of the country. When Georgia was incorporated into the Russian Empire, some twenty families, including my own, had their titles confirmed as co-equal to Russian princes, none of whom predated the 9th century!

Ironically, the most famous Georgian princes in the United States were the 'Marrying Mdivanis,' who were not real princes at all, and gave the lot of us a bad name. Their father used to say, "My sons are princes but I'm not!" I trust the old gentleman benefited from the money from Barbara Hutton and the others his sons married. He deserved it.

While our fellow Christian neighbors, the Armenians, are well known throughout the world, having emigrated and established colonies for centuries, until the recent emigration of about 30,000 Georgian Jews, there were only 3,000 Georgians outside of the USSR. Most of these lived in Paris, and perhaps 300 in the United States, and only about ten in Washington, D.C., where I live. Most are employed by the Voice of America.

By the 18th century, my line of Chavchavadzes were established in the

6

eastern Georgian province of Kakhetia, a wine producing region, on an estate called Tsinandali, not far from Kakhetia's capital of Telavi.

My great-great-great-great-grandfather, Garsevan Chavchavadze, was an important official at the court of the last great Georgian king, Irakly (Hercules) II, and was sent as his ambassador to the court of Catherine the Great. The king was desperate for Russian protection against the Persians, and Garsevan negotiated a treaty with the Russians under the terms of which the Georgian king became a vassal of the Russian empress in return for this protection. This was in 1783. In 1983 the Soviets made a big thing of this anniversary, omitting to mention that Georgia became independent after the 1917 revolution, and was conquered by the Red Army under Dzhugashvili-Stalin in 1921, in violation of treaties.

Nationalist dissidents demonstrated in 1983, calling the 1783 treaty a sell-out. It wasn't, because Russian help was desperately needed. However, in 1795, when the Persian Shah totally sacked the Georgian capital, there were no Russian troops on hand to help. They did not take the field until the following year, and in 1801, when Irakly II's son, George XII died—the last of the Bagration kings—the Georgian monarchy was abolished and Georgia made part of the Russian Empire. My father always told me that this was the will of King George XII, perhaps because he had so many unruly sons and uncles. So there was never a military conquest of Georgia by Imperial Russia. Even a Georgian nationalist admitted to me that survival outside of Russia had become impossible by 1801, there being only about 100,000 Georgians left.

Pondering the 1983 anniversary, it suddenly occurred to me that I was the only person descended in equal degree from all three of the leading figures of 1783—Garsevan Chavchavadze, Catherine the Great and King Irakly II! They would have been amazed, I'm sure, to have a descendant in common.

In 1956 Marvin Kalb wrote that the most famous families in Soviet Georgia were the Dzhugashvilis (Stalin) and the Chavchavadzes. In the old Georgian pecking order, there were a number of families ranking above the Chavchavadzes, but under the Soviets the others were ignored or down-played, while the Chavchavadzes were written about, and the wine of Tsinandali was famous. We owed this publicity to Ilya Chavchavadze, a writer from another branch of the family for whom a long boulevard in Tbilisi is named, and to Garsevan's son, Alexander, and the latter's daughters. In 1987 Ilya Chavchavadze, who died in 1907, was actually canonized by the Soviet controlled Georgian Orthodox Church!

Alexander was born in St. Petersburg in 1787, during Garsevan's ambassadorship, and Catherine the Great was his godmother. He grew up tri-lingual in Georgian, Russian and French. He served as a Russian officer during the Napoleonic wars and became a general in 1829 for having taken the famous Turkish fortress of Bayazet. But his fame now rests on the fact that he was the leading Georgian poet of his day, and the central figure of Georgian culture.

He was also in close touch with the Russian literary lights of his time, most of them tied in spirit if not in fact to the Decembrist uprising of 1825. The poet Lermontov came to Tsinandali, and the poet Griboyedov was a great friend. Alexander was exiled twice to Tambov in European Russia, once as a suspected supporter of an uprising by some of the Georgian royal princes. Actually, he thought this sort of thing was doomed. The second exile, which also did not last long, was for his liberal pro-Decembrist connections.

Nowadays he is remembered as much for his daughters as for his role in bringing Georgian and Russian culture together. His wife was born Princess Salomé Orbeliani. This family, though not rulers of an independent principality, were sort of Georgian Dukes of Norfolk, the senior peer in England, and so prominent in Georgian history that a medieval king ordered all the Orbeliani males castrated. However, the royal castrator evidently did not do a thorough job, because the Orbelianis kept turning up in later generations, back in their prominent role. They claimed descent from an emperor of China, and considered themselves to be the oldest family in Europe, the Caucasus being included in Europe on old maps. Salomé and Alexander had three children: Nina, David and Catherine. Nina, at the age of sixteen, married her father's friend, Griboyedov, who was thirty. Even though he had written a very liberal book called *Gore ot Uma* (*Woe from Wit*), which was banned by the censors, Nicholas I appointed him Russian minister to Tehran, and he departed for this post in 1828 shortly after his marriage, fortunately leaving his young wife behind. She was widowed before having any children.

According to a treaty, Russia had the rights of protectorate over Christians in Persia, and a number of Armenian and Georgian harem inmates (including a eunuch) took refuge in the Russian legation. The ayatollahs stirred up crowd indignation and the Legation, defended by a troop of Cossacks, was attacked, sacked, and everybody in it massacred, including Griboyedov. This incident was discovered by some American newspapers several weeks after the taking of the U. S. diplomatic hostages by Khomeini's minions in 1979. Perhaps someone should have studied history a little earlier!

Griboyedov's body was shipped home by the Persian shah, horrified that Nicholas I might make war on him again, and I believe he gave the emperor a priceless diamond as part of the apology. But Nicholas I had a war with Turkey on his hands and did not avenge the sacking of his Legation. Griboyedov's teenage widow, Nina, always stayed true to the memory of her husband, and I doubt if there is a young girl in the Soviet Union who does not know this story. They are buried together in a crypt on the Holy Mountain in Tbilisi, which is still pointed out as a tourist attraction today.

Nina's sister, Catherine, achieved fame in a totally different way. She was married to David Dadiani, the ruling prince of Mingrelia, a part of western Georgia not yet annexed by Russia. After his early death, acting as regent for their son, she personally led the Mingrelian forces against the Turks. While Nina was meek, but full of common sense, Catherine was full of courage, but not attuned to reality. Mingrelia was finished as an independent principality. It was annexed to Russia in 1857, and Catherine left for France, never conceding the loss of her son's throne to the Russian crown. There, her daughter married the grandson of Napoleon's Marshal Murat, one-time King of Naples, and produced for us some unexpected French relatives.

Alexander Chavchavadze did not live to see the drama of Mingrelia or Nina's death. In 1846, at the age of fifty-nine, he was killed in an accident. On the steep street in Tbilisi where he lived (now named after him), the horses of his carriage were spooked and bolted. He tried to help the coachman hold them and was thrown under the wheels.

Alexander's son, David, my great-great grandfather, married Anna, a granddaughter of Georgia's last king of the Bagration Dynasty, George XII. In 1854 she was at the height of her beauty, tall, dark, extremely well formed in spite of having borne six children, but very reserved in manner.

That summer the family's usual departure for Tsinandali to get away from the oppressive heat of Tbilisi was delayed by rumors of impending raids on Kakhetia by Shamil's warriors. During the eastward spread of the Russian Empire, the most serious resistance by far was put up by the Moslem mountaineers of the North Caucasus. They spoke a baffling variety of languages, but united to fight the Russians for thirty years in the 19th century. Each *aoul* had to be taken by storm, one by one, with fearful losses. Their leader was Shamil, Imam of Chechnya and Dagestan, a charismatic, noble figure who still inspires loyalty among the descendants of his peoples, and was much respected by the Russians who fought him. Until 1934 the Soviets called Shamil a heroic fighter against tsarist oppression. After that, the official line became that he was an agent of Anglo-French-Turkish imperialism.

To the Christian Georgians of Shamil's time, his mountaineers were age-old Moslem enemies and the Georgians enthusiastically supported the Russian effort of conquest.

On assurance from the Russian commander, General Read, that everything was under control, Anna and her entourage set out on the hundred mile journey. With Anna were three of her daughters: Marie, Salomé, and the infant Lydia, her sister Varvara Orbeliani with a little son, numerous servants and even a French governess, Mme. Drancey, imported to instruct and tend little Marie and Salomé.

The great house in Tsinandali was a semi-circular, three-story building with a columned portico. When the family convoy of carriages and carts reached it, it contained a total of twenty-one women and six children. Anna's husband, David, was about twenty miles away in command of a body of troops.

Things here did not seem as safe as they had to General Read. The Tsinandali villagers sensed trouble and prepared to flee. Though the Alazan River was high, a raiding party from the mountains could easily find a ford where they could swim across. Evading the Russian troops would not be hard, particularly at night.

Anna decided it was too dangerous to stay. The whole party could make it on foot to Telavi, where there was a Russian garrison, walking through deep woods impenetrable to horses. They would leave at dawn, it was decided. Too late! At first light Shamil's horsemen, probably of the Lesghin tribe, with hawk-like faces and turbans around their fur hats, wearing *cherkesskas* with daggers slung in front, surrounded the house and broke in. Seeing that they were dealing only with a score of terrified women they relaxed and began to ransack the house. Some appeared with ladies' bonnets over their turbans. But this was no chance raid. It had been scouted out, and the mountaineers knew they had valuable hostages who must be delivered alive to the Imam Shamil.

The women and children were forced to mount in back of the horsemen, their right hands tied to each man's belt. Anna held the baby in her left arm, and off they galloped to get back across the Alazan as quickly as possible. As the overloaded horses were swimming the river, five-year-old Marie, who, out of fatigue, had given up pummeling her captor with her left fist, was still alert enough to yell in French to her governess, "Madame, you are losing your skirts!" To her mid-Victorian horror, Mme. Drancey, tied to the back of what she called *un sauvage*, emerged from the river in chemise and corset.

Even the Victorian mind would admit this greater horror. Anna's left arm could no longer stand the strain, and the infant Lydia crashed to her death on the rocks.[1]

The abduction was much publicized in Europe, and a couple of years after the event, Alexandre Dumas came to see Anna in Tbilisi. He wanted to write a novel called *Les Princesses de Tsinandali*, but he was sent packing after a cup of tea. What an outrage to be featured in a French novel! What a pity, my father always said, we could have been on bookshelves next to *The Three Musketeers*!

The hostage operation ended successfully for Shamil. The prisoners spent almost ten months in his eyrie in the mountains, always well treated, and coming to respect their captor. More than a half-century later little Marie told her grandson, my father, that she could remember Shamil a bit. He had a long beard dyed henna and had dirty little caramels in his pocket, which he would feed to the captive children.

Princess Anna drew an impressive profile of the Imam, with his turban and long straight nose, which has been reproduced in several books. There was no question of rape at any point, if only because the mountaineers were convinced that the women's husbands would never pay ransom for damaged goods.

The Crimean War was in progress, and British and French agents arrived to try to coordinate Shamil's operations against the common Russian enemy. Shamil would have nothing to do with this. He was fighting his own *gazavat*, a holy war, and he could not understand that other war in which the Turkish Sultan was allied with two Christian monarchs (one in skirts, yet!) to fight the Christian Tsar.

For years Shamil's oldest son, Djemaleddin, had been held hostage in Russia, a personal ward of Emperor Nicholas I. Now he was grown up and actually commissioned in the Imperial Guards under the name of Cornet Djemaleddin Shamil. He could hardly remember his old life in the mountains. But now, in exchange for the Chavchavadze and Orbeliani hostages he was to go back to his father. This fine young man was one of the greatest tragedies of the whole affair. He was totally honorable, and destroyed by incompatible loyalties. He deeply disappointed the Imam when he said he could not bring himself to fight against the Russians he had been brought up among, and the Emperor who had been a foster father to him. Still, father and son made some sort of peace, and Djemaleddin became something like chief justice of the mountaineers' government. He died of tuberculosis, still very young, and much respected by both sides.

But Djemaleddin was not the only ransom. Shamil demanded a million

---

1.   *Souvenirs d'une Captive de Chamil.*

10

rubles in silver, a huge sum that he himself could not even visualize. Finally, a ransom was set in terms of so many cart loads of silver, which he could visualize. It was much less than a million, but it ruined the Chavchavadzes. The money was raised by ceding Tsinandali to the crown lands, but under a typical arrangement for the period, a member of the family continued to reside there and run the estate, and the family had first option to buy it back. This did not happen until shortly before World War I. Meanwhile, the imperial crown lands administration had started a winery there in 1885. Before that the family had only made wine for its own use.

Shamil finally surrendered to the Russians in 1859, and later died in Mecca. His people, according to the surrender treaty, were exempt from military service, but many of their descendants volunteered for service in World War I in a specially formed Caucasian cavalry division known colloquially as the *Wild Division*. Anna and David Chavchavadze's grandson, my grandfather, commanded the Circassian Regiment of this division. In World War II Shamil's people were expelled from their ancient *aouls* by Stalin for collaboration with the Germans, and indeed many had greeted the Germans as liberators and fought on their side, in contrast to World War I.

In 1856 David and his newly liberated wife Anna had built a long, rambling house (according to my father), and their gutsy little daughter, Marie, grew up in Tsinandali. Her parents wanted her to marry another Chavchavadze, actually the senior of the whole line, a man many years older than herself. Zakhary Chavchavadze had already made a brilliant career in the Imperial Russian Army. He lived in a house on the other side of the village of Tsinandali. Zakhary was the son of Gulbat Chavchavadze, famous throughout Kakhetia as *the Drinker*, whose fame is still alive. That is quite a title for Georgians to bestow!

In his early days Zakhary had been quite a drinker too, but once, after he had thrown his orderly out of the second story window, he called the man in the next morning and said to him in his heavy Georgian accent, "You are a fool. You don't think I did anything wrong to you. But I swear to you that I will never take another drink as long as I live!" He kept his word. Not only was he the only Georgian teetotaller I ever heard of, he was also something else totally un-Georgian—a tightwad! Years later, when his daughter was nominated to be a lady-in-waiting to the Empress of Russia, he sat with clenched teeth through a reading of the expenses for clothing this would entail. He finally drew the line at the shoes.

"If anybody lifts your skirts I'll kill them," he said, "and if they don't, you don't need special shoes!"

Marie did not want to marry Zakhary. The little dark-eyed girl who had hammered her fist on the back of one of Shamil's horsemen was not afraid to tell him so. She rode over to his house and stated quite simply that if they got married she would make his life miserable.

Nonetheless, the marriage took place. They produced a number of children and there is no record that she made him miserable. She came to love him. He died in 1906, one of the men honored to carry the canopy over the last emperor in the coronation of 1896, and one of the highest ranking generals in the army. There was a time when songs were sung about his conquest of Chechnya and Daghestan and his leap off a cliff into a river at the head of his troop, for which he got his first Cross of

11

St. George. Now he has been forgotten in Tsinandali, though a memory of his father, the Drinker, lingers on. Marie died in 1920 in Tsinandali, during Georgia's brief independence after the Revolution.

Their son, Alexander Chavchavadze, my grandfather, was born in 1870, the eldest son of this union of the old general and the young girl. He had blue eyes and a prominent, straight nose, very much like his great-grandfather and namesake. For reasons not clear to me, he did not speak much Georgian. Russians had always treated the Georgian aristocracy as equals, without any of the British type snobbism toward 'native' princes, and some of them had become Russified.

Like so many 19th century Chavchavadzes, my grandfather began his military career in the Nizhegorodsky Dragoon Regiment. It had been with the previous Alexander when he stormed the Turkish fortress of Bayazet, and one of its troops had followed Zakhary off the cliff into the river.

This was one of the several dragoon regiments founded by Peter the Great in 1702. Through the years it had come to be considered the senior cavalry regiment of the army. Four times it had been offered the honor of joining the Imperial Guards, and four times it had refused. Nicholas II was its last honorary colonel. In this connection an anecdote is recorded—A sergeant-major of the Nizhegorodsky argues with his opposite number of Her Majesty's Lancers of the Guards about whose regiment is the best. After going through a lot of regimental lore, the Nizhegorodsky dragoon wins the argument by pointing out, "One thing you can't deny, our honorary colonel screws your honorary colonel!"

My grandfather was the first of our branch of the Chavchavadzes to marry a Russian, Marie Rodzianko. In order to be in St. Petersburg with her, he transferred from the dragoons to His Majesty's Hussars of the Guard. They had three children: my father Paul, George—who at one time was a well-known concert pianist—and Marina, who has devoted her life to good works in England. They all grew up speaking Russian, English and French, but not Georgian!

When World War I broke out, my grandfather was given command of the Circassian Regiment of the newly formed *Wild* Caucasian Cavalry Division. There were six regiments of volunteers, each representing one of the mountain peoples: the Circassians, Kabardins, Ingush, Chechen, Daghestanis, and the Tatars, the last being from what is now known as Azerbaidjan. For the most part the enlisted men could only speak to those in their own regiment. Russian was used as a *lingua franca*. They were all, of course, Moslems. Some of the officers were also Moslem, like the Guireys and Natirbovs in the Circassian Regiment, but others were Christian Georgians like my grandfather, and still others were Poles, Russians, and there was even a Russianized Italian marquis called degli Albizzi. This martial babel of tongues was commanded by the emperor's brother, Grand Duke Michael, which gave a great deal of chic to the whole enterprise.

The division had a brilliant war record, fighting on the Austrian front. After the February revolution of 1917, and the abdication of the emperor, most of the army began to disintegrate, although Kerensky tried to carry on the war, but the soldiers deserted en masse. Those who stayed had councils which could veto their officers' orders, not exactly an efficient way to run an army, but the Wild Division remained solid as a rock.

Two scenes from this period stand out in my mind. One was when the Circassian Regiment was ordered to take a village in Roumania, occupied by Hungarians, who by this time thought the Russians totally incapable of offensive action. My grandfather said to his officers, "Gentlemen, this may be the last page in the history of our regiment. So let us do it properly." He ordered the regimental band to play marches while the regiment charged on horseback, driving the Hungarians out. The Austrian high command must have scratched their heads in wonder at this nutty outfit which could still stage a cavalry attack with a band playing as if it were 1814.

The other scene involved the arrival of Alexander Kerensky at this part of the front, hoping to use his golden oratory to urge the soldiers to fight. A disorganized mob of 15,000 unruly, armed, and largely drunken troops, crowded into the main square of a Roumanian town to hear him. Who could possibly guarantee any security for Kerensky? My grandfather thought that the first troop, 100 men, of these wild Caucasians, in this case the Circassian Regiment, would do the trick, and it did. Under the command of Captain Sultan Kadir Guirey (who was later to start a fashionable riding school in New York, and whose sons were great friends of mine), these 100 perfectly disciplined mounted men in their Cherkesskas somehow cowed the huge mob into a semblance of order. Guirey rode alone through the crowd to report to Kerensky and then back again. Any one of that crowd could have blown his head off.

Later, the division took part in General Kornilov's attempted takeover of the Provisional Government, and still later, most of them fought with the Whites during the civil war and evacuated to Constantinople with General Wrangel in 1920. Some of the Circassians, under the leadership of the legendary Ulagai, became freebooters and were instrumental in putting King Zog on the throne of Albania.

My grandfather, however, left the division in 1917, and went to Georgia. He and my grandmother had been divorced, and he had personal reasons for going back to the country of his blood, whose language he did not speak. What he did not expect was an approach by a delegation of Khevsurs, during a congress of Trans-Caucasian peoples in Tbilisi. They wanted him to go up into their mountains and be their ruling prince. "It's a pity you don't speak Georgian," they said, "but we'll teach you."

The Khevsurs were a curious group of mountaineers who spoke a dialect of Georgian and practiced a religion which combined Christianity, Islam, and Judaism, giving them very long weekends indeed! Their entire economy was based on cattle and they lived in very primitive hovels made of cow dung. The most curious thing about the Khevsurs was that all the men were equipped with medieval chain mail and weapons, which they wore on their numerous feast days. There are theories that they were descended from a lost group of crusaders. More likely, perhaps, some of them had served the Byzantine Emperor in Constantinople and returned with their armor and weapons. There was a tradition among the Khevsurs that the Chavchavadzes, centuries ago and under another name, had been sovereign princes over them. My father remembered them coming to Tsinandali with voluntary tribute of cheese. Molly van Rensselaer Thayer, who wrote a column for the *Washington Star* for many years, actually visited the Khevsurs in their mountain retreat in the

13

1920s, and frequently told me that she was annoyed with my father because all that he could remember about them was that they smelled bad!

My grandfather turned down the Khevsurs' offer, not being able to envision life for himself Khevsur-style. I often wonder whether, if he had accepted, he would have had many more years of life hidden away in the mountains by his loyal subjects. As it happened, however, he was put in prison after the Bolshevik conquest of independent Georgia, and spent ten years in confinement. During this period, when his former wife and children were already in England, a message was somehow received that he could be bought out. The price was 100 pounds Sterling, at least $10,000 in today's money. The family could not come up with this money until Marina, at a posh ball in London, related the story to her dinner partner. This gentleman immediately fished out 100 pounds from his wallet and gave it to her. She danced the rest of the evening clutching the money—her father's life—in her hand.

But it didn't work. My grandfather was actually released and put on a train, but then re-arrested when he accepted a letter from some woman who begged him to mail it abroad. Possibly a staged provocation. In any case, in 1931, after ten years of prison, my grandfather was shot by the Bolsheviks. I was already seven years old then, and I can remember what consternation this news caused in the family. Thirty years later a Soviet colonel had the fairness to tell me that this was a raw deal. "If they had to shoot him," he said, "they should have done it before those ten years in prison."

My father, Paul Chavchavadze, the first of the family to have Russian blood, was born in St. Petersburg in 1899. Blue-eyed, as were most Chavchavadze men (until I came along), but also blond and totally lacking the Georgian features of his father and younger brother, George. By the time World War I broke out, when he was fifteen, my father had led a rather chopped-up existence, living in St. Petersburg, Tbilisi (while his father was aide to the governor-general) and from 1905 to 1910 mostly on the Adriatic Coast of what was then the Austro-Hungarian Empire, his parents having separated. They got together for a while after this, but later divorced. His education was an equally confused series of schools and tutors, which did not prevent him from acquiring a deep level of culture and knowledge. Totally unmilitary by nature, he aspired to be a writer and finally achieved a literary career, but not until after World War II, in the United States.

Not wanting to stay in St. Petersburg after her divorce, my grandmother jumped at an invitation for herself and the children to stay in Kishinev, in what is now known as Moldavia, and here my father finished his formal education by graduating from a *gimnazia*, equivalent to two or more years of college nowadays.

The Russian revolution broke out when my father was eighteen, actually saving him from army call-up, or more exactly from a quickie wartime officers' training school. Kishinev turned out to be a blessing in disguise. The Roumanians marched in and took Moldavia, eliminating the necessity for a dangerous escape like the ones other people had to endure.

My father visited Tsinandali only twice—once when he was six, for the funeral of old Zakhary, and again when he was eighteen. On that occasion he upheld the glory of his great-grandfather, Gulbat, by knocking down a horn containing two

14

quarts of the good wine of Tsinandali. If there had been no revolution my father would have inherited Tsinandali from his childless uncle, Maximilian, who had bought it back from the crown with his rich Moscow wife's money.

In 1918 my father spent several months in Tbilisi with his father, the only chance the two ever really had to know one another. They were very different—my grandfather was the officer who ordered that last attack on the Austro-Hungarians—my father was totally turned off from the military. My grandfather was a gourmet (probably one reason why he turned down sovereignty over the Khevsurs); my father did not care what he ate and could not describe it the next day. But he learned one lesson from his father, which he drilled into my head. "Of course you hate the Jews," he said to his father one night. At that time Jews and revolutionaries were equated in the minds of many people. He received an unexpected lecture.

"How can you hate a whole people? Do we hate the Chechens and Lesghins who sacked Tsinandali? Did I hate those magnificent Moslem Circassians whom I commanded? Do we hate the Russians who have done plenty of nasty things over the years? Do we hate the British and French for the Crimean War and Napoleon? And never forget that our lord Jesus Christ and every one of his apostles were Jewish!"

Father and son took leave of each other forever at the Tbilisi railroad station. It was not easy to ship my father off to Roumania to join his mother, George and Marina. It was arranged through the Germans, who were occupying part of Georgia and were operating a passenger ship from Poti to Odessa. It was not easy for my grandfather to approach Count Werner von der Schulenberg, because he had been the German consul in Tbilisi in 1914 and my grandfather had been sent to place him under arrest when the war started. But Schulenberg held no grudge and gladly arranged my father's passage. This same Schulenberg became German ambassador to Moscow and was there when the war started in 1941. He was involved in the unsuccessful conspiracy which culminated in the near assassination of Hitler in 1944, and had the conspirators managed to take power, Schulenburg was on their list to become foreign minister.

Before leaving Tbilisi, my father was blessed by his grandmother, Marie, the little captive of Shamil. They knew for sure they would never meet again.

PRINCESS MARIA CHAVCHAVADZE
Neé Rodzianko
Dressed for the famous 1903 Ball

MARIA RODZIANKO - 1880
Author's great-grandmother

MARIA (Babady) CHAVCHAVADZE
with Marina, George and Paul

PRINCE ALEXANDER CHAVCHAVADZE
(Author's grandfather) his sister Sophia, and children Paul, George and Marina

TSINANDALI

GEORGE XII
Last King of Georgia

STROGANOV - GOLITSIN - RODZIANKO

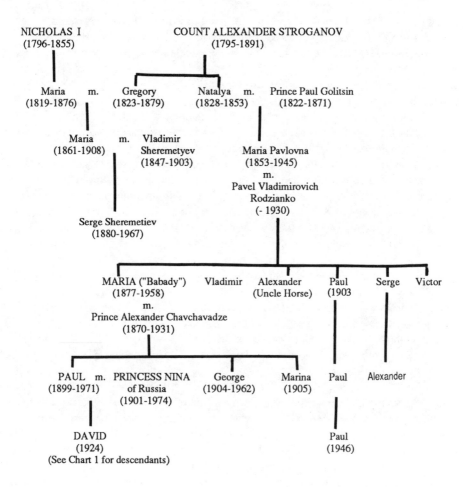

CHAPTER II

Through my grandmother Marie Rodzianko, there comes another historical Russian line—the famous Stroganovs.

Early in the 19th century four tall, strapping brothers called Rodzianko arrived in St. Petersburg from their native Ukraine, where they held land and where their forebears had been among those famed Zaporozhian Cossacks who once ruled the Ukraine and fought Pole and Turk and Crimean Tatar.

Perhaps due to their outstanding horsemanship, looks, and general athletic ability, it did not take the Rodzianko brothers long to be accepted at the top levels of St. Petersburg society, and they promptly began to make brilliant matches for themselves and to produce numerous descendants.

One of these, Pavel Vladimirovich, was to become my father's maternal grandfather. His brother, Michael Rodzianko achieved lasting historical fame as president of the Duma (Russia's parliament) during the crucial turning point of 1917. Statesmanship, however, was not Pavel Vladimirovich's cup of tea, or, more accurately, glass of champagne. Although he served in the guards and even became a general, Pavel Vladimirovich specialized in whooping it up with the Gypsies and playing elaborate practical jokes. He had considerable musical talent, and composed a march called *Casse Tout* (Break Everything!), which was played whenever he entered a Petersburg night club. At the sound of these stirring chords everybody in the know would hurl all the plates on their table to the floor, and the damage would be placed on Pavel Vladimirovich's check. All one had to do to follow him around town (as his wife frequently did) was to look for broken crockery in restaurants and night clubs.

This style of life required a great deal of money, and Pavel Vladimirovich did not really come into his own until he made a rich marriage to Princess Maria Pavlovna Golitsin, my great-grandmother, who, however, was already married to a gentleman called Khitrovo when they met.

Cute, rather than beautiful, in her youth, she had sparkling black eyes and so much personality that right up to the time she died in 1945, in her nineties, young men would travel to Lausanne, Switzerland, specially to see her. At one point, when she was thought to be dying, somebody gave her a spoonful of champagne. She opened her eyes, remarked, "Since when is champagne served in spoons?" and lived for several more years.

Maria also had a will of iron. When Pavel Vladimirovich met her not only was she married, but may have been pregnant, or soon became so. Falling head over heels in love with Pavel, she determined to shed her husband and created a scandal practically without precedent in the 1870s. She demanded a divorce from Khitrovo on the grounds that she was pregnant by Pavel Vladimirovich.

Her pregnancy was not in doubt, but who was the father? Had she really been naughty with Pavel? Whatever the case may have been, she obtained her divorce and quickly married Pavel, and produced a daughter who was christened Marie Rodzianko.

For many years the jilted Mr. Khitrovo begged my grandmother to acknowledge him as her father, offering to make her his sole heiress, and he was a very rich man. She kept refusing, pointing out that she really had to take her mother's word as to her paternity. Had she accepted it would have changed all of our lives, because Mr. Khitrovo had a fortune in Italy which he never withdrew to Russia during World War I. Instead of going to London penniless my grandmother would have taken her children to Italy. Would my parents ever have met; and would I have had to serve in Mussolini's army?

Maria's family, the Golitsins were a very prominent line of Russian princes, descended from the 14th century Lithuanian Grand Duke Gedimin. Like the Obolenskys and Trubetskoys, they had proliferated and there were several lines who were hardly related, except by inter-marriage. Maria Pavlovna's mother was a Stroganov. The Stroganovs were not as illustrious in ancestry as the Golitsins, but were much richer, and very prominent long before their name was attached to a culinary delight!

In the 16th century they were merchants who built a great fortune by mining salt in the Urals. They hired an army of Cossacks to conquer western Siberia, which they then presented to Ivan the Terrible. Ennobled for this, the Stroganovs were later made barons by Peter the Great, and counts by Catherine II. The Siberian coup was not the first service the family had rendered to the crown. One hundred years earlier they had paid the ransom of Grand Duke Vasili (the Blind) of Moscow, captured by the Tatars. In every reign, especially from Peter the Great on, at least one member of the family played an important role.

Maria Pavlovna's uncle, Count Grigory Stroganov, caused quite a stir by marrying one of the daughters of Emperor Nicholas I. This was the first instance of a Russian subject marrying into the Imperial Family since the days of Peter the Great, and Grigory's father never forgave him for such audacious behavior, but his strict father-in-law, the emperor, did not seem to object at all.

The Stroganov whose chef invented Beuf Stroganov (actually as a quickie dish for picnics) was Russian Ambassador in London during the reign of Queen Victoria. At one point he was joined by two other Russian emissaries—Longinov and Putyatin. This gave rise to the apocryphal story that these three gentlemen were once presented to the Queen as follows: "Your Majesty, the Russian ambassadors are here—Long-enough, Strong-enough and Put-it-in."

The Stroganovs continued to be immensely rich. When my great-grandmother, Maria Pavlovna, inherited one fifteenth of their fortune, she became one of the richest women in St. Petersburg.

Maria and her beloved Pavel Vladimirovich and their daughter lived at Furshtadskaya 10, in St. Petersburg, and in time five sons were born, all with unquestioned paternity.

The eldest, Vladimir, served in the navy, but quit in disgust after the defeats in the Russo-Japanese War. The second son, Alexander, became a general in World War I, and was second in command of Yudenich's White Army during the civil war.

The third, Paul, trained the Irish horse team for the Olympics after the war. The youngest two, Sergei and Victor, were young officers in World War I and the civil war. They were only a little older than their nephew, my father, testifying to the undying mutual attraction of their parents. Sergei became a portrait painter and a well-known expert tennis player in London. In general, all the sons were great horsemen, athletes and soldiers, like the earlier Rodzianko brothers. The whole family survived the revolution and continued life as emigrés.

With the portion of the Stroganov fortune his wife inherited, Pavel Vladimirovich had the means to live to the fullest his life of a Hollywood-style Russian nobleman. Crockery shattered every night to the tune of *Casse Tout*, both downtown and out in Novaya Derevnya, where the Gypsies played and sang. Once, Maria followed the trail of broken dishes and found him in some far-out place at four o'clock in the morning, sleeping at the head of a table lined with a number of ladies of the evening, also asleep. He woke up and cried: "My darling, you have come back to me!"

His capers became legendary. Once in Berlin, after a three day disappearance, he was found feeding champagne to the lions in the zoo and promising them their freedom. In Switzerland he made a tremendous fuss with the Russian Legation and almost sent a telegram to the tsar over a sign he claimed to have seen: "This park is off-limits to dogs and Russians." He was incensed that Russians were listed after dogs!

Sometimes Pavel Vladimirovich would order a nightclub redecorated at his expense, or confer a large sum of money on a sick child. During the Russo-Japanese War of 1904-1905, he financed, equipped, and commanded a hospital train, loaded with champagne as well as medical supplies, and was almost captured. He showed a great deal of ingenuity getting the train, wounded, champagne and all out safely.

In more peaceful times he once hired a boat equipped with Gypsies as well as champagne and took his guests out on the Neva. What they did not notice was a small cannon concealed in the bow. At four in the morning, Pavel announced that he was going to fire a 21-gun salute in honor of some German princess whose palace the boat was passing. The cannon boomed. When the police launches came out, fearful of revolutionary disorder, he was highly indignant: "Since when is a Russian nobleman not permitted to fire salutes in honor of foreign royalty?" he roared.

In his way, he was a quintessential Russian. He needed space and extremes. In Switzerland, which his wife so adored, he felt cramped. "You can't spread your arms without knocking down a tourist or a cow!" he complained.

His behavior became more and more bizarre and expensive. At the insistence of his older sons, he was put on an allowance. Then he and Maria separated, but she always insisted that his nightshirt be laid out on the bed beside her. When he occasionally hired a troika to ride up and down Furshtadskaya, she made her sons prevent her from looking out. "He is too irresistible!" she cried.

After the Revolution, like so many others, Pavel drifted south and was eventually evacuated to Constantinople. He lived another twelve years in Yugoslavia, penniless, but still served by a loyal old batman-soldier called Ivan. The last news of him came from a letter written by Ivan to Maria Pavlovna in Lausanne.

This last day started with his asking Ivan to put out a fancy velvet-lined box to receive all the telegrams and congratulations he would receive on this day, the 50th anniversary of his commissioning in the Chevalier Guards Regiment of the Imperial Guards. He sat by the box all day, immaculately clad in a white suit. But it was 1932, and nobody knew, or cared, and nobody came or sent anything. Finally, at dusk, his mind grasped the reality.

"Close the box, Ivan," he said. "The world has passed me by."

In the evening, as Ivan described it, he sat up in bed loudly calling God's blessing down on everybody in the family, beginning with Maria Pavlovna and ending with me, his only great-grandson. Then he said, "Ivan, I am no more."

Ivan ended his letter thus: "His Excellency then deigned to pass to a better world."

Apparently this strange man had a talent for painting as well as music. Hanging on my library door is a very well executed icon of King David of Israel, signed in Latin, "P. Rodzianko, Ano 1925." It was the year after I was born.

Pavel Vladimirovich's daughter (at least officially), Marie Rodzianko, was to become my grandmother, and I will henceforth refer to her, in family tradition, as "Babady", somebody's baby talk for *babushka*. She was born in 1877 and one of her first clear memories was of Russian soldiers returning from the Turkish War of 1877-78. She also remembered the assassination of Emperor Alexander II in 1881, and his killers being taken to their public hanging, a very rare sight in the Russia of those days. She was brought up primarily by an English nanny called Emma, and also by a French governess. At that time it was thought that Russian nurses were too kind and spoiled children terribly. There was perhaps some truth to this notion, as my own upbringing was to show.

As a little girl, in pre-Furshtadskaya days, she lived in the 18th century Stroganov palace in St. Petersburg, and at various country estates. She also stayed in Odessa, where she grew close to her great-grandfather, Count Alexander Grigoryevich Stroganov, who had been born in the reign of Catherine the great, in 1795, and lived until 1891. As an aide to Alexander I, he said he had been there when this mystical emperor officially died in 1825, and was an eye-witness to his death. He insisted there was no truth to the persistent rumors that Alexander I had lived on for years afterwards as the *starets* Fedor Kuzmich.

I checked up on Stroganov's presence in N. K. Shilder's very definitive biography of Alexander I, which lists every person present down to the last servant, but no Stroganov. Whether or not Alexander I died in 1825 is still debated among Russian historians.

Stroganov might have had a motive for supporting the official version of the death. His son married the daughter of Nicholas I, over his objections, and if Fedor Kuzmich (who outlived Nicholas I) had really been Alexander I, it would have cast a shadow over the whole reign of Nicholas I.

Babady remembered this Stroganov as a formidable and severe old man, tall, gaunt, and majestic, with penetrating grey eyes. But he was capable of kindnesses. Once, when he was governor-general of Odessa, a civil service clerk was called on the carpet before him for reading *Kolokol* (the Bell), a revolutionary journal published in London by Alexander Herzen. The clerk, who expected at the very least to be fired, was amazed to hear Stroganov say: "If you read *Kolokol*, at least don't do it in front of your colleagues."

Babady met her future husband, Alexander Chavchavadze, in Kislovodsk, in the Caucasus, and he followed her to Finland where her parents had a summer place. After a swift courtship they were married in 1896. Since Babady had been appointed Maid of Honor to the two empresses, her parents wanted to put off the marriage until after the coronation of the new emperor, Nicholas II, so that Babady could take part in its as a member of the court. The young people were in a hurry, however, and were married at the Stroganov palace, working in a quick honeymoon in Odessa before going to Moscow for the coronation. While Babady, as a married woman, could no longer be a Maid of Honor, her new father-in-law, old Zakhary Chavchavadze, was one of those carrying the canopy over the sovereign, along with Finland's future Marshal Mannerheim.

Unfortunately, family lore has not preserved how or even whether Zakhary, the tightwad teetotaller, had approached Paul Vladimirovich, the big spending champagne guzzler, to ask for Babady's hand for his son. In the case of his second son, Maximilian, Zakhary did approach the father of the bride-elect, a very rich Muscovite, with these words in his strong Georgian accent: "My second fool wants to marry your daughter!"

The coronation turned out to be a day of evil portent: hundreds of people were killed in Khodynka field in Moscow by falling into a ditch when the wooden bridges over it collapsed. They were rushing to get the traditional presents from the new monarch. After the coronation services, it was the custom for the new Tsar to have presents distributed to thousands of ordinary citizens, in this case enameled cups decorated with the imperial initials, and free beer hauled in on carts.

Babady attended the coronation ball that night, which should have been cancelled in view of the tragedy. The French Ambassador, however, had laid-on tremendous expense for the ball, even to transporting vast quantities of silver plate for the affair, and Nicholas' uncles—Grand Dukes Vladimir, Alexis and Serge— argued that it would cause an incident should he not attend. The Emperor and Empress did attend briefly, then departed early, a fact for which they were sharply criticized later. Babady thought the most beautiful woman at the ball was the young Queen Marie of Roumania..

After the coronation, the newlyweds got away for a long trip to Europe—Vienna, London and Paris. In London my grandfather insisted that English was merely a mixture of French and German and would be no problem, but he soon had to depend on his bride as an interpreter. From Paris they took the Orient Express to Constantinople, where they saw the Turkish Sultan going to the Mosque, followed by carriages containing his harem. Then they went across the Black Sea to Batumi, by train to Tbilisi, and on to Tsinandali.

They approached Tsinandali on a phaeton drawn by four horses. The distant mountains no longer held menace, but a mounted escort met them at Telavi as a courtesy. As they approached the Tsinandali Babady's new husband, Sasha, pointed to a "grand old white house," and said it had belonged to his maternal great-grandfather, but now belonged to the government. Unfortunately, Babady, usually so strong on description, says nothing more about this house in her papers. In the village, they were greeted by the peasants, all of whom wore the Georgian national costume, *cherkesskas* (*Chokha* in Georgian), while the women were in long tunics, tight at the waist and open below over a petticoat.

After three weeks of Georgian hospitality they returned to Tbilisi, where Babady met Shamil's main captive, Princess Anna, and the other little captive daughter of forty-two years before, Salomé, who had married a Baltic baron called Osten-Sacken.

After this marvellous honeymoon, Babady was depressed at having to return to St. Petersburg, and, at the command of her parents, to live in a small apartment at Furshtadskaya, made out of her girlhood rooms on the first floor.

Later, when my grandfather became a Guards Hussar, the couple were able to spend a marvellous summer at Tsarskoye Selo with its horse races and the sunset parades and grand maneuvers at Krasnoye Selo, which Kaiser Wilhelm II was visiting that summer as a guest of the Tsar.

Eventually, when my grandfather began working at the General Staff, Babady got her way and the couple moved into their own apartment on St. Isaac's Square, in St. Petersburg, facing the gold-domed cathedral. There on June 27, 1899 my father, Paul, their first child, was born as the roar of cannon saluted the birth of Nicholas II's third daughter, Marie.

They spent some time in Georgia after this, on an estate owned by old Zakhary, near Gori, Stalin's birthplace. Once, while Babady was there alone, she got word that a band of brigands were hiding in the vinyards. They were led by a local Robin Hood, who specialized in robbing the rich and helping the poor, or at least leaving them in peace. Seriously worried, Babady began to count the weapons in the house and wonder how long it could withstand a siege. However, the person who had originally warned her, delivered a reassuring message from Robin Hood: "The leader sends you his compliments and begs leave to shelter in the vinyard overnight. He says that he so respects the family of Prince Zakhary that he would never dream of hurting them or their property."

The drama of the situation appealed to Babady, and she replied: "Tell him they may stay until morning, but must never tell anyone. It must remain a secret!"

Shots rang out in the morning, but the brigands escaped. The shots came from two parties of Cossacks in pursuit, shooting at each other by mistake.

The old Caucasus was full of such incidents. My old friend, Murat Natirboff, the son of an officer in my grandfather's World War I Circassian Regiment, tells how his Circassian family, true to the ancient and unbreakable code of hospitality, received a stranger and seated him at their table. During dinner the house was surrounded by a troop of Cossacks. The host, though himself an officer in the Imperial Army, passed out rifles to the guests to help him defend the house should the Cossacks attack it to capture the stranger. Etiquette was observed all around, however, and the stranger gave himself up to the Cossacks, and the Cossack captain had the sense to bide his time and not make an attack. Absolutely no legal action was taken against the family, since the authorities realized that no member of the family could ever have dishonored himself by violating these age-old traditions of the Caucasus.

Babady having lost another round to her parents, the couple moved back to the house in Furshtadskaya. In 1903, when my grandfather was away on his increasingly frequent trips, the famous Imperial Court costume ball took place. Every guest was to wear an authentic 17th century court costume, with the emperor himself dressed as his forebear Tsar Alexis, Peter the Great's father. Even the guard regiment on duty was clothed in the uniform of the old *streltsy*, and carried weapons of the period. Muscovite Russia was much in vogue at that time.

Preparations went on for months. Babady borrowed an ancient tall brimless hat called a *Kichka*, which was embroidered with pearls and had a piece of sable hanging down the back. Her dress was of stiff brocade, long and straight, with a wide sable border and wing sleeves falling down from the shoulders. The collar was round, stiff, and shoulder-wide and covered with jewels. There was a soft silk undergarment with long narrow sleeves. She wore the family emeralds, two-inch stones, all around the collar and down the front of the dress.

Babady's mother wore the tall Russian *Kokoshnik* headdress, with pearls covering the forehead and heavy pendant diamond earrings. Pavel Vladimirovich looked smashing as a tsar's attendant, in a red and gold tunic tipped with fur.

Many books identify these costumes as normal Russian court costume, but it was strictly a one-time affair, which had never happened before, and was not to be repeated. Although nobody knew it at the time, this was the last great bash of the old Imperial Russia. 1903 was the last normal year of the autocracy, followed as it was by a disastrous war with Japan and the 1905 revolution, and then twelve years of semi-constitutional monarchy until the end. It is strange that this extravaganza should have occurred precisely in 1903.

Babady played a very small but perhaps significant role in the Russo-Japanese War. While Pavel Vladimirovich took off with his nurses, bandages and champagne, Babady and other ladies sewed white tunics for the troops under the direct supervision of the Empress Alexandra in the Winter Palace. A general staff officer approached Babady and pointed out to her that the traditional white tunics of the Russian soldiers might have been all right in the 1877 war, but they made beautiful targets for the weapons of 1904. The subject had been raised in the army, but no decision had been reached.

The next day Babady approached the empress. "Your Majesty," she said, "I have heard that these white tunics make an excellent target for the enemy, who are themselves scarcely visible in theirs. The General Staff is begging for a change, and His Imperial Majesty's decision is anxiously awaited."

"I have heard something about it," replied the empress, looking very serious as she almost always did, "but so far nothing has been decided."

"In the meantime how many lives are being lost? The white material keeps coming in, and each day brings more casualties," Babady insisted.

"I will speak to the emperor," said the empress.

The next day Babady again approached the empress.

"I have spoken to the emperor," was all she said.

"Does His Majesty see the urgency?" Babady asked, as the empress frowned.

"I have told you that I have spoken about it, is that not enough?"

Babady felt thoroughly put down. The dowager empress never treated people like that. But it worked! The next day the workroom was full of bales of khaki cloth, and the same thing must have happened in the factories where most of the tunics were made. So perhaps Babady saved a few lives.

In 1904 Babady gave birth to her second child, George, and the following year to her third and last, Marina. After that the family was transferred to Tbilisi, or Tiflis as was its official Russian name, where my grandfather had been appointed aide-de-camp to the Viceroy of the Caucasus, Count Vorontsov-Dashkov.

This was a time of great unrest in the Caucasus as well as in the rest of the empire. Once a stray bullet went through the tall headdress of a Russian nurse who was holding Marina close to a window in Tiflis. In the middle of all this, old Prince Zakhary died, and was transported to Tsinandali, with all dissident elements holding off to allow the passage of this much respected man to his final resting place.

During the funeral proceedings, Babady was much embarrassed that no telegram had come from her mother in Switzerland. One of Maria Pavlovna's idiosyncrasies was that she at all times had an evil looking little dog called Bobeche sitting on her lap. When one Bobeche died, he would be replaced by an identical clone, also called Bobeche. Finally a telegram arrived in Georgia, much to Babady's relief. "Bobeche is dead. Pray for me," was the entire text! Not a word about old Zakhary.

The was the last Chavchavadze family gathering that Babady attended. From that time she lived mostly abroad with her children, until the outbreak of war in 1914. Her marriage was on the rocks. My father remembers overhearing a quarrel between his parents and his father saying: "She is of no importance." In 1910 they tried living together for a while in Tiflis, but "She" was still in the picture. Nobody knows who she was, but it seems that she stuck by my grandfather until the end of his life by a Bolshevik firing squad. They may or may not have married, and there are rumors that they had children, but nobody knows their fate.

In 1908 in Rome, at the age of nine, my father was taken to a dance at the British Embassy. In those days everybody from eighteen down was labeled a "child". A seven-year old girl, Princess Nina of Russia, was also there and, as royalty, had the right to choose her partners.

"I want to dance with that little boy," she said, pointing at my father, who was interested (he once told me) in some little redhead. They danced and forgot all about it. This incident was pointed out to them fourteen years later, in London, when they were engaged. That is how my father met my mother for the first time.

At the beginning of the 1914 war, the family found itself in Abbazzia, on the Gulf of Fiume (now Rijeka, Yugoslavia) in the Austro-Hungarian Empire. Their money, as enemy aliens, was cut off, and they barely escaped internment by making it to a neutral Greek freighter, thanks to a Greek friend Babady ran into by chance on the street. After a short time in Greece they took an Italian ship (also still neutral) through the Dardanelles to Constantinople. There they transferred to the last Russian ship that left before Russian and Turkey were at war, which was declared the next day, and so made it safe to Odessa.

From Odessa they went to Kishinev, where they were to stay until the revolution. Babady's divorce from my grandfather came through, and, still in 1914, she married a childhood friend, Prince Peter Troubetskoy. This stepgrandfather of mine, whom I knew in his old age in the 1950s, was half Georgian, as his mother was a Princess Bagration-Mukhransky. He was a veteran of the Russo-Japanese War, in which he had lost hearing in one ear, and he was a well-traveled and educated man. Serving the Ministry of Agriculture, he had taken numerous trips gathering insect specimens in foreign lands, all the way to the Tibetan border.

During the revolutionary demonstrations in May 1917, he was the only officer on General Brusilov's staff who refused to wear a red rosette or armband. Yet, when I first met him after World War II, he had become a complete communist fellow traveler, even to the extent of reading that most boring of journals, *Bolshevik*, later renamed *Kommunist*. I slipped anti-communist leaflets that I had picked up in Berlin into this reading matter, hoping that he would think that Soviet printers had stuck them there, or at least that he might open his eyes a bit. He had totally fallen for Stalin's use of Russian nationalism to acquire support during the war. He was not the only one. I was somewhat affected by this too, for a time. But with him it went on indefinitely. In 1953 he said to me, "It's a shame that Prince Zakhary's grandson (he missed a generation there) is an American spy against Russia!" I don't know if this was just a shot in the dark or not, as I had only been in the CIA for three years at the time, and thought I had pretty good cover. I knew instinctively, though, that there was no point trying to convince the old entomologist that working against the USSR was not the same as working against Russia, so I let it pass.

During the 1914-1917 period, Babady went back and forth between Kishinev and Kiev to be with her new husband, leaving the children in Kishinev. Kiev, a major headquarters, was a good listening post for what was going on the the country.

Particularly disturbing to Babady was the influence of Rasputin on the empress, whom Babady had no reason to love. This "man of the people" was indispensable to the empress because of his ability to alleviate the tsarevich's hemophiliac pain. Now she was running things in St. Petersburg with his advice, while the emperor was in command of the troops at general headquarters.

Babady's uncle, Michael Rodzianko, was president of the Duma. They were never in touch, but she agreed with him that the only solution was for the emperor to make his ministers responsible to the Duma, in other words, a full constitutional monarchy. Nicholas II refused to do this in spite of the advice of most of his relatives. There was always his oath to the autocracy, and his wife writing him letters to "show who is master," and exhorting him to follow the advice of "our friend"—Rasputin. In Kiev and elsewhere many people accused the empress of being pro-German, but Babady absolutely denies this, correctly as I believe.

The Rasputin phonomenon discredited the monarchy very badly, and in hindsight one can say that thes emperor should have stayed in St. Petersburg, being much less under Rasputin's influence. But people like Babady, Michael Rodzianko, and most of the politicians who wanted Russian to win the war (as opposed to the extremists who hoped for a defeat so they could take power) instinctively knew that the monarchy must be saved. Not necessarily Nicholas II, but the monarchy. It was still such a powerful symbol among the masses, whether they loved the tsar or just feared him as the lynchpin of law and order. "If there is no tsar, I am not a corporal and you are not a lieutenant." Anarchy. Hurrah! No more rules, no more police, everything is up for grabs! This is exactly what happened when the monarchy

31

suddenly disappeared in March 1917, leaving in charge a bunch of perhaps well-meaning, but inexperienced intellectuals incapable of keeping the country in hand, and totally vulnerable to well-organized extremists. The best organized and most ruthless of these, the Bolsheviks, took over with little trouble eight months after the fall of the monarchy, overthrowing a government so free and democratic that it was incapable of defending itself or coping with the situation in the country.

Kishinev was not far from the Austrian front, and in 1916 and 1917 my father, George, and Marina visited their father just behind the front three times. My father was even taken to within 200 yards of the Austrian lines. The younger children were accompanied by their English governess, May Southby. They hugely enjoyed the Caucasian parties thrown by these officers of the "Wild Division," when they were in reserve. As little Marina danced the *Lesghinka* with some officer, the rest would fire their revolvers until the windows had to be opened to let out the smoke and the people downstairs had to be paid for their shot-through milk buckets.

In 1917 the quiet old town of Kishinev was no longer so quiet. There were robberies and murders by men who called themselves Bolsheviks, though nobody knew whether they were real Bolsheviks, Ukrainian nationalists, or just criminals giving themselves political cover.

On night Babady was woken by a flashlight in her face and a revolver at her temple. She was sleeping with Marina and said to her in English: "Don't be afraid, they have only come to search the house and will depart peacefully." The intruders, having obviously received inside information, assumed that Babady must be the English governess, Miss May Southby, who was known to sleep with Marina. They said that they would leave in peace, but the princess must die. Nevertheless, Babady spoke to them in Russian and they realized they were dealing with the princess.

With the courage that so many of those Russian ladies showed when the chips were down, Babady said to them, "You can't scare me with that old-fashioned Smith and Wesson revolver, and if you want me to get up, just hand me my slippers and dressing gown over there and I will do so."

The leader, surprisingly, lowered his revolver and handed her the robe. He indicated that he wanted money, and his men began a thorough search of the house, tearing up mattresses and turning everything upside down. They brought in young George, aged thirteen, and asked him where his mother's money was, holding a knife to his side. George looked the leader full in the face.

"If I came and asked for your mother's money," he said, "what would you do?"

"Brave boy," replied the leader and let him go.

Most of the valuables were in the bank. They took Babady's rings and pearl necklace. As they were doing this, she told them, "Here you are, twelve armed men, and I am a woman alone and unarmed. Yet I have one advantage over you. You can believe every word I say, while I cannot believe anything you tell me. I give you my word that the money is not in this house."

"Well," said the leader, "money or no money, we must judge you because you are a landowner."

"Where are my lands?"

"In the Caucasus."

"Those are not mine any more."

"You are still a princess and we are Bolsheviks," he said. "So we must kill you. You will die by the knife."

They sat her on a sofa and bound her hands with a towel. She thought her last moments had come. A priest had been killed in a similar manner not long before. Resignedly she thought to herself: 'Well, every chicken is in the same position at the hands of the cook.' Then, as the knife was being held to her throat, she began to pray.

According to Miss Southby, at this point the leader said, "Leave her alone," and made Babady a bow. "We have robbed many titled ladies, but never such a brave one."

The men left at 4:15 AM. The police arrived and said this was a gang of deserters who had murdered many people. Both Babady and May Southby, they said, owed their lives to the fact that they had kept cool and not screamed.

My father had missed this drama, as he was in St. Petersburg with his grandmother. In view of the revolutionary conditions, she was making economies. The butler, to whom she announced her new policy, expected to be fired, and was vastly relieved when she commanded: "No more spinach!" Actually, she had always hated this legume.

As usual, Maria Pavlovna Rodzianko rattled off whatever was on her mind. Why did her daughter ever give up that charming Sasha Chavchavadze for this man who went all the way to Tibet just to look for insects?

Once, while walking with my father, she came across a soldier addressing a crowd. He was pointing at the Cross of St. George on his chest, the highest decoration for valor, and orating: "See this cross? Bloody Nicholas pinned it there with his own hands, and so now I spit at it!"

Maria Pavlovna marched up to the soldier and wagged a finger in his face. "Take it off, damn you! You got it for bravery and now you lose it for meaness, you low-down, good-for-nothing scoundrel!" She tore the cross off his tunic and walked away with it. Nobody in the crowd moved.

"I am sure Kerensky would have slapped his ugly face," Maria Pavlovna remarked to my father. She greatly admired Kerensky at the time.

She threw a party at a restaurant for my father's eighteenth birthday. He had never been to a fancy restaurant before. Walking in, Maria Pavlovna immediately recognized the crystal chandeliers.

"Where did you get those" she demanded of the proprietor. "I have been looking for them everywhere."

"But Pavel Vladimirovich gave them to us," the man protested.

"That's all right. They are mine, but I give them to you. Pavel Vladimirovich's gifts were so costly!"

After Lenin's October coup, Maria Pavlovna was thrown in jail because her brother-in-law had been president of the Duma, and her second son, Alexander, was second in command of Yudenich's White army, moving from the Baltic states toward St. Petersburg. She was put in a cell with seventeen men, who had all been cowed by a sadistic jailer. But, as luck would have it, the jailer turned out to be a former orderly of Pavel Vladimirovich, and changed his attitude entirely when Maria

Pavlovna arrived, even standing at attention and calling her, "Your Excellency," when none of his comrades were about.

She made her seventeen male cell mates, many of them acquaintances, turn their backs every day while she made her toilet, and then, for weeks, she amused and cheered the lot of them.

Her connection with the jailer did not spare Maria Pavlovna from interrogation and torture. The torture consisted of sticking pins under her fingernails. The Bolsheviks could not believe that she had not spoken to the president of the Duma for ten years, but it was true. She had not heard from her son in over a year. She fainted under the torture, but refused to incriminate herself.

Thanks to the Red Cross and the Nansen League of Nations refugee organization, Maria Pavlovna Rodzianko was allowed to emigrate and lived until 1945 in her beloved Switzerland. What a pity for me not to have met this great-grandmother, but we could never afford a trip to Europe in the 1930s, and then the war interfered.

My father left St. Petersburg before the Bolshevik takeover, and went to stay with his father in Georgia, and then rejoined Babady, George and Marina in Kishinev in June of 1918. It had already been annexed by Roumania. There had been resistance in the town, including a strange group of cavalry (nobody knew which party they belonged to), who had been billeted in Babady's house. The arrival of the royal Roumanian Army was, of course, the saving grace for the family, who suddenly found themselves outside of Bolshevik control and part of the Kingdom of Roumania.

The Roumanians were intent on Rumanizing (if no such word exists, I am coining it!) everything about Bessarabia/Moldavia, which meant that Russian schools were in trouble. Babady went to to see King Ferdinand and Queen Marie (that beautiful girl she had so admired in Moscow during the 1896 coronation) at Jassy. They were sympathetic, but had little control over the actions of the government.

Not quite true. Queen Marie (a granddaughter of Queen Victoria) had an improbable lover, who was practically running the country. This was a Canadian colonel called Boyle, who had grown rich in the Klondike. He had rescued the entire Roumanian Senate from the Bolsheviks, who had fled to Russia to avoid the Germans.

Babady thought he was the most wonderful man she had ever met. He went to the Klondike with $18 and came out with eighteen million. He was also an intimate friend of Jack London, in whose book, *Call of the Wild*, he had been mentioned as the man who had killed another man for beating a dog. Naturally, this appealed to the dog-loving Babady, so she arranged for my father to be his interpreter. The fact that my father spoke no Roumanian didn't seem to matter, since everybody of consequence spoke French.

My father's first interview with Boyle was in a hospital where the colonel was recovering from a stroke and getting better by the minute through sheer will-power, and against all medical opinion.

My father asked how Boyle had rescued the Roumanian Senate from the Bolsheviks. "Well, it was just to please Her Majesty," Boyle answered. "Those bearded clods had fled to Russia when Roumania entered the war, hoping for the tsar's protection. Instead they found themselves in a Bolshie jail in U-Patria." (This was the way Boyle pronounced Yevpatoria in the Crimea). The Colonel had simply landed there with a few men, and in full Canadian uniform had bulled his way through a few commissars and evacuated the whole bearded senate to his ship.

When Boyle left the hospital, my father went with him to Bicas, where the queen was in residence, and he listened to many evenings of Boyle's Klondike stories, all of which the queen had heard before, but obviously wanted to hear again. Meanwhile, my father carried on an unsuccessful flirtation with one of her daughters, ending in heartbreak when he saw the object of his affections driving a motorcycle with a musician from the palace orchestra in the side-car.

The colonel was no has-been yet. When not story-telling he was planning another expedition to the Crimea, still in White hands, using a Roumanian ship to evacuate the dowager Empress Marie of Russia. He took my father along on this voyage, but for once the Terror of the Yukon was defeated. The empress refused to budge! She was staying at an estate called Harax, which belonged to a Russian grand duke whose daughter was the little girl who had picked my father to dance with in Rome! So my father's last look at Russia was of Harax, my mother's home, and the cliffs of the Crimea from the deck of Boyle's Roumanian ship.

Eventually the Roumanian government succeeded in getting rid of Colonel Boyle, who died in London in 1922, ruined financially by his escapades on behalf of his fairy queen. The dowager empress was taken out of Russian in 1919 on a British warship, the *H.M.S. Marlborough*, and lived in her Denmark until she died in 1928.

In 1920 Babady, her three children, and Peter Troubetzkoy, moved to London from Bucharest. One reason was Uncle George's musical education. From early babyhood he had shown extraordinary musical talent.

In London Babady opened a boutique, heavily weighted in the direction of hats. Babady always wore huge hats. Notoriously unpunctual for everything except trains, which did not have the decency to wait for her. She once arrived for a train but, finding her hat too big to fit through the door no matter what contortions she went through, she announced to the children that the trip was off until the next day!

Uncle George told me that once Babady, typically an hour late for some posh reception in London, told her name (Princess Troubetskoy) to the man who banged his staff on the he floor to announce guests. The man went in, banged, and proclaimed: "Princess Truboko." Nothing happened. He disappeared, re-emerged and banged again: "Princess Trubiki." Again nothing happened, and he disappeared once more, only to reappear and call out: "Princess Trubshich." By this time a hush had fallen on the whole company, which expected three exotic princesses to make their entrance. But Babady swept in all alone, saying to the servant in a kindly voice, "Wrong again, you silly man!" At the end of the same reception, Babady came up to the host and said, "Call me a taxi, my good man!"

"I beg your pardon!" exclaimed the host.

"Oh, I'm so sorry," said Babady, "I thought you were my husband."

Indeed, when they had retired to Dorset to breed Welsh corgies, Peter Troubetskoy always drove their ancient vehicle, while Babady sat in the back seat wearing a fairly large hat, but not in the same league as those of yore. When he wasn't reading *Bolshevik* he did all the cooking and housework while Babady sat back and sometimes sang delightful old Russian songs, accompanying herself with graceful gestures on a lute. Peter Troubetskoy had a secret admirer, a local British lady who waited for him to emerge every morning to go shopping, then she would sink to the ground in a low court curtsy. "I know how to behave with royalty," she boasted to her friends, none of whom knew that Peter's title was not royal. Or perhaps they just didn't want to spoil her fun!

My first memory of Babady was in 1934 when I was ten and she (without Peter) came to visit us in New York. We went to Farmington, Connecticut, where Babady had a touching reunion with a Mr. Riddle, who had been American Ambassador to St. Petersburg.

His wife, Theodate Pope Riddle, had survived the sinking of the Lusitania in 1915. She later founded an Eton-like prep school called Avon Old Farms—candle light and stiff collars. She never forgave my father for not sending me there.

In order to supply her London boutique, Babady insisted on going to the New York garment district. My parents warned her how tough the place was, but she was not deterred. She had seen tougher situations. They nervously awaited her return, however. She came back, large hat askew, and admitted it had been a very difficult experience.

"But I told those very rude people off," she said.

"What did you say to them?"

"I told them: You are all knaves!"

Babady loved New York, and on her last night there she nightclubbed in Harlem on orangeades, though on special occasions (almost anybody's saint's day or birthday) she was known to knock back a thimble full of vodka.

When she got back to London, she called together a small coterie of female friends—ladies who still wore Queen Mary hats—to a tea party, where she pulled out her lute and announced:

"Now I want to sing you an American song which I learned from my American son in America.

Aunt Marina was there, pouring the tea. She reported that the ladies smiled in anticipation as Babady sounded a few chords on the lute, then began:

> "Said the big red rooster to the little
> white hen:
>   Why don't you lay us an egg now and
> then?
>   Said the little white hen to the big red
> rooster, Why dontcha come around as often as
> you used-ter?
>   Said the big red rooster with a lordly
> stride:
>   These days I'm getting my fun outside!

Babady paused to say to her glazed-eyed audience, "So true, isn't it? and finished the song:

"Said the little white hen with a nervous
twitch:

And so am I, you son of a bitch!"
By this time the big-hatted ladies were close to fainting.

Babady died in Dorset at the age of 81, in 1958. My father was able to be with her at the end. Most of the credit for caring for her in her last years belongs to Marina, whom, I'm afraid, she often took for granted as 19th century ladies usually did with unmarried daughters.

In the fall of 1921 my father finally met my mother again, and began to court her under the strict chaperonage of her English nanny, Miss Bell. Though it was the beginning of the flapper era, my mother's mother, Grand Duchess Marie, had extremely strict Victorian ideas. Actually, Miss Bell was rather easy going, considering her generation. She sat on the sidelines while the young couple roller-skated, and would occasionally grant them three minutes alone. Nana Bell was one of that nearly extinct breed of indomitable British nannies. She later became nurse to the future King Peter II of Yugoslavia, and finished her very long life at the estate of Don Arturo Edwards in Chile. As a child I was gently forced to write to her.

On New Year's day, 1922, my father proposed and was accepted, during one of those three minute breaks allowed by the chaperone.

My mother's family found the match perfectly suitable, but some of them worried about the lack of funds in my father's family. At that time my father was making four pounds a week in an advertising agency. God knows what, if anything, Babady's boutique was bringing in. My mother was only twenty, and though very independent minded, was still frightened at the family's reaction. Her mother accepted the match only after a considerable grumble.

The only relative of my mother's to take action to stop the marriage was her uncle, Grand Duke Michael Mikhailovich, who had been living in London for years, exiled from Russia by the emperor for a morganatic marriage. He even complained to King George V, who luckily did nothing. Then the grand duke invited Babady for lunch.

He ranted and raved, and even accused my mother's mother of wanting to get rid of her in order to get married herself. But the basic thing was that my father was very poor.

Babady looked the grand duke straight in the eye and said:

"Your Imperial Highness, you are quite wrong. We are very rich indeed!"

The grand duke was astonished. "Do the riches come from your side of the family?"

"Certainly," said Babady and took leave of her host.

My twenty-three-year-old father, a nervous wreck by the time she came home, heard all this and asked his mother how she could have lied in such a manner.

"I did not lie!" answered Babady with indignation. "I told him we were very rich. And so we are, in spirit!"

HARAX

GRAND DUKE GEORGE
(Apapa)

MARIE PAVLOVNA RODZIANKO
neé Golitsin
(Author's great-grandmother)

GRAND DUCHESS MARIE
(Amama)

AUTHOR and GRAND DUCHESS XENIA
Windsor Castle, c. 1926

PRINCESS MARIE and GRAND DUKE GEORGE
(Author's Grandparents)

ROMANOV CHART
(simplified)

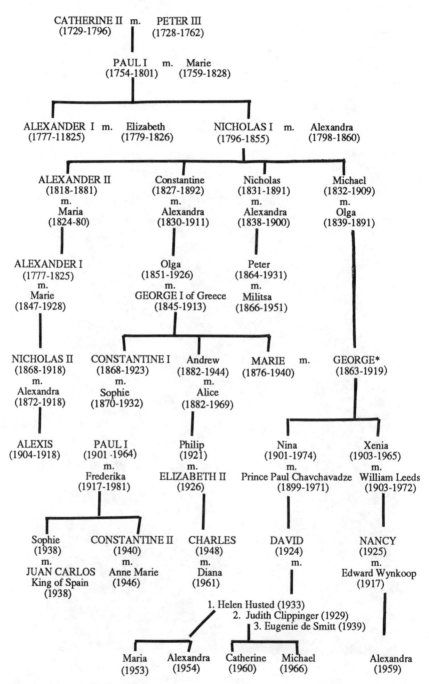

CATHERINE II m. PETER III
(1729-1796)   (1728-1762)

PAUL I m. Marie
(1754-1801)   (1759-1828)

ALEXANDER I m. Elizabeth   NICHOLAS I m. Alexandra
(1777-11825)   (1779-1826)   (1796-1855)   (1798-1860)

ALEXANDER II   Constantine   Nicholas   Michael
(1818-1881)   (1827-1892)   (1831-1891)   (1832-1909)
m.   m.   m.   m.
Maria   Alexandra   Alexandra   Olga
(1824-80)   (1830-1911)   (1838-1900)   (1839-1891)

ALEXANDER I   Olga   Peter
(1777-1825)   (1851-1926)   (1864-1931)
m.   m.   m.
Marie   GEORGE I of Greece   Militsa
(1847-1928)   (1845-1913)   (1866-1951)

NICHOLAS II   CONSTANTINE I   Andrew   MARIE   m.   GEORGE*
(1868-1918)   (1868-1923)   (1882-1944)   (1876-1940)   (1863-1919)
m.   m.   m.
Alexandra   Sophie   Alice
(1872-1918)   (1870-1932)   (1882-1969)

ALEXIS   PAUL I   Philip   Nina   Xenia
(1904-1918)   (1901-1964)   (1921)   (1901-1974)   (1903-1965)
                m.   m.   m.   m.
                Frederika   ELIZABETH II   Prince Paul Chavchavadze   William Leeds
                (1917-1981)   (1926)   (1899-1971)   (1903-1972)

Sophie   CONSTANTINE II   CHARLES   DAVID   NANCY
(1938)   (1940)   (1948)   (1924)   (1925)
m.   m.   m.   m.   m.
JUAN CARLOS Anne Marie   Diana   Edward Wynkoop
King of Spain (1946)   (1961)   (1917)
(1938)

1. Helen Husted (1933)
2. Judith Clippinger (1929)
3. Eugenie de Smitt (1939)

Maria   Alexandra   Catherine   Michael   Alexandra
(1953)   (1954)   (1960)   (1966)   (1959)

* Grand Duke Alexander, brother of George m.
  Grand Duchess Xenia, daughter of
  Alexander III

CHAPTER III

The Romanov family, which was to rule Russia for 304 years, started out modestly enough in the 14th century under various names (Kabyla, Koshka, Zakharin-Koshkin), achieving some prominence in Muscovite Russia, not to be compared with the old Ryurik and Gedemin princely lines. They became boyars but had no title. A girl of the family, Anastasia, married the young Ivan the Terrible in 1547. She was his first and favorite wife, the mother of his eldest son Ivan (whom he killed in a fit of rage long after Anastasia's death), and his second son Feodor, the last ruler of the Ryurik dynasty. So the Romanovs were blood relatives to this last tsar of the old line, who produced no heir by his wife, Irina Godunov. Her brother, Boris, was elected tsar to succeed Feodor by a national assembly called the *Zemskiy Sobor*, which was probably more representative of the population than even the English parliament of that period.

Electing dynasties, which was to happen twice more, was a very unusual feature of Russian history and rare anywhere. The Romanovs' turn came in 1613, eight years after Boris Godunov's death, and after a confused period of anarchy and Polish invasion, known as the "Time of Troubles."

Moscow was freed from the Poles in 1612 by a Russian army raised in the provinces and another *Zemskiy Sobor* was elected (with some peasants represented) to choose a new dynasty. Feodor Romanov would have been the leading candidate, but he had been forced into the church as a monk during the Time of Troubles, and had become patriarch, and so was not eligible to be tsar. The *Zemskiy Sobor* elected his sixteen-year-old son, Michael, to be tsar in 1613, and it was understood that his father would be the real power behind the throne as long as he lived. Michael reigned until 1645, and was succeeded by his son, Alexis (1645-1676).

Peter the Great was Alexis' third and youngest son. The career of this gigantic man (physically as well as in other ways) is well known, but there are some things which are less well known. While capable of great cruelty in putting down rebellions and pushing through his great projects, Peter was a democrat in picking his assistants. He cared nothing about their genealogies, and did away with the incredibly complicated and debilitating protocol system of Muscovite Russia.

Two examples are Alexander Menshikov, who started out as a pie salesman in Moscow, and became Peter's right-hand man; and the poet Pushkin's great-grandfather, a black child from Ethiopia who was presented to Peter by the Turkish sultan. He was sent to France by Peter for military training in engineering and became the chief engineering general of the Russian Army under the name Peter gave him: Abraham Hannibal.

For the first time the titles "count" and "baron" appeared in Russia, awarded for ability, often to people with humble origins. Peter also created new princes (Menshikov was one), and this had never been done before.

Peter insisted on one thing that lasted until the end of the empire: titles meant nothing as far as protocol was concerned. Earned rank was the only criterion. Thus, Colonel Popov would always sit above Captain Prince Obolensky. In this Peter was way ahead of Western Europe.

Peter upped his own title to "emperor," a slap in the face to the Habsburgs, who until then had been the only emperors in Europe. The word *tsar* continued to be used widely, but the official title was *imperator*.

Peter's second wife started out as a servant girl in Lithuania. She first married a Swedish sergeant; when the Russians occupied the area she went up through the ranks until she became the mistress of the commander-in-chief, Sheremetyev. Peter's right-hand man, Menshikov, took her away from Sheremetyev, only to have Peter take her from him! I look at her portraits—a fairly comely brunette, but nothing special—and wonder what it was about her personality that led to such an incredible career.

When Peter died after diving into the Neva to rescue a number of sailors, he did not leave a will, although he had changed the law to allow the emperor to appoint his own successor regardless of primogeniture. He lifted his hand and started a sentence: "Give all to . . . " and then expired. The year was 1725.

His wife's old lover, Menshikov, quickly arranged for her to be proclaimed Catherine I, Empress of all the Russias, the first woman to occupy the throne in her own right, but by no means the last. The servant girl from Lithuania, still illiterate, had become an autocrat. The guards regiments supported her because they remembered how she, along with Peter, had shared their dangers in the Turkish wars. With three exceptions in the 18th century, all of the future Romanovs were, and are, descended from the curious union of Peter and Catherine, through their daughter Anna.

After Catherine I's death in 1727, the succession, until 1762, can best be described as a complicated mess of palace revolutions. Through one of these, Peter and Catherine's beautiful younger daughter, Elizabeth, finally made it to the throne in 1741. Unsnobbish like her father, she took for her lover and secret husband, a humble but handsome Ukrainian choirboy called Razumovsky. For her official heir she made the disastrous decision of picking her nephew, Peter of Holstein-Gottorp, the son of her older sister Anna, and hence Peter the Great's grandson, but lacking any of the latter's qualities.

By dynastic accident, this young man, who was not quite right in the head, had rights to the thrones of Russia, Sweden and his native Holstein, which was the only place he really wanted to be. He made no secret of disliking everything Russian and loving everything German, particularly Frederick the Great, whom he called "my king and master."

Elizabeth made up for her gaffe by choosing a first rate bride for her nephew Peter, an obscure German princess called Sophie Augusta Fredericka of Anhalt-Zerbst, whose maternal uncle Elizabeth had once been engaged to. Sophie came to Russia at the age of fourteen, had her name changed to Catherine, and married Peter, who was her second cousin and also German, but they had nothing else in common. Unlike her husband, this talented girl plunged into learning and appreciating everything Russian.

In 1754 she produced a son, Paul, who according to her memoirs was the result of a liaison with a courtier named Saltykov. Her husband, again according to Catherine, had never consumated the marriage and she was still a virgin after eight years. If this is true, Peter was the last of the Romanovs. However, there is considerable doubt about the whole thing. Peter definitely had an operation (like Louis XVI) which enabled him to have sex in time to be Paul's father, and Paul physically and mentally resembled his official father greatly, and looked nothing like Saltykov, who was known as the handsomest man at court. Peter and Paul both had a tendency toward insanity, both adored drilling troops in ultra-Prussian style. If Paul was more intelligent than Peter, he did, after all, have a brilliant mother. Furthermore, Catherine had a motive for discrediting her son, whose throne she usurped and whom she planned to disinherit.

When Elizabeth died in 1762, Russia and Austria had brought Frederick to his knees and occupied Berlin. Frederick was saved only because of Peter III, his greatest fan, who now sat on the Russian throne. Peter promptly pulled Russian out of the war. In April 1945 the Nazis in Hitler's bunker remembered this episode and prayed for a similar miracle, which they thought had happened when Roosevelt died.

Peter III proceded to plan a war against Denmark for the interests of his beloved Holstein. The fact that he was drunk most of the time might have been overlooked in Russia, but not all this. A conspiracy started, and the guard regiments moved again, placing a fourth woman on the Russian throne, Catherine II. She was as popular as Peter was despised. By rights she should have been regent for her son Paul, and this is something he never forgave his mother. Peter III abdicated and was soon choked to death by Catherine's favorites, the Orlov brothers. This was convenient, but it is generally agreed that Catherine had intended to let the miserable chap go home to his beloved Holstein.

Catherine the Great ruled for thirty-four years. In spite of all that can be said against her—that her liberal ideas and correspondence with Voltaire and Diderot did the serfs no good; that she partitioned Poland with Austria and Prussia; that she had a great many lovers—she was one of the greatest rulers of either sex in the history of the world, a woman of genius, and an ancestress to be proud of.

Catherine the Great died from a stroke in 1796, just before signing a manifesto passing the throne directly to Paul's son, Alexander. So Paul I became emperor, thirty-four years after he thought he should have.

Intelligent, well-educated and well-meaning, Paul had spent those thirty-four years stewing in resentment, not only at the loss of the throne, but because his mother never took him into her confidence and never gave him anything responsible to do, like Queen Victoria with her son Edward VII. He spent most of his time drilling a small private army at Gatchina. Luckily, he had a happy marriage with a princess of Württemberg, rechristened Maria Feodorovna, with whom he produced four boys and six girls, all healthy and good looking.

Paul I immediately issued a law of succession, which continued to the end of the empire, a strict father to oldest son succession. Women could only ascend the throne if there were no males left in the family.

Paul I followed an erratic foreign policy, first sending troops across the Alps to fight the French in Italy (Russian marines actually took Rome for five days in 1799), and then switching into an alliance with Napoleon Bonaparte. On the positive side, he was the first emperor to help the serfs substantially, by limiting the time they had to work for their landlords to three days a week.

But his behavior grew increasingly bizarre. He issued regulations on what people could wear—long trousers were taboo—too Jacobine. He terrorized his troops in the most savage Prussian style, banishing officers to Siberia right from the parade ground for minor infractions of drill or dress. Ever more paranoid, he built himself a castle surrounded by a moat in the middle of Petersburg. Shortly after he moved in, in 1801, he was murdered by a group of nobles who had easy access to him. This was the last of Russia's palace revolutions.

Paul I was succeeded by his oldest son, Alexander I, twenty-four-years old, who had been a party to the conspiracy to dethrone his father, but he had never intended murder. For the rest of his life he would have to live with the ghastly scene (at which he was not present) when Paul I had been strangled on his bed.

Alexander I's reign is well known for his early liberalism, his successes against Napoleon, and his later period of reaction and mysticism. By 1825 he was fully informed on the conspiracies forming in the army and the guards against himself, but he enigmatically did nothing about it, and did not even tell his heir. But who was his heir?

He had no male children. His official heir was his brother Constantine, brought up like himself directly by their grandmother Catherine. But Constantine, happily ensconsed in Warsaw as viceroy and married morgantically to a Polish woman, renounced his rights. This, for reasons known only to himself, Alexander kept secret, even from the next brother, Nicholas. But he frequently talked of abdication.

Officially Alexander I died in 1825 at the age of forty-eight, in an obscure Black Sea port called Taganrog. Although it is possible that he did not die, and lived until 1864 as a wondering holy man, Fedor Kuzmich, one wonders how such a conspiracy could have been pulled off without some of the numerous people present in Taganrog bringing it to light, if only on their deathbeds. Fedor Kuzmich was obviously a very unusual person, and looked like Alexander I. My mother's uncle, the professional historian, Grand Duke Nicholas Mikhailovich, absolutely denied the Kuzmich story in his biography of Alexander I, but according to my mother he privately believed it was true.

My mother's father, Grand Duke George, was present when the graves of all the emperors were opened in St. Peter and Paul, before the revolution, and he said Alexander I's coffin was empty[1]. There was a story that Alexander I was evacuated from Taganrog on a British yacht belonging to Lord Cathcart, with the log mysteriously blank for this period. The Cathcart family supposedly had papers about this which were sealed. In the 1970s a friend of mine wrote the present Lord Cathcart, who replied that there were no papers and his ancestor never had a yacht on the Black Sea.

---

1.   There was an official report in 1920 which says that when Lenin ordered all of the Romanov tombs opened and any jewelry removed, that the tomb of Alexander I was empty. This report also stated that the workmen fled when the tomb of Peter the Great was opened—because he suddenly sat up in the coffin, fully preserved.

Whatever happened, the official death in Taganrog caused havoc in St. Petersburg. Nicholas ordered alliegance to be sworn to "Emperor Constantine I," while Constantine ordered everybody in Warsaw to declare fealty to "Emperor Nicholas I." Couriers galloped back and forth during the interregnum, and total confusion resulted—the perfect time for the officers belonging to the secret societies to strike. They led the Guard units they commanded onto Senate Square, next to the Winter Palace, and ordered the men to shout "Constantine and Constitution!" The men did as ordered, but assumed that Constitution *(Konstitutsiya)*, must be Constantine's wife! The enlisted men had no idea of what was going on. In any case, this was a phony slogan, since there was never any indication that Constantine would have granted a constitution had he accepted the throne.

Through that short, cold December afternoon, the new young emperor and those loyal to him faced the rebellious officers and their bewildered troops. Finally, when the Decembrists had refused several offers to disperse and had shot down a hero of the Napoleonic wars, Miloradovich, Nicholas I dispersed the uprising with a whiff of grapeshot and a cavalry charge. This was the first political revolution, as opposed to palace coups and peasant uprisings, in Russian history. Poorly organized, penetrated, and leading to nothing, it has still achieved an enormous symbolic significance.

Nicholas I never got over the shock of the first day of his reign. Many of the Decembrists came from the most aristocratic families, and he had served with them in the Guards and knew them personally. Over 150 officers were arrested and personally interrogated by Nicholas, five were hanged. There had not been a public execution in Russia for so long that a Swedish hangman had to be imported. The rest of the Decembrists were exiled to Siberia. Nicholas put out an order (very un-Soviet in spirit) that none of their relatives were to be discriminated against. The Decembrists ranged from constitutional monarchists to Jacobins determined to kill the Imperial Family, but they were highly idealistic young men, whose loyal wives followed them to share their exile. Ironically, they are heroes to the Soviet government as well as to most of the dissidents of today.

Perhaps if there had been no Decembrists, Nicholas I's reign would have been different. But, as it was, his thirty year rule (1825-1855) was characterized by strict autocracy and police measures.

The Marquis de Custine, a French traveler, left a description of the police measures of the time in a book which was rediscovered by Beedle Smith, American Ambassador to Stalin's Russia, after the war. He and many others immediately jumped to the conclusion that Russia had always been a police state, Imperial or Communist, totally ignoring the great reforms of the next reign (Alexander II), and the sixty-two years between the death of Nicholas I and the 1917 revolutions, which included a semi-constitutional monarchy and the significant land reforms of Stolypin. To analyze Russia in this simplistic way is a dangerous delusion. George Kennan correctly evaluated Custine as having written a poor description of Russia in 1837, but a very good one of the Soviet Union in 1937. Custine never noticed the flowering of Russian literature that was going on in spite of the censorship.

In fact, Nicholas I acted as the personal censor of Russia's greatest poet, Pushkin, and when the latter was killed in a duel in 1837, the emperor paid his gambling debts and assigned a pension to his widow. He also authorized, attended, and applauded Gogol's play *The Inspector General*, a satire on his own bureaucracy!

Physically, Nicholas I was an extraordinary specimen. One Englishman thought him the most majestic being ever created. Even Custine commented on the "beauty of his classical head." But he has had such a bad press that I feel no guilt in calling attention to the good sides of this great-great-grandfather.

He was totally devoted to his country, and his duty, perhaps too much so. Nowadays we would say that he did not delegate enough authority. He realized this himself. The problem was a serious lack of competent and honest officials for the government. He tried to remedy this in the long run through a build-up of educational facilities. This strict autocrat told his family, according to a daughter, Olga, who became Queen of Württemburg, that he though a republican form of government was higher than a monarchy, but that it would be many years before Russia would be ready for it.

He knew that reforms would have to come, including the abolition of serfdom. That is why this 'arch-reactionary' appointed as chief tutor to his son and heir about the most liberal man available, the poet Zhukovsky. His son, Alexander II, indeed did institute basic reforms, and thanks to his father's spade work, was able to liberate the serfs six years into his reign.

The dissolute Bourbon King of Naples, Ferdinand II, was very eager to meet Nicholas I, thinking to find a kindred spirit. Instead, all he got was a severe lecture on the duty owed by a monarch to his subjects.

Nicholas did not lack the common touch. There was, for instance, the story of Private Agafon Sudeykin—Sudeykin and a group of his buddies got drunk in a pub one night and started a brawl. The pub keeper tried to calm them down by pointing to a picture of the emperor behind the bar. "Who cares?" yelled Sudeykin, "I spit on his portrait!" and proceeded to do just that. The incident was reported to his first sergeant and all the way up through channels to the emperor.

Back came the emperor's reply: "I wish Private Sudeykin to be called front and center before the regiment and told the following: First, I spit at him too. Second, since the man was drunk and did not know what he was doing, there will be no punishment. Third, imperial portraits are not to be hung in pubs."

It is said that Sudeykin never touched a drop for the rest of his life.

Nicholas I liked to take long, unaccompanied walks through St. Petersburg. Once he happened across a humble wooden coffin being drawn to the cemetary by a scrawny nag and followed by a lone woman, the widow. The emperor began to walk at her side, and gradually a whole crowd collected to give the humble man's body a proper send-off.

Nicholas I believed that while as an autocrat he could change the law, he was subject to those already on the books. For instance, he scrupulously observed the constitution of Finland and Poland granted by his brother. Poland actually had one of the most liberal constitutions existing in Europe at the time, but in 1830 the Poles, wanting full independence, revolted. A large part of the peasantry kept out of the revolt, believing that they would be worse off under their own nobility's unchecked rule. Nicholas, of course, did not hesitate to suppress the rebellion, regarding the Poles in violation of the law and the Congress of Vienna settlement of

1814.

Faithfulness to his brother's Holly Alliance was what led Nicholas I to intervene in Hungary in 1849. The Hungarians had rebelled against Hapsburg rule, and were doing quite well. While I don't expect any Hungarian to be cheered by the fact, Nicholas I's invasion of Hungary was not to add it to his own empire, but to return it to what he regarded as the legitimate sovereign of Hungary, the Emperor of Austria. He extracted a promise from the young Franz Josef that none of the Hungarian ringleaders would be executed. The promise was not kept.

Nicholas I died in the middle of the Crimean War at the age of fifty-nine. Some say he committed suicide, regarding himself as an obstacle to the degrading peace he knew had to be made in this lost conflict.

He had enjoyed a very close and loving family life, married to the beautiful Princess Charlotte of Prussia (rechristened Alexandra Feodorovna), the daughter of King Frederick William III and the enchanting Queen Louise, who had vamped Napoleon. They had seven children. All the later Romanovs are descended from their four sons, Alexander II, Grand Dukes Constantine, Nicholas and Michael.

Alexander II is my favorite of all the rulers of Russia. Yet, the Tsar-Liberator, as he was justly called, fell victim to a terrorist bomb in 1881, one of the saddest days in Russian history. On his desk lay the project of a constitution, ready to be signed. The last two emperors of Russia, Alexander III and Nicholas II, were his son and grandson.

The second son of Nicholas I, from whom I am descended through his daughter Olga, was the first grand duke to devote his career to the navy. He was the most liberal-minded of the brothers, surrounding himself with reform-minded people in his capacity as head of the navy and the Geographical Society. This was all right with his brother, Alexander II, but his nephew, Alexander III, regarded him as a thorn in his side, and gradually pushed him out of public life.

The third brother, Nicholas, commanded the Russian armies advancing in the Balkans in the Turkish war of 1877. After the war, it is said, he had a passion for attending every fire in Petersburg, day or night. His son, Grand Duke Nicholas Nikolayevich, Jr. was the hugely tall commander-in-chief of the Russian armies in the first years of World War I.

The fourth brother, and youngest son of Nicholas I, was my great-grandfather, Michael, born in 1832.[2] For much of his long life, by Romanov standards, he was closely involved with the Caucasus. At the age of thirty he was appointed Viceroy, with headquarters in Tiflis, and commander of the Army of the Caucasus. In both these jobs he replaced the aging Prince Baryatinsky, the field marshal to whom Shamil had surrendered. Incidentally, Baryatinsky arranged to have Shamil settle near his place of retirement so that the two old warriors could discuss the campaigns they had fought against each other.

When Grand Duke Michael became viceroy, though Shamil was gone, there was still fighting in the western part of the mountains, and it was not until 1864 that the Caucasus was fully pacified, or conquered, depending on one's point of view. For the next few years Michael was engaged in the peaceful task of trying to

---

2.　　　Thus I am doubly descended from Emperor Nicholas I.

promote the prosperity of the Caucasus as a whole, without trampling on the sensibilities of the numerous peoples under his control. For all practical purposes, he was free to do as he saw fit. He saw to it that serfdom was eliminated in the Caucasus, first in Tiflis province in 1864, and then in the recently independent Mingrelia (1867), the troops of which Catherine Chavchavadze Dadiani had led against the Turks a decade earlier.

In the Russo-Turkish War of 1877, the main Russian forces under Michael's older brother, Nicholas, advanced almost to the gates of Constantinople, liberating the Bulgarians from the Turks in the process. While secondary, the Caucasian front against the Turks was important and also a huge success. This front was commanded by Grand Duke Michael. The Russian troops were augmented by numerous volunteers from various parts of the Caucasus, a fact very pleasing to Michael and the Russian government. There were also, however, small scale revolts by Moslem elements.

The most spectacular success of the Russians on the Caucasian front was the night attack and capture of the huge Turkish system of fortifications around Kars. Garrisoned by 25,000 Turks and supplied for a siege of many months, it was designed partly by European engineers and was considered impregnable in western military circles. The Russians took it in one night, attacking from seven sides simultaneously, with a loss of only 500 dead.

This was the last war won by Imperial Russia, and it was a stunning victory. For his part in it Michael was made field marshal and given the Order of St. George First Class, the highest military decoration of all, and very rarely bestowed. When he died he was the last man in Russia to have it, and also the last field marshal, for none were created either in the Russo-Japanese War or in World War I.

Later Michael was inspector-general of artillery, and under his nephew, Alexander III, he served as president of the Council of State, which made him the most influential grand duke in the government. However, a fellow member, Polevtsev, states in his diaries that Grand Duke Michael would really only perk up when either Caucasian affairs or the artillery were mentioned, and refers to him as "my sweet and cowardly grand duke," meaning that he was not inclined to stand up to his nephew the emperor.

He lived thirteen years into the reign of his grandnephew, Nicholas II, by far the oldest member of the family, and the last surviving son of Nicholas I. My mother remembers this grandfather as a gentle old man in a wheelchair, who liked to take her on his lap and called her "my little angel." She was eight when he died in the south of France in 1909. The French staged solemn ceremonies, and a Russian battleship came to take the old man home.

Grand Duke Michael, whom my son is named after, used to refer to him as "the guy with the long beard", was married to Princess Cäcilie of Baden, rechristened Olga Feodorovna, about whom I know very little except for her utterly fantastic geneology. Through her mother she was descended from the Vasa Kings of Sweden, the Kings of England from George II back, the Kings of Scotland, of course, and many Kings of France and various parts of Spain. Through the mother of Mary, Queen of Scots, she could trace her lineage through the crusader Kings of Cyprus and Kings of Armenia to the Great Kings of Persia—Xerxes, Darius, etc.—to the 7th century B.C., thereby besting the Caucasian side of my family. If it is true, as recently stated, that the Queen of England is descended from Mohammed, then Olga Feodorovna, and therefore I, must be too.[3] It goes along the same line. I don't think my Georgian ancestors would have been pleased at this development!

To this junior branch of the Romanovs, Olga Feodorovna also brought the blood of Ryurik, which was something they conspicuously lacked when they were elected to the throne in 1613. But Olga's descent from him was most curious. It ran through the Kings of France back to Philip I, whose mother was Anna Yaroslavna, daughter of Yaroslav the Wise, Grand Prince of Kiev in the 11th century, of the direct line of Ryurik, the founder of the dynasty. Incidentally, Anna Yaroslavna was literate, while her husband Henry I of France was not, and she regarded Paris as a dump compared to Kiev. Which it probably was 900 years ago.

Grand Duke Michael and his geneological wonder from Baden produced six sons and a daughter. The daughter, Anastasia, not to be confused with Nicholas II's daughter of the same name, married the Grand Duke of Mecklenburg-Schwerin, and became the mother of the last German crown princess. There was talk in the family that the blood of Catherine the Great ran strongly through Anastasia's veins, and she would leave the provincial court of Mecklenburg for a sexual romp in Paris for a month each year.

The eldest son of Grand Duke Michael was Grand Duke Nicholas Mikhailovich, the eminent historian referred to previously, a man who never married (but had numerous illigitimate children), and a socialist, which did not prevent the Bolsheviks from shooting him in 1919.

The second son, Grand Duke Michael Mikhailovich, lived in England because of a morganatic marriage. This, of course, was the gentleman who gave Babady such a hard time over my father's engagement to my mother.

My grandfather, George, was the third son, but before we get to him, let us deal with the fourth son, Alexander Mikhailovich. This was one of the few grand dukes who had a career in the navy, and one of those who survived the revolution. I remember seeing him when I was a little boy in New York. He was called Uncle Sandro, the Georgian nickname for Alexander, typical for this Caucasian-minded branch of the Romanovs. Uncle Sandro, judging from his photogrtaphs, must have been one of the handsomest men of his time, and he stood out even among the Romanovs, whose men, after Paul I, were an extraordinary good looking group. With the Romanov women these genes for good looks appeared less often, with some prominent exceptions.

Uncle Sandro traveled widely in the navy—to Brazil in time to meet the old Emperor Dom Pedro II; to the United States, and to the Far East, including Japan, where he spent enough time to pick up some Japanese from a girl there. When he dined with the Emperor and Empress of Japan, he was seated next to the empress and decided to try out some of this, let's face it, whorehouse Japanese, on her. He did not realize the extent to which Japanese had various levels of politeness, which I

---

3.   I now have a geneological chart of this descent, which goes through Spain to the Moslem world. It would probably surprise them, but a number of prominent Americans have this discent from Mohammed, including Robert E. Lee, Presidents George Washington, Benjamin Harrison and George Bush.

was to learn at Yale at least half a century later. The empress colored deeply and covered her face with her fan. Uncle Sandro also went out through the Suez Canal to Siam and French Indo-China on his yacht, *Tamara*, taking along some botanists and entomologists.

He was about the same age as Nicholas II, and they were great friends. Then they became brothers-in-law as well, because Uncle Sandro married Nicholas' sister, Grand Duchess Xenia. This was the first and only double Romanov marriage. From it came another family typical of the Romanovs, except for that of Nicholas II, six sons and one daughter. Both parents and all the children survived the revolution. The daughter, Irina, married Prince Felix Yusupov, the chief organizer of Rasputin's murder in 1916.

In World War I Uncle Sandro commanded the Russian air force, which contained the first two engined and four engined planes ever built, designed by the same Igor Sikorsky who would later produce airplanes and helicopters in the United States.

After the revolution Uncle Sandro wrote three widely read books, *Once A Grand Duke*, *Always a Grand Duke*, and *The Twilight of Royalty*. My parents said these were ghost written, and although they contain much fascinating information, there are also errors of fact in them. Uncle Sandro died in 1933.

My grandfather, Grand Duke George Mikhailovich, was the first of Michael's children to be born in Tiflis, in 1863, shortly after his father's appointment as viceroy. I will refer to him as *Apapa*, a Danish nickname for grandfather, which entered our branch of the family through Apapa's future marriage to a princess of Greece and Denmark. As a child he and all his brothers were brought up in the Spartan way established by his grandfather, Nicholas I, who liked to sleep on an army cot and wanted his descendants to be just as simple and soldierly. There were also interminable lessons from tutors.

Since Grand Duke Michael remained viceroy for twenty years, Apapa grew up in Georgia and loved it. As a young man he fell in love with Nina Chavchavadze, the youngest daughter of David and Anna, the same Princess Anna who had been kept captive in the mountain headquarters of Shamil. Apapa wanted to marry Nina, but her mother, Princess Anna, ever mindful of the fact that she was a granddaughter of the last King of Georgia, forbade the match. If Nina married a grand duke, she would have to be his morganatic wife, and not a grand duchess, and proud Princess Anna could not bear the thought that any descendant of the Bagrations would have to yield precedence to a bunch of minor German princesses who had become grand duchesses. So Apapa did not get his Chavchavadze bride, and did not marry until he was thirty-seven. Nina too waited many years before she married. This story did not surface until after my parents were married in 1922, and once again gave them the feeling that they were fated to be together. Apapa, I am sure, would have been delighted had he lived to see his daughter bearing the exact name of his first love, Nina Chavchavadze.

Like all of the grand dukes, Apapa entered military service, his regiment being Her Majesty's Lancers of the Guards. An early leg injury prevented him from making much of a military career. He was a passionate coin collector and became one of the greatest numismatic experts in the world. His collection included practically every coin ever used in the territory of the Russian Empire, from the ancient Greeks on. His monographs can still be found in American libraries today. After the revolution, part of this coin collection was smuggled out of Russia. After many peregrinations through Yugoslavia and Greece, and long after World War II, the unpilfered residue ended up in the United States, and now reposes in the Smithsonian Institution in Washington.

With this scholarly collector's bent, it was no wonder that Apapa was appointed curator of the Alexander III Museum in St. Petersburg, still very much alive as the "Russian Museum," one of the leading museums in the USSR today.

Like all the Romanovs except Nicholas II, he was very tall. He had brown eyes, a thin, very straight nose, and a big bushy moustache, but no beard. Hence he was called "the guy with the moustache" by my little son. He began to bald at the turn of the century and was quite bald by the time he was fifty. Luckily, this gene did not come to me, although I have read that male baldness usually comes from maternal grandfathers. "The guy with the moustache" seems to have been a very nice person. I have heard and read adverse comments on most of the grand dukes, but absolutely none about Apapa. Everybody who knew him liked and respected him.

He was four years older than Nicholas II, and also a close friend, though not as close as Uncle Sandro. Still, the emperor knew that Apapa would not disguise the truth from him, and for an honest ruler this is supremely important.

In 1900 Apapa married a first cousin once removed, Princess Marie of Greece. She was the daughter of King George I of Greece, a Danish prince called to the Greek throne in 1863, whose sisters became Queen Alexandra of England, and Dagmar, the Empress Marie Feodorovna of Russia, the mother of the last tsar. So Amama was actually more closely related to Nicholas II than was his fellow Romanov, Apapa. Amama's mother, Queen Olga of Greece, was born a Russian grand duchess, daughter of Apapa's uncle, Grand Duke Constantine.

Apapa was very much in love with Amama, but the passion was not returned. When he proposed to her, standing at a billiard table, she accepted but kept dodging around the table to avoid being kissed. In her memoirs she refers to this rather significant moment in her life very laconically: "The Grand Duke George of Russia proposed to me and was accepted."

Amama had no desire to leave her beloved Greece for the cold north, even though it was her mother's country, and had the same religion. Nevertheless they were married at Corfu with all due pomp, and in 1901 my mother Nina was born, followed in 1903 by her sister Xenia.

The girls were princesses of Russian and "highnesses," rather than grand duchesses and "imperial highnesses," so at birth they rated only a twenty-one gun salute instead of 101. I once met an old general in Berlin after World War II who had been a young officer in the battery that fired those twenty-one guns for my mother's birth on that June day in St. Petersburg.

The reason for these lower titles in this generation was not primarily to save powder for the Russian artillery, but it was largely economic all the same. Around 1886, when for the first time the wife of a grandson of Nicholas I was expecting a child, Alexander III became concerned that the number of grand dukes and grand duchesses would get out of hand with this new generation, and that they would all have to be supported in grand ducal style. So he changed the law. Only the sons, daughters, grandsons and granddaughters of emperors could be grand dukes or grand duchesses. This sensible rule avoided a situation like that in Austria, with its endless collection of Habsburg archdukes and archduchesses.

Apapa and Amama and the two girls first lived in old Grand Duke Michael's palaces, one in town and one outside, both large enough for individual apartments for the old man's numerous sons. My mother remembers bicycling through the halls to pay calls on relatives!

Later, Apapa and Amama bought land in the Crimea and by 1906 had built themselves a house. The estate was called by the Greek name of Harax. It was right on the rocky coast, close to the estates of various relatives, including Nicholas II's Livadia. The fact that the ancient Greeks had lived there soothed Amama's heart. It was Harax, rather than Petersburg, that was home to my mother. In old age she used to say that while she would never want to visit the Soviet Union, she would love to be on a ship looking at the rocky coast of Harax, the same coast that had been my father's last glimpse of Russia from Colonel Boyle's Roumanian ship.

I have the guest book from Harax[4] with many interesting signatures. The great operatic basso Chaliapin came and drew a caricature of himself, clearly recognizable even though the view is of the back of his head. Nicholas II and Alexandra were frequent visitors with their children.

On one occasion a general arrived for lunch and remarked that the emperor really looked very Russian. He had just passed a private soldier on the road who looked very much like him and had drawn himself to attention and saluted the general. A short time later the emperor was announced, dressed as a private, with full pack and rifle. He had taken the hike to test out on his own body new equipment for the Russian troops.

There was a groom at Harax, a Crimean Tatar called Hussein, who used to take my mother and Aunt Xenia out riding. In the 1930s he was driving a cab in New York and presented me with the princely present of a bicycle. I met him forty years later and listened to his stories for a whole wonderful evening. He told me that he used to meet the emperor frequently on the back paths leading to Harax. Nicholas II always stopped to chat with the young lad and always remembered his name.

When the war broke out in 1914 Apapa offered to send Hussein for aviation training.

"Thank you but no, Your Imperial Highness! Nobody will ever get me off the ground where Allah decreed that we live!"

Apapa then sent Hussein to be trained as a driver, which may well have saved his life, because Hussein spent the war and the civil war driving generals around in staff cars. This training helped him get taxi driver jobs in Constantinople and later in New York. Eventually he retired to Florida.

Touchingly, this old man took buses from Florida to Cape Cod for both my parents' funerals. He could have afforded to fly, he told me, but he still refused to

---

4.   This book was brought out of Russia in 1919 aboard the *H.M.S. Marlborough* by
        Empress Marie.

leave the ground.

My mother was something of a tomboy at Harax, playing with her numerous first cousins, the children of Uncle Sandro and Grand Duchess Xenia, and also with the emperor's children, although the poor little tsarevich was extremely limited in what he could do because of hemophilia. She loved them all, except for the youngest daughter, Anastasia, whom she considered nasty to the point of being evil. Anastasia was two days older and could not forgive my mother for being taller than she was.

Perhaps she was touchy about height because her father was so much shorter than all of the grand dukes and most of the guards officers. Nicholas II certainly had a complex about this height, the opposite of the classical Napoleonic complex. He once said to Amama, "Nobody likes to take orders from a dwarf!"

In June 1914 Amama decided to take her daughters on a three month visit to Harrogate in England where the climate was considered beneficial to little Xenia. And so on a railroad platform just before the start of World War I my mother parted forever from her dearly beloved father. Judging from her diaries, I think she somehow knew that she would never see her father or Russia again.

Apapa, who had been out of the army for so many years, was given a staff position with two star general's rank. He was something like an inspector general in view of the emperor's trust in his judgement and truthfulness. It seems that he acquired a number of enemies during the war by reporting mismanagement when he came across it, and there was plenty of that. In his letters to his family in England he expressed more and more disgust with what he saw. Luckily, he enclosed numerous photographs, so I have a whole album of Apapa in World War I.

In 1915 he was sent on a mission to Tokyo, to call on the Emperor of Japan. The Japanese, so recently victorious over the Russians, but now allies, were somewhat embarrassed by the tall stature of Apapa and his aide. They solved that by producing a gigantic Japanese wrestler who was even taller, which made them feel better. They were also very discrete. When the ship carrying Apapa to Japan crossed the spot where the Russian Baltic Fleet had been destroyed in 1905 they left the Russian delegation strictly alone with their thoughts. On the way back from Japan, Apapa inspected many places in the Russian Far East and Siberia, where grand dukes seldom if ever appeared. He wrote that he was impressed with the morale of the troops there, and the lack of revolutionary propaganda as compared to European Russia.

During his inspections Apapa also decorated hundreds of soldiers with the Cross of St. George, always particularly appreciated if bestowed by a member of the Imperial Family.

In 1916 Apapa, convinced that a revolution was inevitable, was one of the grand dukes who urged the emperor to grant a full constitution. The advice was not taken.

After the Bolsheviks toppled Kerensky's government, Apapa managed to go to Finland and almost got on a British ship, but the British Labour government at that time was adamant against helping any members of the former imperial family. If he had kept a low profile long enough, he might have been saved by Finnish independence. But he made the mistake of applying for exit papers at the local soviet. He was soon arrested and shipped back to Petersburg, where he was interrogated by the head of the local Cheka, Uritsky, who was shortly to be assassinated by a member of a rival socialist faction. There was a period of exile for Apapa in Vologda and then imprisonment at St. Petersburg. Apapa's cell, which he diagrammed in a letter to England, was precisely the same as the cells now shown to tourists there, except that some of the plumbing has been removed since his time. On the back of this diagram, someone else wrote what "Citizen George Mikhailovich Romanov" was entitled to in the way of breakfast. Not bad by later standards.

Apapa was joined in the next cell by his cousin, Grand Duke Paul, the youngest son of Alexander II, his brother Nicholas (the historian), and another cousin, Grand Duke Dimitri Constantinovich. Many attempts were made to save these grand dukes by foreign diplomats and even by people involved in Lenin's regime. The writer Maxim Gorky, fighting especially for the life of Nicholas the historian and socialist, obtained an order from Lenin not to execute the four grand dukes, who had never been involved in politics or repressive acts. Lenin told Gorky to take a train to Petersburg with the order, but when Gorky got to the station their execution had already been announced in the press. Whether Lenin fooled Gorky and sent a telegram ahead, or whether the local commissars in Petersburg decided to carry out orders they already had, I do not know.

On January 30, 1919, Apapa and the three other grand dukes, were shot in the Fortress of St. Peter and Paul. They were the last Romanov victims of the Bolsheviks. One can imagine what this well publicised news did to my mother and her sister in England.

Apapa was not yet fifty-six when he was shot, younger than I am now. It happened five years before I was born so, obviously, I never met him. Yet, somehow I felt close to him in childhood because of everything my mother told me, and because we had so many pictures of him, including the mission to Japan and his inspections in Siberia.

Toward the end of World War II I had a dream which was so vivid that it was more like a vision than a dream. Unlike any other dream I ever had, I can remember every detail. I saw Russian officers standing about in the snow near a log cabin wearing long greatcoats and fur hats. I assumed that they were Soviet officers in Alaska; I had just returned from being an American liaison officer with them.

Suddenly I realized that instead of lieutenant's bars, I was wearing shoulder boards too, and a sabre at my side, and I heard myself saying, "Lieutenant Prince Chavchavadze requests an audience with His Imperial Highness."

I was allowed into the cabin where Apapa sat at a desk with his long moustaches and bald head.

"Oh, it's you," he said. "Come and sit next to me!" He caressed my head as I sat by his side.

I tried to speak quickly because I realized that I was in the wrong time and place, and had very little time to stay with him. About all I managed to say before the dream dissolved was, "At least I can tell Mama that we have met!"

KING GEORGE I
and
QUEEN OLGA of GREECE

PRINCE GEORGE OF GREECE

GREEK ROYAL FAMILY - 1950
Princess Irene, Queen Frederika, Crown Prince Constantine, King Paul,
Princess Sophia

QUEEN LOUISE
(Eilers Collection)

KING CHRISTIAN IX of DENMARK
(Great-Great-Grandfather of Author)

David 1938

PRINCE DAVID CHAVCHAVADZE
Knickerbocker Grey - 1938

1922

PRINCESS NINA

THE HOUSES OF DENMARK - ENGLAND - GREECE - RUSSIA
(simplified)

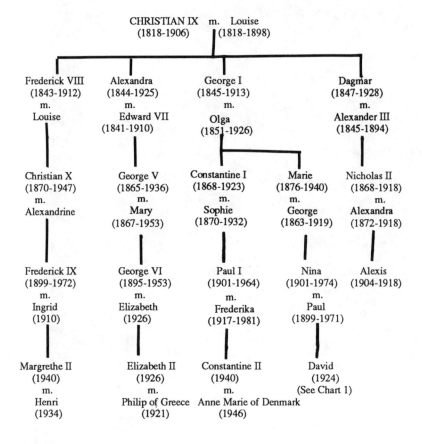

CHRISTIAN IX m. Louise
(1818-1906)   (1818-1898)

Frederick VIII
(1843-1912)
m.
Louise

Alexandra
(1844-1925)
m.
Edward VII
(1841-1910)

George I
(1845-1913)
m.
Olga
(1851-1926)

Dagmar
(1847-1928)
m.
Alexander III
(1845-1894)

Christian X
(1870-1947)
m.
Alexandrine

George V
(1865-1936)
m.
Mary
(1867-1953)

Constantine I
(1868-1923)
m.
Sophie
(1870-1932)

Marie
(1876-1940)
m.
George
(1863-1919)

Nicholas II
(1868-1918)
m.
Alexandra
(1872-1918)

Frederick IX
(1899-1972)
m.
Ingrid
(1910)

George VI
(1895-1953)
m.
Elizabeth
(1926)

Paul I
(1901-1964)
m.
Frederika
(1917-1981)

Nina
(1901-1974)
m.
Paul
(1899-1971)

Alexis
(1904-1918)

Margrethe II
(1940)
m.
Henri
(1934)

Elizabeth II
(1926)
m.
Philip of Greece
(1921)

Constantine II
(1940)
m.
Anne Marie of Denmark
(1946)

David
(1924)
(See Chart 1)

CHAPTER IV

King Christian IX of Denmark, who died at age eighty-seven in 1906, was known as the "Grandfather of Europe." He was born into an impoverished branch of the Danish royal house known as Schleswig-Holstein-Sondeburg-Glücksburg, and had few prospects. He could hardly have dreamed of the dynastic successes in store for him and his issue. The main Danish line died out, and Christian became King of Denmark in 1863. Before he did, however, in the same year, his eldest daughter Alexandra married the Prince of Wales (Edward VII), and his second son, William, was elected King of the Hellenes, as George I. Three years later Christian's second daughter Dagmar married the future Emperor of Russia, Alexander III. Marie Feodorovna, as she was rechristened, became the mother of the ill-fated Nicholas II.

Christian IX's grandson became the first King of Norway in the present line as Haakon VII, and another grandson, Prince Andrew of Greece, fathered the Duke of Edinburgh, Queen Elizabeth II's husband! In a political sleight-of-hand thought necessary at the time, Prince Philip of Greece assumed his mother's name of Mountbatten before marrying the Princess Elizabeth in 1947, so, strictly speaking, when Prince Charles succeeds his mother this once obscure house will have become the dynasty of Great Britain, as well as Denmark, Norway and Greece.

My mother never could remember that mouthful of names, which was never normally used anyway. When she obtained her American citizenship in New York in 1937, she was asked for her father's name.

"Grand Duke George of Russia."

"No, I mean what was his last name," the official said.

"Romanov."

"Mother's maiden name?"

"Princess Marie of Greece."

"Now cut that stuff out, Lady. What was her last name?"

"I don't know," said my mother.

She is listed in the immigration archives as Nina Chavchavadze, daughter of George Romanov and Marie LNU (last name unknown.)

As for my father, he was handed a form and told, "OK Prince, go in the next room and abdicate."

At the age of seventeen, my Danish great-grandfather, Prince William, became a king; embarrassingly, before his father did. The young man was a cadet at the Danish naval academy. His parents tried to hide the offer from him, regarding the Greek throne as a very chancy affair at best, in a far-off, unstable country. Besides, they knew he was the adventurous type and would jump at the challenge. His parents were right. The Prince, who was brown-bagging it at the naval academy, chanced to read about his election in the piece of Danish newspaper in which his can of sardines was wrapped.

He became King of Greece without knowing the language and somehow managed to stay on the throne for fifty years, no small feat in that part of the world. He took the job very seriously, traveling about the country and speaking to as many people as possible. He instinctively understood the Greeks, and his role as a non-Greek referee among a very political minded people.

Actually, the Greeks had wanted Queen Victoria's son, Alfred, to be their king, but this was impossible if only because Britain was then one of the "protecting powers" of Greece. My great-grandfather was a second choice, and owed his election to the fact that his sister would one day be Queen of England.

After four years without leaving Greece, the handsome, young, and very amiable king journeyed to St. Petersburg to visit his other sister. There he met and fell in love with the sixteen-year-old Grand Duchess Olga, whose father was that liberal Grand Duke Constantine, second son of Nicholas I. The feeling was mutual. Years later she told her daughter, "I fell in love with the man, not the king."

They were married, and the new Queen of Greece, upon arriving in Athens, was frequently in tears out of sheer shyness at having to receive ladies of the court. She still played with dolls. This great-grandmother was also my godmother, and actually held me at my christening in 1924. She died two years later, an almost saintly person, really loved by all who knew her.

In 1868 the teenage Queen Olga gave birth to a son, and thousands of Greeks outside the palace yelled out the name "Constantine," because with a new Constantine on the throne some day they felt that the great days of the Greek (Byzantine) empire would be restored.

King George II of Greece and Queen Olga had four other sons, George, Nicholas, Andrew and Christopher, and two daughters, Alexandra, who married Grand Duke Paul of Russia (later shot with Apapa), and died in childbirth, and my grandmother Marie, born in 1876. All of these children were brought up speaking Greek, deeply steeped in Greek history and culture, and all of them very strong Greek nationalists. My grandmother cried when she first learned that she had no Greek blood.

I have met many Greeks who complain that their royal family is foreign. They should have known them personally. On the other hand, I have met Greeks who insist that a foreign referee is useful in their political process.

King George I mingled with his people for fifty years with little or no security precautions, but in 1913 he was assassinated in Salonika, recently acquired from the Turks in the Balkan War. He was succeeded by his eldest son, Constantine I, my grandmother's brother. Constantine was immensely popular at that time because of his role in commanding the Greek Army in the Balkan Wars. This king was to have enormous political problems, particularly with the Allies in World War I. For one thing, he was married to Kaiser Wilhelm II's sister, and everything he did, even though he was thinking only of Greece, was suspect in their eyes. Generally, toward the end of World War I, the Greek dynasty entered a long period of abdications, restorations, re-abdications, re-exiles, re-restorations, and again exile, lasting to the present day.

King Paul I, was the fifth ruler in the dynasty, and succeeded his brother George I on April 1, 1947. He had wanted to marry my mother in the early 1920s in spite of being her first cousin. She liked him a lot, she told me, but only as a cousin. She always said she would have made a terribly queen! She also turned down a chance to be Queen of Yugoslavia when the future King Alexander I proposed. He later married Princess Marie of Roumania.

I have only a vague memory of Amama, through whom I was so closely related to all these people, from when I was three in London. She was looking at me through a lorgnette, being very nearsighted, and murmuring, "Chavchavchavchavchav . . . ." It was obvious that she was not thrilled by my mother's marriage, because all she says in her memoirs is, "My daughter Nina married Paul Chavchavadze, a Caucasian prince." Period. This must have offended my father, whose penciled note on her manuscript is still there. He changed it to read "Prince Paul Chavchavadze, a member of a prominent Georgian family." This was really quite unlike him, but I cannot blame him, he was even left out of the index! However, he always told me that he got on splendidly with his mother-in-law after the first awkward period. I wonder if he saw a letter, now in my possession, that Amama wrote to a friend in 1922: "Nina is engaged to young Prince Paul Chavchavadze, a very nice boy, though a Russian. Perhaps it is his Georgian blood or the excellent influence of his mother, one of the notorious Rodzianko family."

When I was nine in 1933, Amama came to the United States. I remember her as a very amusing person, very easy going and funny with her grandchildren, my cousin, Nancy Leeds and myself, quite unlike the way she had been with her daughters.

I did get into big trouble once, when I got mad at Amama and said something like, "Shut up, you old Greek!" As my father threw me out of the room I heard Amama's explosive laughter.

She enjoyed being called a Greek because this is what she considered herself to be. Even though in her childhood, English, Danish, German, French and Russian were spoken all about her, all of her journals and diaries were kept in Greek, except, fortunately her memoirs, which she typed in English.

At one point, after she was married to Apapa and living in Russia, some protocol arrangement required that she ride in the same carriage with King Ferdinand of Bulgaria. She refused to ride with this "Bulgarian pig," who was a Coburg from Germany and had no more Bulgarian blood than she had Greek. She was forced to take this ride, however, which she did in complete silence, then afterwards had the coach fumigated. As a Greek she hated Bulgarians, all of them. What a classic case of late 19th century chauvinism!

Although she married Apapa without much enthusiasm, her memoirs contain a lot of respect, if not love, for him. Living in Russia from 1900 to 1914, she never learned to speak Russian very well. She spoke French to her husband and English to her daughters, both of whom spoke Russian to their father. They were just as nationalistically Russian as their mother was Greek. My mother hated the frequent trips to Germany to visit relatives and always claimed she had this prejudice long before World War I.

When Amama took her daughters to England on the eve of the war, it was probably a trial separation.

At Harrogate, Amama started a hospital for wounded soldiers, first with twelve beds, and later growing to three different buildings, financed partly by herself, the Russian Red Cross, money from her aunt the dowager Empress Marie Feodorovna, and a lot of support from the British royal family, particularly from her other aunt, Queen Alexandra. This hospital, known as Grand Duchess George's, lasted five years, during which time only eight patients died. A lot of wounded were Canadians, and Amama made up whole scrapbooks of letters written to her by former patients, all of them, British and Canadian enlisted men, and she cherished the little presents they gave her.

One present, which I still have, was not from the hospital patients. It is a black, very British looking umbrella, inscribed around the handle as follows: "To HIH the Grand Duchess George of Russia from the 11th Battalion, King's Own Yorkshire Light Infantry, as a Momento of HIH's visit, 8 May 1915."

I know what Chekhov said: "If you hang a rifle on the wall in the first act . . . ." This umbrella, which would have been a sword had she been a man, will make another appearance.

In 1916, while still running her Harrogate hospital, Amama took a house in London to further her daughters' education. She found herself in a very difficult situation with her dual nationality. Her brother, King Constantine I of Greece, was being accused of being pro-German or at least anti-Allied, and even Emperor Nicholas II was somehow suspected of plotting a separate peace with the Germans, a calumny if there ever was one.

People began to consider Amama some sort of spy or dangerous element, but she had the constant support of her aunt, the dowager Queen Alexandra, a Dane who could be under no suspicion whatever, having loathed the Prussians since their 1864 attack on Denmark.

There had been no safe way for Amama and the girls to return to Russia when war broke out. The only plan that was made in this regard fortunately misfired because of Amama's tardiness. They missed the boat, and the boat was the ship carrying Lord Kitchener which disappeared, presumably torpedoed by the Germans. I still don't know why Lord Kitchener, a very prominent British general, was going to Russia. There was a lot of mystery about it between the wars, and still is.

As often happens with siblings, my mother and her sister Xenia had totally different memories of the British phase of their childhood. Aunt Xenia liked it. My mother thought it was horrible. She, always a rebel, thought of Amama as an impossible Victorian and repressive mother, and her thirteen years in England as a mixture of underheated houses and boring young men talking about horses.

Young man at ball: "Do you hunt?"

My mother: "No."

Young man: "Oh."

Even the excitements of World War I, passing tanks and troops and Zeppelin raids were spoiled for her by someone or other forcing her away from the windows. She should have lived with Queen Alexandra, who drove everybody crazy by refusing to observe blackouts and always watching the fun from her windows at Marlborough House.

My mother missed Russia and her father terribly. Probably Aunt Xenia did too, but she was younger and much better adjusted to her mother's way of doing things. With the revolution of 1917, it became obvious that there would be no more Russia for them, although perhaps their father could join them. The financial situation became extremely serious, and Amama was able to survive largely through the help of a rich American lady, Mrs. Nancy Leeds, who was about to marry Amama's brother, Christopher of Greece. Four years later, Mrs. Leeds' son, William, married Aunt Xenia.

King George V of England was a very grouchy man, but an excellent constitutional monarch. This put him in a very difficult position in regard to his cousin, Nicholas II, and the rest of the Russian Imperial Family, because of the attitude of the new Labour government. He had to obey his ministers, but he could have done more to save the imperial family.

After the murder of Emperor Nicholas II and his immediate family in July 1918, a memorial service was planned in the Russian Orthodox Church in London. The king refused to attend, and here is where the umbrella re-enters the story. Amama, first cousin of both George V and Nicholas II, literally charged into Buckingham Palace with it and, intimidating servants right and left, stormed the sitting room where George V and Queen Mary were having tea. There is no record that she used the umbrella on them, but in any case her indignation produced results, and the king and queen did attend the service at the Russian church, Labour government notwithstanding. After all, it could be treated as a purely family matter.

Meanwhile in Greece other family matters tied to complex politics had been going on. King Constantine was accused by the Allies of being pro-German because he refused to enter the war. Amama always insisted that he was really pro-Allied, but wanted to keep Greece neutral in view of the losses she had suffered in the pre-1914 Balkan wars.

Tremendous intrigues went on between the French (with an assist from the British) and the Greek politician Venizelos. It even came to the point of Allied ships shelling the royal palace and a French division occupying Athens.

Constantine was forced to leave the country in 1917 with his heir, the future George II. Constantine's amiable but inexperienced second son Alexander, aged twenty-four, was placed on the throne as a figurehead. Three years later he died of blood-poisoning from the bite of a pet monkey.

Meanwhile Venizelos took Greece into the war on the Allied side, and, after the war ended, started a new one with Turkey. At the death of King Alexander in 1920, Venizelos decided to call an election. He was soundly defeated, and a plebiscite followed in which the still immensely popular King Constantine was returned in triumph. The Allies refused to recognize him and he inherited the war with Turkey. During the interlude between Alexander's death and Constantine's restoration, my great-grandmother and godmother, Queen Olga, acted as regent, and was thus the last Romanov to rule.

An so, in 1920, Amama, her daughters, and two of her brothers, Andrew and Christopher, headed for Greece in great joy. What must have been the feelings of her Russian daughters at the news that General Wrangel's White Army, in that same year, had been forced to evacuate the Crimea (and, of course, Harax, their home)? It was the end of organized resistance to the Bolsheviks, except in the Far East.

Amama does mention this, in passing, but her feelings for Greece were, as always, triumphant. Now a widow, she vowed to marry the first Greek she met. By this she did not mean literally the first one, since there were hundreds of them swimming around the ship on which they arrived in Corfu, and others generally overwhelming the brothers and sister of the restored king with exceeding enthusiasm, but she did eventually marry the captain of the Greek destroyer *Ierax*, which had been sent to take them through the Corinth Canal to Piraeus. His name was Pericles Ioannides, and he had been jailed for three years by Venizelos for his loyalty to Constantine.

My mother, who never thought much of monarchy or monarchists, could never forget the enthusiasm of the Greeks on both sides of the Corinth Canal and throughout the rest of the journey, and the king was not even aboard. The celebrations in Piraeus and Athens were even greater, and when the king returned, escorted by the same destroyer, there was no containing the crowds.

This restoration was an amazing event in an epoch when thrones were crumbing. Amama remarks that the British nurses employed by members of the royal family wrote a collective letter to *The Times* of London describing the public jubilation, knowing the dim view the British government held of the whole thing. *The Times* regretted that there was no way their letter could be published.

Greece was at war with Turkey, and during this period my nineteen-year-old mother worked as a nurse taking care of the Greek wounded. The experience was valuable when she did the same with Americans at Fort Dix, New Jersey twenty-three years later.

In the fickle world of Balkan politics, Constantine did not last long after his triumphant restoration. The war with the Turks was going badly, and he was again forced to abdicate, this time in favor of his eldest son, George II. He died three months later, of a broken heart, Amama wrote.

By that time, however, Amama and her daughters were gone from Greece. Aunt Xenia married William B. Leeds, Jr. in Paris in 1921, given away by Uncle Sandro. Their only child Nancy (now Mrs. Edward Wynkoop) and I have always been close, although we fought like wildcats as children.

Amama and my mother returned to England, and there my mother met my father, just in from Roumania. My mother was terrified to tell Amama of the engagement, so she picked a strategic moment to break the news. They were going up the stairs of a double-decker London bus, and my mother called up to Amama, "I'm engaged to Paul Chavchavadze!"

By the time Amama had found a seat and arranged her skirts, she had calmed down and even consented to have the young man to dinner.

My parents' wedding took place on September 3, 1922 in the Russian Church in London, in the presence of Queen Alexandra and Queen Olga, whom the British would allow into the country for only twelve days because of continued political complications with the Greek Royal Family. My parents spent their honeymoon at Warwick Castle, lent to them by one of Amama's friends.

Her daughters safely married, Amama got married herself to the destroyer captain, now an admiral, but retired because of further Greek political events. Until the death of Amama's aunt, Queen Alexandra, they lived at Sandringham taking care of her. Then they moved to Rome. I have no idea what her life with the admiral was like. He was not with her in New York in 1933, and I did not meet him until long after her death. Always very outspoken, Amama made no secret of her dislike for Mussolini. Her friendship with the Italian royal family protected her for awhile, but in 1940 Mussolini ordered Amama and the admiral out of Italy. They returned to Greece, Amama already a very sick woman. Shortly afterwards, Mussolini attacked Greece, and Amama lived long enough to know about the magnificent stand her beloved Greeks made against the Italians, who had to be rescued by their German allies. She died as the Germans were approaching Athens, just in time to avoid capture. She was buried in the royal crypt at Tatoi, one of her childhood homes, before the royal family had to evacuate Greece, as we found out later from the future Queen Frederika.

NYANYUSHKA
(Vera Nagovsky)

CHAPTER V

On Sunday, 3 September 1922, among the people attending mass at the Russian church in London there was a very short woman with long golden hair done up in a bun, gray eyes, thirty-two years old. She heard that some sort of important royal wedding was taking place after mass, but that because of security the congregation would not be allowed to stay for it as they normally would have. She decided to stay anyway, and, being so small, she concealed herself behind a column, and thus watched my parents being married, never dreaming how this marriage would affect her life.

Her name was Vera Alexandrovna Nagovsky. She was born in 1890, the third child and second daughter of a priest who ran the village church in Samokrazha, about twenty-five miles north of Novgorod, in the heart of old Great Russia. Although the village then had a population of about 100 people, it must have once been more important, because Father Alexander's church was an impressive three story building of stone. The priest himself, although he claimed relationship to the family of Maria Nogaya, Ivan the Terrible's last wife and the mother of the ill-fated Tsarevich Dmitri, was very much the hearty village priest so common then throughout Russia. His greatest joy was to go out in his boat in a nearby lake and fish for pike. Once he brought back a thirty pounder, which he had his children fillet and distribute to the villagers.

He also had to bring up his children himself. His wife, who died in 1899, bore him a total of five. By church law he could not remarry. He could have become a monk, and possibly a bishop, but his children came first, and he preferred the country life in Samokrazha to a monk's cell or the responsibility of high church office. His daughter summed up in four words what he taught his children: love, kindness, pity and good sense.

In spite of the loss of her mother at the age of nine, Vera remembered a happy childhood. There was plenty of work to do. There were horses, cows, pigs and chickens to take care of, a large vegetable garden, picking wild strawberries that covered the fields like a red carpet, and, of course, the great Russian sport of picking mushrooms in the woods. These things were marinated and stored for the winter. Hay had to be stacked in the barn. Vera remembered it all lovingly, including the winter with its magic snowfalls.

She attended the village school, and in the evenings her father read aloud from books he had bought in Novgorod, including not only Russian classics but translations from French and English. Her sister attended a school run by nuns in Novgorod, and this was where Vera was supposed to go. She had been there several times and met the nuns, but somehow she wanted something better and less religiously oriented for herself.

As in the fairy tales, her godmother came to her rescue. She was the wife of a prominent St. Petersburg doctor, and she arranged a scholarship for Vera for the eight-year course at a girls' school in the capital called the Patriotic Institute, one of several such schools founded by Catherine the Great. At this time it was under the patronage of the Dowager Empress Marie Feodorovna and Nicholas II's second daughter, Tatiana.

Vera was the lucky one in her family. There was no way then to predict that the old way of life would disappear within twenty years, in war and revolution. Both of her brothers were wounded in World War I, and lived on somehow under the Soviets with the stigma of coming from a clerical family. Vera's younger sister, Shura, though, lived on in Samokrazha, through revolution, collectivization, World War II and German occupation, never marrying and cultivating her little "private" plot until her death in 1980. Vera helped her by sending packages and money from England and the United States. Shura was her only link with home and Russia.

Vera enjoyed the Patriotic Institute. There were only eleven girls in her class. Her teacher was a very cultivated woman, the daughter of the famous artist Serov. The girls got to attend St. Petersburg theatres, opera and ballet, seeing all the stars of the time, including Chaliapin and Anna Pavlova. When she graduated in 1908 Vera easily had the equivalent of today's American B.A. At graduation the senior class was presented to the dowager empress and her granddaughter at the Winter Palace. Vacations were spent back in Samokrazha, or at Vera's godmothers' Chekhovian estate near Luga. On one Christmas trip to Samokrazha, Vera had the classical Russian narrow escape from wolves while being driven in a sleigh from Novgorod.

Vera wanted to become a teacher, but an illness in the summer of 1908 prevented her from getting such a position in the coming fall. Instead, she became a nurse/governess, and that's what she did for the rest of her working life. A terrible profession. One forms attachments to other people's children, who inevitably grow older, and one has to move on. Governesses never seem to marry, and Vera was no exception, although she had her chances. At best they can expect to retire in some employer's household, see their ex-charges occasionally, and putter around with surrogate grandchildren. In Russia this possibility was shut off by revolution, but it scarcely exists anywhere any more.

In those days St. Petersburg was swarming with British and French governesses, with the British drawing ahead of the French in the highest social circles. They could impart a desirable language and they were strict. Russians were not in great demand.

Nevertheless, Vera got a job in Moscow in the family of an engineer with three children, Kolya, Natasha, and Vasya, whose adventures I knew by heart as a child. A second job followed in 1913 in a British Moscow family who wanted their children to know good Russian. These were called Tom and Lilly (Tomik and Lilka, Vera called them), and I know endless stories about them, too.

In 1914 while in the employ of this family, Vera was given a ride by a guest of the house, an Englishman, and the only romance in her life took place. He followed her to Riga, where the family summered on the Baltic. Then the war broke out. The Englishman, whose identity Vera always kept secret, went off to serve King and Country, and was killed in one of the first battles in France. Even in her eighties Vera could still cry at the thought of him, and she became an Anglophile (a rare thing among Russians) for life.

In the 1930s when she lived with us, Vera received two proposals of marriage. One was from the wonderful Crimean Tatar Hussein, the ex-groom at Harax. Her answer, "You are out of your mind!"

This was perhaps understandable, Hussein being a Moslem. But the second proposal came from a penniless Russian artist on Cape Cod, who was certainly a Christian. Her answer was the same.

Judging from the expression on her face when she told me the facts of life (not very accurately), sex did not turn her on, yet she was so proud of her long, golden hair, which she could wrap about her like a cloak when it wasn't pinned up in the omnipresent bun.

Tomik and Lilka's family returned to England, and Vera got her final job in Russia, taking care of a five-year-old called Eileen Don, whose mother had died the year before and whose father was the British representative of Eastman Kodak in Moscow. The luck of working for Mr. Don manifested itself after the revolution. By 1918 Vera could see arrested people being led under guard just by looking out of the window. Armed, drunken sailors entered apartments and helped themselves. Finally Mr. Don decided to return to England, still hoping to return to Moscow later. He asked Vera to come along. She agreed, provided that she could take leave of her family in Samokrazha, or whatever was left of it.

The trains in those days, when they ran at all, were jammed with people, inside, on top and between cars. To get a ticket at all was next to impossible, but tiny Vera persevered. She had a lot of strength in emergencies, or when she thought something was her due. When she retired to Florida in the 1950s she insisted on registering and voting as a Republican, in spite of the extremely bad time the southern Democratic officials gave her. She got her way. She was a Republican because of her admiration for Herbert Hoover's work in Russia to alleviate the severe famine of 1920. When he left the White House in 1933 she tearfully predicted, "He will return!"

A long way in time and space from Florida was that train to Novgorod in the winter of 1919. It was full of drunken soldiers. Vera rode between the cars and arrived frozen, not far from death. She was chopped loose and revived by a kindly conductor, and managed a farewell with her father and sister Shura that lasted for only two days.

The Soviets needed Mr. Don for trade with Britain and granted Vera a passport without difficulty. Mr. Don arranged a British visa for her in Petersburg, where some foreign diplomats were still functioning. Both Eileen and her grandmother were extremely ill by the time they all crossed the Finnish border, after a very severe shake-down by Soviet customs on the border. Vera managed to retain the icon with which her mother had blessed her on her deathbed.

In Finland Mr. Don's mother died, his daughter was at the point of death, all this after the loss of his wife and probably his business. The poor man went temporarily out of his head, and was committed to a Finnish sanatorium. So Vera was left all alone as she tried to nurse Eileen back to health. Leaving Eileen with some Finns, she took a train to Helsinki to try to find a British representative and on the train ran into friends of the Don family! These good people took care of Eileen and Vera until poor Mr. Don had recovered his senses and Eileen recovered from typhus. Vera's luck held as usual. She always called it 'God's help'.

By August 1919, after a stormy sea journey by way of Copenhagen, they were safe in England. I don't know how much English she spoke when she arrived, but when I knew her she spoke it quite fluently, but with an unbelievably classic Russian accent which she retained to the end of her long life. Every sound she made called Cyrillic letters to mind. Eileen turned ten in 1921 and the custom of the time decreed she must go to boarding school. Again Vera's heart was wrenched to part with a child, particularly this one with whom she had gone through so much.

In London, as opposed to old St. Petersburg, Russian speaking nannies and governesses were in demand. Vera had three offers through the still-functioning Kerensky consulate. One in England, another in Iran and a third in Ireland. She elected to stay in England.

In 1923 she was hired by a British-Russian family to take care of a little boy called Sasha Daddington, who was eighteen months old and "nervously ill," it was alleged. Both parents worked, his mother helping the famous Constance Garnett to translate the Russian classics. Two years with Vera was enough to cure Sasha of his nervous condition, whatever it was, and Vera again headed for the clearing house of the Kerensky consulate.

There she placed a notice on the board, and it so happened that my parents were looking for a Russian nurse for me. I was one year old, in the charge of a rather nasty British nanny, who insisted on calling my parents "Your Majesty." My father, not wanting to disaffect her, kept saying: "Nanny, we are not kings yet!" When Queen Olga of Greece came, and Nanny could have properly said, "Your Majesty," she bobbed and demoted the queen with a, "Your 'Oiness!"

I was on the point of speaking English, probably with dropped "H's" when Vera arrived. With her on the scene I grew up speaking Russian exclusively until the age of five. It was classical, correct Novgorod Great Russian (I still get compliments on its purity from Soviets and ex-Soviets), but it differed somewhat from the Petersburg aristocratic Russian my parents spoke. The difference was mostly in the stress of certain words and in my parents' avoidance of most diminutives, which Vera loved. After considerably more than half a century I still sometimes get confused as to whether I am speaking Novogorod or St. Petersburg.

Vera Alexandrovna Nagovsky became my *Nyanyushka*, diminutive for nanny in Russian. This is what I called her. She stayed with me for thirteen years, even after we moved to New York and she could have made five times as much elsewhere.

She taught me to read and write in Russian using the old orthography; she read aloud to me from the Russian classics and taught me Russian grammar. She even read to me from American classics like *Tom Sawyer*, translating into Russian as she went along. I still mentally pronounce names like "Amy Lawrence" and "Becky Thatcher" with her accent. She even did this with *Alice in Wonderland*, but a lot must have been lost in translation. She told me stories of rural Russia, of birch trees and mushroom hunting, of those far off children whose fate is unknown—Kolya, Natasha, Vasya, Tomik and Lilka, of her own childhood, her father, her brothers and sisters—a Russia very different from that of my parents.

76

She enveloped me with love, tenderness and affection. My relationship with my parents was always good, but they spent very little time with me, turning over my upbringing largely to Nyanyushka. Yes, she was very permissive, and those old St. Petersburg ladies had been right about Russian nannies in that respect. She also was straight-laced, looking down on my parents' fun-loving mode of life, which did not prevent me from following in their footsteps when my time came! I cannot imagine what childhood would have been like without Nyanyushka. She, more than anyone else, put Russia into me. Yet, she would always stand up when the *Star Spangled Banner* was played over the radio.

Without her I probably would have spoken the language to some extent, though almost nobody I knew of my generation and similar background in New York spoke Russian, or they lost it after entering American schools. I occasionally rebelled and came out with English, but basically I was proud of my heritage and put up with all the extra work because I wanted to speak Russian well. This all-important motivation came from my parents as well as from Nyanyushka.

Nyanyushka was a remarkable human being. She had about four more jobs with children after our very tearful parting in 1938 (obligatory boarding school again), and then she retired to Florida, living very modestly on social security and the proceeds from a small insurance policy. For years she prepared for her death in a very orderly manner. There was a letter on her desk to her sister announcing that she had died. Since postage had gone up over the years, the envelope was plastered with more and more stamps. As it turned out she outlived Shura by about a year.

Un-Russian as it was, she loved the warm climate of Florida. Perhaps it was the memory of having to be pried loose from the outside of a railroad coach in the Russian winter of 1919.

Nyanyushka died eighteen days short of her ninety-first birthday. She left all of her modest savings to me. She always had saved when she could. There would have been more, but Anglophile that she was, she transferred her savings in the 1930s to a British bank. Her funds were frozen during World War II, and returned to her much reduced in value. Until the end, although she had trouble walking, she could take care of herself and her mind was totally clear. She died peacefully in her sleep. God rest her soul!

PRINCESS NINA and AUTHOR

1916

PRINCESS NINA

MARUSYA, PRINCESS NINA, SASHA

IVAN OBLENSKY and AUTHOR

THE NOURMAHAL
The Astor Yacht

AUTHOR and HIS COUSIN NANCY LEEDS

CHAPTER VI

My mother always thought that her life went in cycles of thirteen years—thirteen years in Russia, thirteen years in England, thirteen years in New York—but then the cycle broke down. Most of the rest of her life was spent on Cape Cod.

That she disliked England has already been stated, but probably the worst part of it, as she grew older, was the discipline imposed by her mother. For instance, she couldn't stand wearing black for months at a time in mourning for some relative or other, and Amama was such a Victorian product that when my mother got married she did not know the facts of life; all she knew was that you were supposed to sleep in the same bed as your husband!

Unlike her sister Xenia, she was always a rebel. She had a mind of her own and very strongly held opinions. My father used to say that she was one of the few royals in existence who totally lacked what he called "royal beetles," by which he meant that all the other royals he had met, no matter how charming, intelligent and well-meaning, had to various degrees this thing on their minds, that they were royals, and one could sense this.

Mama always chuckled and said that her refusal of the two proposals which would have made her a queen prevented the premature fall of those monarchies, Greece and Yugoslavia. In London, she and her sister noticed that the Prince of Wales (later King Edward VIII and Duke of Windsor) went out of his way to be rude to them, and they realized that they were considered possible future brides for him. Both Mama and Xenia despised him thoroughly. Of the four sons of George V, their favorite by far was the youngest, the Duke of Kent. This time, I believe, Xenia took the initiative. She said to him, "David, neither of us would marry you if you were the last man on earth!" After that he became much more amiable.

Politically, my mother was very liberal, always for the underdog, and she thought monarchy was silly, in principle. But there were areas totally off limits to this liberalism. No personal criticism of Emperor Nicholas II was permitted, for instance, and she refused to meet Kerensky (an angel compared to Lenin) because she believed that he had been rude to the emperor. She was anything but a racist, except when it came to Germans. It did absolutely no good to point out that most of her blood was German. In this respect, she resembled Amama and the poor Bulgarians.

When this beautiful brown-eyed girl married my father in 1922, I have no doubt that it was a love match and, despite some difficulties, they stayed together and were very close. I do have a feeling that if my father had not come along at more or less the time he did, she would have married somebody else, as long as he wasn't likely to be a king, because marriage was the only route by which to escape from her mother. The young couple may have been rich in spirit, but in nothing

83

else—except wedding presents. Amama was comfortably off, but my mother and father were dependent only upon themselves. The Romanov fortune, as well as the Chavchavadze and Stroganov wealth, was gone in the flames of revolution.

Luckily, a lot of people gave checks and they had 3,000 pounds [$150,000 or more today] on which they got through the next five years. They were also given an elaborate chandelier, which they sold, only to come across it years later in somebody's house in New Hampshire! My father could only get odd jobs in London. He once ran a movie projector in a theatre and had a bit part in an episode of *The Perils of Pauline*!

Still, they managed to live in a house on a street appropriately called Moscow Road, with a cook named Mrs. Smith, and later a nanny for me. Of course, there was a boarder—Russians are big on boarders—to help defray the expenses. This was a young Russian called Count Vladimir Kleinmichel, who had been an admirer of my mother. For some reason he was called "Uncle Vanya." One of my earliest memories is being lifted up by Uncle Vanya to a map of Russia in his room and told to point to and touch the city of Kursk, which he considered his home. This was easy to do, because Kursk was a greasy mess from being touched previously by me. I used to think of this when the great battle raged around Kursk in World War II. Uncle Vanya worked for the Bank of England and used to hand pound notes to my parents, which I assumed he manufactured there. Actually, he handled the accounts of Grand Duchess Xenia, the sister of Nicholas II.

The Grand Duchess, who was now separated from Uncle Sandro, and her numerous children had been evacuated from the Crimea by the British.[1] Their last home in Russia had been Harax, and she was given a grace and favor house by the King, near Windsor Castle, called Frogmore Cottage. She had numerous grandchildren my age or older, and I used to go out there frequently with Nyanyushka. I tried to talk to the Guards at Windsor Castle in Russian, but they wouldn't answer, not even in English.

One day, as Nyanyushka was wheeling me in my pram, King George V rode by on horseback and asked Nyanyushka whether the Grand Duchess was at home.

"Yes Your Majesty," she replied in her overwhelming Russian accent, "and I am sure she would be very glad to see you!"

Innocent Nyanyushka did not realize that the grand duchess would probably have rather hidden under a bed than receive a call from her grouchy first cousin. Undoubtedly she resented his not trying harder to save her brother, Nicholas II, and his family.

While I was toddling with my cousins, my parents were having a very good time with the numerous other young Russians in London. The spirit of the twenties was very much on all of them, and none of them lost time moping over what had been lost in Russia. In my entire life I never heard either of my parents complain about their material losses, no matter how tough finances became.

---

1.   At the time of the Revolution there were sixty-one Romanovs alive. Eight of them
       were lucky enough to be abroad. Eighteen were murdered by the Bolsheviks, and
       the remaining thirty five managed to escape between 1917 and 1920.

They loved parties, but that emphatically did not include stuffy affairs at court. They began to refuse such invitations, known as "royal commands," and were soon dropped from the Buckingham Palace list. My father did go to one court ball alone because my mother was in her last stage of pregnancy with me. This one was rather interesting because the Labour government was in power and the wives of the ministers were ogling the regular court crowd, which they had never seen before. The Prince of Wales was supposed to start the dancing, but for some reason was in no hurry to do so. As a hush settled over the crowd King George V, in his quarterdeck voice, bellowed at his son across the ballroom, "Dance, damn you!" He did.

The King was himself stung on a different occasion. At that time the assorted Bertie Woosters of London amused themselves by playing a game called "Beaver." This consisted of sticking a finger in the ribs of some bearded gentleman and calling out, "Beaver!" Points were awarded according to the importance of the victim. The young Duke of Kent won hands down by poking his father in public and yelling, "Royal Beaver!"

My parents' generation—people born plus or minus 1900—have always been dear to me. They were the last people to receive the old, pre-World War I upbringing, which gave them great strength and principles, and yet in their youth they were rebels in a great generation gap. In old age, many seemed to revert to the old world. There are not many of them left. The Russians among them are of special interest, because when they die there will be nobody left to remember old Russia as it actually was.

My parents and their Russian crowd in London, strange as it may seem, never thought then that they would be emigrés for the rest of their lives. They remained very Russian, although each gradually gave up the dream. They could never become British or French or German or Czech or Yugoslavian. While they did not expect a restoration, they expected that Russia would somehow become free enough for them to live in. To become Americans, my parents thought, was a different story.

My mother's dislike of England was part of it, plus the fact that they liked most of the Americans they met. The decision to move came when my father landed a job in the New York office of the Cunard Line, in 1927. Amama was horrified. She imagined that the Wild West, or at least gangsters, started when one left Manhattan.

Among my few memories of the London phase of my life was this talk about America. I confused it with Aunt Merika, a relative of ours whom Uncle Vanya moved out of the house to marry. I knew we were going by ship, but to me this meant something like a barge on the Thames, with one man smoking a pipe, and a little dog aboard.

I have a flash of memory of riding on a train to Southampton, one of my grandmothers with us. June 1927. I had just passed my third birthday. The barge on the Thames looked more like a skyscraper—the great old Cunarder *RMS Aquitania*, my personal *Mayflower*.

Nyanyushka was seasick throughout the six-day trip. I remember people waving on the dock in New York and my mother pointing out my father, who was already there. I could not see him, only handkerchiefs waving.

My parents and Nyanyushka were still stateless, carrying so-called Nansen passports issued by the League of Nations. I, however, having been born in London, had a beautiful blue British passport, respected by all. My parents were admitted to the United States not as immigrants, but to work for a foreign company. That is why it took them ten years to change their status and become U.S. citizens. When they did, my position became unclear. Was I still a British subject or did I become an American automatically through them, as a minor? I always had problems proving my citizenship until I acquired my first American passport through a friendly consul in Berlin in 1946. I remember that at some point we all had actually to go out to famous old Ellis Island to go through some sort of immigration routine, years after we had lived in New York.

We started life in New York in a modest apartment at 55 East 86th Street, a building that is still there, essentially unchanged. When I was six we moved into a larger apartment in the same building. The lease was signed, but the Depression hit. Consequently, coming back from school one day I found that the dining room was blocked off by sheets and two Russians had moved in. The maid's room was occupied by Princess Eugenie Ouroussov. Again, boarders were the solution, all of them friends or relatives.

My parents enjoyed themselves vastly in the New York of the late twenties—acquiring many American friends without losing contact with the Russians, some of whom would tell me stories about the Russian civil war, fought so recently.

Nyanyushka and I walked to Central Park every day and stopped to shop on the way home— the butchers, the fishmongers and the greengrocers. Once on Fifth Avenue we ran into the great basso Chaliapin, whom Nyanyushka had known slightly in Russia, as had my grandmother.

"Fyodor Ivanovich!" she shouted.

Chaliapin stopped, looked down at the diminutive woman, and said, "Where have I had the honor to meet you?"

At the so-and-sos, Nyanyushka explained. "What happened to them?" "All dead in the revolution," she replied. Chaliapin then took off his fur hat, knelt on Fifth Avenue, crossed himself broadly and proclaimed: "*Tsarstvo nebesnoye!*" (heavenly kingdom), which is what one is supposed to say on hearing of a death. He was appearing at the Metropolitan Opera at the time, probably, and it must have been a sight for the passers-by!

My religious education too was left up to Nyanyushka—a priest's daughter after all. She was permissive in this too. Many were the Sundays we missed at the church on 121st Street. Most White Russians lived on the fringes of Harlem then. But the unforgettable Father Vasily Kurdiumov came to give me Bible lessons, spending most of his time describing to Nyanyushka the funerals he had just performed. He was permissive too in the lessons, and later in the confessional.

He had wanted to be a wrestler, but his mother persuaded him to become a deacon of the cathedral of Uncle Vanya's Kursk. He got into all kinds of trouble with his bishop for going to wrestling matches, forbidden to the clergy, and yelling out comments in his magnificent deacon's voice, which most of the town knew. He had never wanted to be a priest, but under emigré conditions there was such a shortage that he was ordained. In New York, at least, he could attend all the wrestling matches his heart desired.

When I was grown up, he told me that his mother had persuaded him by burying two bottles in the ground, one containing holy water. At the end of a year the holy water was still pure, while the plain water had become polluted. "Yes, there is certainly something to it!" Father Vasily sighed. I was shocked. This priest had always been the model Christian for me, and I could never have imagined that his faith rested on such a shaky foundation.

One of my early memories in the United States was a frightening one. I remember suddenly being surrounded by a crowd of adults on the beach at Larchmont, who were saying, "Your father was a king, the king of Russia." Somebody had blabbed that I was a prince, and for Americans this usually means the son of a king. Even at that age, perhaps five, I knew somehow that the "king" of Russia was dead and so was his son, but all I could do was shake my head and say, "No." I did not have enough English to say more. They advanced on me hostilely for my denying what I knew was not true. How could they have been so ill-informed in 1929?

Nyanyushka taught me a little English, and then, in preparation for entering school a strait-laced governess type called Miss Sunderkotter came to give me lessons. Once, in jest, I pretended to attack her, holding a tiny Roman soldier with a diminutive spear. She went all to pieces and screamed, "That barbaric Russian child is trying to give me blood poisoning!" I should have stuck her with the spear!

Miss Sunderkotter was the sister of one of the governesses Nyanyushka had made friends with in the park. We went to the Rambles, where in those days dozens of that ilk, mostly English and Scottish, filled the benches while their charges charged around the rocks and bushes. Some of these Scottish women, invited to tea by Nyanyushka, filled me so full of rather bloody Scottish history that I was caught sleepwalking one night by Nyanyushka, saying in Russian, "Poor Scotland!"

Anyway, by the time I entered first grade at the Lawrence-Smith School in 1930, I could speak English, but with an accent that rapidly disappeared. Still, the teacher, an Englishwoman named Miss Glover, kept referring to me as "the little Russian boy," and not a very bright one, because I once inquired what "Czar" meant in some fairy tale.

"It's like a king," she explained. "You had one in Russia."

But there was a world of difference between the word I knew, *tsar* and this weirdly spelled word pronounced *Zar*.

During vacations Nyanyushka and I were shipped off to people's estates, first to Aunt Xenia's in Oyster Bay, next to Theodore Roosevelt's Sagamore Hill, and after she was divorced, to her house in Syosset. At these places I was with my cousin Nancy, who did not speak Russian but did speak French, in addition to English, thanks to her Mademoiselle. She and Nyanyushka, in strongly accented English, called each other "Ze sharming guest," and "Ze charming hostess," but otherwise stayed away from each other. Mademoiselle, braying like a donkey to illustrate nasal sounds, gave me my first French lessons. Nyanyushka gave Nancy Russian lessons. None of this had much effect. Mademoiselle was anything but permissive with poor Nancy.

Nyanyushka and I also stayed at the nearby Syosset estate of my father's boss at the Cunard Line, Sir Ashley Sparks, where I was taught to ride horseback. In addition there was an estate in Larchmont belonging to a Russophile Italian called Joseph Mercadante. There, before the election of 1928, a very old Irish gardener taught me to yell "Hurrah for Al Smith!" to the disgust of the people in the big house, who were for Hoover, naturally.

Frequently we went up to Rhinebeck, New York, to Vincent Astor's estate, because his nephew, Ivan Obolensky, was close to my age. The most memorable thing there was Mr. Astor's model railroad, built perfectly to scale with a mile of track, about four inches between the rails which were attached to wooden ties by miniature spikes. There was a roundhouse with steam locomotives with which Mr. Astor would occasionally pull a number of flat cars full of adults and children. Ivan and I were barred from using the locomotives, but we were allowed to propel ourselves by hand, lying down on these flat cars, going through switches and over trestles. Nyanyushka and I also went to Bermuda three times with Ivan, once on the Astors' yacht *Nourmahal*, about the size of a destroyer, and the other two times on the liners *Queen of Bermuda* and *Monarch of Bermuda*.

Ivan's father, Prince Serge Obolensky, was a glamorous figure to me, as I saw his handsome form riding in Rhinebeck wearing a Cossack-type hat, and when he told Ivan and me about his World War I experiences. He had been first a private and eventually a major in the Chevalier Guards. In World War II, already in his fifties, he parachuted into Sardinia with an OSS team, and established a relationship with the Italian governor, whose father had once been Ambassador to St. Petersburg. As a result, Sardinia surrendered to the Allies, or rather to Serge Obolensky, without resistance. Between wars and after wars, Uncle Serge, as I called him, was very successful in the hotel business in New York, and continued to be very active in the New York social scene until his death at the age of ninety.

At all these estates, Nyanyushka would pick out a secluded spot and continue reading to me in Russian and giving me grammar lessons. I don't remember feeling the slightest envy about the mode of life at these estates in contrast to our modest apartment. My parents could not even afford a car until 1934, so it all seemed perfectly natural. Some people had it. We had lost it. No regrets.

The only boy I knew of my generation who spoke Russian was not a Russian at all, but a Circassian, Chinghiz Khan Guirey, a descendant of the Crimean khans and Ghenghis (which should really be Chinghis) Khan. His younger brother Azamat and I were great friends, but Azamat, while understanding everything that was said, could only speak a few words of the language. They also spoke Circassian to their father, who had been an officer in my grandfather's Circassian Regiment of the Wild Division.

There were a lot of North Caucasians of various nationalities in New York at that time. They even held an annual ball called *Allaverdy*, only one of which I managed to attend before the war put an end to them. It was sensational. The lights were turned off as all the men, dressed in *cherkesskas*, did their national dances with flaming daggers in their mouths. This was the real thing, not the imitations put on in various Russian nightclubs, usually by Cossacks.

I talked to a lot of them in childhood. I realized that they were not Russian and were Moslems, and that they were descendents of Shamil's gallant men who had resisted the Russians for thirty years, and, as part of the fight, kidnapped my family. Russian colonial policy had been honorable to them, and there was a solidarity between us all in the emigration. They seemed to respect me not only for being the grandson of a Wild Division regimental commander, but also for being the great-grandson of the Russian Viceroy of the Caucasus. It was only after World War II that certain anti-Russian (as well as anti-Soviet) attitudes began to appear among them, including Chinghiz Guirey, reinforced by new North Caucasian emigrés from the USSR.

While my father was totally unmilitary, I was a throwback to all the ancestors. I could not wait until I was old enough to join the Knickerbocker Greys at the age of eight. This was a small corps of cadets that drilled twice a week at the Seventh Regiment Armory and was closely associated with that old New York National Guard regiment. The Knickerbocker Greys, which still exists, was once called the "Social Register's private little army." We did get a lot of publicity, because among the cadets there were scions of all sorts of media: Lowell Thomas, Jr., Truman Talley (Movietone News), Ogden Reid, Jr. (New York Herald Tribune) and Julius Ochs Adler (New York Times). We had parades and sham battles. Actually, all that drill was a great help to me when I got into the real army. We also got to attend the Seventh Regiment's evening parades, with all those men dressed in West Point type vintage 1812 uniforms, some of them hardly sober enough to lift a rifle after the preliminary cocktail parties in each of the many company rooms in the Armory.

Once when I came home in my uniform, an old man in a top hat and cutaway waved his furled umbrella at me and shouted, "Are you Knickerbocker Greys? My great-grandson was Knickerbocker Greys!"

We became great friends. His name was Charles le Boutillier, and he had been in the Seventh Regiment, but he had been too old even for the Spanish-American War. He remembered, as a little boy of eight, watching the Seventh Regiment marching off to the Civil War, which meant he was born around 1853. As a teenager he was in Paris when the Prussians were approaching in 1870. While there were many Civil War veterans still around, I never met one, and Mr. le Boutillier was about as far back as I could get in time, among people I have known. We used to go to Seventh Regiment parades together, and sometimes we played cribbage. He used to write me letters in Latin, addressed *Carus Dux*. We lost touch after I went away to prep school and he died in the early 1940s.

The Russian cocoon I lived in was by no means designed to isolate me from American life, and I suddenly was exposed to new vistas of it. In 1934 a spot was discovered on my lung, and Nyanyushka and I were shipped to Tucson, Arizona, to stay with a friend of my parents, Mrs. Anderson. We traveled by car, with Mrs. Anderson's chauffeur, Jack Warner and me in the front seat, and tiny Nyanyushka with heaps of baggage in the back. This was the first time I saw Washington and the White House, and then we drove through Virginia, Tennessee, Arkansas, Texas and New Mexico, staying in tourist homes and rest cabins which occasionally popped up along the two-lane roads of that time.

In Tucson I was quickly equipped with Levis, then unknown in the East, and enrolled at University Heights, the only public and co-ed school I ever went to. Unfortunately, at the age of ten the boys were supposed to, and did, ignore the girls. The girls, however, did not ignore the boys. On weekends I rode horseback with my Knickerbocker Greys Rifle Club .22, and even shot a rattlesnake! I also learned a lot of cowboy songs and how to play the harmonica.

I was determined to get a rattlesnake, having promised snake skins to practically every kid I knew in New York. It was with great difficulty that I persuaded the cowboy with me to bring the thing back to the stable. It kept writhing, shying the horses. When I brought it into the house Mrs. Anderson and my mother, who had driven out to see me—she loved long drives—screamed and almost fainted. "Get it out of here!" I tried to put it in the frigidaire, but the cook also had a fit. Sadly, I started to bury it in the back yard. At this point Nyanyushka came to my rescue. With the skills acquired at the Patriotic Institute in St. Petersburg, she expertly skinned the Arizona snake, and the skin hung over my desk in New York for years, until it finally disintegrated. In April 1935 we returned the way we had come. Some American life, a chauffeur in 1935!

Two years later my mother and I drove out to Valley Ranch, Wyoming, near Cody, a dude ranch my mother was supposed to write up for some magazine. We drove through a plague of locusts in the midwest. The sky was dark with them, and the road slippery. Every window and vent in the car had to be closed, but I still had to help pick them off of my mother's jeans.

Two years later, in 1939, when I was fifteen, I was packed off with a younger friend, Columbus O'Donnell, in a station wagon driven by a twenty-year-old lad called Jimmie Dooly, with instructions and funds from Columbus's mother to go anywhere in the United States we wanted to, as long as we did not stay on the East Coast. We had camping equipment. We drove to California by the northern route, visited San Francisco and Hollywood, returned through northern Arizona and back to Vermont where we had started. Columbus' mother was miffed that so many places we went I had Russian relatives or contacts, whereas Columbus had nobody to look up. She did not understand the White Russian diaspora. There was Count Tolstoy in Detroit—a Romanov cousin, Prince Rostislav in Chicago, another one, Prince Vasily, in San Francisco, and a Prince Golitsin in Hollywood. A few days after this trip, World War II broke out in Europe.

In 1940 there was still another trip, this time with Ivan Obolensky to a dude ranch north of Cody, Wyoming. So by the time I was sixteen I was extremely well traveled in the United States but had never been to Europe, not counting those shadowy beginnings in England.

During this rather privileged childhood, was I aware of the Great Depression going on all around me? Certainly, but in a removed sort of way. I remember my friends in the park making up tall stories about seeing people jumping out of skyscraper windows. One boy said he had seen a gentleman float down, making a parachute out of the loose pyjamas he was wearing. These were echoes of real suicides on Wall Street. I also remember the many men sitting on the sidewalks behind boxes, selling apples at a nickel a piece. Nyanyushka would always buy one and give it to me, saying, "We must always help the unfortunate."

When my parents said that Uncle Vanya Kleinmichel might emigrate to the States, but wondered what he would do here, I suggested that he could sell apples. Big laugh from the adults present.

Aside from estate-hopping, travel and schools, there were other American influences in my life. In the summer of 1932, my parents decided that Mama, Nyanyushka and I should go to Provincetown at the tip of Cape Cod. In those days there were fairly large ships that went from New York to Providence, Fall River or New Bedford, and a train to the end of the Cape. I did not realize why my parents were so sentimental about those overnight trips until later. The ships went beyond the three-mile limit and prohibition was lifted for the night!

I have never met anybody my age who saw the inside of a speakeasy, but I did. It was called the Club Unusual, in Provincetown. My mother, while she had a drink, gave me some nickels to play the slot machines. Since the whole thing was illegal anyway, why not slot machines too? A year later came Roosevelt and repeal. My mother, who would not normally walk more than a couple of blocks, marched in the Beer Parade in New York, agitating to make beer, at least, legal. I wore a little foaming stein as a boutonnière.

My parents were told that free fish and blueberries were available in Provincetown, in addition to a large group of intellectuals. The intellectuals were there all right; the blueberries were available for picking if you could stand the mosquitoes; but the fish—my first morning in Provincetown I was given a pail and told to get some fish from the fishermen at the main wharf. My fellow eight-year-old Portuguese kids made out like bandits, but the fishermen just laughed at me, and I came home with an empty pail. Street-wise I was not. It was a pity though, because perfectly edible fish like whiting were dumped into the harbor in those days, there being no market for it. The whole harbor stank at low tide.

Some of the New York boarders came along to defray expenses and by coincidence the house across the street was full of Russian artists, including Nicholas Afonchikov, Nick Afon to the locals, one of the two unfortunates who proposed to Nyanyushka and was told they were out of their minds.

I played the role of an Indian child in a very corny movie, in which the Indians met the Pilgrims on the main wharf. The Pilgrims filed down the gangplank of the Boston boat, the *Dorothy Bradford*, considerably larger than the original *Mayflower*. Decades later an actual replica of the *Mayflower* sailed from England and was going to ignore Provincetown, where the Pilgrims had first landed. Harry Kemp, known as the Poet of the Dunes, organized a posse of Portuguese fishing boats and sent a cable to the Queen of England threatening to force the phony *Mayflower* into the harbor if necessary. The expedition yielded. When I was in my teens I used to spend the night in Harry Kemp's cabin on the dunes by the ocean, listening to incredible mystical stories and being forced to sleep with my head pointed north for some metaphysical reason.

Then there were five summers in Truro, the next town from Provincetown. No electricity or plumbing. The customary two-holer privy out back. Lots of wild parties during which Nyanyushka and I were banished for the night to somebody else's house.

My best friend in Truro was Archie, a brilliant boy, who had been brought up as an orthodox Marxist-Leninist by his mother, who came from a wealthy Chicago family. When his mother went to Russia around 1934 and came back disillusioned, Archie and his sisters merely labeled her a hopeless Trotskyite and went on being Stalinists. Their father, a successful lawyer, who kept divorcing and remarrying their mother, put up with all this in a very good-natured way.

In the summer of 1936 when Archie and I were twelve, my parents and I stayed in Wellfleet in the house of Lothrop Weld, who, much later, fathered Tuesday Weld. Mr. Weld gave me a job weeding his garden at ten cents an hour. Archie rode his bike down from Truro to organize me. I was being exploited and I should strike for more pay. I struck—and was fired. "I don't really need you," said Mr. Weld. "I thought I was doing you a favor because you needed the money." This taught me something, but Archie just said to wait for the revolution.

From 1939 to 1941, when Hither and Stalin were allies, Archie went about playing anti-war records, like:

"I hate war, and so does Eleanor," and
"No desire do I feel to defend Republic Steel,
I'm a young boy and cannot leave my mother."

All of these records disappeared on 22 June 1941, when Hither attacked the Soviet Union. Archie became a fighter pilot in the U.S. Army Air Corps and performed heroically. He was shot down in flames, his handsome face hideously burned. It was later partially restored by months or years of agonizing plastic surgery. Luckily his sight, hearing and basic health were saved and he could live a normal life. I don't know whether he thought he was fighting for Stalin or for the United States, and I suppose it really doesn't matter.

At a dinner party in Truro I heard my mother predict that Stalin-Hitler alliance a year before it happened, to the indignant disagreement of the other guests. "Both bastards are birds of a feather and they will make a deal," she said.

On the Cape we were surrounded by people who thought, in the middle of Stalin's most ghastly bloodbaths, which were no secret, that the USSR was some sort of Utopia. There were exceptions, like Edmund Wilson, who had also gone there and became disillusioned. It was amazing how my staunchly anti-Soviet parents managed to get on with these people, but they did.

My mother tried to avoid politics with them, being so fond of them in other ways. During this period of the Spanish Civil War, which was fought verbally on Cape Cod and other places, I was somewhat confused. My parents supported Franco, not for any liking for fascism or his Italian and German allies, but because they thought the Spanish Republic was being taken over by Stalinist Communists, which to them was worse. Most of my friends in New York felt the same way, but on the Cape we were totally outnumbered. I knew better than to discuss the issue with Archie.

In 1938 that house in Truro, which somebody had christened the *Villa Pismire* (a species of ant, believe it or not), was especially loaded with non-Russian boarders, or p.g.'s. Some of them, unknown to me then, wanted to join the International Brigade in Spain, but kept putting it off, discussing the war over drinks on the Cape being easier. None of them ever did get to Spain, but I had the bad taste to bring a kid my age into the house and say, "Can you imagine, this guy is for the

Loyalists!"

"And who are you for?" somebody asked.

I told him, and a Spanish Civil War battle commenced. My mother, shooting me a dirty look, defended the Franco side valiantly against all the indignant armchair international brigadiers, and a female p.g. who belonged to something called the Agricultural Socialist Party.

Politics aside, that summer, when I was fourteen and about to go away to school, was great fun. My favorite p.g., Harl Cook, whose father had founded the famous Provincetown Players and had later become a shepherd in Delphi, helped me publish a weekly gossip sheet called the *Truro Terror*, which I printed on a small mimeograph machine. Harl and I also bought a large, decrepit sailboat in Provincetown for $15, and somehow hauled it to the yard of the Villa Pismire. For about two days all of the p.g.'s, overcoming their hangovers, worked on it with enthusiasm and then forgot about it. It remained in the yard as an outdoor cocktail lounge, christened *La Belle Pismire*. During my parents' anniversary party on September 3, I ran a national Russian Tricolor up the mast. Some leftist at the party tried to tear it down. I was so furious I ran for my BB gun. It was that White Army veteran, Nicholas Afonchikov, who calmed me down. In Russian he pointed out to me that (1) the guy was drunk out of his mind, (2) this symbol only meant something to four people present, and, (3) that some day these people would wake up.

For the arrival of my father for his vacation, all the p.g.'s worked on huge placards, which we planted on Longnook Road. One said "Villa Pismire by the Sea, Exorbitant Rates, Russian Cuisine, Chamberpot Music with Meals, Madame Nina, Prop." The other read: "Two Holes with every Privy, one Piano with every Spivy." Spivy was a New York nightclub entertainer who every summer arrived at the Villa Pismire with a tiny piano in the rumble seat of her car. Unfortunately, the cops made us take the signs down, considering them indecent.

There was wonderful singing at the Villa Pismire when Spivy was there with her little piano, and my father with his guitar. At other times, Afonchikov, who was not a p.g. but an unpaid dishwasher, would sing, also with guitar, and by the time I was fourteen I could accompany myself with a ukulele and knew most of the songs.

After 1935 Nyanyushka no longer came up with us to Cape Cod. This was a deliberate move on my parents' part to wean me away from her. It was probably wise, since I had to part with her in 1938 permanently, boarding school in those days being *de rigueur*, even if one couldn't afford it. Thank God it wasn't England, where they ship boys off at seven.

We were still together during the school year and during those visits to peoples' estates before and after Cape Cod. She proudly saw me make cadet colonel of the Knickerbocker Greys. This promotion produced a telegram addressed to "Colonel Prince Chavchavadze," in which my mother's cousin, Grand Duchess Marie Pavlovna, said that she was proud of me as a Russian and a relative.

My regular school was first rate in every way. I can still remember the names of all of my classmates, including Albert Herring, killed in Bastogne in 1944, and Warren, a rich, fatherless only child, brought up by two nagging harpies, his mother and grandmother. Eventually they had him committed to an asylum. He was let out, but overhearing them plotting to commit him again, he strangled them both with his pajama top. I trust the rest of the class had better lives. There were no reunions, because the school folded shortly after I left, perhaps because Mr. C. Lawrence Smith, the founder and headmaster, had been generous enough to let the likes of me go through free. In 1930 my parents had merely identified themselves to Mr. Smith, explaining their circumstances, and asked for a full scholarship for me.

Nyanyushka and I finally parted in June of 1938, in Syosset. I cried for two hours, then pulled myself together and headed for Cape Cod for that marvellous summer. What else? I was never given any choice.

When that summer was over my parents drove me to Andover, twenty miles north of Boston and left me. This time I cried again, but for a shorter time, dried my eyes and went downstairs to meet my classmates. I had had no choice of schools, nor the option of staying in New York. My father was nice enough to write that if I was unhappy, something else could be arranged.

In 1939 the theoretical option of New York entirely disappeared. My parents bought a house in Wellfleet, built in 1780 with thirteen acres of land for $1,800, most of it paid for by a broach in the shape of the old Russian crown of Vladimir Monomach, inherited by my mother from Queen Olga. The house had not been occupied since 1913, and, lifting up mats from the floor I discovered a Sunday supplement from some 1913 newspaper featuring one of Mama's first cousins, a daughter of that tiresome Grand Duke Michael who had made a fuss over my parents' wedding. A strange thing, meaning to us that the house had been waiting for us all this time.

With the outbreak of war in 1939 my father had a perfect excuse to quit his job with the Cunard White Star Line, which had never been his idea of a career. While my mother and friends were working on the new house he sold fruits and vegetables to chefs in New York restaurants (one chef remembered Pavel Vladimirovich, which aided the sale), and then he worked for the Tolstoy Foundation, recently founded by Tolstoy's daughter and still going strong today. At that time it was trying to aid Soviet prisoners in Finland, abandoned by Stalin and branded traitors.

I began to work my way through Andover, being a KP in the "Beanery," selling the services of kindly old Mrs. Robb the laundress, selling the New York Times and delivering it, being an office boy to the Headmaster, at thirty-five cents per hour, moving the furniture and raising the curtain for the Saturday night movie show, and being a proctor at meals for the younger boys. I also acquired a number of scholarships, so that I didn't cost my parents a cent after 1940, which is lucky because they could not have paid.

At Andover there was absolutely nobody to speak Russian with. I had a few books with me, which I read occasionally. The problem was that despite all Nyanyushka's efforts two pages of reading in Russian was about all I could stand at one sitting. But when we were assigned *War and Peace* in English class, I decided it was ridiculous for me to read it in translation, particularly since Nyanyushka had read it to me when I was ten. The nightly assignment of pages was rough, but I forced myself and suddenly found that something snapped in my mind, and ever since then I have been able to read Russian almost as fast as English.

In addition to working my way through school, and the tough academic work, I was also active in extra-curricular activities, both the school newspaper and literary magazine, the debating society and the Glee Club. It is a mystery to me how I could have worked all that in, with my natural laziness, and still made honor roll grades, which resulted in a four-year full scholarship to Yale. Going to Wellfleet for vacations in winter, or even in spring, was for the birds as far as I was concerned, but my parents were quite understanding, and let me go to New York for part of the time.

In 1940 my father's brother George arrived in the States with his rich French wife and her two daughters. He had married the Comtesse Elizabeth de Breteuil, a widow who came from the French branch of the wealthy Philadelphia Ridgways. They rented a mansion in Bernardsville, New Jersey, but also came up to Cape Cod several times. Uncle George at that time was a very successful concert pianist—Carnegie Hall and all that. My parents and I spent a lot of time in Bernardsville, which was a center for what was known as the "St. Regis refugees." Some of them were Free French (Gaullists), and others pro-Vichy. But they all despised the United States for its "lack of culture." Of course, all they saw of the States was the horrible Jersey flats between New York and Bernardsville.

We had many good times there as Uncle George was a genius at arranging imaginative, good parties, but the attitude of these French, who were living better than 99% of the American population, infuriated me. Besides, to them I was an uncultured lout because, despite my background, my French was not very good. My mother felt the same way I did, but my father, who spoke perfect French, was more at home. It never occurred to any of these people that it was a major miracle that I spoke good Russian, but this was not important to them.

I remember a conversation I had with Uncle George's eldest stepdaughter. I told her to relax, enjoy herself. My parents were perfectly happy in the United States. Her answer was typical, "Yes, but they lost Russia, we lost France!" In her mind it was worse to lose France for three or four years than to lose Russia forever, and for all I knew, I would soon have to liberate their France at the point of a bayonet and maybe die doing it.

Pearl Harbor came when I was a senior at Andover. Already members of my class had gone off to join the Canadian Air Force, or the RAF. George Bush joined the U.S. Naval Air Arm right after graduation in June 1942. I was not a close friend of the future president, but he was well liked in the class. I went on to Yale in July, entering the first wartime accelerated class, called 1945W. In late June I hitchhiked from Cape Cod to New Haven, having spent the night in Yarmouth with my classmate Bill Coffin, the future Rev. William Sloane Coffin.

On June 24 I made a trip to New York where I met my first king, not counting my encounter with George V of England while in my baby carriage. This was King George II of Greece, my mother's first cousin, who had become king after his father Constantine's second abdication in 1922. He had himself been exiled then restored, and, although still king, was again in exile due to the Nazi conquest of Greece. Because of the Greeks' strong resistance to the Nazis and the king's fighting withdrawal to Crete, Hitler had declared him Germany's "public enemy number one!"

King George was staying at the Waldorf Towers, guarded by two men in plain clothes and quite a number of uniformed police. My father, Aunt Xenia, and Princess Margarethe[2] of Denmark had dinner with him there in his private suite. I noted in my diary how strange it was to hear the words, "Dinner is served, Your Majesty," and also that Uncle Georgie struck me as being very modest, unstuffy and amiable.

I was sitting next to my father, who noticed that the king was sitting on a cushion that looked like the Italian flag. "Rather appropriate," my father remarked to me, "that the royal fanny of Greece is sitting on an Italian flag! I wonder if he's doing it on purpose?" Appropriate it was too, since Mussolini's Italians had been the first to invade Greece, much to their regret.

Toward the end of the meal an exotic looking desert appeared, and I asked my father what it was. "It's *kaka*," he replied, using Russian baby talk for crap.

This caused the waiter carrying the desert to double up with laughter and stagger back into the pantry.

"Uncle Georgie, " I asked the king, "Does *kaka* mean the same in Greek as in Russian?"

"No," he replied, "we have a better word—*skata*."

Unfortunately, this scatalogical conversation is all I remember about the dinner. Later that night, at a bar, I tried out my new Greek word on the Greek bartender.

"Ha ha," he laughed, "where you learn that word?"

"From the King of Greece."

"Ha ha! You big joker, kid!"

The rest of my summer of 1942 was spent at Yale. What glorious independence after Andover, and how easy academically! Very little outside work to do because my $1,000 scholarship covered almost everything, and the ever-present feeling of eat, drink and be merry, for tomorrow we die! The New Haven girls yelled "slacker" at us, but my main worry at the time was that I could not get into the army because of my nearsightedness.

My old friend Chinghiz Guirey was there, two classes ahead of me. Together we sought out Yale's small Russian colony—Professor George Vernadsky, the famous historian and his wife Nina; George Fedotov, the theologian and his family; and Countess Sophia Panin, who had been a super-liberal in the old St. Petersburg days, and her half-brother Professor Petrunkevich, too busy being the world's leading spider expert to bother about politics.

Chinghiz and I founded a Russian cultural society. All of these people took part, except the spider specialist. Our great coup was successfully inviting Alexander Kerensky. At that well-attended session he was savagely attacked by the professor of Russian at Yale, who was clearly taking a pro-Soviet point of view. Kerensky ably defended himself in his very poor English. This was embarrassing, because both Chinghiz and I worked for this professor as "native informants," at the princely pay of four dollars an hour. We spent most of our time tactfully persuading the students to pronounce words our way and not his. Such was the effect of the

<hr>

2.   Princess Margarethe was the daughter of Prince Valdemar, and wife of Prince René of Bourbon-Parma.

American-Soviet alliance that we seriously considered inviting somebody from the Soviet consulate in New York to our Russian cultural society.

I took a course in Japanese. This was a pretty silly thing to do. I already had Russian, and quite a lot of French, and if I needed an enemy language, I could have gone on with German, two years of which I had taken at Andover. I had no desire to go to the Far East, and plenty of desire to go to Europe. The whole Japanese class was taken into the army as corporals and sent to Signal Corps, except me. At that time for a clearance the army demanded that even your grandparents had to be American born. Even the presidency does not demand this! I was upset at the time, but it was a lucky break. I would have spent the war either on Japanese codes, or on some Pacific island interrogating the few Japanese who surrendered.

I joined the Army Enlisted Reserve, after a hassle in proving my citizenship. This was supposed to let you stay in college until graduation, but in small print it said that the army could call you anytime it needed you.

The small print was activated in February 1943, just after I had completed my freshman year.

GRAND DUCHESS MARIE, AUTHOR
PRINCESS XENIA - 1933

PRINCE PAUL (Author's father) and AUTHOR

NANCY LEEDS and AUTHOR, 1945

CHAPTER VII

My roommates at Yale hung a star on our door, and my father presented me with a *charochka*, a ceremonial drinking cup to be drained in one gulp, using a verse written for his father: "Hurrah for the prince our commander, the whole Caucasus is proud of him!" Quite a send-off for a buck private in the U.S. Army.

At Fort Devens, Massachusetts it seemed as if all of Yale had been called up. The barracks was full of Yalies in preppie civilian clothes listening respectfully to a Harvard man demonstrate how to make beds the army way. The soda jerk in the PX had taught me English literature at Andover.

In less than a week we were uniformed and herded to a train. The cars had "colored" and "white" signs on them, so we knew we were going South, but that was all we knew. I was deposited at Camp Croft, South Carolina, not far from Spartanburg.

I found myself in an infantry basic training platoon where the cadre was all from Brooklyn. Here, my fellow trainees were mostly from the University of New Hampshire, caught up in the same enlisted reserve call-up. We were persecuted by the company drill sergeant, a reformed drunk who hated anybody who had been to college.

There was a girl's college, Converse, in Spartanburg, which was off limits to enlisted men, but Hawkie Harrison, a fellow Yalie from Virginia, marched a few of us onto the campus, demanding to see the dean. His name, plus the fact we were all from Yale, opened all doors and the Dean immediately made us welcome and authorized dates with her charges.

In May 1943 after I had been in infantry basic training for two months, some IBM machine in the newly built Pentagon noticed that I spoke Russian, and I suddenly received individual orders to report to a place called Camp Ritchie, Maryland, to military intelligence. This machine may have saved my life!

When my orders came through I became a general object of envy. "You'll be wearing Class A's the whole time," they said. Ha! It would have done them good to see me a few days later on KP in greasy fatigues for a whole week.

Camp Ritchie was located near the present Camp David, just across the state line from a Pennsylvania resort town called Blue Ridge Summit. My bus arrived at dawn, a fog blanketing the beautiful mountains surrounding the camp, just in time for breakfast. I found a chow line and stood in it.

Being sleepy, it took me a few minutes to realize that there was something strange about this chow line. Most of the soldiers wore German uniforms, and furthermore they were Germans, though they addressed each other in heavily accented English.

Camp Ritchie was loaded with German speakers, many of them recent refugees from the Nazis. There were also a few squat figures in German uniform who were totally silent. These turned out to be American Indians, who were supposed to creep through the woods without snapping a twig to ambush trainee patrols. The only trouble was that the army, in its wisdom, had selected Hopis from Arizona for this purpose, who in civilian life had hardly ever seen a tree, let alone a twig. The noise they made stumbling through forests was to be a great help to us later on. After breakfast I was directed to Company E, 2nd Battalion, Military Intelligence Training Center.

A sergeant with a Cockney accent assigned me a bed. He actually let me go to sleep in it in mid-morning because he had heard my uncle give a piano recital in Albert Hall! This sort of pull did not go very far. The next day I found myself on the list for a week's KP and spent my nineteenth birthday scrubbing G.I. cans in that damn mess hall.

Company E was a holding company for a huge conglomeration of linguistically qualified yardbirds, many of them Ph.D's, who were fair game for every lousy detail in camp while waiting for a class to start in the Combat Intelligence School (Companies F and G). German and Italian were in great demand, but I was told there might be a long wait for a Russian class. A long wait in Company E seemed like a jail sentence.

Sasha Sogolow, one of the first fellow Russian speakers I met at Ritchie gave a party to celebrate landing the job of permanent latrine orderly in his barracks. He soon had a toady, also Russian, and a corporal at that, who was cultivating Sasha, convinced the latter could get him promoted.

I too made a try for permanent status. During the interregnum when a new sergeant took over the barracks, there was considerable confusion with people departing to enter the school. During this afternoon of anarchy I noticed that the barracks orderly room was empty and, through judicious questioning, I determined that that aristocrat of all yardbirds, the barracks clerk, had been transferred to school. I quickly donned sun-tans, occupied the little office, and began to type lists of fictitious names.

Presently, behind me, I heard a musical bass voice with a central European accent, "Who are you?"

"I am the barracks clerk. Who are you?"

"I am the barracks sergeant," said the benevolent looking middle aged man with a circlet of silvery hair around his bald pate. "I am Sergeant Denes."

That blessed man of music, that most noble of Franz Josef's ex-officers, let me get away with my fait-accompli. My star was in its ascendancy. Even Man-Mountain Dean, the famous wrestler who was our detail sergeant, called me into his private room and said, "Kid, I like you. You got class. You don't have to go on kitchen police no more."

The bubble burst within five days. Returning to the barracks full of beer from our favorite hang-out beyond the gates, a place with the unlikely name of Chocolate Park, I heard the benevolent bass voice of Sergeant Denes intone, "Chavchavadze eez a tragedy!" A horrified gaze at the bulletin board confirmed it—one week's KP for me, starting at 0530 hours.

During one of those weeks on KP I scrubbed G.I. cans with an aristocratic Prussian named Fritz Kramer, who later became known for discovering Kissinger and making a prominent career in the Pentagon, but all that was far ahead. He wore a monocle with a black cord, which dangled over his fatigues when it wasn't in his eye. The mess sergeant approached and addressed a number of obscenities to this circumstance, which somehow offended him. With great dignity Fritz looked up from the can and said, "Zargent, my occultist has prescribed a monocle, zerefore I wear a monocle."

Going off KP one evening I recognized my night shift replacement, a new soldier in the barracks. It was Dr. Walter Hasenclever, who had taught me German at Andover.

"My God, Dr. Hasenclever," I mumbled.

"Considering ze zircumstances," he replied, "you may call me Walter."[1]

I was trying to visit my father who was about to go to England with the Red Cross, and I finally succeeded in getting a three day pass from an unexpected source, having been turned down several times by the Maryland mafia who ran the camp. After that last week on KP was over, I found myself building a pier in the lake. When we were not in the water we were hauling telephone pole sections to use as piling for the pier. I got my finger caught under one of these. The lieutenant in charge of the detail drove me to the hospital, griping the whole way at my goofing off from the job on medical grounds.

The finger turned out to be fractured, but instead of sending me back to the company on limited duty, they made me occupy a bed in the ward. The limited duty or walking-wounded concept had not reached Camp Ritchie. I cannot say that I objected to this enforced vacation. My friends came to visit and we sang Russian songs together. Best of all, a helpful nurse arranged a three day pass. I could not go back to the company, but I could go to New York, finger sticking out in a rather irreverent gesture.

My father was a Red Cross field director with the assimilated rank of captain. It was great to be in uniform together and do grown-up things like whooping it up in Spivy's Roof until 4:00 AM. Spivy ran this night club from 1940 to 1950; her erstwhile rumble-seat piano was now in the elevator, and Spivy and we sang to its accompaniment while the last guests rode down at closing time. Papa left for Scotland soon afterward, and I did not see him again for two years.

It was announced that the Tenth Class at Camp Ritchie would have a Russian section, and so on July 24, 1943 I was transferred to Company G.

Most numerous were the Germans who were eventually to make up teams for the interrogation of prisoners-of-war. There were also a number of Italian sections, and one each Russian, French and Spanish. This was the make-up of the Tenth Class. We all studied the same thing.

The Italians did not last long. On the third day they marched out of Ritchie with real, honest-to-God M-1 rifles slung on their shoulders, waving at us with sheepish, unhappy faces, pointing at the weapons which had become so unfamiliar

---

1.   This incident was used in *Once to Every Man* by the Reverend William Sloan Coffin as if it happened to the author. Bill did study under Dr. Hasenclever and was at Camp Ritchie in 1943, but, as he told me, he chose to appropriate what he thought was a good story.

for Ritchie inmates. The Italians were needed in a hurry for the invasion of Sicily.

At first we memorized the organization of armies—U.S., British, Soviet, German and Italian. Data on the Red Army was classified confidential, because it was obtained solely from German POW sources. The Soviets wouldn't tell their allies anything.

Section 7-D, the Russian section, was composed of about fourteen men, including one student officer, a Russian named Grant. Nobody dared ask him what his real name was. Only Len Gmirkin, a boy my own age who had come to California by way of China, and I spoke straight English. In those days it was practically impossible to find a non-Russian who had learned Russian. At nineteen my Russian was fluent and fairly correct, but this was my first exposure to Russian speakers with backgrounds so different from my parents' circle and Nyanyushka. I learned a lot of new words, including the all-important cuss words.

They came from all over. Young Dmitry Dvoichenko-Markov, who had just made it out of Roumania via Spain, could hardly speak English at all. He had been drafted on arrival, and he was probably the first person I ever met with whom I had to speak Russian, there being no other language in common.

Boris Tumarin, a much older man, had lived in Latvia, but in recent years had produced plays in New York. Anatole Chelnov was from Belgium. Nicholas Baranov was an actor who looked and conducted himself like that distinguished-looking drunk with white hair and moustache who was always draped around a lamp post in 1930s movies, and was a veteran of Wrangel's White Army. Nicholas Ryazanovsky, though only nineteen, already had the professorial dignity of an old-time Russian intellectual, and was to become a prominent historian. There was a mysterious Russian called Montague, who wouldn't tell anybody his real name. Sasha Rubenstein, who could charm anybody in minutes, was to become a great asset to our section. Ilya Wolston, our guardhouse lawyer, had lived in Lithuania, Germany, France and England. Another older man, Alexander Bozhko, had been raised in China with a heart loyal to the Ukraine.

Wherever they were from, all soldiers then could acquire U.S. citizenship in three months. Some poor clerk in the Hagerstown, Maryland, courthouse was regularly confronted with a mob of eighty of ninety guys with crazy names and accents. The man was so overworked that some of this business had to be transferred to Frederick. At this point one could also have a name change for free. Chelnavsky became Chelnov, Tumarinsons became Tumarin, and there was even a fellow with the perfectly good name of Orlov who changed it to Rubin! Our man Ilya Volfovsky wanted to change his name to Elliott Wolston. The clerk wrote in all four names—Ilya Elliott Wolston-Volfovsky, and Ilya came out stuck with all that and hyphenated like a baron for duration plus six. After that he compromised and became Ilya Wolston.

Every morning at the reveille formation, during which we tended to be talkative, our commander Corporal Peter Eider, glancing fearfully toward the center of the company, would emit an anguished Russian whisper, "*Tishe, tishe, radi Boga!*" (Quiet, quiet, for God's sake!) The top sergeant is coming! Oh my God the company commander is with him and even a lieutenant-colonel! I'll be restricted! (This came out as *restriktovan* in Russian.) Then switching to his English parade ground voice, "Sakshon 7-D. AttanSHON! Dress right, DRESS!"

From organization of armies we went on to map reading, terrain mapping, and night problems involving compass readings. The maps were printed in German, Italian or Japanese. If you misread your compass you could end up wandering around all night.

They took us up on hills and let us watch whole formations of "German" infantry, artillery and tanks go by. There was even a cavalry section. We had to write reports on precisely what we had seen, when, where, how many and moving at what speed in what direction. There was unarmed close combat and an infiltration course under live machine gun fire. Wolston drew the line at this. "Sergeant," he announced, "I have a definite agreement with my draft board that I am not supposed to be exposed to live ammunition!" It was no use. Minutes later tracers were zipping centimeters above his ample hindquarters.

With all this marching and counter-marching through the beautiful countryside, Section 7-D developed considerable esprit de corps. Baranov taught Eider how to give commands in Russian. As in all Russian armies, the best singers marched at the head of the column. We got so good at singing soldiers' songs on the march, both Imperial and Soviet, that people would come specially to hear us.

With all our tremendously varied Russian backgrounds, political arguments were to be expected, but there were very few. If anybody worried about our alliance with Stalin he did not say so. In general we were enthusiasts for the war, felt a certain pride in Soviet victories, and were willing to let bygones be bygones—at least for the time-being.

There was so much we did not know. We had no idea of the number of Soviet citizens who had at first greeted the Germans as liberators and the number of people who begged the Germans to let them fight Stalin. We did not know that at that very moment there was a camp outside Berlin, in some ways resembling Ritchie, full of young Russians who wanted to fight Stalin with German arms, there being no other way. They were probably singing the same songs as we were. Traitors, we would have called them then.

Behind us on the march was the Spanish section. I guess the idea was that we might still invade Spain or be allowed through Spain to get at the Germans. They were all Puerto Ricans, they had an awful lot of rank, and most of them were named Rodriguez.

The Rodriguez clan was rather touchy about their rank. Once when an instructor addressed them as "men," Lt. Colonel Rodriguez stepped out of ranks and said with indignation, "We are not men, we are gentlemen!"

Because of all that rank, the Rodriguezes found themselves leading most of the patrols in the infamous Two Day Problem, which was a forty-hour march from point to point in a wide circumference of the camp. The student patrols had to find their way with maps and compasses. At night security discipline was to be maintained—no loud talking or lights. Those noisy Indians were out in the woods to ambush us. There was one place where if you missed your compass bearing by a couple of degrees you ended up somewhere in the Cumberland Mountains, lost for days.

My patrol hit this area after dark, commanded by one of the Majors

Rodriguez. It had become evident that azimuth-following was not his strong point. He was not alone in this. I became conscious that the woods were alive with thrashing humanity, matches being lit all over the place, flashlights beaming, and the din of Hispanic oaths. Then the crash of rifle fire as the Indians, noisy as tanks, crashed through to nab a luckless patrol.

We somehow found our azimuth. It began to rain, harder and harder. When we finally arrived at the next point we were entitled to a four hour sleep break. There was a nice big ten there, but it was for umpires only, and a cadre lieutenant stood at its entrance, directing us to sleep in the rain. Here Major Rodriguez showed his true mettle,. With a savage cry of, "My men will not-a sleep in the rain!" he shoved past the lieutenant and we all followed under the shelter of his blessed golden oak leaves. We found the tent already full of other patrols whose Rodriguez commanders had shown the same sterling qualities of looking after their men.

The climax of the course was the Eight Day Problem. This was a cleverly conceived exercise which reproduced the intelligence elements of an army corps G-2, several division G-2s, and some regimental and battalion S-2s. The students changed assignments every twenty-four hours to experience every level of operations. Those assigned to battalion level actually went out on patrol to pick up bits of information from the Hopis and the rest of Camp Ritchie's private Wehrmacht. Prisoners-of-war, realistically garbed and tagged, were interrogated in German at various levels. Civilians were also interrogated in the various languages. It was assumed that Western Maryland was inhabited by a mishmash population speaking Russian, French and Spanish. In order to force each headquarters to exercise local security, mount guard, circulate passwords and protect documents, the woods at night were infiltrated by "subversives" whose function was to bomb the various headquarters tents with fire crackers or tear gas, or sneak in and erase the all important situation map overlays.

The Russian Division G-2 (in those days nobody bothered to say Soviet) was run with the most realism we could manage. Russian symbols were used on the situation map; the language was exclusively Russian, and we ignored the rules against snapping to attention and saluting visiting officers. We even drew red stars on our American helmet liners. Since there was only one student officer among us, we all got to play the role of colonels or other field grade officers several times.

One night our boy Sasha Rubenstein came in out of the moonlight and reported that he had met, and established considerable rapport with, some subversives skulking in the woods. They proposed that we join them in an attack on the corps headquarters, and he showed us the firecrackers they had given him as a token of trust.

In a council of war we decided that collaboration with subversives to that extent was unthinkable for wartime allies. However, we decided not to reject this fortuitous contact entirely. Rubenstein was dispatched into the night to parley further with the subversives. In return for our neutrality, failure to report their impending attack on the corps, they were to do us a favor, later, at our convenience. Smilingly Sasha returned and motioned for silence. "Bang!" An explosion came from the direction of the corps tent. Those of us off duty dashed over there in time to see the whole complement of corps G-2s pouring out of the tent with streaming eyes, led by the Rodriguez in command, while gas-masked subversives destroyed all the vital documents and map overlays.

Our payoff came the following night when we received a visit from some senior officers, including the camp commander, Colonel Banfill. As we went through our routine of ramrod attention and reports through an interpreter, Sasha Rubenstein slipped off into the woods and moments later a tear gas bomb exploded in the tent. It shook up and temporarily removed the visitors, but we quickly donned our gas masks and went on working through the fumes. We received a citation for our coolness and presence of mind in contrast to the performance of the corps the night before. The value of good intelligence cannot be overestimated. Viva Rubenstein!

The Eight Day Problem was the end of the course and, at the zenith of our morale, the end of Section 7-D. We were transferred to Company H, perhaps for a long stay, as Russian speakers were not in demand. Company H was a prelude for overseas and war. It was commanded by a second lieutenant called Zamorello, whose bulletin board was always surrounded, because fantastic things would be announced there—furloughs, promotions, shipments to England, all by order of the second lieutenant. Seven of us from Section 7-D did not receive the customary post-school furlough. Meanwhile, Len Gmirkin and I had been selected to go to Fort Benning Infantry Officer Candidate School.

Finding me on KP again, Sasha Sogolow dashed in yelling to me in Russian, "Go look at the bulletin board right away." I took off, the corporal in charge screaming in rage behind me.

I could not believe what I was reading. By order of Second Lieutenant Zamorello I had become a staff sergeant, and the other six of us had also been showered with stripes. I dashed down to the PX, bought chevrons, sewed them on with a couple of stitches and returned to the kitchen, arms akimbo, suddenly outranking everybody except the Lord Mess Sergeant himself. My recent torturer, the corporal, was puzzled. "Pardon me, Sergeant, but didn't I see you somewhere this morning?" he asked.

"That was this morning, Corporal. Carry on!"

Sasha Sogolow was green with envy. "You milksop—nineteen years old and all that rank!"

A sense of the fabulous hovered over Company H. The new stripes meant we were going somewhere. They also meant that Len Gimrkin and I were not going to OCS at Benning. With those beautiful new stripes in hand, who cared about a possible gold bar in the bush?

The alert barracks in Company H was festooned in disorderly fashion with rifles and other rare items recently issued to those about to leave. The ruler here was a Teutonic master sergeant known to all as Goulasch-Kanone. The inmates liked to provoke him roguishly, because his predictable roars were entertaining, "Zere are a lot of new non-coms here, but remember, your stripes are not tattooed on!"

It turned out to be Alaska for the seven of us—Ilya Elliott Wolston-Volfovsky, Len Gmirkin and me, plus our new leader, Staff Sergeant Nicholas Baranov, late of Wrangel's army, appropriately heading for the place his namesake had developed for Russia in the 18th century. Baranov's character ran to extremes, à *la russe*. You were either in his favor, in which case you were addressed as "toots," or you were out of it and were addressed as "you preek."

In the case of Zamorello's promotion mill there was no doubt of Ritchie's efficiency. In an almost inconceivable bureaucratic tour de force, the stripes we had received were the precise vacancies in the table of organization of a tiny detachment in the far off Alaskan Department, the very slots the men there had been hoping to fill for many months. As a result, we almost lost those prized stripes when we got there.

Baranov received our sealed orders to proceed by rail to Fort Lawton, Washington. Goulasch-Kanone briefed us—we would not receive furloughs before shipment; we were not to speak Russian or mention Camp Ritchie; if we had to refer to it among ourselves, we should say "CP."

During those last days at Ritchie, two of my best friends had turned up, both assigned to Company E—Chinghiz Khan Guirey and William Sloan Coffin, fresh from infantry training, full of energy as usual and fond of doing bayonet exercises with broomsticks.

No furlough, so my mother came to see me off. She was delighted to see Chinghiz and Bill, both of whom went AWOL under the fence to pay their respects. She was also delighted with my new stripes. She had never understood why I had not even made Pfc in seven months, being ignorant of the ways of Ritchie. Besides, now while at her job in the PX, she could wear a little staff-sergeant's insignia, explaining with pride that it was her son, not her husband, who was "old sarge." When I eventually became a lieutenant she was furious. Any green kid could be that, but staff-sergeant had a mature ring about it.

I brought my mother into the camp and parked her in the PX beer garden while I went off to round up my friends. When I returned she was surrounded by our fat, sleepy Hopi friends. They stroked her arm and called her "Mom," and bought her beers. They were delighted with her and she with them, as she had been to their reservation in Arizona!

At the bar there stood, in his customary smashed condition, a French prince in an American private's uniform, Gaeton de Bourbon-Parme. He looked up, and after some difficulty in focusing, perceived my mother, whom he did not recognize, and the Indians. He sounded the alarm, "Mon Dieu! A white woman surrounded by savages! Help!" He was subdued by two Russian veterans of the *Ballet Russe de Monte Carlo*. There was nothing like Camp Ritchie, anywhere, ever. We should have had a post anthropologist.

On an October afternoon a Western Maryland train pulled out of the tiny depot near the camp, bound for Baltimore and carrying seven new sergeants bound for Alaska and my mother, whom I had tipped off—the hell with Gouslasch-Kanone and his security. She rode with us in silence, because we had all gone to sleep. Soldiers always did that. I woke up in time to say good-bye to her on the Baltimore station platform. Baranov clicked his heels and kissed her hand, promising to take care of me. It was not long, however, before I was "you preek" to him. Mama made the sign of the cross over me, dry-eyed. I think she was vastly relieved that Alaska was my destination.

After three weeks at Fort Lawton, Washington, we were loaded on a transport, an old ship made in Germany before World War I. We had no naval escort, so technically we were bait for Japanese submarines. It took several days to get to the port of Whittier, Alaska, a beautiful place with Norwegian looking fjords. Moving on to Fort Richardson, outside of Anchorage, we found ourselves in a large tent with a lot of other troops, all earmarked for the 11th Air Force, then operating against the Japanese from the Aleutian Islands. The tent was very cold in spite of a large stove in the middle. What were we doing in the 11th Air Force? Six of us shrugged philosophically, but not Wolston. He announced that this was a SNAFU and he would get to the bottom of it.

Wolston did not lack *chutzpah*. The way he got to Camp Ritchie in the first place was by walking cold into the Pentagon as a buck private, then wandering around until he found somebody interested in soldiers who spoke languages. This time he took off on foot and walked around for miles on the huge post until he saw a building with a sign, "G-2, Alaskan Department." There he found a very worried Captain George Kisevalter, commander of the Interpreters/Interrogators Detachment, who could not understand what had happened to the seven enlisted men he had requisitioned from Camp Ritchie. Wolston told him. They were in a tent in the 11th Air Force!

Thanks to Wolston we were shifted into a warm barracks belonging to Headquarters, Alaskan Department, General Simon Bolivar Buckner commanding, and we met our new C.O., Captain Kisevalter, who had led a company into combat against the Japanese in Attu. He was a Russian from New York who had met my father and mother. Although this put me on Baranov's "preek" list for awhile, it probably helped the captain decide not to reduce us to privates without prejudice, horrified as he was to find that Ritchie had given us all of his vacancies.

He told us we were members of the "I and I" Detachment under the Alaskan Department. We never saw the second "I" part (Interrogators) because they were all Nisei Japanese speakers out on the Aleutian Chain. We were the interpreters, and we were to be stationed in Fairbanks, Nome and one place in between, to facilitate the movement of lend-lease aircraft to the Soviets. Those bases belonged to the Air Transport Command, but we were ground troops because the Alaskan Department was responsible for the security of all of Alaska. As G-2 men we were to keep an eye on the Soviets, but our main duty was to facilitate good relations with them.

We were stationed at Ladd Field outside of Fairbanks. This was a well winterized place, which even had heated underground tunnels connecting the main buildings. We met our colleagues in what we all referred to as the *Ay-yay-yay* detachment. Some of them were Russians from San Francisco who had emigrated through China. Others belonged to a national guard regiment in New York. When he was organizing the Detachment, Kisevalter knew he would find Russians in that regiment in Alaska and liberated them from various coastal artillery positions. As a New Yorker, Kisevalter knew this regiment had had a Russian battery which, before U.S. recognition of the Soviets, used to march down Fifth Avenue with the Russian national colors flying, and was sometimes reviewed by my mother's first cousin, Grand Duchess Marie Pavlovna.

Since 1942 there had been a Soviet military presence in Alaska, some 200 officers, enlisted men and civilians, and so at nineteen, I met my first Soviets! They were in Alaska to receive lend-lease aircraft from the U.S. and fly them from Fairbanks to Uelkal and Anadyr on the other side of the Bering Straits. The planes were flown to Fairbanks through Canada from Great Falls, Montana by U.S. military pilots; their white stars were painted red, sometimes using Texaco stencils. The Soviets gave them a thorough mechanical examination before accepting them.

From Fairbanks, the flying was then done by the Soviet First Aviation Ferrying Regiment, which took them across to the USSR. The Second Regiment, which never came to Alaska, took them on to Novosibirsk, from where the Third Regiment flew them to the front. The planes could thus be in combat three days after leaving Fairbanks. Between 1942 and 1945 the Soviets received about 12,000 aircraft through this ALSIB route—B-25 bombers, A-20 attack bombers, P-39 and P-63 "cobra" fighters, and the trusty C-47 war-horses.

When I was fifteen, the 1939 World's Fair had opened in New York, and I spent days in the Soviet pavilion overhearing interesting snatches of conversation. Even at that age I could see the extravagance of propaganda in the exhibits, for example—1913, no private radio sets; 1939, X-million private sets. Who had radios in 1913 anywhere? I also watched the free Soviet movies over and over again, until I could fully understand the sound track. I particularly remember the picture *Chapayev*, about a Red Army cavalry hero of humble beginnings who is now, probably unfairly, the butt of numerous jokes in the USSR in which he always appears as a dumbbell.

But now, in Alaska, I was meeting my first Soviets in person. It was enormously interesting to me. I had no feeling of resentment toward this generation, and if they liked the system they had, let them have it, was my attitude. I was determined to work at my mission of facilitating good relations. My pride in the way the Russians were fighting, plus healthy curiosity about them, succeeded in overcoming my anti-Soviet upbringing for several years.

A short time before, Stalin had introduced the shoulder boards of the Imperial Army to replace the collar insignia of the Red Army. This was one of his tricks to put Russian nationalism to work in an army which had obviously not been eager to fight for the Party or international communism. I did not know that then, and it was a thrill to see my first Soviet officer standing in front of the cigarette counter in the PX looking so much like the countless photographs I had seen of my relatives in World War I. Actually, the Soviet commander in Fairbanks, Colonel Machin, was offended by this un-Bolshevik innovation and wore no insignia whatever for a few months.

It was exciting that I had no difficult talking with them; some words and stresses were different, but there was no basic change in the language. I tried to adapt to their way of speaking, but still got compliments from them on the purity of my Russian.

Basically there were two jobs for the enlisted American Russian-speakers—to interpret in the tower for landings and take-offs, and to interpret between mechanics in the hangars.

The whole procedure of aircraft acceptance by the Soviets caused endless bickering. The Americans were irritated because the Soviets were so sticky in signing for and taking over this largesse. They did not realize that if a plane developed mechanical trouble on its way to the front, the Soviet mechanic who had signed for it was held responsible, and if it crashed, the consequence for him could be very serious.

Members of the Ay-yay-yay were also stationed in Nome, where there was a small permanent party of Soviets and also at a small emergency landing field called Moses Point, a real place of exile for those who did not cherish the great outdoors.

Our headquarters in Fairbanks was called the Base Foreign Liaison Office. In addition to Captain Kisevalter there was Lt. Michael Gavrisheff from Washington, D.C., a Russian speaking non-com, in effect, the first sergeant of the detachment, and a clerk called Fox, whose name was translated as Lisitsyn, the only Russian word he knew. In Nome there was also an Ay-yay-yay officer, Lt. Igor Gubert, from San Francisco.

Shortly after arriving I was appointed to the non-com slot in the Liaison Office. It made sense, because I had been educated in English. It did not sit well with some of the boys that the youngest milksop of all had been appointed their first sergeant. Baranov assumed it was because Kisevalter knew my family.

The Liaison Office was sort of an embassy between the Soviets and the American command. We had to handle everything from arguments over aircraft to small housekeeping details. We also acted as a consulate, keeping track of the names of the Soviets coming in and out of Alaska and those stationed in Fairbanks and Nome. Nobody else in the government was doing this.

One thing was a big surprise—on my way to Alaska I had worried that my particular background would make me a pariah among the Soviets. The opposite was true. They turned out to be snobs about the whole thing, calling me a historical personality and often calling me prince or even "Comrade Prince!" How did they know my title? The NKVD men there, of course, had their special sources. Most of them, however, knew because they had studied the same book on literature in which there was a footnote stating that the Russian poet Griboyedov had married Princess Nina Chavchavadze!

Through this job I met all of the Soviets in Fairbanks, but outside of hours I was restricted to the enlisted men, who were in the minority, most of them mechanics. We ate together in the mess, but there was almost no social life. They never went to town. They had a little club in one of their winterized barracks, but the only time I got to see it was while acting as interpreter for a *Yank* Magazine correspondent. There were a few tables and chairs, a short bar with a mirror behind it where a picture of Stalin, clipped from *Look* magazine was stuck carelessly in the corner. We got along fine on the whole. I still have a series of pictures of us engaged in snowball fights with Soviet sergeants during lunch hour.

They must have been lonely and bored. Every night for almost two years there came from the Soviet enlisted barracks the sound of an accordion always mournfully playing the same Russian tune, *Siniy Platochek*, the *Little Blue Kerchief*. This song always reminds me of Fairbanks and the iron curtain already present there, though nobody had as yet coined the phrase.

This was brought home to me with special clarity when one of the Soviet master sergeants came down with syphilis and was committed to the U.S. base hospital. All contact with him from other Soviet personnel ceased. He was a pariah. I visited him every day and brought him reading materials in Russian, mostly *Novoye Russkoye Slovo*, the New York daily which still flourishes today.

He read it all gratefully, but without comment. The gratitude was in his eyes; he hardly talked to me. The Soviets accused him of having contracted VD from a woman in Fairbanks, and fraternization was forbidden. He claimed it came from a native woman on the Chukhotsk Peninsular. He acted like a condemned man, and he probably was, because in the wartime Red Army men contracting VD in foreign countries were sent to punishment battalions at the front, where they were used, among other things, to explode mines by crossing fields—a great time saver. If they survived they could be reinstated in rank and returned to their old units, having done their penance, but the chances were small.

The only time this sergeant opened up to me was just before one of his examinations by an American medical officer, at which I was to act as interpreter. He begged me to persuade the doctor to falsify the diagnosis—anything but VD! I tried, but all I got was "Impossible. Medical ethics. Medical ethics." Shortly after this the sergeant was shipped back to the USSR, his comrades still avoiding him. It still bothers me that I could not have done more, but we were not accepting defectors. I still remember the poor fellow's name—Yevdokim Prozora.

We avoided political discussions with the Soviets, though some of our boys were unreconstructed Whites. Years later Kisevalter told me that one Soviet officer had tried to defect in Alaska, and with a sore heart Kisevalter had talked him out of it.

In the spring of 1944 Captain Kisevalter was transferred to the Pentagon, leaving the newly promoted Captain Gavrisheff in charge. A replacement officer arrived, Second Lieutenant Kyrill F. de Shishmareff, from Camp Ritchie. Everybody assumed that he had to speak Russian with a name like that, and nobody bothered to test him. It turned out that he only spoke a few words, very well pronounced, like "good morning," "Greetings," and "good-bye," enough to snow the Soviets for awhile as he passed them on the street. He was a tall, impressive looking man in his forties, terribly ashamed of his rank, and he began to hint that he was really a major whom Eisenhower had sent to clean up Alaska. He had been, he said, an officer in the French Foreign Legion. Upon arriving in Alaska he began to complain in writing that he was malassigned, since he did not speak Russian. This turned out to be my great opportunity.

Gavrisheff did not know what to do. First he directed me to give Kyrill Russian lessons, but this turned out to be hopeless. Actually, we both liked Kyrill, who was an amusing man of the world beneath this overlay of bluff, but there was no way he could run the outfit during Gavrisheff's frequent absences accompanying VIP's. So I ran it, including even the officer in Nome, getting Kyrill to sign papers now and then. He was not easy to get hold of, because he had found a lady friend in Fairbanks at whose house he spent his days writing a book about the Foreign Legion. I also was reading all the army regulations that we received, and I realized that the Commanding General of Alaska, an official theatre of war, could grant "battlefield" commissions to enlisted men.

Here was the solution—if Shishmareff were to leave, another few months would pass before we received a replacement, and there was no guarantee that he would be able to speak good Russian either. An officer was desperately needed. If I were to be commissioned, already completely familiar with the job, everybody would gain.

Gavrisheff agreed to give it a try. Shishmareff also supported the scheme enthusiastically. It would help him leave Alaska. So Gavrisheff wrote a letter to the Commanding General.

It was unbelievable, but three weeks later on a Sunday morning, some sergeant from Base Headquarters woke me up and when I complained said, "Get your clothes on. You won't be disappointed." I found myself being sworn in as a second lieutenant in the Army of the United States, in July 1944, at the age of twenty! It was even more thrilling than my sudden promotion to staff sergeant from the kitchens at Ritchie.

Sundays the PX was closed, and I could not buy insignia. Kyrill gave me enough, and clothes too, to get me by as an officer. I walked into my barracks to collect my worldly goods. I was immediately surrounded by my friends, who demanded to know, in Russian, if I was out of my mind impersonating an officer! I convinced them that it was true, realizing then that it would not be easy to be an officer in the same outfit in which I had been an enlisted man.

Shishmareff departed a few days later without waiting for Gavrisheff to return from a trip. Heavy is the head that wears the crown. I have often wondered what the Soviets thought about this sudden promotion, and what they reported to Moscow. Probably that I was a political character to be watched carefully.

During those difficult days there was a certain continuity in the person of our only civilian, Eugene Serebrennikov. Eugene had once taken a trolley car to the front in the city of Kazan to fight on the White side. A man of at least my father's age, he was well educated in Russian and English, and was very valuable to the Ay-yay-yay detachment. We called him the Merchant, army slang for civilian being "feather merchant." He gave me some much needed fatherly advice on the problems I was now being confronted with. There were problems with the Soviets at all times.

"Captain Gamov, how do you read me?" one of our boys said in the control tower, clearly seeing his plane circling over the field.

No answer. Question repeated. No answer. Phone call to the Base Foreign Liaison Office.

"He's a major now," I say. "He made major last week."

"Major Gamov, how do you read me? Over."

"This is Gamov. I hear you perfectly, *Priyom*."

On another occasion a Soviet pilot was being petulant with one of our tower interpreters because the tower had authorized a few American take-offs ahead of him, although he had been first in line. This time the problem was solved by the short, stout figure of Colonel Vasin, the commander of the First Aviation Ferrying Regiment. He appeared in the tower with his steel teeth flashing in the low Alaskan sun. He had lost his own teeth ramming German planes with his Stormovik.

"This is Vasin," he barked over the microphone.

"Yes, Comrade Commander!" replied the pilot, now aware that he was no longer talking to one of our interpreters.

"What the hell kind of democracy are you trying to spread? You've made your pile of shit, now sit in it! *Priyom!*"

I had a run-in with this Colonel Vasin that I have never forgotten. In 1944 a group of allied military attaches from Ottawa came to Fairbanks. There was a big banquet at which I, the only junior officer, had to interpret between English, Russian and French. The Soviets gave the banquet and I was seated next to Colonel Vasin. Everybody got drunker and drunker as we emptied, Soviet style, water glasses of vodka in honor of Stalin, Roosevelt, Churchill, etc. By the time we got down to the Grand Duchess of Luxembourg, I felt that one more toast would send me under the table. I respectfully requested to pass up the next toast. Vasin was furious. In pidgin English he asked the nearest American colonel to order me to drink. This worthy affably issued me a direct order to do so. In desperation I resorted to the liaison flip—a deft movement past the right ear with the vodka ending up harmlessly against the wall, if one was lucky enough not to hit a waiter. Nobody noticed, of course, except Colonel Vasin.

"Your ancestors were honorable Russian officers," he said to me in fury, "and you are a piece of shit. If you were under my command I would have you shot for that!"

He was not kidding, and in wartime Soviet officers did have this power. How I thanked God for the "U.S." on my uniform. For the first time I was looking into the eyes of the type who would not have hesitated to shoot my grandfathers for belonging to a class, or me for trying to stay sober enough to do my job. Colonel Vasin never addressed a pleasant word to me after that evening.

More than thirty years later I told this story to two prominent Soviet dissidents who had been thrown out of the country and got two different reactions. Vladimir Bukovsky, just out of GULAG, said he would have shot me too for wasting 150 grams of vodka! Former General Grigorenko said that in my place he would have knocked the bastard's stainless steel teeth out. The latter reaction perhaps gives a clue as to why Grigorenko, though in command of a whole Soviet division in 1945, held the rank of lieutenant-colonel only.

There was no shortage of problems for the Base Foreign Liaison Office. An American senator was quoted by a well-known columnist as quoting the Soviet ground commander in Fairbanks that American aid was insufficient. Colonel Kiselev must have been reprimanded to the edge of Siberia, because after that the very mention of the appearance of an American journalist or congressman would cause him to turn green and become so hostile that no one outside of our office could understand him. Once he even threatened to break the camera that some newsreel photographer was pointing at a jeep load of Russians.

Normally Kiselev was a pleasant man. I once took him into Fairbanks to meet the chief industrialist of the town, old "Cap" Lathrop, who owned the movie theatre, the radio station, the newspaper and a lot of other property. He was a self-made man, an old Alaskan pioneer, and it was interesting to translate this conversation between the leading local capitalist and the representative of the so-called Dictatorship of the Proletariat.

The meeting was cordial and smooth. The Soviet colonel was a technician,

114

a tough man who had been around, and both men instinctively respected each other. On the way back to the base Kiselev had nothing bad to say about the capitalist. He was absolutely amazed at Lathrop's control of all the media in town and that these outlets were not plugging any particular line. The colonel said, nostalgically, that he would like to retire to Fairbanks, build a house for himself, and maybe open a rival radio station!

In Alaska the Soviets never gave signs of dissatisfaction with the regime. This was a picked group, carefully briefed. Even the sergeants wore officers' uniforms, except for their shoulder boards. The only thing I heard along this line was a Soviet lieutenant colonel telling me that he would never have another promotion because he was Jewish. I was amazed, because I was under the impression that a large number of Jews still held high positions in the USSR. When *Time* magazine stated that one of the Soviet marshals was Jewish, the claim caused general mirth among the Fairbanks Soviets.

After I was commissioned I saw a lot more of the Soviets because they used our officers' club. We were always in great demand with them, to translate, or just for company. They particularly yearned for us in the movies. All the interpreters dodged them there, because it was no easy task to translate, for instance, one of Bob Hope's gags, while the whole audience was laughing and objecting to the hum of translation. Occasionally they brought in some of their own movies.

During the three years of the ALSIB operation, three Soviets were killed in plane crashes in Alaska. Two more were rescued by Americans, to whom they presented money as a reward. They were amazed when it was turned down. Sometimes I hitched rides to Nome on Soviet planes, that is, Sovietized American planes, always hoping that Nome would be socked in and I would have to land in the USSR, but this never happened. With an American aboard they had orders to turn back to an American air strip.

Nome's temperature was higher than Fairbanks', but the latter was dry while Nome usually had a terrible wet wind from the Bering Sea. Just walking from one building to another once, my trousers became two columns of ice, and it wasn't even raining. Our boys were not happy there. They complained that relations with the Soviets were poisoned by the presence of a very obnoxious and obvious NKVD officer.

In Fairbanks the NKVD officers kept a low profile. Once in 1945 a major said to me, "You'll be one of us some day!" using the familiar form. Was this a pitch, as we used to say later in the CIA? If so, it was never followed up. Perhaps they were recruiting agents among the Alaskans. Mostly, I think, they were interested in keeping their own men and dependents in line. The Soviet officers permanently posted had wives and children there, but not the Americans, since it was officially a theatre of war.

In addition to all our other duties there was VIP travel on this main route between the U.S. and the USSR. Foreign Minister Maxim Litvinov and his wife came through; Vice President Wallace stopped in Fairbanks on his way back from Siberia, and played volley ball with our Soviets. He later wrote a book describing how Siberia had obviously been built up by free men, although his hosts had been the GULAG chiefs of the area and he saw plenty of camps with their watch towers.

We also had to deal with those formidable Marxist females, Lillian Hellman and Anna Louise Strong.

Some of this travel resulted in trips "outside" as the Alaskans said, for members of the Detachment. Wolston, for instance, accompanied Molotov to San Francisco for the conference originating the United Nations. My break came earlier, in August 1944. Andrei Gromyko, then Soviet Ambassador to Washington, arrived from Moscow on his way to the Dumbarton Oaks conference, the first one regarding the United Nations. He was accompanied by a delegation of nineteen caricatures of Soviet bureaucrats. The bucket seats of his C-47 had been replaced by passenger seats, but the plane, through poor maintenance, was almost ready for the glue factory. This did not in the least dampen my ardor for the trip. If Gromyko could make it from Moscow, the chances are we would reach Washington.

The plane had a Soviet crew of three—Captain Vozdushny the flight engineer, Senior Lieutenant Ivanov, and the radio man, a twenty year old called Tolya Iskrov[2]. He was dressed in a junior lieutenant's uniform, but it later turned out he was really an enlisted man, so dressed because the Soviets did not want him off alone during our stops, eating with Americans and sleeping in their enlisted quarters.

In Fairbanks the plane was joined by an American pilot, Captain Schwartz, a Pfc radio operator, Jim Haight, almost twenty like his opposite number, and a liaison officer/interpreter. That was me.

Things started off badly before we even left Fairbanks. No agreement had been reached as to which pilot would sit on the left, and hence command the plane. Schwartz and Vozdushny argued about this, using me as interpreter, eying each other with hostility. Finally cables were sent to the Pentagon, which decided, typically for 1944, in Vozdushny's favor.

It was a beautiful August day when Andrei Gromyko solemnly boarded the airplane, followed by his nineteen assistants and then by the six man Soviet-American crew. Gromyko was then in his late thirties, a slim, dark haired man of medium height, with a dour expression that made him look much older than his years, which is why forty years later when his face had become word famous, to me he still resembled the young man he had been, absent a few wrinkles.

At every landing disembarking led to considerable confusion and disorder as the delegates in the narrow aisle tried to reverse their order of rank and let Gromyko out first. Shortly after take off Captain Vozdushny removed his tunic, revealing a sky-blue undershirt, turned on the automatic pilot, and went to sleep. The three twenty year olds grew friendly immediately. Ivanov, a mild, harmless man with balding blond hair, regarded us benevolently, but Captain Schwartz was still smarting over his defeat in the seating battle, and was a very nervous man. So, from the time Vozdushny's nap was over, I had to stand leaning over the seats of the two pilots, translating. Vozdushny was as bland and stubborn as Schwartz was nervous.

"Tell that son of a bitch that if there's bad weather in Edmonton I will ride

---

2.   I have changed the names of the Soviet crew for their protection, and those of the Americans for my own.

116

the range down," Schwartz stated.

"Nyet," Vozdushny replied.

"For Christ's sake, tell him he doesn't know how to ride the range down."

"In the Soviet Union we learn quickly. Show me the diagrams," Vozdushny answered.

Luckily we had good weather all the way.

In the middle of the first landing Ivanov stuck his hand down to lower the landing gear. American procedure was to have the co-pilot do this, so Schwartz smacked Ivanov's hand. Ivanov, in a hurt voice demanded, "Why is he insulting me?" Meanwhile, Schwartz was yelling "flaps!" and I was trying to think of the Russian word, *shchitki*, which I'll never again forget, and trying to soothe Ivanov's ruffled feathers.

We landed at Whitehorse and Fort Nelson, Yukon Territory, and Edmonton, Alberta. Next stop was Minneapolis, and here was an issue upon which the whole crew could agree. We wanted to spend the night there. The Americans had heard that Minneapolis teemed with young, willing girls, and the Russians probably just wanted to sleep, although they were undoubtedly fascinated at the prospect of seeing a large American city for the first time. It was up to me to sell Gromyko on this plan.

"Mr. Ambassador," I began after entering the passenger compartment and standing before him, "the crew has decided that it is extremely desirable to spend the night in Minneapolis."

He lifted his serious, expressionless face and looked at me calmly. "Nyet," he said. There it was, one of the nyets for which he would become famous at the United Nations and then as foreign minister for decades.

"Secretary of State Stettinius," he continued after a moment, "is expecting me and we cannot spare the time."

"But Mr. Ambassador," I tried to conceal my desperation, "the Soviet crew is extremely tired."

He lifted his hand, forefinger extended, and placed the finger against his forehead in deliberation. "This must be taken into consideration," he concluded. "Call the flight engineer."

I stuck my head into the cockpit and called for Ivanov. With violent movements the gentle little man checked the buttons on his tunic and smoothed his sparse hair before appearing on stage at rigid attention.

Gromyko put Ivanov through a calm but perceptive interrogation on the state of the Soviet crew's fatigue. Luckily for the plan, Ivanov could not have looked more tired. Finally Gromyko dismissed Ivanov.

"*Yest, tovarishch posol* (Yes, Comrade Ambassador)," the little flight engineer barked, turned on his heel and disappeared forward.

"Lieutenant," Gromyko turned to me, "we will land in Minneapolis for the night, but on condition that we are on this plane and ready to take off at five o'clock sharp tomorrow morning."

"Yes, Mr. Ambassador," I replied and made myself scarce.

The atmosphere in the cockpit was not at all dampened by the news about the ghastly hour for tomorrow's take off. The two captains went so far as to exchange half smiles. The twenty year old club rejoiced. Not only had we been the instigators of the whole idea, but there had been an added reason for it that only Tolya Iskrov among the Soviets knew about. It was Jim Haight's twentieth birthday!

In a stately procession of twos, Gromyko and his delegation entered the Nicollet Hotel, followed by the crews, while I fussed about the desk checking them all in. Soon they were safely registered and we were free, and in the States!

I will limit myself to very few comments on the events of that evening. First, the Soviet crew was ordered by Vozdushny to stick together and go off separately from us. Secondly, Jim Haight took off with Texan directness to a destination known only to himself. Thirdly, Captain Schwartz and I walked off together, soon separating, and the number of girls around, to our Alaskan eyes, was truly staggering. I imagine Gromyko and his followers stayed in the hotel.

Bleary-eyed, at four o'clock the next morning, I stood in the lobby of the Nicollet counting Soviet noses. All present. A bus took us to the airport, almost an hour away.

It was only after the Soviets had entered that tired C-47 that Schwartz and I discovered with horror that Jim Haight was missing. We called the hotel. After a tremendously long series of clicks as the operator buzzed his room, a sleepy voice answered. Our Texas birthday boy explained that he had celebrated quite hard and had been escorted back to the hotel by an MP patrol car. If the desk had called to wake him up, he had not heard it.

Schwartz and I held a worried *conseil de guerre* in the operations office. It would take Haight a good hour to get here and it was already 5:15. Gromyko had been so insistent about his blasted take off, too. To my relief, Schwartz agreed with me that it was better to delay the flight an hour than to leave Pfc. Haight behind to face AWOL charges. Besides, it would take that long at least to dig up a substitute radio man. Iskrov was no good to us without English. Then Schwartz said, "You're the liaison officer. You've got to do something and also explain to Gromyko."

I looked out of the window and saw a group of soldiers loading box lunches on our aircraft. I sent word to them to unload the lunches, and then load them on again. No, don't ask why, just do it. They did it, three times. The Soviet delegates at the rear of the plane probably began to think that a diabolical plot was afoot to poison their food.

5:40 AM—a worried Ivanov emerged from the plane and ran around looking for us. What could we tell him? Weather? A more beautiful dawn could not be imagined, and already Vozdushny had turned over the engines. They ran perfectly. Ivanov returned to the plane without finding us.

6:00 AM—I could just make out Gromyko's head in the forward window of the passenger compartment. He was looking out at frequent intervals.

Ten minutes later a car roared up and out stepped Jim, sheepish, apologetic, and terribly hung over, dragging his B-4 bag. We dashed out of the operations office, joined him without a word, and boarded the plane.

Schwartz and Haight made it into the cockpit. I was moving quickly, but Gromyko reached out a hand and would have grabbed me by the belt if I had not stopped at his words, *Gospodin Leytenant!*"

"Yes, Mr. Ambassador?"

He brought his wristwatch up with a majestic motion and showed me what I already knew all too well—it was 6:15 AM.

"Do you remember the condition under which we spent the night in Minneapolis?"

"Yes, Mr. Ambassador."

"Will you be so kind as to explain?"

I thought fast, watching his expressionless face, but no new ideas came to me. I had considered them all during that hour in the operations room. There was a secret weapon—the truth!

"Mr. Ambassador," I said, trying to be light and humorous, "this may be the first time in history that an important international conference has been held up by a Pfc." I then explained exactly what had happened to Jim Haight, that it had been his birthday, and that we were unwilling to leave him in the clutches of military justice.

To my surprise, the stern face relaxed into a smile, and Gromyko actually chuckled.

In the many years of nyets since then I have often wondered whether he understood and sympathized, or whether that chuckle was caused by the thought of what they would have done to a Soviet Pfc under similar circumstances.

We flew to Washington, none of us in good shape. Jim Haight suffered in silence, resting his head on the radio. As we made our approach into Washington National Airport, I looked down and saw a company of troops in formation and the tiny figure of Secretary Stetinnius, the sun glinting on his white hair and smiling teeth. We landed, and the usual turmoil took place as the delegation tried to get in protocol-prescribed order. The door opened and Ambassador Gromyko walked out into the cameras.

We all formed a line as the honor guard passed in review. The National Anthem was played and we saluted. This was followed by another piece of music, totally unfamiliar to me, and obviously to the Soviet crew, but since everybody was saluting we shrugged and saluted too. It was the new Soviet anthem which had just replaced the *International*.

After this I was free, on the East coast, and for an indefinite period! What a wonderful feeling! I was attached to the plane, but had nothing to do with the Dumbarton Oaks conference. I hitched a ride to New York on a general's plane, made my way to Wellfleet and walked in on my mother. She was not as surprised as I had hoped. Some newspaper had mentioned that Gromyko's liaison officer on this trip was a relative of Emperor Nicholas II, and this had been called to her attention!

Every few days for the next two weeks I would call the Soviet Embassy in Washington to ask about our dear C-47. At first I was amazed how rude they were to me. Then I tried speaking English and explaining that I was in the American army. Their attitude changed entirely. About two weeks later they told me the plane was leaving, though the conference was still in session.

There was a new American pilot, much more relaxed than Captain Schwartz. We left Washington with the same Soviet crew, but no passengers. We got as far as Edmonton, and there the decrepit ambassadorial lemon absolutely refused to take off. It taxied out to the runway, but could not make it off the ground. Since it belonged to the Soviets, I, as the only American officer present who could read the inventory, had to sign for one C-47 and equipment, received from the government of the USSR by the United States Army Air Corps. For years I was afraid of receiving a bill for God knows how many thousands of dollars.

The Soviet crew and I got back to Alaska on an Air Transport Command plane, sitting on boxes, and on those boxes, when the others were out of earshot, one of them surprisingly asked me to sing *God Save the Tsar*!

As for Gromyko, one of our Cape Cod friends, Norman Matson, used to say that he was probably the only true *Homo Sovieticus* the regime had produced. Years later, at the United Nations, he said in answer to a reporter's question, "My own personality does not interest me." This, Norman Matson said, should be embroidered on the Soviet flag, as well it should, but I once got a chuckle out of this super *Homo Sovieticus*!

CHAPTER VIII

In January 1945 I pointed out to Captain Gavrisheff that my gold bars were turning green! I had only been commissioned since July, but I was wearing some of Shishmareff's old brass.

"You bastard," Gavrisheff said.

Nevertheless, on February 15, 1945 I was promoted to first lieutenant, and in March I became eligible for RRR—forty-five days leave. I had not been in Alaska for two years yet, but why argue? They give—you take.

My father was in Germany, and my mother was working as a full-time nurse's aid at Fort Dix, reviving her experiences from that long-ago war between Greece and Turkey, and her mother's hospital at Harrogate during World War I. I saw her once a week on her days off, and we whooped it up on Spivy's Roof. One night we went to Harlem to sample a new, exotic Italian dish called "pizza," and watched it being made.

My cousin, Nancy Leeds, was in New York working as a volunteer hostess in a private club for officers, and we became close friends, as opposed to childhood. We often visited her father, "Uncle William" Leeds, whom I had not seen since the early 1930s. His name was anathema to my mother, but he had always been nice to me and continued to be. This time he offered to fix me up with a call girl!

"Of course, David old boy, for God's sake, take him up on it," said Wrangel. "Think of how you'll kick yourself back in Alaska if you don't!"

George Wrangel, with his silvery hair, guardsman's moustache, British accent, but also speaking fluent Italian, French and Russian, was a man-about town and bon vivant of an extinct type. Practically every day during this RRR I lunched with him at "21," where he had his own private wine cellar with the Wrangel coronet—eleven balls instead of nine—embossed on the leather cover of his private wine list. We didn't just lunch. He talked Italian to the waiters; his mother, Aunt Maroussia, had been born in Russia into the Neapolitan ducal family of Ruffo. He also consulted with the chef in French, saying, "David old boy, for God's sakes, a chef is a creative artist!" The chef, coloring with pleasure, would retire to the kitchens to make us something magnificent. There was nothing phony in Wrangel's knowledge of food and wine.

Who was Wrangel? Well, he was a relative of mine, Baron George Wrangel, who later became famous as the original Hathaway Shirt man with the eye-patch. He too had once fixed me up with a call girl, at the request of my father, when I was a freshman at Yale. He even sent telegrams the way he talked, "David old boy for God's sake I'm giving a party for you Friday," this one read. Sensing what was in the wind, I arrived at his suite in the Park Chambers Hotel in a rather nervous state. "David old boy for God's sake," said Wrangel handing me a scotch, "Rome wasn't built in a day. Don't give it a second thought!"

Wrangel could be described then as an honorable gigolo. Gigolo because he had a fabulously rich mistress drinking herself to death on Long Island—honorable, because he spent every evening except Tuesday with her and tried to make her cut down on her drinking. He used the money to support his mother and sister, as well as blowing it at "21" and other places. On Tuesdays he liked to spend the night with an Orpheum girl, whose ambition was to acquire her own fancy western saddle, boots, etc. at a New York State dude ranch.

By the time I arrived in March 1945 this arrangement was coming apart at the seams. Wrangel had fallen in love with a beautiful British model, Betsy, tall, blonde and penniless by his standards. Betsy was no gold digger. She insisted that he break off with the mistress, but he was dragging his feet. He used to hand me $40 and tell me to take Betsy out, which I would do, going through the Wrangel routine at "21" as best I could. Eventually, he married Betsy and later divorced her. Meanwhile the rich lady on Long Island had acquired another gigolo, dishonorable this time, who encouraged her drinking until she died a year later, leaving him all of her money.

After the cut-off of this money, Wrangel, who was not penniless for the first time, used his initiative, contacts and know-how and sold furs and jewels, and later got into modeling. But not Hathaway Shirts right away, that was the culmination of his modeling career. He appeared first draped around two pages of *True Story* magazine, holding a young girl in his lap. The caption said: "Jody, Jody," he said, "and his eyes were wet."

"David old boy for God's sakes," said Wrangel to me in 1947, "come and see Wrangel emoting!" He took me up to his tiny room in the cheapest hotel in New York with any chic, the Sutton, and showed me this copy of *True Story* and I took him to lunch, but not at "21." There he told me, "David old boy for God's sakes, you have no idea how difficult it was to hold that girl in my lap for hours while they were taking the pictures. Such a delightful little bit of fluff!"

Later, I used to see him in the *New Yorker*, advertising whiskey. "That's Dawson," says another character in the ad, "he knows. Its Calvert's Reserve for him!" Actually, even in his flush days, Wrangel was picking up money on the side with this sort of thing. He would always order whiskey by brand name, then he would suddenly switch to another brand, brushing aside my questions as to why the change in taste.

The Hathaway contract enabled George to live comfortably in Spain, spending only February in New York for the photography.

Back in the spring of 1945, however, on April 12, I was sitting around with Wrangel and his mother and a Russian from Newport, when Wrangel's Orpheum girlfriend called.

"Roosevelt died," Wrangel announced returning from the phone.

"Thank God," said the Russian from Newport.

I burst into tears and was stroked on the head by Aunt Maroussia, who also restrained me from slugging the Russian. At that time I had positively monarchical feelings toward Roosevelt, who had become president when I was eight years old. To have this titan replaced by a little unknown man with funny glasses in the middle of a gigantic war was disastrous. I canceled a date with a girl that night. She was very understanding, but surprised that I was so affected by the event.

I was probably the first person in New York to sing the latest Soviet wartime songs, so free of the pre-war propaganda. This led to arguments with some of the older generation. The old, "right-wing dinosaurs," as I called them, accused me of being pro-Communist.

"Isn't it true that the Soviet DP's in Europe don't want to go home?"

"My father writes that most of the ones in the camp he is running want to go."

"Some of them don't, isn't that true?"

"Yes, but those are the ones that have collaborated with the Germans and are afraid."

"Prince Chavchavadze, you sound like a Soviet citizen!"

I must admit my last remark was all wrong, and a reflection of what I had been told by the Soviets in Alaska. The truth was much more complicated. My father's DP's perhaps did not suspect that they would be punished for the mere fact of being in the West, whether they actively collaborated or not. The whole question of collaboration, as I would learn later, was not just a Quisling-like phenomenon—millions of Russians and other nationalities looked to the Germans as liberators from Stalin, and were committed to the German side before they realized that the Nazis were in no way liberators. Some went on regarding Hitler as enemy number two, the only way to get rid of enemy number one, Stalin and his Bolsheviks.

The "dinosaurs" whom I despised in those days were right about one thing, "Don't forget," they said, "that you are still dealing with Bolsheviks. Don't be taken in by Stalin's national trappings. A leopard doesn't change its spots!"

Shortly after Roosevelt died a *Te Deum* was held for him in the Russian church on 121st Street, Father Vasily conducting the service. He, who had given me Bible lessons when I was a little boy, was then, unknown to me, doing the same thing for a little six year old girl called Genia, who would one day be my wife!

On this occasion, after the service, Father Vasily made a little eulogy in which the greatest thing about the late president turned out to be the fact that his mother had once attended a service in this very church and had said, "Please Father Vasily, pray for my boy Frank. He good boy!"

The Russians in that church suffered from the New Yorkers' syndrome of not being able to form a line, even to kiss the cross. Instead, they crowded around. Father Vasily's long arm reached over the heads of a few, stretching the cross to me to be kissed.

"That's my spiritual son, Prince Chavchavadze," he explained to the indignant heads in between.

In back of the church was a wonderful little restaurant with good Russian food and cheap vodka, and a banquet hall where, around this time, a reunion banquet was being held for the Imperial Guards Chevalier Guard Regiment, under the chairmanship of my great uncle, General Alexander "Uncle Horse" Rodzianko. I was a little miffed that he did not invite me to this, so I said, "By order of President Truman, the Chevalier Guards have been mechanized!"

"Ill-mannered young man," the old general muttered.

This was not the only smart aleck remark that I lived to regret. One day I spotted a Georgian relative, Prince Tenghiz Dadyshkiliani, standing by the Plaza Hotel in doorman's uniform, job courtesy of Serge Obolensky no doubt. A man of great strength, Dadyshkiliani was famous for having torn apart several pairs of handcuffs the French police had placed on him after some pre-war brawl in Paris. "Back in uniform, eh Uncle Tenghiz?" I said.

"Get out of my sight and go back to helping your Bolsheviks," Prince Dadyshkiliani replied in his thick Georgian accent.

On 56th Street, between Sixth and Seventh Avenue, stood another doorman, guarding the entrance to the Casino Russe in his *cherkesska*. This was a wonderful old Cossack called Fedor Danilovich Gamali. He always embraced me warmly, and he would say, "Listen to me, don't go near the front if you can help it." I did not tell him how far from the front I had been all along, not being proud of it.

The Casino Russe, connected inside and under the same management as the still famous Russian Tea Room, featured a singer called Maroussia Savva. She was touched to learn that some of the Soviets in Alaska had somehow obtained her records and loved them.

Over on 52nd Street, among all those jazz joints in the cellars of brownstone houses that have since been swept away, was another Russian place, the *Yar*. Here the permanent fixture was another Cossack in a *cherkesska*, Zakhar Martynov, who threw daggers with his mouth onto a board on which the customers placed dollar bills. In spite of his loud but phony invocation of Allah, he often missed, but would pick up the bills anyway. Zakhar had served in one of the Imperial Guard Cossack regiments, and I often listened to the tall stories he told Americans at the bar.

"In 1914 Tsar say to me, 'Zakhar, don't go to front. Stay with me!' I say to Tsar, No, Your Imperial Majesty, is my duty go to front! Tsar say, 'Nu, OK, Zakhar, but come back after war.'"

The glorious, and occasionally inglorious, forty-five days were coming to an end. My mother and I went up to Spivy's roof for a final evening together and there ran into by chance, and made friends with, a very amiable colonel called Rankin Roberts, who had served with General Stilwell in the China-Burma-India theater, and was now in the Pentagon in Army Ground Force Public Relations.

This chance meeting had extraordinary consequences for me. Colonel Roberts was looking for somebody who had had experience with the Soviets to appear at a rally in Madison Square Garden to boost the Soviet-American alliance. As a result, instead of returning to Alaska I got a reprieve. I was ordered to the Pentagon, as it happened, on the day of the German surrender, May 8, 1945, V-E Day.

There was a false V-E Day the day before, so I did not miss out on the business of kissing every girl in sight. I was right there on Times Square when they all poured out of the buildings, not knowing that the press reports were premature.

The evening of the real V-E day, Roberts and I had a drink at a Washington hotel, the occasion being spoiled by the fact that the waiter refused to serve me, unimpressed by my silver bars and the fact that I had only twelve days to go to attain the age of twenty-one.

After a few days at the Pentagon I was ordered back to New York, to 90 Church Street, so I took up residence with Wrangel, this time commuting to work by subway. The event we were working on was called "Salute to the G.I.'s of the United Nations," to take place in Madison Square Garden under the joint sponsorship, believe it or not, of the War Department and the National Council of Soviet-American Friendship!

My job was to relate my Alaskan experiences to a writer, who would then put together my speech for the great rally. The writer turned out to be Warrant Officer E. J. Kahn, Jr., who was to make a considerable name for himself as a writer for the *New Yorker*. He and his wife Ginny, a WAC officer in a neighboring office, and I became friends and spent some of our evenings on Spivy's Roof, where the whole caper had started. Both of them were very familiar with the Cape Cod scene.

Jack Kahn also wrote the speeches of the other two lieutenants who were to participate; one who had met the Soviets on the Elbe River, and the other who had been freed by them from a German POW camp.

As the great day drew near I noticed one puzzling circumstance—we were told that Madison Square Garden had been totally sold out for the rally, but I had never seen it advertised anywhere. Yet Aunt Maroussia, Wrangel's mother, seemed to have no problem getting tickets for it. What kind of contacts did she have, and why? While I did not recognize it then, the entire event was run by communists!

The rally was preceded by a dinner at the Soviet Consulate. I put down my mother's name as my date and she received an invitation. For me this whole thing was a lark, and I was used to being with the Soviets in both official and unofficial situations. But Mama, to her credit, hesitated. After all, no member of the Imperial Family had ever attended an official Soviet function, and not, to my knowledge, has since. She felt it was not the right thing to do, but curiosity to see what the Soviets were like won out. I talked her into it, another youthful stupidity I now regret.

She was seated, protocol-wise, in the lowest possible position, appropriate for the lady of a first lieutenant. There were no incidents, no rudeness on the part of the Soviets, and, luckily, no publicity later about the dinner. My mother and the Soviets chatted amiably and if they knew who she was they gave no sign of it.

There was plenty of vodka, very welcome I must say, considering what was to come. At the Consulate I met the other two lieutenants who were to appear at the rally with me for the first time, and I was relieved to note that these two combat officers were suffering from acute spasms of terror, as bad if not worse than my own.

At Madison Square Garden the other two lieutenants, my mother and I were ushered into a bare dressing room furnished, however, by an unknown angel with a bottle of Scotch. In the few minutes before the band music started, our cue to appear in the arena, all four of us were able to supplement the Soviets' vodka with good Celtic fluid and marched to our seats with great aplomb. Thousands of faces surrounded the flood-lit rostrum, located where the boxing ring was on less political occasions. Flags of the United Nations all over the place. We had not been told the order of speakers, and to my surprise, the announcer, John Huston, called me first, only slightly mispronouncing my name.

I walked up to the rostrum with considerable bravado, eyed the thousands of heads through a pleasant haze, the visibility further obscured by spotlights, and began to read the immortal words of E. J. Kahn, Jr.: "I have come here tonight," I boomed through the microphones, "to dispel a vicious rumor being circulated about our gallant Russian allies. . . ."

A deafening roar of applause shook Madison Square Garden, but they had not even heard the end of the sentence. At that point I knew, even in my 1945 political naiveté, that something was wrong. I waited for the applause to die down and then finished the sentence, ". . . .and the rumor is that they do not like pin-up girls!" Of course they liked pin-up girls, when they could get them, particularly Deanna Durbin!

This time they laughed; it brought down the house. The rest of the speech, with more laugh-lines provided by Jack Kahn, went very well. As I was returning to my seat a person I had known in Alaska and who was known to be pro-Communist hugged me and said, "Splendid, Chavchavadze, you told the whole truth!"

Oy! And there was to be more.

The speech of the Soviet military attaché in Washington, delivered in a scarcely comprehensible English monotone, was received by the audience with ecstatic convulsions, while the British military attaché, speaking amusingly in clear English, was applauded in a perfunctory manner. Other cooly received speeches were delivered by General Walton Walker, later killed in Korea, and Mrs. "Vinegar Joe" Stilwell, filling in for her husband.

The mere sight of Paul Robeson caused an ovation before he even sang.

Between speeches, just as the procession of flags was about to enter, a burly American master-sergeant double-timed to where Colonel Roberts was sitting and saluted. "Sir," he said, pointing to an enraged functionary of the Soviet-American Friendship Society who had run after him, "this bastard wants to carry the red flag in front of the American flag!"

"Quite right, Sergeant," the colonel answered. "On American soil our flag goes first."

I could see that Rankin Roberts was under considerable strain, undoubtedly aware of the strange things going on. There was an argument, hard to follow, in which the Society representative pleaded that the music was written in a certain way, and, besides, at the last rally the red flag had been carried in first.

"The hell it was," snapped the master sergeant. "You tried, but didn't get away with it last year either!" The victorious sergeant led the procession carrying the Stars and Stripes.

All that vodka and scotch had taken their effect and I don't remember much else that went on. Paul Robeson sang, beautifully as usual. Somebody asked me for my autograph. Suitable sentiments were voiced about carrying on the war against Japan.

Three years later, E. J. Kahn, Jr. wrote an article in the *New Yorker* entitled *Reflections on a Subversive Past*. He pointed out that if the current definition of subversive activity were followed, like being in the same enterprise as Paul Robeson, it would fit not only himself, but a "White Russian of princely origin," and Eisenhower. I don't remember Ike's involvement in this affair, but he probably sent a telegram. Most ironic of all, I received a commendation from a major-general for my part in the rally, which entitled me to wear a commendation ribbon on my uniform.

During the few days in Washington Rankin Roberts had taken me to the War College, and there we ran into a grey-haired officer. It was only when I was close to him that I saw the four tiny stars on each shoulder. It was "Vinegar Joe" Stilwell. He took an interest in me because I spoke Russian, and later I was told that he was about to be sent to Moscow on some sort of mission and wanted to take me along as an aide. Just at that time, General Simon Bolivar Buckner, the man who had signed off on my commission, was killed while commanding the Tenth Army in Okinawa, and Stilwell was sent to replace him. The mission to Moscow was scrapped, as were my dreams of arriving in Fairbanks with four-star general's aide insignia and saying, "Sorry boys, but I'm going on to Moscow."

Three days later I was back in Alaska, but not as I had hoped.

There was a new C.O. of the Ay-yay-yay Detachment, Captain Eugene de Moore, who had replaced Michael Gavrisheff. He was a good-looking, dapper man, in the style of Ronald Coleman. For some reason he had changed his name from Count Muraviev-Amursky. He was very much a Russian, moody and running to extremes. While his English was adequate for conversation, it was deficient for reading and writing, which turned out to be an advantage for me.

My old friend Wolston was back from Nome and now in the first sergeant's slot, managing to incur de Moore's wrath every day.

"Davidka, I bahst Wolston," de Moore would threaten.

"You won't bust Wolston," I replied.

"Why I not bahst Wolston?"

"Because you don't know how."

The point was, he could do nothing without someone to put it into proper Army English. However, he went to Anchorage and got himself promoted to major!

Some unusual travelers were coming through Fairbanks—Russian Orthodox Bishops, both Soviet and American, traveling in both directions. Stalin was holding an election for Patriarch!

"Ha ha," Colonel Kiselev laughed. "Peter the Great abolished the patriarch and the Bolsheviks are restoring him!" He did not mention the fact that one was elected in 1917 whom the Bolsheviks shot. So the Soviets in Fairbanks had to learn how to address bishops. I have a picture of one getting off a C-47, his robes covering the ladder, and it looks as if a Soviet sergeant is preventing him from floating upwards.

The atom bomb dropped on Hiroshima and the USSR entered the war against Japan. I congratulated our Soviets on being allies again, and was struck by their lack of enthusiasm. However, their war lasted about five days, and they suffered something like 5,000 casualties. Yet, some of them had the nerve to say that they had beaten the Japanese in five days and we had been fighting them for four years!

In mid-August it was all over. The official peace would not be signed until September 2, but we began to celebrate, long before office hours were over. Soldiers and WACs greeted officers with, "Hi, civilian," instead of a salute. The Soviets were not in much of a mood to celebrate. Perhaps they were afraid to go home, and they were disturbed by all this anarchy.

In the early evening I proposed a trip to Fairbanks to three Soviet officers, all dressed up with brass buttons and gold shoulder boards. They agreed after some hesitation. On the main street pandemonium reigned. G.I.'s, happy and plastered, were wandering around in the middle of the street, sitting on car hoods and on the sidewalk, wearing civilian hats and ties. Alcoholic sweetness and light was in the air.

The Soviets stayed in their jeep, watching in horror as a group of ten G.I.'s stopped an American captain and with the best good-will in the world proceeded to strip him of every bit of brass on his uniform from cap to buttons, slapping him on the back and acting in a very revolutionary manner. The captain adapted quickly, accepting swigs from the soldier's bottles. It was a surrealistic imitation of a revolution, but there was no way the Soviets could understand this unusual bit of Americana.

Savoring every word, I said to them, "Gentlemen, the revolution has begun. Let us dismount and face the triumphant soldiery!"

They didn't think it was funny, and they knew their shoulder boards and brass would have special souvenir value. They let me out and their jeep roared off, as if under fire. The sun reflected off their three pairs of gold shoulder boards, almost identical to the ones that hostile mobs of soldiers had pulled off of, or nailed to, the shoulders of Russian officers almost three decades earlier.

Within a few yards I was given the non-brass treatment, receiving a blue tie with red polka dots in compensation. I was a private again, or perhaps a civilian. The atmosphere of universal friendship and equality began to affect me. My favorite bar, the Allies Room, was full of friendly soldiers and WACS. It occurred to me that I no longer had to act as an officer nor observe the no-fraternization rule with enlisted women. I began to flirt with an attractive WAC at the bar, on whom I had cast a frustrated eye at the base. She seemed receptive. The sergeant on the other side of her was not paying much attention.

That's what I thought.

The next thing I remember is waking up in my own bed, still wearing that polka-dotted tie. It was late morning. I scraped up enough insignia for an officer's uniform and headed for the officer's club, my head not in the healthiest condition. There was an aching sensation around my jowls.

I went to the mail clerk's desk. She was a small WAC who spoke in the soft accents of Georgia, the one next to Alabama, I mean. She inquired with solicitude whether I had gotten home all right the night before. I replied that I had, but I would appreciate any light that could be thrown on how this had been accomplished.

"Well, suh," she said, "I can fill you in on that. You were getting kinda amorous with one of our girls from the Third Platoon, and the sergeant who was with her didn't take kindly to that at all, Suh, and so he laid you out on the floor with a blockbuster. He musta started swinging from the floor mats."

I regarded her with fatalistic interest.

"Well, Suh," she continued, "I saw you lying there on the floor. You weren't the only one, but I sort of noted you because you always smile and joke when you pick up your mail. So I organized a couple of the boys to carry you outside and send you back to the BOQ in a cab. I hope everything went all right!"

By October only a skeleton crew of Soviets remained in Fairbanks. Then suddenly, with no warning whatever, a plane load of seven Soviet naval officers and seventeen enlisted men, complete with beribboned caps, landed in Fairbanks.

Every so often we had been visited by Soviet naval pilots, always headed east to pick up some sort of seaplanes and deliver them, probably by way of Africa and Iran. I had partied with them and learned some naval songs, but this group was different. They had nothing to do with flying; they were from the Baltic fleet.

"Where are you going," I asked the senior ranking officer, a lieutenant commander called Firsov.

"To Groton," be answered pleasantly, stressing the last syllable.

"What state is it in?"

This threw him. For some reason the Soviets did not seem to realize that the U.S. was a collection of states. My first thought was that some exotic program had developed at the Groton School, where Roosevelt had gone, but I dismissed this as unlikely. We sent a cable to the Pentagon. In a few days an answer arrived that they were going to a Coast Guard small boat training school in Groton, Connecticut, next to New London, but they were early and to keep them in Fairbanks until you hear from us.

A period of excruciating boredom ensued for them. The officers at least had our officer's club, but the only amusement for the sailors was the incomprehensible nightly movie. I made friends with the officers—not a bad group, except for one obviously political type. After a couple of days, keeping my activities quiet from the officers, I began to concern myself with the sailors. Ruled over by a petty officer in his forties, the rest of them were about my age, and they were a hand-picked group. Physically, mentally, and in their relaxed and humorous approach to life, they were far above the Soviet enlisted men I had met in Alaska, or the ones I would meet in Berlin. I had a far better time with them than with their officers.

A routine soon developed. I would dine at the club with the officers, turn them over to Major de Moore, pick up a couple of cases of beer and go to the sailors' quarters. The beer we killed, sitting around a large table, talking and singing in soft harmony, giving me a still greater repertoire of Soviet wartime songs. A close relationship developed. For them I was the only link with the impenetrable outside world.

My one man USO campaign to keep up the morale of the Baltic Fleet branched out into excursions into Fairbanks night life. In the ancient Nash which de Moore and I had bought jointly, I transported eight or nine of them at a time, slowly, so the ones on the roof and running boards wouldn't fall off, then make a second trip for the rest. One night it snowed heavily. My totally atrophied windshield wipers were replaced by two sailors sweeping the windshield with their arms, but I still drove into a ditch. All nine sailors quickly emerged and, counting in loud, military cadence, hoisted the venerable vehicle back onto the road, laughing happily. What was snow to these Leningrad boys? And what a fine thing it was to own a car, even this heap without wipers!

Two weeks went by without word from the Pentagon. On one of those afternoons, the last of the Soviets stationed in Fairbanks—the commanding officer with his wife and two little boys, the timid little civilian bookkeeper, and the NKVD officer—boarded the last of the red-starred C-47s. They posed to be photographed with Major de Moore and myself, and soon the C-47 was a speck in the sky flying toward Siberia.

As de Moore and I walked away along the landing strip, I broached the subject of accompanying the Baltic Fleet contingent to the States. He admitted it was a logical idea, especially since Firsov, the only one who spoke a little English, could not even read a menu. Besides, I could go to the Pentagon and try to get us all transferred from Alaska now that the Soviets had departed, I argued, and I would be back in a week.

All of this was true except the last sentence. I have to admit deviousness in this affair. One of us three Ay-yay-yay officers would have to stay in Alaska to handle any business that might come up, and none of us had enough points for discharge, not having been in combat. Captain Gubert in Nome, with the most time in Alaska, should be the first to go. He actually did leave a few weeks later. I should have been the next one, but de Moore was a major and wanted to go home desperately. If he stayed, he wanted me to handle the paper work for him.

Here my secret weapon of reading all of the junk mail and regulations again paid off. There was a new regulation that any officer coming into the continental limits of the United States, even on temporary duty, had to be reassigned there and could not go overseas again, and Alaska was considered to be "overseas!" Naturally, I did not mention this.

When the order to move the Baltic Fleet finally came through de Moore smelled a rat, perhaps. As I was saying good-bye to him, he pulled a .45 automatic out of his foot locker, laid it down and said, "David, if you don't come back, sooner or later I'll shoot you!"

My conscience was eased by a genuine resolve to get him and the boys out of Alaska when I got to Washington, and I did try, as I had once before during the RRR, through Major Kisevalter, without any success either time. All of them left soon anyway, except for de Moore.

I took a final look at the familiar Ladd Field hangers and the Alaskan range in the distance and lugged the B-4 bag containing my worldly goods on to an American C-47, after the twenty-four members of the Baltic Fleet had boarded. This time I did not have to interpret between pilots, but it was the same old series of landings in the Yukon and Edmonton.

I sat next to the Soviet senior officer, Firsov, a well-educated little man who had recently taken part in amphibious operations in Roumania. In a friendly way we argued about (a) the October Revolution, and (b) the activities of the Soviet secret police. Firsov's idea was that the only reason the American secret police were not obvious was that they had perfected so many electronic gadgets of control.

We landed at Great Falls, Montana, and were driven in an army bus to the railroad station where we boarded a train to Chicago. I had to do everything from buying the tickets to ordering the meals.

For hours I sat with the officers on the back of the observation car watching the Great Plains go by, answering their numerous questions about the United States. I had to keep my relationship with my real friends, the sailors, down to a formal level. They showed their understanding by their winks and smiles and by the fact that I could never lift my B-4 bag if it had to be moved. One of them would always grab it.

We changed trains in Chicago, and there were a few hours to wait. Forming a column of twos, we marched out of the station and eventually along Michigan Avenue, stopping traffic wherever we went. The sailors, with their cap ribbons hanging and blowing in back, suddenly reminded me of a column of French schoolgirls, as drawn by Ludwig Bemelmans, walking two by two through the Place Vendôme.

Back at the station I counted noses. One sailor was missing. Only forty-five minutes until train time! I alerted the MP's, and jeeps sped in various directions, but twenty minutes later the missing sailor appeared, walking slowly and thoughtfully toward us.

"Mr. Lieutenant," he said, "I have been talking to a man who presented me with this book; I couldn't understand a word he said, but he wrote something in the book. Will you translate it for me and tell me what the book is?"

He handed me a black book, on the fly-leaf of which was written, "To my dear Russian friend. May you find God." It was signed Rev. so-and-so. I can't remember the name. The book, of course, was the Bible. The sailor listened to my translation solemnly. None of the others said a word. The sailor was still carrying the Bible when we boarded the train.

In New York we were met by one of the Soviet naval attachés from Washington. He explained that the officers were to go with him to Washington for a briefing, then he said, "Lieutenant, if you don't mind, will you take command of the sailors and see that they get to Groton?"

We exchanged salutes. Mind! Even the fact of being back in New York took a back seat to this—I had been officially given command of a body of Soviet military, even if it was only seventeen men! No member of my family had commanded Russian troops for a quarter of a century, and probably nobody else in the emigration either.

Again in a column of twos I led the sailors out of Pennsylvania Station. As we walked east on 34th Street the men broke ranks and crowded around a taxi. The driver was showing them a newspaper and trying to explain something. When I approached he quickly hid the newspaper and looked sullen. I explained that I was only trying to help him get his message across. Somewhat reluctantly he fished out the *Daily Worker*. He was trying to tell them that he was a Communist. When I translated this, there were shrugs from the sailors. Either the sight of a Communist was too commonplace a phenomenon to excite them, or they merely thought him a fool. Or both.

We marched to the Empire State building and went up to the observation deck. They stared in silence at the great city spread before us. "This is not a city, this is a super-city," one of them murmured. Others exchanged very long and serious glances with me. It was a long way from Alaska or anything they had ever seen before.

Again in a column of twos, ribbons fluttering, we marched to Grand Central and through the coaches of the Boston train, to the amazed stares of the passengers, right into the club car. There we tried to recreate those evenings in Fairbanks—beer, songs and all.

After a couple of beers the chief petty officer stood at my elbow and said with formality, "Mr. Lieutenant, we would like to express our pleasure at your being in command. Thanks, for everything."

I tried not to cry in my beer, with only limited success.

In New London I formed the column for the last time. A Coast Guard bus took them to Groton, Connecticut, United States of America.

My reading of the regulations turned out to be correct. At Fort Dix I was given another forty-five days RRR, before reassignment in the U.S. What incredible luck! Two RRR's in one year without hearing a shot fired in anger. But what of de Moore? After my unsuccessful trip to Washington he stayed in Alaska for another eighteen months, itching to shoot me the whole time, I suppose. About two years later, when I was finally discharged from the army and sporting my new captain's bars, I stopped off for a drink at the Russian Bear on Lexington Avenue, and who was there? Naturally, Major Eugene de Moore, in civilian clothes. I thought my last moment had come, but he didn't shoot me. He merely tried to convince me that he had made lieutenant-colonel.

At the start of this new RRR, I went to Cape Cod to see my parents. My father was back from Germany with many interesting stories, getting ready to go to Korea and China, still with the Red Cross. I told them about my Soviet naval friends; they arranged for the officers to be invited to dinner at a friend's house in New London, and we drove down. The dinner was not a great success because of the smart-alecky behavior of the officer I had picked out in Alaska as being NKVD. My mother didn't need to be told. "That one is from the Cheka, or whatever they call it now," she said.

Most of all I wanted to see the sailors. The snow in New London was as thick as it had been in Fairbanks in October. A friendly petty officer showed me the barracks where my seventeen friends were housed. When I asked him how they were, he enigmatically replied, "OK. No sweat."

I was sure that they would be as restricted by their own authorities as their air corps compatriots had been in Alaska. It was noon when I walked into the building and there they all were, taking a nap in their blue and white striped undershirts. They had told me once that Soviet naval infantry used to attack with nothing over those undershirts, and it produced some sort of hypnotic effect on the Germans. They added that everybody on both sides was drunk, having been issued a generous shot of raw spirits. I shook one of the sailors, Zhenya, a tall boy from Western Siberia. He opened a gray eye. "O-o-okh! *Gospodin Leytenant*! Hey, comrades, get up. Look who has come to visit us!"

Bodies hurled out of bunks. I was surrounded, beaten on the back, embraced, kissed. The meeting lasted only a few minutes because they had a scheduled class to attend. They were pulling on their uniforms as they talked. There was so much to say. Finally, I had a chance to ask whether they ever had a chance to go to town and have a good time.

"Good time!" Zhenya acted as a spokesman. "Why do you think we are taking a nap at noon? Mr. Lieutenant, you never told us that the city of New London contained a college for girls, for girls only, can you imagine that? And such wonderful girls. Konektikut College. And some of them are studying Russian! They have adopted us! And they all have cars, cultured cars, better than the one you had in Alaska, if you will forgive me. We drive all over the place with them. America is wonderful!"

I would give a lot to know what happened to those sailors. They must have returned home in an atmosphere in which Stalin was handing out at least "prophylactic" exile if not worse to anybody who had been in the West, even as a forced laborer in Germany—and my sailors, with their "Konektikut" College girls, and with that NKVD type watching them. . . .

But I will never forget them. I remember them every time I walk on Michigan Avenue in Chicago, near the Art Gallery, or walk out of Pennsylvania Station in New York, or drive by the Groton signs on my way past New London to Cape Cod.

Late autumn and winter of 1945 found me back in New York, where there was much euphoria and more lunches with Wrangel, and quantities of debutante parties.

In the middle of this Lucullan existence, I learned from my mother that my grandmother's eldest surviving brother, Prince George of Greece, had arrived in New York and wanted to see me. As a small child I had met her youngest brother, Prince Christopher, to whom I had said in Russian—not knowing he understood—"Uncle Christopher, you look like a big behind with glasses." He exploded with laughter.

On my way into the Plaza Hotel where Prince George was staying, I saw the familiar figure of Alexander Tarsaidze, a New York Georgian who had been a naval cadet in Russia, and who was the author of several very interesting books on Imperial Russia. I asked him what he was doing there.

"Don't you know," he said, "that whenever your great uncle Prince George of Greece appears, we of the Russian Imperial Navy honor him, because not only did he serve in our navy, but he saved the life of our emperor when he was heir to the throne?"

I hadn't known, and so Tarsaidze told me a little of the story, enough to whet my appetite for more.

Uncle George turned out to be delightful, with gray moustaches with a wing-spread of about ten inches, very tall, and speaking in a whisper because of an operation on his vocal chords. From 1896 to 1906 he had ruled Crete as the appointed representative of the Powers, including Russia. He told me that his main problem had been with the "exceeding drunkenness of the Russian sailors stationed there."

As we were waiting for the elevator to go down to lunch Uncle George approached an elderly worker who was filling some sort of hole in the wall. "What are you doing?" he asked in his whisper.

"I'm filling this hole," the worker replied in a very similar whisper.

"I have to talk like this," whispered Uncle George.

"So do I," the worker whispered back.

Uncle George was curious about everything. At lunch he tried to question the waitress and make little jokes, but she could not understand his brand of archaic continental English.

Back upstairs in his room I asked him to tell me the story that Tarsaidze had mentioned. Looking out over the skyscrapers of New York he related the events of fifty-three years earlier.

"I went on this long trip which Nicky, as tsarevich, took to the Far East in 1892. While riding in a carriage in some Japanese city, not Tokyo, Nicky was attacked by a berserk Japanese policeman who hit him a glancing blow on the head with his sword. No satisfactory motive for this, other than insanity, has ever been established. The Japanese emperor was horrified."

Before the assassin could strike a second blow, the twenty-two year old giant that Uncle George was then, smashed the man with his walking stick, knocking him cold, thus probably saving the future tsar's life. The original blow had not done much damage. It is strange to think how different world history would have been if Uncle George had not prevented a second blow.

"The Russian sailors," Prince George continued, "on the cruiser *Avrora* threw me up and down in delight. But the horses (cavalry officers attached to Nicholas) were exceedingly scared of what Uncle Sasha (Alexander III) might do to them, and they sent a telegram to Petersburg that I had taken Nicky to a bordello, which had exceedingly offended the sensibilities of the Japanese. I had to leave the party and return to Europe through the United States. When I reached Chicago, I was greeted by a great many exceedingly enthusiastic Greeks, but the newspapers said under my photograph, 'Famous Australian boxer arrives in Chicago'. When I got to England the Queen (Victoria) refused to receive me because of the bordello story, but Uncle Bertie (the future Edward VII) was exceedingly nice to me, and later Nicky had a special medal made for me."

I saw this delightful old man once again in Paris in 1947. He was married to a very learned psychiatrist and friend of Freud, Marie Bonaparte, and they had two children.[1] Uncle George died in 1957 at the age of eighty-eight. Shortly before his death I saw a picture of him in a newspaper, taken just as a sea gull had landed on his head. I am sure this would have pleased the old sea-dog!

My forty-five days leave ended on Christmas Eve, so the army magnanimously extended my RRR until January 4, at which time I was supposed to report to "Fort Sto. . .", the rest was missing, so I had to go to 90 Church Street again to look at a list of all the posts in the country, discovering that they wanted me to go to Fort Story, Virginia, on Virginia Beach near Norfolk.

"What do you do?" asked the adjutant when I had found the place.

"I am a Russian liaison officer."

He looked at me rather puzzled. "No Russians here," he said. "Would you like to be assistant PX officer?"

I expressed a lack of enthusiasm and went over to look at the post organizational chart, where I discovered a German prisoner-of-war camp in a box to one side.

---

1.   Prince Peter, who was third in line to the Greek Throne until the birth of the present
        King Constantine's children; and Princess Eugenie.

134

"Sir, I took two years of German at school. Perhaps I could be of use in your POW camp?"

"Well, if you want to live in the boonies, maybe that's a good idea," he said, relieved to get rid of me. Thus I found myself in a little place called Camp Ashby, one of seven officers, commanded by a puritanical old major who had been a prewar sergeant, with 1000 prisoners.

My best friend turned out to be the German *Lagersprecher*, or camp spokesman, who spoke English and had been a judge in Germany until he fell afoul of the Nazis and found himself as a non-com in Rommel's Afrika Korps. His name was Hans Kohlmann.

In addition to frequent tours as duty officer, I had only odd jobs to do, including that of POW welfare officer. I had a modest fund with which to buy things to make the prisoners' life a little happier. Musical instruments, for instance.

This had unforeseen and rather touching consequences. Many years later Hans Kohlmann somehow got hold of my address and wrote me a letter from his home in Germany. He said the prisoners who played the instruments had never stopped thinking of me as their great benefactor. After we had released them, the Belgians forced them to work there for another year. The Belgians had confiscated all the PX supplies the prisoners brought from Virginia, working on farms at eighty cents a day, but not the musical instruments. So when they finally returned to Germany they were a band, well rehearsed for years, and immediate employment was theirs.

As we gradually released prisoners, I had to interview them on exactly where their home was in Germany. This was important, because it established which zone of occupation they would be sent to, and naturally those who lived in the Soviet Zone tried to disguise their place of origin. In retrospect, I am entirely disgusted with myself for my zeal in pinning them down. This is what I was supposed to do, but I should have known better. I was still under the spell of the wartime alliance, and a number of individuals who could have lived in West Germany were condemned to live in East Germany because of me.

I was also detailed as guard commander on trains taking prisoners from other camps to New York, and by ferry to Staten Island, where they were loaded onto ships.

Meanwhile, I was trying to get to Europe myself. Finally, through the efforts of an Ay-yay-yay Detachment friend, now an officer in Berlin, I received orders to go to New York and ship out for the old enemy capital.

Arriving in New York on my twenty-second birthday, I spent it at "21" with my mother and Wrangel, my father having already departed for Korea. The next day I boarded a transport for the ten day trip to Bremerhaven. The ship was full of officers returning to Germany from leave. They couldn't wait to get back, and they did war-dances of pleasure when the ship came into the range of the Armed Forces Network and their favorite program, *Luncheon in München!*

ORTHODOX BISHOP "FLOATS" TO THE GROUND

SEEING THE LAST SOVIETS OFF FROM ALASKA - 1945
Author on left, Major de Moore on right

DAVID CHAVCHAVADZE

ALASKA - 1943

l. Baranov, Gmirkin, Dvoichenko-Markov, Tumarin (seated), Wolston, Author

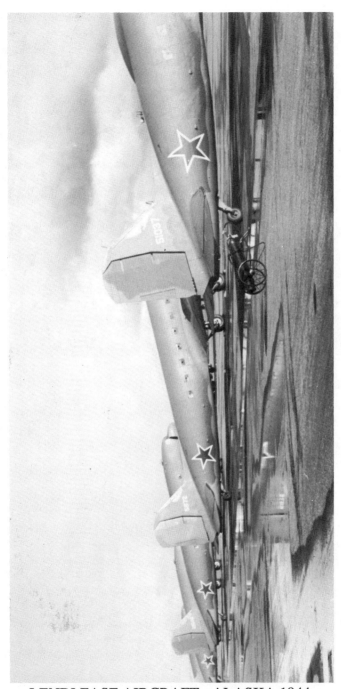

LENDLEASE AIRCRAFT - ALASKA 1944

SPIVY and AUTHOR

CHAPTER IX

On June 1, 1946 I set foot in Continental Europe for the first time. Everything was vastly exciting—the European trains with windows you could open and look out; the German railroad men with their Kaiser Wilhelm moustaches; the cars from all over Europe, including some draped with red flags; British troops here and there; Polish refugees, organized into some sort of para-military uniforms, with whom I could communicate in Russian, and who were trying to do black market with us.

After a night on a siding, the train deposited me at a replacement depot somewhere near Kassel. That night a sergeant with whom I was having a beer offered to introduce me to a friend of his Fräulein. We went to a housing project, and my Fräulein turned out to be somewhat older than my mother and not very attractive. Before I could explain that this was not my cup of tea, loud knocks were heard at the door. Two strapping veterans of the Wehrmacht barged in, addressing my date as "Mutti." Her sons! The sergeant pushed them out, locked the door, and said to me cheerfully, "Well, Lieutenant, I guess we'll have to fight our way out of here!"

So we each took a load of firewood, grabbed "Mutti" between us, and walked down four flights of stairs in total darkness, waiting to be jumped any minute. What a stupid situation. My second night in Europe, and I was about to be killed or wounded by the German Army for something I had not even done, but the attack failed to come.

The following night I was on the military train to Berlin, seeing Soviet troop formations for the first time and hearing Russian spoken. Somehow I could not conceive of Berlin as a city. I suppose I thought we would all be living in a quadrangle, such as in Ladd Field, Alaska. A quadripartite triangle, with the city off to the side somewhere, like Fairbanks.

Instead, I found myself in a suburb called Dahlem, being assigned a billet in a requisitioned private house, and drawing sheets and blankets in some warehouse. All this on foot, with no idea of the geography of the place. I was told by the German woman who handed me the bedding that I could get to my billet by riding three stops on the subway.

What she did not bother to mention was that I could have stood on the street holding up a cigarette and any German driver would have stopped to take me to my destination. In June 1946, a carton of American cigarettes, costing fifty cents in the PX, was worth 1800 Reichsmarks on the black market, or $180 at the legal rate of exchange. By the time I got there the real racket was over. We could no longer send $100 money orders home until we got writer's cramp, but we could still send our entire salary plus 10% home, and use the cigarette money to live off. Everybody had so much money it was hard to pick up the check for anything.

Nobody who sold a few cartons was considered a criminal. It was the big wheeler-dealers who dealt in cars, diamonds and tens of thousands of dollars that the CID was after. This army organization might call on you if you ordered 100 cartons a week from the U.S. (at one dollar a carton), and enquire politely whether you were really such a heavy smoker. But they were too busy to investigate something like twenty cartons a month. For four packages of cigarettes you could hire a German orchestra for an entire evening. No wonder the G.I.'s used to sing, in pidgin German, to the tune of *Lili Marlene*:

> *"Schlafen in de Bahnhof, Amerikan Soldat,*
> *Viele Cigaretten, viele Schokolat. . . ."*

In addition to Hitler's Reichsmarks, still circulating, the Allies printed entirely different looking Allied marks, which the Germans could use at par with the old money, but the PX and other American installations would only accept Allied marks. The Allies gave the plates to the Soviets, who churned out marks by the millions, giving their troops months of back pay at no cost to themselves. These were also accepted by American stores at the rate of ten cents a mark, and we could use them to send money orders home. The only way you could tell which were Soviet was by a dash in front of the serial number. In the end the U.S. Treasury paid for the whole mess.

Having found my billet, I went over to Michael Gavrisheff's house, my former commanding officer in Alaska, for a party. Gavrisheff told me that an Armenian black marketeer would probably show up. He did, trying to sell a 1939 Mercedes-Benz. His price was twenty-four cartons of cigarettes. Tempting as it was, we refused. I was to meet this Armenian again seven years later, by which time he was an established East-West trader, and a multi-millionaire who served caviar sculpted in the form of life-sized pheasants.

I also met a Russian that night who was in the French civil service, Serge Zvyagintsev. We sang Russian songs until dawn, accompanied by a German musician to whom Serge would occasionally throw a cigarette and yell in Russian, "Don't stop playing, you German scum!"

We were all under OMGUS—Office of Military Government, U.S. The Germans thought this meant bus in English because it was painted on the sides of double-decker Berlin buses requisitioned by the Americans. OMGUS headquarters was in Dahlem, but I worked at the Allied Control Authority (ACA) several miles away in a palatial building which had once been the Prussian Supreme Court. This was the seat of the Quadripartite Military Government of Germany. It was a short-lived institution; the Soviets walked out on it at the end of 1947, but in 1946 it was full of American, British, French and Soviet officers and civilians. Even the latrines had signs in the three Allied languages, but none in German.

I was assigned to the Liaison and Protocol Section of the American Element of the Allied Secretariat. This was a pool of interpreters and translators, officers and civilians, Russian and French speakers. We Americans were more or less assigned at random on a daily basis to any meeting that happened to be in session—anything from de-Nazification to venereal disease. The other three powers' interpreters were assigned to specific directorates so that they came to know a specific field well, a more sensible system. The interpreting was all consecutive, that is, there were no microphones or booths. You sat next to your delegate taking notes like mad and trying to stop him from talking too long. The rules required that the American interpreter translate what his delegate said into Russian, while the Russian Interpreter had to translate his delegate into English.

My first day at ACA was a disaster. I was assigned to the Finance Directorate, not my strong point in any language. The American delegate, a brigadier general, made a long statement which I did not fully understand even in English. I politely asked him to repeat what he had said.

"Young man, I don't remember what I said," the general replied.

"He doesn't remember what he said," I translated to the Soviets. I was lucky not to have been on the next train out of Berlin.

Mr. Shepherdson, the British interpreter, saved me. He was brought up in Russia in one of those British business families living there before the revolution. He translated for me while I made notes of unfamiliar words. Mr. Shepherdson had the reputation of being the best interpreter at ACA. He was excellent, but he had the advantage of knowing his subject and British policy on it as well as his delegate did. In many meetings the British delegate would drone on and then say, "Mr. Shepherdson?"

"Oh no, Sir, do go on!"

'   Finally, Mr. Shepherdson would make his own speech in Russian. In general terms it coincided with his delegate's statement, but not in any way word for word. No one could tell but the brotherhood of interpreters, and they kept silent. Interpreting for all of us became so automatic that we could come out of a long meeting with very little memory of what had been said. We usually reported to work at 10:45 AM, in time for the 11:00 AM start of most meetings. We would become furious at our long-suffering secretary, Miss Christiansen, if we pulled an occasional assignment at the ghastly hour of 10:00 AM or earlier.

Every month the chairmanship at ACA rotated to one of the four powers. The typical meeting would go on for an hour or so, and then the chairman for the month would invite everybody to a rather alcoholic lunch in the ACA mess. After lunch the meeting would last until 3:00 or 3:30 PM, then we were free to go home. Occasionally a meeting would last far into the night, but this was rare. As if these liberal working conditions were not enough, we also were free on the holidays of all four powers, something like twenty days a year, plus, of course, Saturdays and Sundays.

The quadripartite meetings were slow because of all the interpreting in three languages, but we soon noticed the Soviets were dragging their feet. Often a whole meeting would go by in arguments about the minutes of the previous meeting. "The Soviet Delegation agrees in principle, but has certain reservations of a textual nature."

How often we heard that phrase! Or else they would not agree, not even in principle. Almost always, on every subject, it was the Soviets against the three western powers. I can remember only one case in which the vote went differently. In one committee, Public Safety, the French would sneak in a point on the agenda

143

every time. They were determined to blow up the monument to the Prussian victory over Napoleon III in 1870. This very tall column was located in the British Sector, and the British let the French fly their flag at the top of it, but they were not satisfied.

The Soviet delegate gave a party, and had a cake made in the shape of the monument in question, cleverly seeded with explosives. At the height of the party the Soviet colonel pressed a button and blew the cake to smithereens. At the next meeting of the committee he moved to have the point taken off the agenda because, "as we all know, the monument has already been destroyed!"

This was an unusually cute quadripartite reception. To attend these affairs and translate was very much part of the job, but to me it was all so glamorous and interesting that I never thought of it as work, even when no cakes were blown up. At times I would find myself translating chitchat between General Lucius Clay and Marshal Sokolovsky.

Once I went to a huge Soviet reception in Potsdam in the Cecilienhof Palace, once belonging to Crown Prince Wilhelm. Later, I was able to describe to his son, my cousin Louis Ferdinand, what silver the Soviets were using in his old home. This reception featured suckling pigs and huge mounds of caviar. On the way to it the road was lined with Soviet troops, in a purely ceremonial way, to salute the foreign visitors. Nevertheless, we got confused about a turn in the road and I asked one of the soldiers how to get to Cecilienhof. He looked very frightened and said, "I won't tell!" Their security indoctrination was superb, and ridiculous.

Among the suckling pigs and caviar I bumped into a genuine Soviet war hero, Marshal of the Tank Forces Rotmistrov, who latched on to me and used me as an interpreter all evening. He was much more amusing and lively than the usual run of Soviet generals I met.

At the end of this reception I performed one more Liaison and Protocol function—calling for VIP cars through a microphone. A Soviet full colonel was doing the same thing. He was pale and haggard and had such a tragic expression on his face that I immediately understood he was in some sort of very deep trouble. The rest of the Soviets were ignoring him, and he wouldn't talk to me. The situation was somehow familiar, and then I remembered that master sergeant with syphilis in far-off Alaska.

Finishing my car-calling, I ran into an unfamiliar Soviet captain.

"Your name is Chavchavadze?" he asked.

"Yes."

"Your family owned thousands of hectacres of land?"

"I really don't know how many."

Turning to a row of Soviet enlisted drivers standing at the wall he said, "Comrades," in agitprop tones, "this man and we have only one thing in common—the language. His parents were shot by the people!"

The enlisted men looked indifferent, reminding me of my Baltic Fleet sailors when the New York cabbie told them he was a Communist.

I let it go. It was time to go back to Berlin, and I had developed marvelous rapport with Marshal Rotmistrov. Why make trouble? My job was to smooth relations. This incident, so rare for the period, still bothers me. I could really have nailed that captain

Liaison and Protocol sometimes led to off-beat assignments. Once I was ordered to report to headquarters in Dahlem at the crushing hour of 9:00 AM. A very good-looking WAC major handed me a spaniel and asked me to take it to get shots. She turned out to be Eisenhower's friend, Kay Summersby. So I drove off in a staff car, holding this dog, got a shot for it at some vet's office, and grandly returned it to Major Summersby.

There was the mysterious business of the Englishman who avoided the British in Berlin, and somehow arranged to have an American staff car, with me as the interpreter, take him to Soviet headquarters in Karlshorst. He was a man in his sixties, and like a fool I did not make a note of his name; he described himself as past president of some British labor organization, but the Labour government was in power, so why was he avoiding the British? And why did some American official go along with this?

We were met by three typically bull-headed NKVD types who understood as little as I did what the man was driving at. He seemed to want to arrange some sort of class-solidarity contact with the Soviets, he being a socialist. I suppose he was in the same league with the famous Red Dean of Canterbury, whom I later heard at Yale preaching bits of wisdom like, "But I know there is freedom of religion in Roumania, because the Minister of Religion told me so himself!"

This conversation was much more nebulous:

Englishman, "Why don't you send a football team to play us?'

Soviet, "But we did send a football team to play you."

Englishman, "No, no no! You were playing a upper-class team, an establishment team."

Soviet, "Tell this type that we sent a team to play a team representing England.

Englishman: "But you don't understand. That team did not represent the working classes!"

Soviets among themselves: "What the hell is all this talk about sports?"

Never have I heard a more inconclusive conversation. Nobody understood what he wanted. He was glum all the way back to West Berlin. I should have asked him some questions, but I didn't. I also should have told him that he had been received by state security officers right out of central casting. Even then I could spot these, in or out of uniform. I could also spot ex-Imperial Army officers. I went up to a major at ACA and asked whether he had served in it.

"Right," he said, "the 85th Vyborg Regiment of His Imperial and Royal Majesty the German Emperor and King of Prussia!"

We became friends because I happened to know about this regiment. For years Alexander III had avoided making Wilhelm II honorary colonel of a Russian regiment. Finally, he had to give in, and the Kaiser, proudly reviewing this regiment, went up to the band and asked the leader why the band had silver trumpets.

"For the taking of Berlin, Your Imperial Majesty," the bandleader replied, referring to 1762, and thus Alexander III put down his disliked relative.

The Soviets at ACA could not get over all the titled and historic names among the interpreters in the three western armies.

"There goes Prince Naryshkin," a Soviet girl said to me about a British officer.

"The Naryshkins are not princes," I replied.

"Counts, or maybe barons?"

"No. The mother of Peter the Great was a Naryshkin, but they turned down a title, saying that they were an older family than the Romanovs."

"My God, what nerve!" she exclaimed. "Were they shot?"

It was I by chance who pulled off the biggest coup along this line at the ACA building. In the presence of numerous Soviets, I introduced two Americans to each other, "Major Barclay de Tolly, may I present Pfc Golenishchev-Kutuzov."

"What a historical moment!" they all exclaimed.

In 1812 General Barclay de Tolly was replaced by Field Marshal Golenishchev-Kutuzov in command of the Russian armies fighting Napoleon, and here wc had Major Nick de Tolly, an American air attaché in Moscow, and our own Pfc. Illarion Ilyich Golenishchev-Kutuzov, aged nineteen. Larik Kutuzov never forgave me for saying, "Pfc," because he went around in some sort of civilian uniform, but that is what he was, and the historical moment was too piquant to pass up. Decades later, Larik went to work for Marshall Field in Chicago, and ruefully referred to himself as Marshall Field Kutuzov!

The Soviets at ACA were, of course, as highly picked a group as the ones in Alaska had been. Still, some of them were interesting. One of these, Misha, a fellow interpreter and lieutenant, became a special friend, with whom I would go to the Soviet *Gastronom* in their sector after work to make purchases. Once, in a frank moment, I asked him whether he would hesitate for a moment if ordered to shoot me.

"Not for a second!" he replied promptly, and we both laughed. But it wasn't really funny. I had the feeling that Misha would have carried out the order of that colonel in Alaska who had wanted to shoot me for passing up a toast. A couple of minutes later, Misha, who must have been doing some thinking, remarked red-faced, "Listen, you understand, service is service and friendship is friendship."

While a bit apologetic, he did not rescind his statement and, in fact, acted as if he expected it would happen soon.

I did not stick to the ACA in my fascination with Soviets.

On my first Sunday in Berlin I took the U-Bahn to the Soviet Sector and wandered about, watching the numerous Soviet military. At the old imperial palace on Unter den Linden, later blown up by the Soviets, I started talking to a private. He was a real wartime soldier from the Second Shock Army, still stationed in Poland. He had come to Berlin because he was a general's driver. He was amazed to hear Russian coming out of this foreign uniform! I was the first American he had ever met. We had a few drinks, and then, to my surprise, he started on Misha's theme, somewhat differently.

"God, I would hate to have to shoot at you!"

"But there isn't going to be any war between us."

"Yes there will be!"

"Come on, we are friends, allies!"

"I tell you there will be a war!" he insisted, tears in his eyes.

Like most of them, this soldier was a very warm individual. He insisted on giving me a photograph in memory of our "historic" meeting, and then he asked me my rank.

"Senior lieutenant," I told him.

His attitude changed immediately, and he became stiff and reserved. It took quite a bit of doing to convince him that I could not care less that he was a private, and to restore some of our camaraderie. Here was a specimen of the so-called classless Red Army!

I became friends with another Soviet enlisted man, a sergeant called Nikolai, a peasant from Byelorussia. He knew I was an officer and always, at least when sober, addressed me as Mr. Lieutenant. Nikolai yearned for a simple, old-fashioned peasant life. For whatever reason, he was unhappy with his time and place.

"You know, I was born at a terrible time," he said to me in his cups. "Junk and disorder everywhere. If I were born a hundred years from now, maybe I could fly around on my own little wings, but now, first we spit at the old days; then we are told to respect certain parts of the old days. If I had been born a hundred years ago, I would have put my Maria Kazimirovna on a wagon, taken her to the bazaar, and there would have been all those relatives and godparents, and what else would I have needed? But now. . . ." and he delivered himself of a string of expletives.

What a pity that I avoided politics with the Soviets in those days! About the only exception was when I slipped my interpreter friend Misha, at his request, a copy of the defector Kravchenko's book, *I Chose Freedom*. He read it, returned it, and said, "No comment," in English. I had been expecting a tirade against it.

The ACA building was guarded by American sentries who would present arms with loud clashes for any officer who walked by. At this immature stage of my development, I must admit it was most enjoyable, particularly when a Fräulein of the night before saw me off to work. In the rear entrance, which we normally used, there were also British, French and Soviet soldiers. The Soviets consisted of about a squad of men, commanded by a senior lieutenant, who were billeted in the American Sector, in a house all by themselves. Even then this struck me as strange. They could have lived in the Soviet Sector and been just as close to the building where they worked. Less than two years later it would have been impossible. I became fast friends with this group.

Over the lieutenant's bed there was a picture of Stalin, with a slightly larger one of himself underneath. He felt his oats, commanding as he did the only group of Soviets quartered in the American Sector. One morning—I had spent the night after a party—we had breakfast together. This consisted of borsch with a water glass full of vodka. All their food was prepared by an eighteen-year-old soldier whom everybody called *povoryonok* (little cook).

"I am displeased with Povoryonok," the lieutenant said.

"Why?"

"He screwed up yesterday. He overslept and my breakfast was late. I am really going to give it to him!"

"Come on," I said, feeling queazy about what the lieutenant could do to Povoryonok if he wanted to. "He's a good kid and a good cook too. This borsch is excellent!"

"Fuck him," said the officer and yelled, "Povoryonok!"

The good-looking, fresh-faced young soldier, with his hair just beginning to grow back after being shaved all around his skull, appeared out of the kitchen and stood at attention.

"Yes, Comrade Senior Lieutenant!" he barked.

"Povoryonok, you have been fucking up all over the place lately, and I am going to let you have it!"

He stood awaiting his fate, white-faced. I had never before witnessed an internal Red Army disciplinary situation. The lieutenant waited for dramatic effect, then he poured a glass full of vodka and commanded, "Drink this, and that's an order!"

Povoryonok, far from relieved, looked with horror at the six ounces of clear liquid.

"I can't do it, Comrade Senior Lieutenant!"

"You will do it, and bottoms up!"

Povoryonok drank the glass down, gagging a few times.

"Now get out of here and stop fucking up!" the lieutenant shouted.

Povoryonok executed a lurchy about face and half staggered into the kitchen. The lieutenant looked at me with a triumphal smile, as if to say, 'That's how we handle things in this army.'

He had obviously been grandstanding for my benefit, but I doubt that he would have handled the situation much differently if I had not been there, if only because any serious punishment would have meant putting papers through channels, to the detriment of his own position, which was a ticklish one.

This was illustrated not long after at another party. We all sat around the table, with the lieutenant at its head, eating Povoryonok's food and drinking large quantities of vodka. When that ran out, some ghastly peppermint German liqueur which looked like vodka was substituted, and unfortunately, I drank it bottoms up. As I was gagging after this unimaginable horror, I noticed that the other three American guests, enlisted men who also worked at ACA, were in really bad shape, not knowing the Russian trick of eating large quantities of food after each murderous drink.

A couple of them staggered out onto the street, followed by a couple of Russians and myself. One of the MP's dashed at a German woman passing by. Her husband lifted up his walking stick, but had no need to use it. The MP tripped and bashed his head open against a parked car. We took him to the U.S. hospital for some stitches—nothing serious.

Early next morning I got a frantic call from one of the Russians.

"Mr. Lieutenant, there's an American officer here, I think the commander of the guy who hurt himself last night, and he is accusing us of knifing that guy!"

I got over there as soon as I could. I explained to the MP captain what really happened, and offered to write an official document to that effect. I was really frightened for my Russian friends if the incident should get into official channels. Luckily, the MP was reasonable, accepting my testimony orally. I think he also understood the potential seriousness of the incident and did not want that sort of trouble for himself.

After that I could do nothing wrong with that little group of Russians.

Every time I came to work, the ones on duty would leap up and yell, "*Zdravya zhelayu Gospodin Leytenant!*" (wish you health, Mr. Lieutenant). It was not quite the way it would have been said in the Imperial Army, but it was close enough.

As soon as space opened up I switched my billet to Falkenried No. 9, also not far from the Dahlemdorf U-Bahn station. This was an all Russian-American household with four bedrooms, one of them containing an old friend from Alaska, Paul Duncan, and his German girlfriend Klara, whom he eventually married. He was also a first lieutenant. Duncan was his real name, thanks to a Scottish ancestor, though he could hardly have been more Russian—Pavel Pavlovich Dunkan.

My other two housemates, also first lieutenants, were two brothers, Walter Onoszko and George Onoshko, they spelled the name differently. They were sons of an Imperial Army colonel and steeped in Russian military tradition, including all the old songs. Walter, a dapper man with a Peter the Great moustache, had been a member of the Seventh Regiment, New York National Guard, and had served in Iran, another lend-lease route to the Soviets. George's military spirit was so strong that he had actually been an enlisted man in the pre-war U.S. regular army, and had seen combat against the Japanese, leading his platoon while singing his father's old regimental song under his breath. I was by far the youngest of this group.

George, with his short blond crew-cut and perpetual smile, soon developed a live-in Russian girlfriend, whom he also married. Genia was the daughter of White emigrés from Prague. With her warm heart, her turned-up nose and gray eyes, and her lovely singing voice, she became the ideal hostess for Falkenried 9. Living in the basement was another semi-hostess, the owner of this requisitioned house, a Volga German with perfect Russian, Maria Davydovna Naudit. What poor Maria Davydovna had to put up with was being a servant in her own house, and a disapproving witness of our parties and orgies! But still, she was warm, well-fed, treated most cordially by all of us, and living in her own home. Years later she greeted me as a long-lost relative, having forgiven me all my youthful transgressions. The Fräuleins did not bother her so much as the Soviets we occasionally invited. Then, Maria Davydovna would hide in the basement, having quite recently lived through the big rape of Berlin.

In spite of all the free city transport and cigarette-hitch-hiking, transportation was a problem for all of us until the Army put up for sale a bunch of used jeeps. Considering that these things had been through combat—you could tell by their tires, scarred by the tops of C-ration cans, and by the number of times they broke down—the price of $400 each was exorbitant, but what a relief to have wheels!

Duncan and I bought the first two jeeps and drove side by side in them down Unter den Linden in the Soviet Sector, yelling in Russian, "Down with everybody, long live Trotsky!" to the amazement of passing Soviets. Gas was cheap, fifteen cents a gallon, but rationed.

Liquor was rationed too, and there was not nearly enough for us and our numerous guests. This deficiency was solved in three ways—we discovered that Scotch was not rationed for our British friends, but they were wild to get hold of our unrationed canned orange juice. Even the French ordered fruit juice rather than wine at our officers' clubs, so we traded cases of orange juice with the British for a financially equivalent quantity of Scotch. Then we discovered that for a few packages of cigarettes we could get huge quantities of German clear Schnapps, really the same as vodka, somewhere in the French Sector. We had one huge bottle, frequently refilled in this way, that took up the whole back seat of a jeep. There was also vodka available at the Soviet PX, but the basic house drink at Falkenried was clear Schnapps and canned orange juice.

We frequently drove to Frohnau, the Dahlem of the French Sector, for parties at their attractive little *popottes*. By taking a short cut through the Soviet Sector we could see Soviet troops on their evening march, whole companies of them singing. I had never heard Russian troops singing on the march before, and it was breathtaking. Strange to say, the song they most often sang was about the sinking of the Russian cruiser *Varyag* during the Russo-Japanese War, not only a pre-revolutionary song, but one of defeat. I often thought of this years later when Americans, before and during Vietnam, attached such importance to the fact that America had never lost a war. England, France, Germany, Russia had all lost wars, and some of them could even sing about it.

After I had been in Berlin for about six weeks came Bastille Day, and we were all invited to Tegelsee, a lake in the French Sector. Our French ACA colleague, George Bazaroff, handed us 18th century costumes and herded us onto some very small and fragile phony frigates, where we "made legs" and swept our hats off as the generals went by in their motor boat, the Soviet general obviously puzzled by the whole thing. Every time we did this the "frigates" almost turned over, and the stability of the one I was on was not improved by George Bazaroff climbing the mast and yelling, "*Tirez les premiers, Messieurs les anglais!* (Shoot first, gentlemen of England)—a line taken from the Battle of Fontenoy where the British and French went into an Alphonse-Gaston act as to who should shoot first.

The French-Russians also came to Falkenried in substantial numbers, including Serge Zvyagintsev. He was beginning to make ultra-chauvinist Russian noises, going far beyond our shared traditions. He began to sound pro-Soviet. Another of our ACA French-Russian acquaintances was recalled from Berlin and shot by the French for collaboration.

A real Frenchman, whom we called the "shit-digger," was imported by Duncan, who was crazy about souvenirs, particularly firearms. He and the Frenchman did a thorough job on Saturdays of exploring the cellars of Hitler's ruined Reichs Chancellery in the Soviet Sector. I went along on one of these expeditions. Duncan had already found exotic weapons down there, like Roumanian pistols, and the Frenchman had found a roll of $500 in U.S. currency on a corpse. They were less than half burned, so Duncan, when he went home on leave, was able to redeem them.

It was spooky and dark down there, and also flooded from the destroyed plumbing. We used flashlights and built bridges of boards over the flooded parts. I saw one German corpse with its head missing. There was a room ankle deep in iron crosses and other decorations. I also discovered the ladies' cloakroom and lifted some brass coat tags inscribed with the Nazi eagle and the word *Reichskanzlei*. On this occasion I also went down into the bunker where Hitler and company had spent their last days and where Hitler committed suicide. It was totally unguarded. Dim electric lights cast shadows in the small rooms in which this *Götterdämerung* had been played out. The next time I tried to go there, there was a Soviet sentry posted at the entrance, letting nobody in.

"Why do you want to go in anyway?" he asked.

"I want to see where Hitler died."

"Everybody knows Hitler is in Argentina. I personally stormed the Chancellery over there and I never saw him."

The center of Berlin was still so badly bombed out as to defy description, though the diligent Germans had already begun to make neat piles of the rubble and bricks.

For all his military background, George Onoshko was a very kind man. He spoke to all dogs in very polite pidgin German, "Good Hund, setzen Sie down." It was at his suggestion that on Christmas Eve, 1946, he and I filled up our musette bags with PX candy and spent all afternoon walking around handing a candy to every passing child. The look of amazement and gratitude on the mothers' faces, not to mention the joy of the kids, made our Christmas for us.

Changes had begun to be felt. No longer could Allied marks be used in the PX and other establishments. Instead, scrip was introduced; the first issue was colored gray. These were actually American dollars, specially printed for use within the American community in Europe. Occasionally, in a top-secret operation, the scrip was called in and replaced so that Germans and other foreigners would be afraid to use it. This paper money included denominations as low as five cents. The French and British commenced to put out their own scrip, so our wallets were jammed with five types of money. Reichsmarks that we got for cigarettes could only be used in the German economy for buying such things as engravings, silver, etc—a terrible hardship! Scrip was, of course, a smart idea, which saved the treasury millions of dollars.

By the end of 1946, fewer Soviets appeared in West Berlin, except on official business. The last one I met in our sector on his own was a senior lieutenant riding a trolley car with a bag of potatoes over his shoulder.

"I am Jewish by nationality," he told me rather proudly, "and I am doing business with some Jewish friends in your sector." I trust he was selling and not buying those potatoes.

ACA Soviets would still drop in at Falkenried, more often than not begging for the new wonder drug Penicillin for treatment of VD. It was no longer a question of life and death, but an officer could still be reduced to the ranks for it. We could have recruited a few, had we been in the business.

At one party a group of Soviets from some ACA committee came and got very drunk on our "orange blossoms," not being used to sipping drinks with only a few crackers or nuts around. The Falkenried chorus went into action, accompanied by George Onoshko on his mandolin, singing both Soviet and pre-revolutionary songs, which were very well received.

During a break in the music, the chief of this group whispered to me that we had the most wonderful life and atmosphere that could possible be imagined.

"I'm sure it's the same with your life," I replied, still the wartime liaison officer.

"With us it is shit!" and he passed out in his corner of the sofa.

I got up to lead another old song dating back to the Turkish War of 1877. They loved it, but as I drew close to the end I started getting signals from some friends to knock it off before the last verse. The hell with it, I thought, full of orange blossoms myself. "Our favorite one is the unconquerable Tsar!" was the last line of the last verse.

The Soviets staggered to their feet, picked up their chief, and exited carrying him. This in no way spoiled my relations with any of them. Since there were several there, a demonstrative exit had to be made.

One summer night, shortly after I had acquired my jeep, Alex Mikhalevsky, another lieutenant from Liaison and Protocol, and I were returning from a party feeling very happy. I parked the jeep on a side street in the British Sector and we began to harmonize on a Russian song. Suddenly a female Russian voice came out of a window of a partially destroyed building above us.

"There's nothing to eat and you won't even let us sleep!"

She thought we were Soviets. We sobered up and drove away thinking that in those semi-ruined buildings there were our type of people, but without our privileges, eking out an existence on their German ration cards.

Pre-war Berlin had been one of the four great European centers of the White Russian emigration, the others being Belgrade, Paris and Prague. Most of the younger generation escaped military service in the German Army, since, curiously, the Nazis never drafted foreigners, and few of the emigrés had acquired German citizenship. All who could, fled Berlin as the Red Army approached, expecting GULAG or worse if captured. Some had survived the short Soviet occupation of April to July 1945, by posing as Germans. Others returned when West Berlin was safely in allied hands.

It was not long before I began to meet these White Russians. There was a Russian couple next door, Lida and Alyosha Kessler. Lida sang Gypsy songs beautifully, and was much in demand at our parties, when there were no Soviets there. Walter Onoszko had made contacts before I came to Berlin. There was Viktoria Mikhailovna Warrlich, also a very good singer, who lived in the British Sector with her husband, an elderly German ex-diplomat. He had been stationed in Moscow before the war, and with his strongly accented but fluent Russian he tried to set me straight on what the USSR was really like, a total despotism. Their youngest child, a baby then, became a West German movie star, Maria Warrlich.

Through this family I met Baroness Elizabeth Klodt, then about seventy-five, born around 1871. This old lady, who must have been a knock-out in her youth, had been through four husbands. The first, Venedikt Petrov, had been the commander of my family regiment, the Nizhegorodsky Dragoons, at the turn of the century. She was fascinating about life in the regiment in 1902, then celebrating its 200th anniversary. Because of her, I named my jeep *Yakov Semenovich*, in honor of the monkey which had been the regimental mascot in her time. Yakov Semenovich enabled me to supply her and others with coal in the terribly cold winter of 1946-1947. The baroness had a couple of treasures, which somebody had brought out of Lithuania for her at the risk of their life—a Chinese chess set, which she thought was priceless, and a huge ruby. Poor Baroness Klodt! After I left Berlin she was somehow lured to Potsdam and disappeared into the GULAG. The Soviets snatched any emigré they could then.

There was another old lady, a relative, Aunt Sonia Tregubov, born Baroness Osten-Sacken, descended from Salomé Chavchavadze, one of the captives of Shamil. Aunt Sonia, who looked very Georgian, lived for her son, Yury Tregubov. Everybody said he must be dead, but Aunt Sonia refused to believe it, and she was right. One day he walked in from a POW camp.

Yury was well known to the young German-Russians in Berlin, who called him either "general" or "wizard." He had the stiff manners of a 19th century Russian intellectual, something of an eccentric, full of occult lore—vampires and werewolves. Once, when he was spending the night on my couch in Falkenried, he woke me up.

"Listen, do you hear that?"

I heard a dog howling and said so angrily.

"It's not that often that a werewolf comes to Dahlem, and you object to being woken up to hear him!"

There was also the business of never sitting between two mirrors, because you could get lost in the infinity of side passages. How much of this he took seriously it is hard to say. Perhaps it was a cover for looking us over, the strange group of Russians from over the Atlantic, and trying to figure out where we stood politically, and whether there was any hope of turning us into an active anti-Soviet role. He went about all this very subtly. He said he had been in the *Volksturm*, that collection of old men and young boys whom Hitler had thrown into action at the end of the war. He said his combat activity had consisted of firing one panzerfaust at an American jeep, and missing, and then surrendering his battalion to the Americans. All the senior officers had taken flight. He had tried, in his old-fashioned way, to tender his officer's dagger to the American commander, who, to his disgust, genially waved it aside.

Yury never told us that he had been an officer in Vlasov's Army, or that he was a member of the anti-Soviet emigré organization NTS. NTS, established in 1930 in Belgrade by members of the younger generation of the White emigration, was devoted to overthrowing the Soviet regime and establishing a more or less democratic Russia with a three sector economy. In the 1930s some of its members made clandestine trips to the USSR. During the war NTS supported the Vlasov movement and recruited many members in occupied Russia, where its nationalist activities were declared illegal by the Nazis, and the NTS leadership ended the war in German concentration camps. The organization revived after the war, and it is active to the present day, now the oldest existing Russian anti-Soviet organization, and the only one that has always kept up a close study of Soviet realities.

I had vaguely heard of Vlasov, but NTS meant nothing to me at the time. Actually, I think Yury was the only member of NTS then in Berlin, and he was trying to get some anti-Soviet operations going. I clearly realized that Yury was in particular danger from the Soviets.

Yury was always falling in love, and always without any success. First it was Gloria Horstmann, the daughter of a former German ambassador, who Yury said was the only pure and innocent Fräulein in Berlin. Then there was the Russian girl, a very gifted painter, who did a portrait of Yury, catching all his mystery, eccentricity, and old-world stuffiness. This Russian Don Quixote decided to risk his life to prove or disprove this girl's loyalty, or perhaps he could not resist playing Russian roulette. In 1947 he accompanied her to a theatre in the Soviet Sector to see *Captain from Köpenick*. NKVD men were waiting for him as they came out, and he spent seven years in GULAG before coming back again. The girl whom he had trusted enough to commit this idiocy for, removed herself to East Berlin.

It was not only Yury who never mentioned the Vlasov business to us. Nobody did. Yet, they all must have known a great deal about it. The part of Dahlem where we lived had been full of Vlasov's men three years before, his own headquarters an easy walk from Falkenried. The German-Russians still did not trust us, as Allied officers, knowing that forced repatriation was still going on. Not even Genia said a word about it. She, coming from Prague, must have known a great deal. It was there that the Vlasov movement was officially proclaimed in 1944, and it was Vlasov's First Division that liberated Prague from the Germans in the last days of the war, before the Soviet troops got there.

Genia and George were about to get married. The night before Captain Sasha Sogolow, from my Camp Ritchie days, came to call. He was the only one of us who was an intelligence officer. Genial, kind, and always amusing, Sasha hated what he had to do—warn George that Genia had bad "traces" on her which could hurt George's army career. These traces had nothing to do with Genia's being pro-Soviet, but were rather the sort of thing that hardly anybody who had lived under the Germans could avoid. Genia and George were terribly upset and furious at Sasha, but they didn't know him the way I did. He was only carrying out a very unpleasant job.

The next day they were married at a local Berlin town hall, followed by a fabulous party at Harnack House, the American officers' club. Falkenried finally had an official hostess. She made George a wonderful wife through the rest of their Berlin days, a tour in Tokyo, and many years in New Jersey until George died.

Sasha's father had been a wealthy Jewish business man in Imperial Russia, supplying uniforms for the army. After the revolution, the whole family fled to Germany, little Sasha being entrusted with a toy walking stick in which the family jewels were hidden. Did the Bolsheviks find the jewels? No, Little Sasha lost the toy cane! This should have made him a failure for life, because his father never forgot it.

In New York, Sasha kept his Russian and German, and acquired English, writing it impeccably but speaking with a slight accent, with amusing slips of the tongue. He graduated from City College, New York, surrounded by left-wing types, with whom he tried to avoid arguments. The depression being on, he worked for a while selling chicken-plucking machines, until he was beaten up by a bunch of manual chicken-pluckers. His greatest ambition then, as he told me, was to get tenure teaching German in New York public schools. World War II came and it killed millions, but it gave some people chances they had never dreamed of. At Camp Ritchie, after the seven of us had departed for Alaska, Private Sasha was enrolled in the German Order of Battle Course, which he finished brilliantly, and became an officer.

The only thing I know about his pre-Berlin army career was that somewhere in France he ruined his uniform, and he was always a natty dresser, by hitting the dirt when personally strafed by a German plane. "I never realized how anti-Semitic they were," he told me.

On July 4, 1945, when the United States forces entered Berlin to occupy their sector, tri-lingual Sasha was in the first jeep. The commanding general ordered everyone to pitch tents, where our Dahlem PX later stood, and put out sentries. Maximum security. It was not only Yury Tregubov who believed in werewolves in those days. There were supposed to be die-hard Nazis using this name who might try to practice partisan warfare against us. Sasha Sogolow knew better. There was not a German alive who would do anything to interfere with the western allies taking over their assigned sectors of Berlin. He took off in a jeep, found the fanciest house in Dahlem, and was immediately welcomed as a liberator. He stayed there for months, until the billeting officer found him another, in which he settled with a bunch of Russian-Americans, Falkenried style. By the time I got to Berlin Sasha was already a captain, and with a real intelligence job. It was no fun. He had to hand back defectors to the Soviets, because our government was still determined not to annoy Stalin.

Toward the end of 1946 my routine at ACA was interrupted by two developments, a two week stretch of duty at OMGUS Headquarters, and a trip to the British Zone.

The first was interesting because I was temporarily running an office which handled all the liaison between the Soviets and the State Department element in Berlin, known as the Office of the Political Adviser, and also sent supplies to the U.S. embassies in Warsaw and Moscow. This job entailed frequent trips to Soviet Headquarters at Karlshorst and to East Berlin's Schoenefelde Airport, to meet or see off VIPs. I remember heading toward Schoenefelde at dawn, into the rising sun, and thinking "Red dawn over Europe." Then it was still just a phrase which did not bother me much.

This job almost resulted in a trip to Moscow, as "officer courier guard," accompanying a State Department diplomatic courier all the way by train and then returning. Diplomatic couriers are not normally accompanied by army officers, and this was some general's idea of putting a more-or-less trained eye on the train. For this trip I needed a passport, and for a passport I needed my birth certificate. I wrote my parents for it, and they got terribly worried because someone told them the only reason I would need it was to get married! But they sent it, without a word about this, and I acquired my first American passport, which forever solved my citizenship problems. But the trip never came off. The Soviets never refused me a visa, but they never granted me one either, until the whole idea lapsed.

In the British Zone I traveled all around in an early Volkswagon bug driven by a British soldier, inspecting factories of all kinds. I was the only interpreter, and had to interpret for the Soviet, British and French delegates.

The Soviet delegate was a colonel who had served as a volunteer in the Imperial Army in World War I. We were thrown together much of the time, since he could not speak to any of the others. With his pince-nez, he looked like the old intelligentsia he had sprung from, but he was totally Sovietized. The drunker he got, the rougher his talk. It was always about shooting people who got out of line. Yet, the extent to which he depended on me and missed me when I was gone, was endearing.

I took a weekend off to visit Princess Luise of Prussia, a descendant of King Friedrich-Wilhelm III, and a distant relative, who lived in a 17th century palace near Münster, which also turned out to be a storehouse for the best 13th and 14th century art in Westphalia. When I returned to the hotel my Soviet colonel was lonely and drunk.

"Did you screw the Prussian Princess?"

"No."

"How dare a Prussian Princess refuse a Russian Prince?" he exclaimed.

Back in Berlin, I was invited to five New Year's eve parties and I went to all of them. The first was British, hosted by an ACA friend, Squadron Leader the Hon. Hugo Stafford-Northcote. Much to my surprise, everybody was in Elizabethan costume. Hugo handed me some clothes and said, "Put these on, Ducky." So I shortly reappeared in very authentic 16th century finery. After a while, tiring of saying "'od's blood," and "i' faith" and things like that, I resumed my 20th century uniform and drove over to the house of some enlisted men I knew, who lived next door to General Clay. They were quite smashed by this time, and several fist fights broke out. I suddenly realized I was the only officer there, and I could just imagine General Clay's aide or perhaps the general himself coming over and holding me responsible for all the mayhem.

So, getting back in Yakov Semenovich, I pushed on to Gavrisheff's house for a few songs and drinks, and then to Tempelhof, where Ilya Wolston was giving a very large party with his beautiful Polish fiancée, Bogumila. Wolston was now a civilian and working for American Airlines. With his usual luck, the airline soon folded, its assets going to Pan American. Another beautiful Polish girl at the party, with whom most of us danced, was shortly thereafter picked up as a Soviet or Polish agent. She not only admitted this, but named as her accomplices every Russian-speaking officer whose name she could remember, including myself and Sasha Sogolow. Luckily, the case landed on his desk, and all that came of it was a lecture on discretion by a bewhiskered colonel aptly named Busby.

The fifth and last party was at the house of the ACA Soviet guards, where there were stiff shots of vodka and Povoryonok's *pirozhki*. By this time I was in no shape to drive. The lieutenant offered me a bed for the night, or a ride home. For some reason I chose the latter. Two Soviet soldiers deposited me safely at Falkenried on Yakov Semenovich.

January 1, 1947. I woke up with the uneasy feeling that Yakov Semenovich was behind the iron curtain. Well, not quite. I pulled myself together and took a trolley to the Soviets' house, where Povoryonok served the lieutenant and me a sumptuous breakfast of potatoes, vodka and beer.

The boys who had driven me home reported on their adventures. Yakov Semenovich had broken down on their way back—he was always doing this, old war-horse that he was—and they had hailed a German driver.

"As you know, Mr. Lieutenant, the Germans are our subordinates."

Probably thoroughly frightened at being stopped by Soviets in the American

Sector, the German driver tied the jeep to his rear bumper, but this ersatz extremity immediately fell off. The boys stuck loyally by Yakov and finally somehow got him home. There he was. Now, what to do?

"No problem," said the lieutenant. "We will tow it to a garage."

"With what?"

"Well, I just happen to have a car here, belonging to one of our colonels. Of course, it isn't registered. . . ."

We hitched Yakov Semenovich behind the colonel's illegal car and the lieutenant got behind the wheel. Strange jerks occurred, resulting in slight collisions.

"What the hell is going on?" I asked, getting out.

"I think I'm doing quite well," the lieutenant said huffily, "considering I only started driving lessons last week."

With many bumps and grinds and thoroughly illegally, Yakov Semenovich was towed to a garage. These guys would never let me down, no matter how much inconvenience it caused them. I felt about them the way I had about my private section of the Baltic Fleet, and that's what they were like when nobody was looking over their shoulder.

On January 2, the Allied Control Authority went back to work, nobody suspecting that it had only about a year more to live as a quadripartite body.

The ACA went on, but our social life changed drastically at the beginning of 1947. Dependents—wives and children—arrived. It amazed me to see Americans, really eager to see their wives, and moving everything they could in the bureaucracy to speed up the reunion, still sticking to their Fräuleins until the very morning the dependents' train pulled in, and sometimes hiring the Fräuleins as maids in their new married quarters!

The American Sector suddenly filled up with attractive generals and colonels' daughters, which meant all sorts of balls and parties and dances. They all arrived with skirts of extraordinary length, "The New Look."

Lots of other countries had military missions, really consulates, in Berlin, and I found myself deluged with invitations from the Belgians, Australians, South Africans, Canadians, Danes, Greeks and others.

The Greeks quickly found out I was related to their king and invited me frequently. Their chief, Naval Captain Papageorgiu, had known my grandmother's second husband, Admiral Ioannides. It was rather odd to hear him say, as I ordered his car—a flunky job I performed at General Clay's receptions—"I will inform His Majesty the King that I saw you!"

The Greeks complained to me that on their national day, March 25, the Soviets called up and enquired, "From exactly which foreign yoke are you celebrating your independence?" Everybody should know, said the Greeks, that it was from the Turks, and besides, these bastards are financing a Communist insurgency against us.

My cousin Xenia, always known as "Mysh," meaning mouse, arrived to be with her American husband Cal Ancrum. I had last seen her when I was a toddler near Windsor Castle. We became fast friends. She is the daughter of Prince Andrew, son of Grand Duke Alexander Mikhailovich and Grand Duchess Xenia.

Mysh and Cal took me to a party attended by Nicholas Nabokov, a cousin of the writer, and a well-known musician, also with the American element in Berlin. He had his ninety year old dependent father with him. The old man, like all the Nabokovs, had been a liberal in Imperial Russia. I observed him going over to some high-ranking Soviets and saying, "You know, I was always on the side of the people!" and then shuffling over to Mysh on the other side of the room with the same ingratiating smile, and saying, "I knew your grandfather, His Imperial Highness, Grand Duke Alexander Mikhailovich very well!" I wondered how anybody of ninety could feel necessity for such hypocrisy!

Berlin was an island, and large as its territory was, one sometimes felt the need to get out. Late in 1946 I managed a short trip to London, my first since the age of three. It was a thrill to meet all those semi-legendary people who had known me then—my father's sister Marina Chavchavadze, Uncle "Vanya" and his wife, Aunt Merika, numerous Golitsin relatives, and the Romanovs—Grand Duchess Xenia, the emperor's sister and her daughter, Princess Yusupov, in her grace and favor house by the maze in Hampton Court.

I stayed with Uncle George Chavchavadze and his uncle, Sergei Rodzianko, all at the latter's girlfriend's house. One day Uncle George suggested that we visit his great friend Marina, the Duchess of Kent, at her country place, Coppins, in Berkshire.

Perhaps the most beautiful woman the Greek royal family had produced, Marina was the daughter of Amama's brother, Prince Nicholas of Greece and Grand Duchess Helen Vladimirovna of Russia. Marina's husband, George, Duke of Kent, was the youngest son of George V, and was by far the most fun of that king's children, according to my parents. He had been killed in a plane crash during World War II.

"Fine," I said. "Let's take the guitar along just in case."

At this point I received a lecture on the deficiencies of my American upbringing—one doesn't walk into royalty waving a guitar.

"Come on, Uncle George," I said. "She is one of my mother's favorite first cousins."

But the answer remained no. Uncle George hired a limousine and chauffeur to make the trip, and the first thing that Marina said was, "Damn it, where is your guitar? I hear you sing very well!"

So Uncle George, the professional concert pianist, ended up by accompanying me on the piano while I sang off-color American songs, much to the amusement of Marina and her ten-year-old daughter, Princess Alexandra of Kent.

My second escape from Berlin was quite different. On Memorial Day weekend 1947, I was invited to ride to Prague by an American couple who wanted a Russian-speaker along, just in case. Passes through the Soviet Zone going south were hard to get, and mine was perhaps helped along because Pravda had just published an article on my ancestor, Alexander Chavchavadze. The Soviet official smiled genially and said, "How can we refuse the descendant of such a great man!"

The Soviet guards on the Berlin border could not understand why we wanted to go to Czechoslovakia instead of America if we had a three day pass. They kept holding our interzonal passes upside down, and they tried to make a fuss, requiring additional documentation, but I talked them out of this. A bunch of morons on that post.

In the Soviet Zone we gathered crowds of Germans wherever we stopped. We passed through the terrible wreck of Dresden. After the ruins we were used to, Czechoslovakia was a dream. Waiters in tails at the simplest places served us eggs and milk. In Berlin even among the Americans only pregnant women could get milk. There were lots of Communist signs around, but Czechoslovakia was not yet part of Stalin's empire. Prague was full of American G.I.s from Bavaria.

Thanks to Nuala and Claiborne Pell, later Senator from Rhode Island, at the American Embassy, I saw a lot of this very beautiful city, including cocktails on the roof of a 17th century building near the Hradcany, as the moon rose over the castle where the word "Defenestration" had originated. The last defenestration had not happened yet. Foreign Minister Masaryk had not yet been pushed out of his window.

At one bar, where a Czeck conjurer kept pulling ping pong balls out of my ear and stealing my wristwatch without my feeling a thing, but always giving it back, the bartender addressed me in perfect English, "Lieutenant, I lived in the States until 1938 and came back here for a visit that year because an American admiral assured me that there would be no war. I've been here ever since, thanks to that son of a bitch!" I am afraid the worst was yet to come for this poor fellow.

In June I made the mad decision to drive to Paris in Yakov Semenovich. My first flat tire was somewhere near Frankfurt, but I managed to pull a switch at an American ordnance depot. Then I spent the night at Wolfsgarten, the old home of the last Empress of Russia, enjoying the hospitality of Peg and Lou Hessen, Prince and Princess Ludwig of Hesse and by Rhine. It was a lovely evening, except that as always in such establishments the servants had unpacked my bag, and I had to repack everything to leave at 5:00 AM, if I hoped to make it to Paris that day.

Right on the border of the French Zone Yakov Semenovich had another flat. The French soldiers smirked as they watched me changing the tire, naturally not offering to help. This left me with no spare. One more flat and I would have to hitch-hike, and Yakov Semenovich would be a thing of the past. Entering France, I drove all over the battlefields of World War I looking for a tire. Wherever I stopped there was a surprised look. "*Mais Monsieur, vous êtes Americain!*" Americans were supposed to have tires growing out of their pockets. Finally, near Verdun, I found a huge French Army depot with thousands of American jeeps, but I could not cajole them out of a tire, and there were too many to try bribery.

All this delayed my schedule and I spent the night at Rheims, where there turned out to be a large Russian balalaika orchestra playing in a beer garden. At my table there were two unmistakable Soviet characters. They were former Red Army prisoners-of-war, or perhaps Vlasovites, trying to escape forced repatriation. It was fascinating to hear anti-Soviet talk from people brought up there.

The next day I made it to Paris, and ran into an American captain who gladly agreed to give me a spare tire. What a relief!

I stayed with Uncle George Chavchavadze's step-daughters, Laure and Hélène de Breteuil, in a wonderful 18th century house on Rue de Belle Chasse. This led to balls, parties, trips to Versailles, etc.

Throughout all this frou-frou I had on my mind the real reason I had come to Paris. My old French Element friend from Berlin, Serge Zvyagintsev, had become a Soviet citizen and intended to go to the Soviet Union with his wife and three children. It was difficult to get hold of him, because he was already working in some Soviet office with the usual stone-wall Soviet telephone manners.

I knew that a lot of Russians from Paris had voluntarily gone back, moved by misplaced patriotism. Among them was a distant relative, Misha Chavchavadze, whose daughter Irina was still in the French Element in Berlin. I did not know then that Misha, after all kinds of Georgian hospitality, was to serve ten years for espionage in GULAG. But in spite of my still very friendly attitude toward individual Soviets, I knew that going back there was not a wise thing to do.

Even before the war there had been such voluntary repatriations of White emigrés. The former Imperial military attaché in Paris, Count Ignatyev, agreed to turn over Imperial army funds at his disposal in exchange for a major-generalship in the Red Army. This, in its time, had inspired the play and movie *Tovarishch*. Stalin kept his word, referring to the new general as "our Count Ignatyev," while the newly Red Count spent the war teaching military cadets how to generally behave like officers.

The case of Ignatyev was probably the key to what Zvyagintsev had in mind. He was Serge's uncle.

Serge Zvyagintsev and I met on a street corner. He introduced me to his wife, a good-looking Georgian whose maiden name was Tseretelli, the name of a prominent Menshevik—not an asset in Stalin's USSR[1]. We climbed into a cab, and Serge immediately spoke Russian to the driver, who answered without the least surprise. A few minutes later Serge leaned out of the cab to ask directions in Russian from some woman on the street, who also replied without surprise. Then he asked directions again, this time from a man, who shrugged and said, "*Je ne parle que le francais.*"

"Fool," said Serge. "He must have lived in this part of town for twenty years and he hasn't learned a word of Russian!"

Finally we found the little Russian place we were looking for, the Mayak. We talked there for hours. I got nowhere.

"Serge, already the Soviets are preventing their soldiers from coming into West Berlin freely!"

"And they're right! Why should our Russian soldiers be exposed to western decadence?"

I realized that I was facing an extreme Russian nationalist, to whom nothing mattered except Russia's current prominence in the world. He weakened only on one point.

"All right, so you don't want to repatriate. You are an American."

"Does that make so much difference?"

"Certainly. I might feel different if I were an American. America is made up of emigrés. But how can a Russian become a Frenchman, a Belgian or a Turk?

1.　　The Mensheviks were the non-Leninist faction of the Russian Social Democratic Party after the Bolsheviks split from it in 1903.

These French bastards would not even issue us gas masks in 1939 because we were foreigners!"

"You are taking three children there. I don't have any yet, but do you realize that our children may end up at war with each other?"

"Never!"

"Several Red Army soldiers have said that to me."

"They don't know anything. They are quite correctly being kept in line so they won't be tempted by the goodies of the West. Russia needs a strong hand at the helm, and it has a strong hand at the helm," Serge insisted.

I also got a dose of chauvinism from another direction. The singer sat down with us and attacked me with extreme savagery because I happened to mention that the Hussar song she had just sung was taken from an Austrian tune.

"You are an ignorant milksop!" she yelled.

"Better a milksop than an old lady." It was one of those things that I should have said, but I didn't. The Zvyagintsevs, who knew perfectly well that I was right, kept silent on this issue.

Shortly after this they left for the Soviet Union. I don't know whether the pull they expected from Stalin's Count Ignatyev worked. Years later I heard they were living in a small provincial city, a fate quite bad enough.

Serge should have had the luck of three Russian princes in Paris who went to the Soviet Embassy to offer their services to the Motherland, since they had had a technical education. Luckily, the consul who received them was an Armenian with a sense of humor.

"Gentlemen," he said, "the Motherland doesn't need fools like you!"

I heard this story in South America, many years too late to be any use to Serge Zvyagintsev.

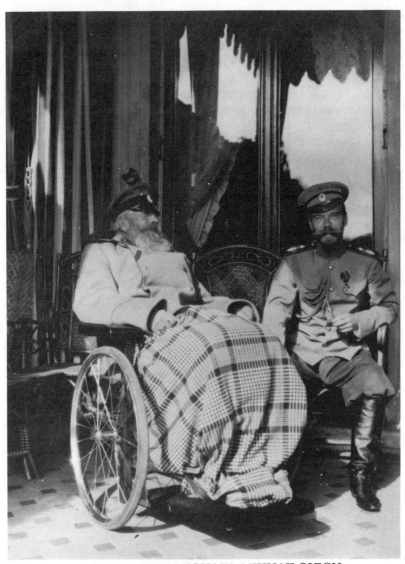

GRAND DUKE MICHAEL MIKHAILOVICH
with EMPEROR NICHOLAS II c. 1908

WALTER ONOSZKO, GEORGE ONOSHKO and WIFE GENIA,
AUTHOR - Berlin 1947

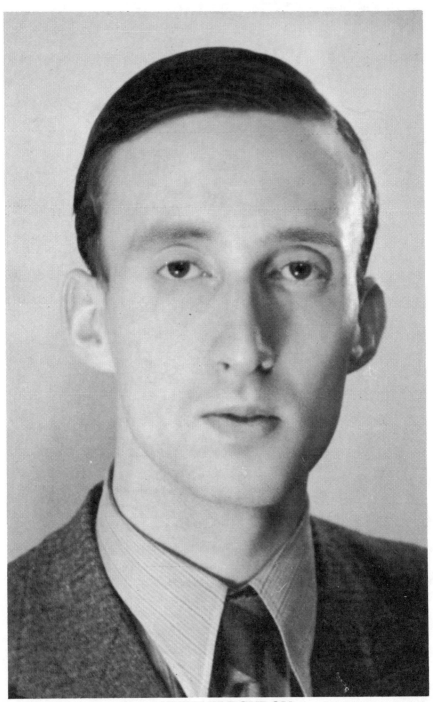

YURY TREGUBOV

CHAPTER X

If I had been three years older, and with a college degree, I would have stayed in Berlin indefinitely. It was heart-wrenching to drag myself away, not knowing that I would be back before very long. One last great tearful blast at Falkenried No. 9, and the following morning I loaded my worldly goods into Yakov Semenovich and took off. It was July 1947.

In the Soviet Zone I stopped to pick up a hitchhiker, a Soviet private. This soldier was on his way to a new unit. He had orders, but transportation was not provided. A thrifty way to run an army. He got off at Magdeburg, and was the last Soviet I was to see in my military career.

Red flags at the Helmstedt checkpoint and I was in the British Zone. I surrendered Yakov Semenovich and myself in the American Bremen enclave for shipment home. Ten days in another old transport.

I was discharged at Camp Kilmer, New Jersey, and promoted to captain, still officially in the army for two months terminal leave. Reclaiming Yakov Semenovich at the pier, I drove off in the direction of Cape Cod to rejoin my parents.

I stopped for the night in Westchester County where my friends, the Guirey brothers, were having a party. Azamat, who had been a merchant marine officer during the war, was his old self, but Chinghiz had changed entirely. He was still in the army, also a captain, but he, my only Russian-speaking contemporary from childhood, now refused to speak Russian! He offered no explanation for this. It was later that I learned that he had been involved in the forced repatriations, including that of his uncle Kelech Guirey, and this had made him not only anti-Soviet but anti-Russian. In a book he later published he backed every minority, no matter how small, against all Great Russians, no matter what their regime. Significantly his father, the old Wild Division veteran, did not share his son's new prejudice.

I was looking forward to home the next day as I drove Yakov across Cape Cod Canal, picking up two civilian hitchhikers. Somewhere near Brewster I was flagged down by a Massachusetts state trooper. The hitchhikers made themselves scarce and I was left with the cop, who then discovered that all my orders, except one, said first lieutenant, not captain; that the only license I had was from something called OMGUS, and that I had no insurance. I had no proof that OMGUS had announced that the 1946 plates would be good throughout 1947, and what good were they anyway in the middle of Massachusetts? He had me.

"I am an army officer. Give me a ticket, and I will appear anywhere you say. My family is waiting for me in Wellfleet."

"Don't give me any lip. I was a lowly tech sergeant myself. You're coming to the station," spoke the law in the person of Trooper White.

So I found myself in a cell, my belt and shoelaces removed against possible suicide. Hoping to remove one of the charges against me, I pointed out to the corporal in charge that I had had a Massachusetts license, which was still good for people coming out of the service.

"Right," he said, and checked with Boston. That Athens of the North denied ever hearing of me, the reason being, as it turned out, that my name had been misspelled on the original license. Things began to look worse.

"What kind of a name is that anyway," the corporal enquired.

"Russian." A long silence.

After what seemed like ages the corporal spoke again, "I used to know a Russian once, down in Florida, name of Obolensky—Obie we used to call him."

Obolensky—Florida—ah yes. There were those other Obolenskys, not Serge and Ivan. The mind clicked over fast.

"You probably mean Alexis Obolensky," I said.

"That's right!" exclaimed the corporal, and after a pause, "Hey, are you a prince like Obie?"

"As a matter of fact, I am."

Before I knew it I was out of the cell and getting advice from the corporal and from a bail official who had arrived. They were all on my side now. They told me to wear my Class A uniform and plead *nolo contendere* before the judge and Trooper White would testify for me. Trooper White! For me? Then they bailed me out for $200, but they retained custody of Yakov Semenovich.

At this point Trooper White returned from his rounds, looking very surprised at the cozy scene that met his eyes.

"Whitey," said the corporal, "take Prince Chidziwidzy home!"

My father was furious. "They stick an American captain just back from overseas in a cell and everything changes when they find out he's a Russian prince!"

One of the greatest of all Wellfleet parties took place on September 3, my parents' twenty-fifth wedding anniversary. The most memorable guest was Father Vasily Kurdiumov, all the way from New York. Before his car appeared through the woods, we heard his great archdeacon's voice singing.

"Pour, pour, Prince Pavel Alexandrovich, a ceremonial cup!"

After drinking this down, he blessed the house, and like all Russian priests did a thorough job of it, splashing holy water on all the foundations and on the dogs for good measure. This was forbidden by church law, but Father Vasily remarked that dogs were also God's children. As we followed him up the steep, 18th Century stairs, he started panting, stopped, looked down on us, and for some reason spoke in his Nyanyushka-accented English, "I voz Cadillac. Now I second-hand Ford!" It was the old would-be wrestler mourning for his youthful physique.

My mother wore her 1922 wedding dress, and there was much singing. Father Vasily sat next to the punch bowl, helping himself liberally, and blessing everybody who came close. Most of our Cape Cod friends had never seen anyone like him, and the next day some brought their children to be blessed.

Returning to Yale as a sophomore was a bit of a comedown, but only for a couple of days. I soon discovered old friends, fellow veterans, in various classes, mostly ahead of me, and I was four years older than the non-veterans in my class. This was an advantage at women's colleges. Yale was not co-ed in those days, and I don't know how any of us survived those drunken Sunday night drives home from

Smith, Vassar, Sarah Lawrence, etc. A very pleasant post-war atmosphere was present for a short time. Then Stalin imposed the Berlin blockade, and there was serious talk of a Soviet dash to the English channel; in 1949 China went Communist, and ten days after I graduated the Korean War started.

I had not done any studying for four years, and as a result I drew a complete blank in my first ten-minute quiz on elementary economics. I noticed that the instructor, a graduate student named Newton Steers, was wearing officer's pinks—it was not only fashionable but economical to wear bits and pieces of uniform then. I appealed to him as a fellow veteran and he agreed to disregard the quiz. After this I had no serious academic problems, and, to my surprise, I found myself learning a great deal from excellent professors.

I worked hard enough to get good grades, with plenty of time for other things. In contrast to Andover, these did not include extra-curricular activities, except for singing in the Yale Glee Club and a singing group called Orpheus and Bacchus, in which the latter god had as much influence as the former. I joined DKE and in 1949 the senior society Elihu.

The G.I. Bill of Rights covered my basic expenses, including books, but left nothing for beer, travel and dates. A trickle of income came from the Army reserves, and I found myself in command of a small unit called the "469th Strategic Intelligence Research and Analysis Team." This imposing designation had little content, but I could hold paid drills in the form of seminars on foreign countries, with Yale professors as guest speakers.

I looked into my old freshman job with the Russian Department. It was filled by a recent Soviet emigré called Vladimir Petrov, the first member of the "new" emigration I had met. Petrov had been arrested as a young student in 1934 and spent seven years digging gold in Kolyma. Released in 1941, he went home to Krasnodar in time to be overrun by the Germans, with whom he retreated and made his way to Austria, Italy and after the war, the U.S. In 1947 he was at work on his first book, *Soviet Gold*, which caused quite a stir. I translated one chapter of this book, and then his entire second book, *My Retreat from Russia*, and a number of short articles. At the going rate of seven dollars per 1000 words, this was just what I needed. The translating could be done in my room whenever I had time. The first year of this collaboration earned me $700, quite enough at a time when a round-trip train ticket to New York and a dinner date could be managed for $25!

During the election campaign of 1948 Yale was thoroughly Republican. On election evening, believing like everybody else that Uncle Harry had no chance to win, I went to the movies. When I returned, I found a group of worried faces clustering around the radio.

"Don't worry, the agricultural vote is not in yet," I said, trying to make them feel better. But Truman won, and the next day I had a drink at Deke to celebrate with the only three people I could find who had voted for him—an old Andover roommate, Jack Greenway, William Sloane Coffin, Jr., and Jason, the Deke bartender.   Yale was very conservative. Fruitlessly, I searched for someone to argue with about Communism. I heard that somewhere in the student body there was a character called "Communist Kelly," but I never met him. Thus I was a bit puzzled when in 1950 my classmate Bill Buckley published his *God and Man at Yale*.

Perhaps he perceived among the faculty seeds that would sprout in fifteen years. True, one of my instructors privately admitted being an extreme left-wing socialist, but none of this was evident in his classes.

In contrast to Yale's conservative calm, Sarah Lawrence had a large minority out thumping the drums for Henry Wallace in 1948, and organizing lectures on such subjects as progressive genetics, i.e., the spurious Lysenko theory, supported by Stalin, which had caused the death of some of Russia's best geneticists. Here I had no problems finding political arguments. These Stalinist girls all called themselves liberals, not realizing that it was a bad word in the vocabulary of their idols, Lenin and Stalin. But they were more stimulating company than most of the debutantes I met.

My own political position at the time I re-entered Yale, in spite of all of my experience with the Soviets, was still very naive. The best example I can cite is the time I had dinner with King Michael of Roumania in 1947. He was still king then, though under the thumb of the Communists. He was two years older than me, and a second cousin. His mother, Queen Helen (Aunt Sitta), a daughter of King Constantine I of Greece, was one of my mother's innumerable first cousins. My cousin Nancy, Aunt Sitta's goddaughter, had fixed the whole thing up, and I got through security at the Waldorf Astoria by mentioning her name.

Supposedly Michael and I looked a great deal alike, judging from black and white photographs. I remember thinking this as a child when I put Roumanian stamps with his picture into my album. Michael had actually been king twice—he was declared king as a child, and ruled under a regency after his father, King Carol II abdicated; then Carol returned and reclaimed the throne, replacing his son. During World War II, Carol was forced out, and Michael reascended the throne.

When we met, Aunt Sitta made us stand side by side, but we didn't look much alike at all. He was taller, huskier, and had blue eyes.

He was very silent almost all the time. There were just the three of us, so I chattered away with Aunt Sitta, and what did I chatter about? Things like what fun it was to meet the Soviets, anecdotes about them, asking what Marshal Tolbukhin, the occupier of Roumania, was like, and all this in front of a young king who had managed to switch Roumania from the Axis to the Allied side three years before, but was then overrun by the Soviets and reigned at the pleasure of Comrades Groza and Ana Pauker. They were only biding their time to get rid of him, because his popularity in Roumania was considerable. The Communists finally forced King Michael to abdicate and leave Roumania at the very end of 1947.

I can imagine what he must have thought of me! He did not even tell me his favorite joke, which he related to other relatives. A couple is making love on a railroad track. A train grinds to a halt, almost killing them, and the man says to the angry engineer, "I was coming, and she was coming, and you were coming, but you're the only one with brakes!"

After this, King Michael attended the wedding of Princess Elizabeth and Prince Philip, returning from which, in full uniform, he was squirted with a soda-syphon by another cousin of mine, Anne of Bourbon-Parma, whom I knew well in the Bernardsville days. This led to a romance and he married her in the following year.

In 1948 my Yale friend, Win Briggs, talked me into an odd proposition. Though a man of broad interests, most of all he wanted to be a cowboy! He came from Lake Forest, Illinois, and his sole experience with cowboyism was at a dude ranch in Jackson Hole, Wyoming. He had made a deal with the dude ranch owner to sharecrop a 400 acre parcel of land on the Snake River. After the hay was in, Win and his partner, if he could find one, would own half of it. From the proceeds cattle would be acquired and the place would become a cattle ranch. My role was to invest $600, work with Win that summer, and then leave the rest in his hands, unless I wanted to remain actively involved. I still can't understand why I agreed. We recruited a British artist friend, Tony Vevers, as an unpaid field hand, receiving room and board. More important, Briggs engaged a real cowboy and his wife, Dick and Shirla Pearson, and their four teams of horses.

Tony, Win and I set out for Wyoming in Win's convertible, armed with book matches printed with the enticing legend, "Snake River Cattle Co."

At our ranch the three of us slept in a tent. There was a two bedroom shack, but the Pearsons lived in one room and the other was rented to dudes, a lady from Connecticut and her two children.

Since we could not afford a bailer, all the hay was brought in by horses and stacked, probably the last time in Jackson Hole that this was done. People actually made special trips to watch two of the horse teams pull a huge rake up something that looked like a medieval siege tower and dump the hay on top of Briggs and me, who tramped around like rats in a wheel, trying to square the corners of the stack.

Though technically our employee, Dick Pearson ran the whole show, being the only one who knew what he was doing. He didn't like us very much, except for Tony, who showed considerable manual dexterity. How could he like characters who called their saddle horses, "Franz Josef," "Friedrich-Wilhelm," and "Markgraf von Hippelius?" These horses were useless to the operation, but how could the Snake River Cattle Co. lack saddle horses?

All in all, I preferred basic training and the slave days of Company E at Camp Ritchie. At the end of the summer, however, this oddly assorted company had stacked 400 tons of perfectly good hay. Except for one thing—cattlemen who bought our half of the hay, worth $4,000, would have to bring their stock to the stacks to feed on it, and the dude ranch owner was so unpopular in Jackson Hole that nobody wanted to have anything to do with him and his land. The whole premise of the Snake River Cattle Co. collapsed through poor advance intelligence work. We were saved by the only lawyer in Jackson Hole, on whom the dude ranch owner was very dependent.

"You took these boys," said the lawyer severely, "with a totally unrealistic contract drawn up by some dude lawyer in Greenwich. We don't operate that way in these parts! I suggest you let these boys out of the contract."

The clause that most upset the lawyer, one that Briggs and I had paid little attention to, was that we were supposed to clear twenty acres of land every year. With the equipment, personnel, and time at our disposal, this was clearly impossible. The owner grudgingly obeyed, and the contract was nullified.

Thus ended my experiment in the world of agriculture. Talking about it at the Allied Control Authority had been more pleasant. Win's ambition to become a rancher was totally dissipated. He became a businessman, living in Italy, India, Afghanistan and Hong Kong.

One of my roommates at Yale, George Gorham, had been a platoon sergeant during the campaign in Italy. One day his platoon acquired a new recruit, an American resident of Italy, Jack McMorrow, who did not, however, speak a word of English. George took McMorrow under his wing and made life bearable for him. Realizing that he would have been eaten alive if it had not been for George, McMorrow told him at the end of the war that his uncle, Willi Dombray, ran the Villa D'Este on Lake Como, and George was welcome to come there any time and bring anybody and stay as long as he liked without charge.

George and I set out for Le Havre in the steerage of the good ship *Georgic* in the summer of 1949. This was really much more my bag than Wyoming, let's face it. My father activated an old contact in the Cunard White Star Line and obtained first class privileges, excluding meals, for George and me. Thus occurred my fourth and last Atlantic crossing by sea, which cost, if memory does not fail me, $150.

Via Paris and Switzerland, on third class railroad cars, George and I beat our way to the Villa D'Este. There is not much point describing the beauty of the place and that of Lake Como. McMorrow had not exaggerated. He greeted George like a brother and his uncle extended every courtesy to George and me. It was even intimated to me that I would be welcome the following summer as sort of gigolo-in-residence, for the benefit of the rich Brazilian and Argentine ladies who made up much of the clientele.

Then it was my turn to offer George a freebie. My uncle, George Chavchavadze and his wife Elizabeth, were ensconced in Venice in the Palazzo Polignac, on the Grand Canal near the Ponte del' Academia. Again we rolled out of a third class carriage into a palazzo, via a breath-taking first time trip by gondola. George left after a few days, but I remained for a month, leading the life of a renaissance magnate.

The first morning my uncle's valet, known as Lorenzo the Magnificent, dashed into my room yelling, "Venezia better than Wellfleet, hey?" While this was comparing apples and bananas, I had to admit he had a point. Lorenzo had accompanied my uncle during the latter's obsession with fishing all the ponds on Cape Cod while staying with my parents. Lorenzo had allegedly left a little Venetian behind with a Cape Cod postmistress. More than thirty years later I recognized my room at the palazzo as Sebastian's bedroom in the Venetian episode of *Brideshead Revisited*.

In 1949 there were five private gondolas left in Venice, one of them belonging to my aunt. The gondoliers wore the Chavchavadze coat-of-arms in silver. The chief gondolier was also the head of the gondoliers' union, so all I had to do to locate the family was to ask any gondolier anywhere for Eugenio. Within five minutes the gondolier grapevine would report on the location of our gondola, all by word of mouth.

There were frequent picnics at the Lido. What they called a picnic was a perfectly set table in the sand, at the entrance to a cabana, the food and wines served by gondoliers. One of the first girls I met, Adriana Ivancic, I learned later was the model for the heroine of Hemingway's book on Venice. Another, Afdera Franchetti, was to marry Henry Fonda. Orson Welles was much in evidence, as was King Peter II of Yugoslavia, who was married to another cousin of mine, Princess Alexandra, the daughter of the unfortunate King Alexander of Greece, who had died in 1920 of a monkey bite.

King Peter liked to drink, but never said much. He had also come to the throne as a boy after his father was assassinated in 1934. In 1941 the Regent, Prince Paul, was overthrown and Peter became king in his own right for a matter of weeks, until the Nazi invasion forced him into exile in England. In 1944 he pleaded with Churchill to allow him to parachute into Yugoslavia to join the royalist forces, but was refused. While there was little he could do against Tito or the Soviets, he never gave up hope of being restored, and was continually involved in and exile politics.

I made a side trip to see Rome, and to Mantua to view Isabella D'Este's incredibly designed palace with its 1555 graffiti by Charles V's invading Spanish troops, but I hurried back to Venice. Just exploring Venice on foot was endless pleasure, or riding the Grand Canal's marine buses, the *vaporetti*, crossing the Grand Canal on the gondola ferry, called *tragetto*, one of which was close to our palazzo, or moonlit trips to the island of Murano. I could have gladly stayed for the rest of the summer.

"Why don't you?" asked Aunt Elizabeth, whose opinion of me had risen since Bernardsville days. "This is the best place."

Neither she nor anyone else there could understand that I was being pulled by an even more powerful magnet than Venice—Berlin, representing not only the memories of another legendary existence two years before, but also the real, grim world. Venice was just a wonderful dream.

I was able to bum a ride with Henry and Patty Luce, who drove through Austria to Munich and Nuremberg, and the amazing old walled town of Rothenburg, to Frankfurt. I was no longer entitled to the U.S. military train, so for the first time I flew into Berlin, landing at Tempelhof, newly world-famous because of the recent blockade and Allied airlift.

Some of the momentum of the airlift was still on. Supply planes landed every few minutes. The atmosphere of 1949 was totally different from that of 1947.

Ilarion Ilyich Golenishchev-Kutuzov picked me up at Tempelhof and drove me to the old ACA building, where I had translated that crazy kaleidoscope of subjects. The four flags were still flying in the order of chairmanship, even though the Soviets had long ago walked out. The tri-lingual signs on the latrines were still there, but our old restaurant and bar were boarded up. Gone, naturally, were my friends the Soviet guards.

But there were some friends left. With them, Kutuzov, who occupied a very comfortable requisitioned house with Fräulein-in-residence, did his best to re-create the old days, including an orchestra to play *Fredericus Rex*, but it didn't really work.

Several times I called on Yury Tregubov's mother, Aunt Sonya. Tears rolled down the cheeks of her severe Georgian face. She had lost her son again, was utterly lonely, with nothing to live for, although she lived another five years believing, but not knowing, that Yury was still alive.

I saw no Soviets in West Berlin in 1949, but there were stories about them. A German professor with reason to fear them takes a chance and rides into East Berlin on the U-Bahn. A drunken Soviet soldier carrying a sub-machine gun boards the car. All the Germans freeze. The professor tries to remain calm, praying that documents will not be demanded. The Russian sways for a while and then says, "Hitler nix gut!" Then he looks around the car, grins, and says, "Stalin auch nix gut!" The subway car explodes in relieved laughter.

A Russian emigré woman told me that when the Soviets were still around, some of them flirted as follows, "You are a good girl. I believe that if I slept with you, you wouldn't report anything I said in my sleep!"

I was a genuine tourist in Berlin, but probably nobody believed it. For one thing, I was seen entering and leaving the OMGUS Headquarters compound freely. This was done quite simply—the perforations on my old Army AGO card had been made so low that I could cover them with my thumb and walk through the guard post with no problem. My friends must have thought I was in some intelligence service or other. As a result I received an education in those few weeks.

Michel (Misha) Scherbinine, whom I had known slightly at Ritchie, and during my first Berlin incarnation, had a modest civilian job with the American MP's which kept him busy because of the numerous border incidents requiring bilingual expertise. He also ran a strange menage at Malvernstrasse No. 1, Zehlendorf, a large house with many bedrooms. Puttering around in the kitchen and to some extent ruling the roost was Misha's very old mother, a formidable St. Petersburg grande dame, who disapproved of almost everything that went on under that roof. Malvernstrasse 1 was an unofficial, or perhaps semi-official, defector reception center. Misha was the only American at Malvernstrasse, and had to do the considerable shopping in the PX and commissary himself, probably in large measure at his own expense.

It was only in 1948 that the Americans had begun accepting Soviet defectors and not turning them back. The British were a little quicker to catch on, if only because they realized how much useful information a defector could give.

From my journal of that summer I read, "When you walk into the house, you are apt to be ushered into any one of four rooms by the duty clerk, not an MP, but a Polish refugee. You learn not to bat an eye at the sight of unknown people sitting in the other waiting rooms.

Misha's comings and going are erratic. His little green Volkswagen is always on the go. He spends some time in his office in the MP compound, but not much. One of the most amazing things about him is that he is forty-two, but looks barely thirty. People say he is a poor security risk. Perhaps, because in spite of all his experience, he trusts people too much."

An elderly old emigré couple, Count and Countess Manteufel, also inhabited the house. He had served in a lancer regiment stationed in Warsaw before World War I. She was an affectionate lady with a very bad memory and a taste for drinks. She had been a nurse in the Russo-Japanese War and had gone down with one of the Russian ships sunk by the Japanese, but had obviously survived. She couldn't remember the name of the ship. "Was it the *Varyag*?" I asked her, the famous ship that even the Soviets had sung about on their evening marches in Berlin.

"*Varyag*? It sounds familiar, but I'm not sure. Anyway Grand Duke Kirill Vladimirovich was on my ship. He survived too."

It must have been the *Petropavlovsk*, forty-five years before. It seemed an age to me then.

Misha's mother grumbled, "The countess is a drunk who should learn not to act like a young girl!"

Two defectors were in residence. From my journal: "Valentin, former Soviet lieutenant, tall, blond, much too good-looking for the sake of his character. No brighter or dumber than the average Soviet officer, he maintains an epicurean view of life and his knowledge of it exhibits strange gaps. But Valentin does valuable service as a contact man for other potential Soviet deserters."

It will be noted that I had not yet learned the word "defector." One night I sat up with Valentin until 6:00 AM listening to his reasons for defection. We were both quite drunk and it all seemed convincing, though unfortunately I can remember no details. Eventually Valentin either went back, or was kidnapped by the Soviets, or, as some people said, had been a penetration of Malvernstrasse to begin with.

The other defector was Nikolai, who unlike Valentine, was restricted to the house. This was explained by the story that he had been in Vlasov's Russian Liberation Army. It was only years later that Misha told me he was also a recent defector.

Misha Scherbinine's great heart was his strength and his weakness. He was ready to help any anti-Soviet Russian, White, DP, or defector. He certainly was able to set up a warm Russian atmosphere for new defectors at a time when nobody else was doing it.

I wrote then at the age of twenty-five, "Scherbinine inspired me in a strange way—made me think that perhaps a low-level job like his, which in its actual operations affords opportunities for doing good almost unavailable anywhere else, is worth many a career. If Scherbinine left Berlin today, scores of people would be in actual desperation. His greatness and his weakness is that he is the kindest and most generous person most people have ever met, so they cannot believe what they see. They suspect ulterior motives. When they find out that Misha is just what he seems, they either worship him or victimize him."

I was not so naive as not to understand that the Soviets might find out I was back in Berlin and do something about it. They always assumed that all Russian-speakers were intelligence officers, and obviously had had a file on me since 1943.

My journal relates an incident on August 26, 1949, which would have appealed to anybody's sense of melodrama, my first clandestine meeting. The day before a mysterious German called up, asking for Herr Chavchavadze. When I answered, he said that a matter of great importance to me would be discussed if I came to the corner of Kurfürstendamm and Uhlandstrasse the next afternoon at three o'clock. Thoughts of Yury Tregubov and Baroness Klodt flashed through my head. It was obviously a trap of some sort, but what could they do to me in broad daylight in the most populated part of the British Sector? Perhaps I could learn something.

I gave the phone to Ricki, Kutuzov's girlfriend, so that she could glean all she could from the man's accent and tone. Ricki and the unknown German began to yell at each other.

"Who are you?"

"I am a friend of Herr Chavchavadze."

"Why doesn't he speak himself?"

"Because he doesn't speak much German."

"But he must speak German if he is in Berlin!"

"Please don't forget that Berlin has an Allied occupation!"

"Nein, nein!, Berlin has a Soviet occupation. A Soviet occupation!" Bang. He hung up.

I drove over to Scherbinine's to ask his advice and was told to keep the date, he would cover me. Matters were not helped, and my personal dramatic sense was considerably damaged, by the fact that at 2:30 the next day coming downstairs I hit the cavity where the welcome mat was supposed to be, but wasn't, and sprained my ankle.

Nevertheless, out to Kurfürstendamm went Misha and I in an MP jeep. I got out and, limping slightly, sauntered over to the cafe at the corner of Uhlandstrasse. I tried to look as much like Alan Ladd as possible, cigarette dangling from my lips, but the ankle hurt like hell. Misha kept his eye on me, wandering around the sidewalk. I ordered a beer and sipped at it, looking at the other people in the cafe obliquely, as well as those who strolled by on the sidewalk. Nothing happened. A more anti-climactic story could hardly be told.

I was to learn that a lot of clandestine situations are anti-climactic, and also that anybody who wanted me to meet him would not be so hostile over the phone. Many years later I found out that the whole thing had been a practical joke, staged by Ilya Wolston, whose German was so good that he even fooled Ricki.

Once more the time had come to leave Berlin. There was a tremendous farewell party for me at Malvernstrasse, after which we all went to the military train station at Lichterfelde, where Wolston was supposed to meet me with a ticket and orders for the train that he had promised to conjure up from the State Department, where he now worked. Wolston arrived, but without the papers. So we all went back and finished the party. The following day we repeated the whole procedure, arriving at Lichterfelde feeling no pain. This time Wolston came through. I played the guitar and sang out of the window of the coach until it began to move, with a chorus of old friends on the platform. Then I tossed the guitar to them and tearfully sat down. I became conscious of a gentleman some twenty years my senior, who had been viewing this scene of extravagant Slavic farewells with Anglo-Saxon distaste. I was to see this face and its expression three or four years later, when he became one of my early chiefs in the CIA.

A ghastly Atlantic crossing, my first by air, on a flight which landed everywhere except Greenland, and it was my senior year at Yale.

I was in the honors program of the History Department and had to choose a subject for a thesis. I tried to think of some obscure corner of Russian history that I could illuminate with some original research, but my thoughts kept drifting back to Berlin and Malvernstrasse.

Could I do something as recent as World War II—the Vlasov affair, for instance? I knew so little about it. His followers had been repatriated after the war. Even during the war there had been talk that a certain General Vlasov had defected to the Germans with his whole army, which the Germans had promptly turned against the Soviets.

"Nonsense," said Vladimir Petrov, for whom I was still doing translations. "You were in the army. You know damned well that no general could defect with a unit as large as an army. Besides, if he had, the Nazis were in no mood to turn it around." This was puzzling, but Petrov ought to know; he had worked for the Vlasov movement as a civilian.

For the first time, from Petrov, I heard the basic story. Vlasov was captured by the Germans in 1942 when the army he commanded was destroyed trying to relieve the siege of Leningrad. Afterwards, thinking that the wartime situation was the only chance to get rid of Stalin and his regime, and supported by anti-Hitler German staff officers, Vlasov tried to form a Russian liberation army, which only achieved reality in the fall of 1944 when the Germans were desperate. Before that, the many Russian volunteer battalions were not actually commanded by him, and Hitler had them all transferred to the west, where they had no motivation to fight the Americans and British. Hitler disliked the whole idea, and Vlasov disliked Nazi ideology. He consistently refused to make anti-Semitic statements and protected many Jews. He did receive semi-covert support from the German general staff officers who were plotting against Hitler, including Stauffenberg. They realized that Russia could never be conquered with Hitler's war aims. The only hope for Germany was to overthrow the Soviets with the aid of anti-Soviet Russians and then make peace with a new government, à la 1917-1918. Vlasov had tremendous prestige with the Russians in occupied areas, and in Germany. He had been one of the heroes of the Soviet defense of Moscow in 1941. All Soviet prisoners had been declared traitors by Stalin, so a great number wanted to join Vlasov, though few were allowed to do so by the Nazis, and most died from disease, cold and hunger. Hitler thought of these five million prisoners-of-war not only as *Untermenschen*, but as hopelessly brainwashed Communists. The irony is that so many of them were eager to fight against Stalin.

Somehow a million Soviet citizens did bear arms against the Soviets, in spite of Nazi reluctance to arm them. Behind all this were the feuding semi-independent fiefs of the Third Reich, national minority problems, and God knows what else. Practically nothing had been published in English on the subject. With possible war with the Soviets not far away, it seemed to be a subject of vast importance, a weapon that the U.S. must not misuse or ignore, perhaps the key to everything.

"How can I document anything like this?" I asked Petrov.

"It may not be as hard as you think. Try it," he said.

He put me on to an article about Vlasov in an emigré publication written by the well-known old Menshevik Boris Nikolayevsky, whom I interviewed in New York.

As I quickly ran out of printed sources for the thesis, the quest for human sources became an imperative. I knew it would not be easy. Those who had survived forced repatriation and had made it to the United States had, as a rule, changed at least their date or place of birth, and were reluctant to reveal their connection with Vlasov. Many had been saved by pretending to have been born in

Poland, or somewhere else outside the USSR.

I started by going to our old Russian church on 121st Street. It was a Saturday night, when parties and dances were held in the rooms in back of the church. Father Vasily was still in charge. The cash box was manned by the old Cossack doorman from the Casino Russe, Fedor Danilovich Gamali. But I knew nobody else. Unlike the days before the war, the place was jumping with new arrivals from Europe, some from the old emigration, some from the new, all speaking Russian.

As I stood looking at the dance floor, a short pretty blonde, in that forward way that Russian girls have, asked me why I wasn't dancing and invited me out on the floor. My luck was hard to believe. She had been a civilian secretary at Vlasov's headquarters! Through her I began to meet former officers and soldiers from Vlasov's army, known as the ROA (Russian Liberation Army). She warned me to be very careful in broaching the subject. I mean one did not just come up to them and say, "I understand you were in the ROA." It had to be done subtly, after they came to know you.

This blonde, Marina, not typically for the Vlasov movement, was the daughter of old emigrés, born and brought up in Yugoslavia with its network of Russian schools and cadet corps. She took me to parties in parts of New York where I had never been before, to meet these ex-Soviets, who were really no different from the ones I had met in Alaska and Berlin, except these were free to speak their minds with complete frankness.

Around this time I also met Peter Pirogov, a pilot who had defected in Germany just after the Americans had stopped turning back defectors, and had received a lot of publicity at the time. He told me that during the war he had flown over Vlasov's First Division as it marched south from the front into Czechoslovakia in April 1945, hating their guts as traitors and wishing that his mission was to strafe them rather than just observe them, but now he sympathized with what they had been trying to do.

I remembered all those hints that Yury had dropped at Falkenried. Now I could have talked with him frankly. No. Now he could have talked with me frankly. I had been the blind one. But that Don Quixote had felt the compulsion to ride his Rosinante through the Brandenburg Gate.

While I had collected quite a bit of information with all these contacts, I was still hoping for some original documentary evidence, and this involved a trip to Washington. I was told there were whole boxes of documents from Germany in the old torpedo factory in Alexandria.

Bill Coffin was fascinated with my thesis, having learned excellent Russian during the war. He had been involved in the forced repatriation of members of Vlasov's Second Division in Plattling, Bavaria. Bill suggested that I look up his brother-in-law in Washington, who worked for the government and might be helpful in my quest for documentation.

In Washington I stayed with Senator and Mrs. Robert Taft, the parents of my Yale friend, Horace Taft. They lived in Georgetown, which was then purely residential. You could hardly find a place to have a beer on Wisconsin Avenue or M Street in those days, where now you can hardly find a building without a bar or a restaurant. Senator Taft gave me a ticket to the Senate. I found him a very effective speaker, quite at odds with his umbrella-over-head media image.

The boxes of unsorted documents from Germany in the torpedo factory had all been arbitrarily classified "confidential," and I had no clearance, so I called up Coffin's brother-in-law and was invited to dinner, also in Georgetown. It was a very pleasant evening. I had always been fond of Coffin's sister, Margot, and I had attended their wedding. Did I have a premonition that this evening would change my entire life? No, but it did. My host listened to my spiel about the mistakes the Germans had made in handling Soviets willing and eager to fight for them without much comment. Then he invited me to come to his office the following morning.

Naturally, I went. On his desk there was a sign, "Kindly restrain your enthusiasm." Perhaps I should have paid attention to that sign, but that morning I was recruited for the CIA, and I was enthusiastic about it. What better place to use my experience and languages to protect the United States and to fight Stalin?

I never did get clearance for the German records, and the thesis was finished without them, but it was a great success. It was read by Professor Hajo Holborn, who recommended an immediate M.A. for me, refused through lack of residence time, and by that other professor who had said he was an extreme left-wing socialist. He was complimentary too. If I had stayed around to make a book of it, it would have been the first book in English on the subject. I have since come across my thesis as a source for later books written on the subject of Soviet defection to the Germans.

In June 1950 I finally graduated from Yale, Summa Cum Laude, Phi Beta Kappa, exactly eight years after I had entered as a freshman in the summer of 1942, when New Haven girls called us slackers.

On June 25, 1950, back on Cape Cod, I found myself on a Portuguese fishing boat with my parents and cousin Natalia Golitsin Heseltine, sailing around in a large circle with the rest of Provincetown's fishing fleet, past the Catholic Bishop of Fall River and other clergy who were blessing the fleet in this traditional ceremony. We were all suffering from monumental hangovers. Natalia and I were amusing each other with take-offs on Stalin's extravagantly chauvinistic statements about how the Russians had invented practically everything. "Popov invented the wheel," was our favorite. Then somebody turned on a radio and we stopped laughing. North Korea had invaded South Korea, and President Truman was sending in U.S. troops. Peace had lasted less than five years.

A few days later Natalia, who worked for the UN at Lake Success, had cause for pride. The United Nations had endorsed the American and South Korean effort. Members of the UN pledged troops and the whole fight was carried out under the UN flag. The Soviets had made a big mistake, their delegate was missing when he could have delivered a veto in the Security Council.

I was already too old for the draft in this second U.S. war of my lifetime, but I was a captain in the reserves and could have been called up. On June 26 I got a call from the Pentagon asking, but not ordering, me to take three months of active duty. I refused, not knowing when the CIA would send for me. So began the 1950s, that allegedly bland decade in which nothing happened.

While those poor guys in the American occupation forces in Japan were unexpectedly thrown into mortal combat, I spent my last full summer on Cape Cod, my last extended time with my parents. Yakov Semenovich being but a sentimental memory, Natalia left me her Studebaker when she went to Europe. It looked the same fore and aft, which was why she called it "Countess Torby," in honor of the morganatic wife of Grand Duke Michael Mikhailovich. Some Russian wag had written in verse, "Having seen Countess Torby, I didn't know which was the front and which the back." Countess Torby gave me the mobility for frequent trips to Provincetown and to parties down the two-rut sandy roads of Truro and Wellfleet. Any man who was straight could hardly fail to score with the girls in Provincetown. Every day was made more enjoyable by the fact that I never knew how soon the call from Washington would come. The clearance was taking a long time, but I could hardly blame them.

At the end of August the telegram came. Please report to Washington (address given) on September 5, 1950.

My twenty-four years in the CIA were about to start, and I would be the only Romanov relative actively working against the Bolshevik regime.

CHAPTER XI

There was no CIA building in Virginia in 1950. CIA headquarters was still located in the buildings used by OSS during the war. A small cadre had stayed on, but after the CIA was founded in 1947, a lot of old OSS war horses rejoined the colors. They weren't old really. I found that most of the branch chiefs, division chiefs and higher were still in their thirties, typically ex-majors or lieutenant-colonels from the OSS, many of them Ivy League graduates.

The operational elements of the CIA, later called the Clandestine Services, were located in a row of World War II temporary wooden buildings by the reflecting pool near the Lincoln Memorial. There were no signs, only letters of the alphabet. It was to one of these tempos that I nervously reported. The ratty tempos were also ratty on the inside. No air-conditioning, either, but lots of familiar faces from Ritchie, Berlin and even Alaska. The World War II clans were gathering again. Enthusiasm and esprit-de-corps permeated the hot and humid air.

At first there was no orientation or training. Fascinating classified documents were given me to read. This led to a period of confusion. How to discuss intelligently the international problems of the day outside the Agency and keep straight what I had seen on the inside, and what I had read in the press? After a couple of weeks my mind became compartmented and this problem ceased to exist. There was always the terrible temptation to tell people interesting tidbits, or to hint that I knew something they did not. This would have been a violation of the Great Taboo, an unpardonable sin. The Taboo covered everything learned on the inside, not just classified reports, but even the names of colleagues, the location of buildings or , in the case of covert employees like myself, that one worked for the Agency. The worst thing you could say in Washington was that you worked for "the government." This always led to a loud hoo-ha!

"I am doing some research for the army."

"I know six other guys who are doing that," answered a sixteen year old kid at one party, "but they all really work for the CIA."

The worst thing was that everyone thought that this cover-up was silly. They did not realize we were going overseas under good cover, which could be destroyed before we ever left, and could endanger our lives.

"Why don't you admit where you work like so-and-so does?"

How to explain that So-and-so was an "overt analyst" who would stay in Washington?

Americans always ask what you do. The Great Taboo has put a stamp on me. I never ask what anyone does, not wanting to be asked myself, even though nowadays I can plainly state that I am a retired CIA officer.

In those early days in the tempos, I heard the Great Taboo violated once. A group of visiting boy scouts stood outside the door of Tempo "K" enquiring politely from exiting employees what was in the building. People brushed by in silence, until one man, bolder than the rest and perhaps smarter, told the boys, "This is the U.S. Government's super-secret spy headquarters."

"Aw, come on!" was the reaction of the boys, looking at the decrepit tempo. It was obvious to them that their collective leg was being pulled and they walked sadly away.

Secrecy is second nature to me now. No temptations to reveal anything, besides, in many cases I know better than today's officials what should be kept secret, even after thirty odd years. No dead bodies, no crimes. Merely relationships that could hurt somebody or harm the struggle against the Soviets.

In November I was sent to a training course, located across Independence Avenue. The instructors then had very little experience more than did the trainees, and their wartime experience was mostly not applicable.

We had practical exercises in setting up clandestine meetings between two people unknown to each other, through recognition signals. The trainees thought these up and they were distributed for use by other members of the class. The first set of instructions I received seemed a bit cumbersome, but I memorized them and proceeded to act them out. I arrived in the lobby of the Annapolis Hotel at precisely 10:00 AM, carrying a copy of *Readers Digest* in my left hand and *Life* in my right. I stood in the lobby and switched the magazines from one hand to the other, then I went to a phone booth and pretended to make a phone call. After this I purchased Edgeworth tobacco at the tobacco stand.

At that point a nervous individual approached and said, "What is the way to the Washington Monument?"

"Come to the front door and I will show you," I countered.

"How about a cup of coffee?" suggested "Agent X."

"Fine, there's a cafeteria in the hotel," I snapped back, according to the script.

We retraced our steps past the puzzled tobacconist and sat down at a table. As if this wasn't enough recognition signaling, there was more. I was supposed to pass Agent X a message concealed in a package of cigarettes, but of a specific exotic brand. I have forgotten the name, but Egyptian Queen will do. On my way to the meeting I had made an honest effort to buy Egyptian Queens in at least six drug stores with no success. The druggists just looked at me as if I had just swished my way in from Provincetown. So I bought the next most exotic brand available and pushed that pack at Agent X as we sat over our coffee.

His eyes widened in horror.

"My favorite brand is Egyptian Queen," I explained earnestly, "but I couldn't find them anywhere today.

He looked at that insufficiently exotic package as if it were about to explode. "Take it, for God's sakes," I pleaded.

He wouldn't touch it. He was terribly upset. "Oh my God, I've screwed up!" he moaned.

The instructor said he had been right in refusing. Years later, when I had a tour as an instructor in the Office of Training, I used this story as a horrible example of over-complicated contact instructions and lack of common sense on the part of

Agent X, and equally on the part of the instructor who had ruled in his favor. Common sense is 90% of the game.

Real life contact instructions are apt to be very simple—a minimal recognition signal, perhaps the description of clothes to be worn, and an uncomplicated, but not too ordinary phrase and answer. This almost always works smoothly. I had one once that did not.

I was supposed to meet a young oriental gentleman in the lobby of the Hilton in a European city at high noon. He was to carry a copy of *Paris Match*. That day at noon the lobby of the Hilton was wall-to-wall with youngish oriental gentlemen, a Japanese tourist bus having just arrived. Were they all reading *Paris Match*? No, none of them were, including the one I was supposed to meet—he had forgotten that small detail!

A huge amount of seemingly trivial information about practically everything is essential to a case officer. My colleague on the other side of the world who had issued these instructions should have known that Europe was loaded with Japanese tourists, and also that *Paris Match* is the most popular color photo magazine in the French-speaking world. He had also assumed that giving a simple instruction to an agent was enough for it to be carried out. To this recently, and perhaps not fully recruited agent, the nuts and bolts of clandestine operations probably seemed tiresome, ludicrous and childish. Some training is necessary. Operations officers have to be both psychologists and schoolmasters.

Even during my 1950 training, it was obvious how different real espionage was from all those movie and TV versions—all those shoot-outs, total confusion between the case officer and the agent, usually a foreigner, the man with access to the target, the actual spy—no way resemble reality. In the movies the hero gets his orders from inside headquarters, and then, speaking Arabic fluently, swims the Suez Canal in a burnoose and makes off with the secret or whatever the objective is, after a thrilling chase with lots of boom-boom ammunition expended.

That's not the way it works. My mother, under this misapprehension, kept warning me that good as my Russian was, I could not pass for a Soviet for long. She was afraid I would be parachuted into the USSR, or something like that. She need not have worried. It would never have occurred to anyone in the Agency to use me in that way.

Some organizations, like the FBI, call their staffers "agents," but I am using CIA terminology. An agent is not a staffer, or a case officer, but a person who has agreed to perform some secret task for the Agency, and whose only point of contact to it is through a case officer with whom he meets—never in the official buildings—or communicates.

For all espionage services this point of contact is extremely sensitive. It is the agent's only link with the government he is covertly working for, and it is here that the relationship can most likely be discovered. If it is discovered, the agent pays the price. The case officer may hardly be affected at all, or may be in for some minor unpleasantness like having to leave the post earlier than he had expected. The agent is the real hero in the business. He is the one that could be shot, or in another sort of country, have his career and personal life ruined for having worked for us. To expose the names of agents, as Philip Agee did, was much worse than his naming of staffers, most of whom are blown early in their career anyway if they are active.

In the fall of 1950, while I was playing those games in training, the Communist Chinese entered the Korean War and succeeded in driving MacArthur's victorious forces all the way back to a foothold in Pusan, without any outright Soviet participation. My dread for the future of the country was really much greater than what I had felt after Pearl Harbor. What we were doing was as important as that hot war in Korea. It was good to be at the tip of the spear, or as somebody stated recently, the RAF of the Cold War!

The main danger to a case officer-agent meeting is that it will be observed by a hostile force, or a force that is not hostile but is still a threat, like the security service of a friendly country they happen to be in. Hundreds of passers-by or restaurant patrons are not much of a problem, but a really sensitive meeting should take place in a safehouse or apartment.

Safehouses are a pain in the neck. They have to be located in a suitable place, rented securely, keepers may have to be recruited to live in them. If nobody lives there, a maid may have to be hired. All these are points of danger. Everybody lives in fear of a safehouse being bugged, but if nobody cleans them, bedbugs (sorry!) or other creatures with six legs will move in. I was once opening a safe apartment's door in Germany when a neighboring door opened and a woman said in very passable G.I. English, "You guys ought to use this place more often. The mail is piling up!"

Sure enough, the mailbox was overflowing with two weeks' worth of junk mail and utility bills. Whoever had the chore of swinging by and picking this up was on leave and had not bothered to delegate the job.

Convenient safehouses are those lived in quite genuinely by people with a legitimate occupation, who are specially recruited for this purpose and told to get lost at certain times, but this is another obvious point of vulnerability. Safehouses are expensive, and time-consuming, yet important. You miss them when you can't get them, like in Communist countries, for instance, which is one of the reasons we call them "denied areas." Meetings can be held in cars, with another set of important trivia to worry about. Whose name would come up if somebody checked the license tags?

Then there are hotel rooms, temporary safehouses. For certain types of meetings they are preferable. You hold them only as long as you need them and give them up. Much less expense and bother, but another set of problems—forms and passports going to the local police, observation by the desk in the lobby, maids barging in.

I have often held meetings in hotel rooms rented by agents who have perfectly sound reasons to be in the area, but it's the agent's room, and he has a life of his own. In some parts of the world, you have to bend to local conditions. I once held a meeting with an agent who was staying in a cabana-like attachment to a hotel. The debriefing was constantly being interrupted by safaris of servants bringing in whiskey, soda bottles, and food. I actually had to hide under the bed when the local police chief came for an unexpected social call, which fortunately did not last long. There was also a young man who kept appearing and whispering in the agent's ear. When I asked him who that person was, the agent replied, "That's my pimp, old boy.

He has just fixed me up with the local beauty queen. She is a semi-finalist for Miss Universe. Would you mind not coming over until after ten tomorrow?"

Of course, all this was totally wrong according to the book, but there was no other place to meet, and if he had suddenly barred those multitudes from his room, this would have been suspicious and inconsistent with the life-style of the place. Since this agent was always wheeling and dealing with western businessmen, my presence caused no raised eyebrows. I did not, however, feel like facing the police chief's probable curiosity. With him there had to be an introduction, so I preferred to take a dive under the bed.

Totally unexpected forms of hostile observation sometimes occur. I once arrived at a Middle Eastern airport, expecting to be met by an officer from the local CIA station. It should have been simple. We knew each other. I saw the officer standing there as I made my way through passport control, but as I emerged he suddenly turned away and walked off. I followed at a respectful distance until I saw him enter the men's room. I was about ready to follow him in when out he came, shoved a fat envelope into my hand and disappeared into the crowd. There was a note inside, instructing me to take a cab to the Embassy. This was mystifying. I could have gone there directly and saved him a trip to the airport. The envelope was suspiciously fat, as if it contained a large sum of money. It did, a large wad of small demonational bills worth about ten dollars, thoughtfully included for use with a taxi.

The trouble with this brush pass was that it had been observed by a local policeman, who began to follow me as I went looking for a taxi. On his mind there was terrorism, narcotic smuggling, all the things that make airports dangerous places nowadays. On mine there was incarceration in one of the charming jails of that particular country, until the whole matter had been sorted out. Luckily, he did not stop me from taking the taxi.

Still mystified, and somewhat miffed, I arrived at the embassy. My colleague was there and explained that the whole melodrama had been triggered by an unexpected truly hostile observation. As my plane had taxied to the terminal he had become aware that practically every known KGB officer in town was present in the waiting room, probably meeting an Aeroflot flight. He knew them, from pictures and diplomatic parties, and they knew him. So he had avoided approaching me in order not to be Typhoid Mary, infecting me the moment I set foot in the country.

An infinity of other things can go wrong with operations. I had an agent, a stout, middle-aged man, who looked like Sidney Greenstreet, but had a perpetually youthful, I would say teenage, attitude toward life. He loved working for us. No task was too menial for him. Once, while on an observational mission, his stout posterior overwhelmed the tensile strength of his trousers, which split all the way up and down the seam. Blushing, he flattened himself against the wall to figure out what to do. He belonged to a very clothes-conscious people. He had a sketch pad with him, to give him cover to lounge around anywhere he needed to. On one of these large sheets of paper he drew his lucky number, and contrived to hang it on his back. He then took off his pants and jogged home in his shorts, almost qualifying as a marathon runner, living as he did in a distant suburb.

After a few years of enthusiasm, "Sidney Greenstreet" became jaded and succumbed to temptation. He began to embezzle money from us, fairly modest amounts. With his native ingenuity, he got away with it for some time, but then he had to be terminated.

The press to the contrary, to "terminate" an agent in the CIA means to fire him and get him to sign a quit-claim. To "terminate with prejudice," or with "extreme prejudice," merely means to blacklist him with other agencies who might be tempted to use him.

The greatest threat to clandestine meetings is deliberate surveillance by a hostile organization. This can range from a lone goon on a street corner to the massive Orwellian apparatus of Communist countries, using dozens of people and vehicles and aided by the entire police force.

When surveillance enters the picture, it is usually the case officer who is the threat to the agent, not vice versa. If the agent is under surveillance he is already under suspicion of some sort, and the jig may be at least half up anyway. But the case officer, particularly if he is an official American stationed abroad, is a known quantity. It is easy to learn where he lives and works as starting points for surveillance.

Naturally, a great deal of time is devoted to surveillance in the training of staffers and agents alike. How to spot it without appearing to be tailwise. It takes practice, and there is no substitute for the street. Heightened powers of observation are necessary to spot the same faces, coats, hats and cars turning up about you, without resorting to obvious tricks like stopping to tie a shoe or hanging around shop windows to look at reflections. If you do enough walking and spend time, it is a rare surveillance team that cannot be spotted. The idea is not to avoid it, but just to know it's there. A surveillance team can be shaken off, but this is done rarely.

Once, an agent we were training for a mission overseas got into the tourist line and took a tour of the White House, followed by the entire surveillance team standing in line at a respectful distance behind him. It was my first time in the White House! After this, the agent blatantly jay-walked across Pennsylvania Avenue, heading for Blair House where the limousine of a prominent African chief of state was parked. For a moment we thought we would lose him to the blazing guns of the Secret Service. Oh, how the branch chief, an old friend from Ritchie and Berlin, raved and ranted when we told him. "Playing games in the White House! Blair House yet! You want me to lose my job?"

Still, we learned something about the agent. He was enthusiastic, but too much of a cowboy. He had to be toned down. He was also resourceful. The day before he had invented a new system for spotting surveillance. He stood next to a blind guitarist, feeding coins into his tin cup, pretending to enjoy the music, and looking in all directions for surveillance. Imaginative, but not good. The guitarist's face lit up in beatific amazement, while a crowd began to gather to observe this strange music lover.

Outside their own turf it is not very easy for the KGB and its satellite services to mount much of a surveillance. It takes a lot of bodies and vehicles. Most such scares in western countries in my experience have been false alarms. I remember once in Germany working with a visiting technical expert, not an Agency staffer, who was staying in a hotel near the main railroad station. This man had no experience with foreign countries and was over-excited at the thought of being, even peripherally, in the spy business. Every time he left his hotel he thought he spotted surveillance. I got considerably fatigued tramping around and around the Bahnhofplatz with him until his fears were allayed. We put out people for counter-surveillance and generally wasted a lot of time and shoe leather on him.

Years later I was supposed to meet an agent in a European city. Now here, I was warned, was a special case. The KGB were likely to have great surveillance capabilities. I was to do everything according to the book.

The meeting was scheduled for 10:00 AM in front of the Mercedes Benz dealership on a small square a little way from the center of town. I cased the area the day before, a Sunday. Everything was closed. The next day I appeared at 9:45 AM, wearing a cap low over my eyes to make photographic identification more difficult. To my horror, I saw four cars parked outside the dealership, each car with four men sitting in it. My God, talk about surveillance capabilities! I could not see my agent, but I maneuvered in such a way that he might spot me from a distance. I prayed that he would remember the danger signal we had agreed to use.

At precisely ten o'clock all the doors of all the cars opened, and sixteen men dashed out and headed for a liquor store located next to the dealership! It was just opening its doors. I had noticed it the day before, but I had not realized that the natives had a problem acquiring enough to fill their capacity. All sixteen came out laden with bottles and drove away, but my agent did not show up. The same scene was repeated for two more days with only the slightest variations. I cannot swear that the goons, or just plain drunks, were the same ones, but that liquor store was doing a fantastic business. Where was my agent? He was unable to meet me during those three days and had no secure way of letting me know.

On the other hand, there was a case in Berlin—Berlin had so many intelligence officers, agents and goons in it that they must have made up a measurable percentage of the population. I mean, there were in addition to ourselves and the other American services, at least two services each from the British, French, West Germans, East Germans, Soviets, Czechs, Poles and God knows who else. Nobody had problems assembling surveillance teams. The Soviets had an endless supply of east Germans. According to one British movie of the time, if you opened any manhole cover in Berlin, you would hear the *Third Man Theme* played on a zither!

On a Sunday afternoon one of our case officers was supposed to meet an agent coming out of East Berlin through an elevated railroad station. He called for counter-surveillance. A colleague of mine and I took our wives and a total of five children for a stroll by the station. Just two families strolling on a Sunday afternoon.

Few people were about, which made the goons more obvious. They were there! Staked out like guards at Buckingham Palace, lacking only bearskins and bayonets. A most unprofessional performance, but a fortunate one for us. Obviously, the operation was no good. We signaled the case officer to abort the meeting. We had to be extra careful in those days, because abductions were part of the other side's technique, and those elevated S-Bahn stations were under East German control, even in West Berlin.

Of course, in running an agent you can cut out personal meetings altogether and substitute various forms of clandestine communications, such as dead drops, secret writing, and radio. The danger of surveillance may be cut down, but it remains. Somebody has to mail the letter; somebody has to load the dead drop. Even if loaded without surveillance, dead drops have to be protected against chance threats such as wet or freezing weather, squirrels, and little children, to name but a few dangers. I have seen a perfectly good dead drop disappear because the building it was in was demolished. Once an operation I was involved in almost went up in smoke because some kids found a package in a dead drop, opened it, and, unlike most adults, immediately came to the conclusion that this was spy stuff and turned it over to the police.

While the movies and TV sometimes come out with authentic-looking clandestine films, on one subject all of their realism goes out the window—weapons. No show without a shoot-out. Normally, guns are not only unnecessary, but are superfluous and dangerous and can only get you into trouble. An agent does not carry a gun. If he gets caught in an act of espionage, the chances of his being able to shoot his way out are infinitesimal. He is facing a government, and a gun will deprive him of any hope of alibi or denial.

A case officer doesn't carry a gun either. What for? Maybe they are armed now in certain parts of the world against terrorists, but I would hope that they conform to what other Americans do in their area.

Abduction was always an arrow in the KGB's quiver. Before World War II, they had managed to abduct two Russian emigré leaders, Generals Kutepov and Miller, right out of Paris. These were very complicated operations. In occupied Berlin and Vienna their job was much easier. A few blocks without border controls and their victim was in the bag. As the Shadrin case shows, they were still at it in Vienna in the 1970s.

The KGB in Germany also went in for the murder of emigré leaders at least four times in the 1950s. Two of their murderers defected, one without carrying out his mission. Thirty years later the Roumanian and Bulgarian services were still active in these "wet" affairs, as they are called in the Lubyanka. The victims of these crimes were never western case officers. Nevertheless, we carried guns in Berlin in the 1950s. It was the only period of my CIA service that I ever saw a gun. It was a special situation. We were on our own territory, under Allied military occupation. Under such conditions, perhaps a pistol could have prevented an abduction long enough for the good old West Berlin Police or the MPs to come to our aid. But I know of no cases in which this actually happened.

We had a chief, however, who thoroughly believed in guns. He was an ex-FBI man who always carried two himself, in shoulder holsters. For this reason he would never take off his jacket no matter how hot it got, even once during a steaming mid-summer square dance! He never got to shoot one, and neither did I, except on the range.

I remember sitting in a Volswagon bug with a fellow case officer on an extremely cold night, waiting for someone from the Soviet Sector to emerge from one of those elevated S-Bahn stations. My shivering colleague said, "How's your heater, Dave?'

Striving to be with it, and assuming he was using gangster talk, I replied, "I've got the safety on."

He was merely talking about the Volkswagen's heating system! One night I actually took the safety off. A meeting was taking place in a safe apartment not far from the Soviet Sector border on Potsdamerplatz. The chief was afraid there might be an attempt to abduct the agent right out of the meeting, so another officer and I were staked out across from the apartment house. It was cold and dark. For a time all went well, then suddenly a car with four men in it pulled up and parked outside the house.

The other case officer suggested that I stay put while he got into his car, parked across the street, to prepare to ram these goons if they tried to drive away with a victim. It was his own private car, a nice Mercedes, and I remember having a fleeting bureaucratic thought about what kind of paper work would be necessary before the Agency would pay for any damages. But I had more serious things to think about, left alone on that dark corner. What precisely was I to do if they entered the building? And when they came out? I left off the safety on my pistol and transferred it to my overcoat pocket, and waited, and waited.

Then they simply drove away. Perhaps they had been holding a meeting of their own, or maybe they were black-marketeers. We never did find out. Their West Berlin plates were totally unrevealing when we checked them out. Not much for TV, but what a relief when dramas like this resolve themselves without a climax!

There was one other time when I thought I might have to use my pistol. An agent whose main field of activity was in West Germany used to fly to Berlin from time to time. There was a way to do this without his name appearing on the passenger manifest, but he had to be personally met by a case officer at Tempelhof Airport and escorted there on his return trip. This was my only role in the operation. It was one of those many time-consuming, seemingly menial things we had to do in the name of security.

After a few uneventful trips to Berlin this agent was contacted in West Germany and informed that they were holding his wife in East Berlin. He had not seen her for a number of years. This was a typical case of hostage-blackmail, designed to "double" an agent. I saw several more like it. He reported all this to his case officer, and was sent to Berlin so that our counter-intelligence people could handle it locally.

He had clearly demonstrated that he was still on our side, but you never can tell when a man under such pressure could change his mind. Consequently, when I met him at Tempelhof I was a little uneasy. Suppose he tried to force me to drive to East Berlin, thus delivering one case officer and one vehicle to the Soviets in exchange for his wife?

I had not taken anyone else with me because you do not expose additional case officers to agents, unless there is no other way, and the man who worked with this agent was not available. We were all out on the streets day and night, as we were short-handed, which is why the chief never cared what time we rolled in in the mornings.

I had my pistol, but I was at a disadvantage, being at the wheel. The agent's face was grim when I met him. He immediately started talking about the Soviets holding his wife. This was a good sign. He was in a state of rage against them, and determined to play the game out wherever it led on our side. And he did, although I never learned the details. Years later, in Washington, we unexpectedly ran into each other. We embraced with some emotion. As a gun story, this too was a fizzle, and just as well. Most real-life spy stories are fizzles.

When Truman fired General MacArthur, only one person I knew in the Agency defended the general. I remember the cynical smiles on so many faces when we were listening to MacArthur's tear-jerking, "Old soldiers never die," speech to congress. As for McCarthyism, rampant at the time, we all realized there was a real danger of Communist penetration of the government, but McCarthy was going about it ludicrously, catching nobody, and giving serious anti-Communists a bad name, which they still have thanks to his lingering influence. In this sense he was inadvertently worth a large number of agents to the Soviets.

In that 1950-1951 period, I used to see President Truman quite often—from a distance. Once, when I was taking a taxi to work it drove by Blair House moments after his attempted assassination by Puerto Rican nationalists. It was all the more shocking because there had been no presidential assassination attempt since 1932 when the Mayor of Chicago was killed sitting next to President-elect Roosevelt. I remember reading about it when I was eight.

The first single girl I was introduced to in Washington was Jackie Bouvier—very good-looking, intelligent, with a finishing school veneer under which one felt there was something deeper. We were never close, but once, at a wedding in New York, for no apparent reason she kicked me painfully in the shins. I kicked her back! I think she considered me to be phlegmatic and was trying to get me to react. She was probably right, but I doubt that she expected precisely that type of reaction. We remained on good terms. Jackie and her younger sister, Lee, had many good parties at Merrywood, a beautiful estate that has now been broken up into lots.

On January 21, 1951, at a party in the Society of the Cincinnati Building, I met my future wife, Helen Husted, not yet eighteen, and her two lovely sisters, Caroline and Priscilla, as well as their parents, Helen and Ellery. Nell, as Helen was called, was the middle sister, very beautiful with dark eyes and curly dark hair. She spoke perfect Spanish, from a recent lengthy stay in Mexico, and quite a bit of Russian, which she was studying at Bennington. Actually, Nell was an authentic linguistic genius. Later she learned to speak almost perfect Russian, German and French, and even wrote a dissertation on Georgian phonemes.

I became a regular visitor at the Husted house on Reservoir Road in Georgetown. Nell's parents were delightful. Ellery was a fellow Yale man, an architect who helped design the future Dulles Airport in Washington. I remember him standing over a large, water color sketch of it, pouring a bit of Bourbon out of his glass onto just the right places. He was an artist, as well as an architect, and would probably have been happier as an artist if he could have supported his family that way. He did not really think the law applied much to him, sort of like Pavel Vladimirovich. One day the cops led him off in handcuffs because of over 100 unpaid parking tickets. He also never could get used to income taxes!

Nell's mother, Helen, was one of the most amusing and attractive women I ever met, and continued to be until her death at the age of eighty-five. She and Ellery were the same age, just fifty, shortly after I met them, my mother's age. But there were problems between Helen and her three daughters, which I did not realize at the time. I was crazy about the whole family, but it was only later that I really fell in love with Nell. One of the problems of our marriage was that I loved her parents so much, and she resented that. I wanted her to love mine too, but she didn't like them much, until after our divorce.

On June 1, 1951, I departed for West Germany, which to me lacked the drama of Berlin. My entire baggage consisted of a B-4 bag and a footlocker following by sea. The means of transportation was one of those marvellous Pan Am prop jobs with a bar downstairs from the main cabin, at which you could sit and drink during take-off. The main cabin had births, like an old Pullman, so there were never any of the future jet-lag problems. It took something like twelve or thirteen hours to get to London, with landings, if you were lucky, in Iceland and Shannon, Ireland.

The great German currency reform was firmly in place when I arrived. The new Deutsche Mark (DM) was hard currency, no more of that old cigarette stuff, but with the DM at something like 4.25 to the dollar, life was dirt cheap for us even without the black market.

Rumpsteak à la Meier with potatoes and vegetables and a couple of those wonderful draft beers cost perhaps two dollars at any corner beer joint.

On weekends I would drive to Mainz or Darmstadt, or those wonderful towns on the Rhine, to carouse and sing, linking arms with strangers at the table.

Yet, there was always the thought that Stalin might send his troops over the border at any time. All Americans had standing orders to park their cars at night pointing at the Rhine, equipped with an extra jerry-can of gasoline. I knew only one person who actually did this, however.

There were temporary duty trips to places where a lot of old friends were stationed. One of these was Bill Coffin, who had followed me into the CIA, having been so instrumental in my own recruitment. Since Bill revealed it all in such eloquent detail in his book, *Once to Every Man*, I can say that they were recruiting and training recent Russian emigrés to be dropped by parachute into the USSR. This program went on for three years, with plenty of heroism but not much success. In this day of overhead photography it seems incredible that it was considered necessary then, but there was a real blackout of intelligence on the USSR, and desperate need for it.

I recognized the need for it and knew about it, but I have always been grateful not to have been directly involved—not to have seen, trained, and looked into the eyes of those doomed heroes. Even so, for years I could not look at a full moon without thinking of the phrase, "August drop-moon," or whatever month it was. Coffin speculates that the program was betrayed to the Soviets by Philby, the British traitor who was stationed in Washington at that time. Even without betrayal it was a very difficult operation.

I was doing clandestine things, not normally a matter of life and death, but which I still do not feel free to reveal. The part of my work which I can reveal involved hand-holding and socializing with the latest Soviet defectors, as well as questioning them. Getting information on life in the Soviet Union, and its army, was very much to my taste. These were all military defectors. Stalin's iron curtain was in a closed position, and practically nobody else had a chance to escape. But in Germany and Austria, a Soviet soldier or officer still had a chance to make it, particularly in Berlin or Vienna.

Defectors are an extremely valuable source of information. They can also be a horrendous, time-consuming, maddening and expensive handling problem. In 1951 defector reception and handling had gone an astronomically long way from Scherbinine's home-made center in Malverstrasse in the Berlin of 1949. While there was a fair chance to escape in Berlin or Vienna, it did not always work that way. One night in 1951, when I was in Vienna unsuccessfully trying to persuade a Soviet colonel to defect, a private made it into the International Sector and walked into a military post. Unfortunately, it was a quadripartite one, *Vier in Jeep*, as the Austrians used to call them. There was an American MP on duty there, but he didn't move fast enough or didn't move at all, and the poor Soviet wretch fell into the hands of his own countrymen, who had no difficulty sending him on his first step to GULAG.

Another Soviet private in Berlin was luckier. He was standing guard on the Soviet war memorial in the British Sector near the Brandenburg Gate. He walked off his post, weapon and all, intending to defect and almost immediately found himself lit up by floodlights on the nearby Tiergarten, where a movie was being shot, believe it or not, involving the defection of a Soviet soldier!

As this bewildered real defector walked into the floodlights, the director yelled, "God damn it, the defection scene isn't tonight, it's tomorrow night! Get that idiot out of here!"

It was soon evident that the confused boy in Soviet uniform was for real, and it helped that the director was a second generation emigré from Paris and spoke Russian. The West Berlin police were called and the soldier was safe.

One of the first defectors I met this time was an ex-Soviet armored force captain, whom I shall call Vladimir, an unstable personality. He had defected in Berlin while very drunk, *na avos*, as the Russians say. Loosely translated, this means "screw it—let's do it!"

In West Germany he developed considerable anti-Stalinist enthusiasm and wrote some pretty good articles for emigré magazines.

As I drove him around in my Chevrolet, he would become indignant if anybody passed us, particularly Volkswagens.

"How can you let those Fascist bedbugs pass your good American Chevrolet?"

Vladimir pined away for an East German girl he had left behind. Since we then had the capabilities, and he was a good source, we obliged him in this. I flew with Vladimir to Berlin, without telling him what it was all about, for fear something would go wrong, and we were met at Tempelhof and driven to a safehouse.

After a while the doorbell rang. Vladimir went mad with pleasure when a very pretty blonde wearing green boots walked in and threw herself into his arms. Then it was my turn to be surprised. The pretty blonde was followed by another, a clone, also wearing green boots. Vladimir had neglected to tell us that his girlfriend had a twin sister, and our agents had brought her along for good measure. During the next twenty-four hours Vladimir made love to his girlfriend eight times and also once to her sister, "out of politeness," he explained to me, "so she won't feel left out."

I was sorely tempted to be polite to the sister as well, but I stayed by the dictum that operations and sex do not mix.

It seems incredible now what we could accomplish before the Berlin wall went up, and to what lengths we would go to make a defector happy. I don't remember what happened to those twin blondes in the green boots, but Vladimir's girl obviously did not want to stay with him. They both probably went home.

Back in the West Vladimir went into deep depressions. Once he disappeared for a few days, and then came back. On another occasion he claimed I saved his life, appearing just in time to prevent his cutting his wrist with a razor blade. I had been away in Italy for a few days. He was lying in bed and produced the blade from under the covers, but I think this was a bit of dramatization on his part. He would recover from these depressions and was in a very optimistic mood when the two of us flew to Washington together. There I turned him over to other officers and never saw him again.

Eventually, Vladimir went back to the USSR. No matter how much is done for them, some go back. In some cases they are wooed by KGB-inspired family letters and promises that all is forgiven. All is never forgiven, especially in military cases. Not long ago I met a Russian Jewish emigré who had been in the same concentration camp with another officer defector whom I knew in Germany. This man, in order to hide the stupidity of his voluntary return from his fellow inmates, had concocted a story that the Soviets had kidnapped him out of West Germany. They are capable of this, but it did not happen in his case. The man was serving fifteen years.

Why do they go back? Some cannot face life in a foreign country when they are on their own, no matter how much help they get. The Soviets push the line that defectors are squeezed dry like lemons by us, and then cast aside. This is simply not true, but it may seem so to defectors who, after weeks or months of questioning, are expected to make some sort of life for themselves, even with plenty of aid and guidance.

Others, handled in the same way by the same people, face their problems with fortitude and go on to a relatively happy life. Much depends on personality and the original reason for defection. The man who jumps to escape some particular problem, whether it be a fight with his boss or a drunken car accident, is likely to jump back when faced with a new set of problems. On the other hand, the man who consciously plans his defection for a long time, merely waiting for a physical opportunity, and who has solid, well thought out reasons for leaving, is likely to stay in the West.

In the 1970s one such defector told me that he had read every scrap of information in the Soviet press about returned defectors and managed to derive from these articles a pretty fair picture of how the Americans would handle him. He liked what he learned. For years he practiced swimming, hoping to make it across the Black Sea into Turkey, but eventually he made it dry-shod on a trip abroad, taking one of those fearful taxi rides to an American embassy. He hailed the cab at a moment when he knew his KGB "nursemaid" was in bed with his pants off, giving the defector a few minutes head start. It all ended happily, and he is now an enthusiastic resident of the United States, with a very high opinion of the CIA officers who handled him.

KING MICHAEL OF ROUMANIA and
QUEEN MOTHER HELEN

PRINCESS XENIA ANDREYEVNA and SOVIET SOLDIER
Berlin 1947

PRINCESS MARGARITA and KRAFT
(below) PRINCE GOTTFRIED and MARGARITA
of HOHENLOHE-LANGENBURG
with twins PRINCE RUPRECHT and ALBRECHT

PRINCE LOUIS FERDINAND of PRUSSIA

MARIA, NELL and AUTHOR -1954

CHAPTER XII

In 1951 I made a trip to Venice, where Uncle George and Aunt Elizabeth were still holding court at the Palazzo Polignac. It was only a long weekend, but a memorable one. At a cocktail party in another Grand Canal palazzo, Winston Churchill suddenly walked in. He was not prime minister at the time, but he was elected again later.

Churchill did all the things we had seen in the newsreels—wore a cowboy hat, smoked a long cigar, made V-signs, and he was far from sober. An old acquaintance from 1949 introduced us. I was so overwhelmed to shake hands with this titan of both world wars that all I could manage was a bow. After a time we all went out onto the balcony to watch him depart in his launch, and we applauded. He was so pleased he had the launch make a U-turn on the Grand Canal and go by us again. He was still making V-signs.

It was at this time that Don Carlos Bestigui, who lived across the Grand Canal from us, was planning a huge costume ball, widely publicised and criticised for coming too soon after the war. The denizens of each palazzo planned suitable 18th century costumes. Aunt Elizabeth was Catherine the Great, which meant that Uncle George had to be Peter III.

"Why do I have to be that idiot?" he asked me.

"Well, you're married to her, and you don't look much like Potemkin," I said.

I attended the dress rehearsal for the ball, which was a huge party in itself. The costumed groups arived in gondolas, and it took little imagination to envision the Venice of Casanova's time. There was even a greased pole for the townspeople to climb for prizes, very authentic for the period, and also erected for the dress rehearsal. Lady Diana Duff Cooper was the centerpiece of the whole affair, sitting in costume under a priceless Tiepolo.

I missed the real ball because I was afraid Vladimir, back in Germany, would redefect or something worse, so I returned to the real world.

In the fall of 1951 Nell Husted came to Paris to attend the Sorbonne, and I started going to Paris as often as possible, sitting up on the train on Friday night and returning Monday morning. By this time I was determined to marry her, but it was a difficult and far from happy courtship. She was, after all, not ninteen, while I was at an age when a lot of young men mysteriously develop an overwhelming urge to get married. We were not really suited to each other, a fact she well realized, but which I kept ignoring. We went to Geneva and Vienna together, and even to Berlin on the military train. We were in a semi-engaged state when she returned to Washington in the spring of 1952, and I soon followed her, somehow squaring it with the always kindly bureacuracy of the CIA. We spent some time in Washington then went to Wellfleet to stay with my parents, who were very supportive of me, and besides, they liked her.

We were married in Washington on September 13, 1952 in a Russian Church located in an apartment on a street appropriately called Church Street, near Du Pont Circle. It was one of those ghastly hot and humid days, so hot that my mother, who had a Spartan upbringing as far as standing in church was concerned, fainted and had to be helped outside. The reception at the Husteds' housed turned out to be a marvellous party. Nyanyushka was there as were George Wrangel, Ivan Obolensky and so many other dear friends and relations. After making an official exit from the reception we went next door to a friend's house, changed clothes, and went right back to the party. Nobody wanted to leave. My father and I sang along with Nell, who already knew some Russian songs and had a lovely singing voice. We spent the night at the Mayflower Hotel, and the next day, my leave having run out, we boarded a plane for Germany. We were met on the other side by cheering coleagues, who knew that I had been far from certain of returning with a bride.

We found that it was illegal for us to live in my apartment because it was listed as bachelor's quarters, but it was much better than anything available as maried quarters; so, encouraged by Nell, I arranged a transfer to Berlin. It was amazingly easy to do in those days. Berlin was the place I wanted to be anyway, the point of the spear! West Germany could not compete in any way.

In the late fall of 1952 we drove to Helmstedt and took the military train, as the CIA would not permit us to drive through the Soviet Zone. MPs delivered the car to us in Berlin.

To be in Berlin at that time was perhaps the most prestigious and elite assignment anywhere. The city looked more or less the way it had during my army days, except a lot of ruins had been cleaned up, but what a difference in atmosphere! The Soviets were now the enemy. The Cold War was in full force, and we were on the front line, surrounded in our little island of the three western sectors.

Being CIA, we were not allowed to set foot in the Soviet Sector, but Nell managed to violate this rule the day after we arrived. She took the U-Bahn downtown, missed her stop, and ended up in Alexanderplatz.

"*Amerikanisch*?" she asked hopefully of the man sitting next to her.

"*Nein, Russisch*," he replied. She quickly got out, reversed directions and emerged safely at some station in the British Sector.

Nell could hardly speak a word of German, so she began taking lessons from a Prussian-type schoolmaster, who was scared to death of the little boxer puppy we had acquired. It was not long before Nell was fluent in it. Though no slouch at languages, I lacked Nell's genius for them, and my fluency left much to be desired in 1952.

Ellery Husted's architectural work brought him to Paris, so Nell's parents rented an apartment there, resulting in some wonderful weekends for us. In February 1953 Nell, already pregnant, went off to join her parents in Madrid.

After a *Fasching* party somewhere near Kurfürstendamm, the streets were icy and I slid into a German car from the rear. Unfortunately, the German cops called the MPs, who took me off for an alcohol test. Though I felt quite sober, naturally I flunked the test and had my license lifted for a month.

"Were you drunk, Dave?" the boss asked the next morning. I thought of the drinks he served and drank himself—a bourbon on the rocks consisted of a water glass full of bourbon and a piece or two of ice.

"Well, not really, but I had had a few." A case officer in Berlin unable to drive a car is useless, so I decided that the only thing to do was join Nell in Spain. "Bill, I can't work here without a license. How about letting me take some leave and join my wife in Spain?

"Fine by me, Dave," he agreed. This fine commander looked like Tweedledum and walked with both arms swinging in the same direction, perhaps because of his shoulder holsters.

This was my first trip to Spain, and I was overwhelmed by friendliness and what I can only describe as an inner nobility of bearing on the part of almost all the Spaniards we came into contact with. We went to Madrid, Toledo, Cordoba, Malaga and I made a side trip to Morocco—costing five dollars by air, then it was back to Berlin. Nell did not return until March 16, and was buzzed by Soviet fighters performing ominous acrobatics over the so-called German Democratic Republic.

Stalin died during this time, officially acknowledged by the Soviets on March 6. During those days we really worked around the clock. Agents were coming in from the east to report on the state of mind of Soviet troops, and the East German population. The big surprise was that the Soviet troops seemed stunned and apprehensive, but not overcome with grief or anything like that.

I was at the monument on the British side of the Brandenburg Gate when the Soviet lieutenant commanding the guard addressed a crowd of worried Germans. "*Vsyo budet khorosho*," he shouted with a broad smile. Everything will be fine!

By way of contrast, toward the end of May, we were visited by the pretender to the German throne, my second cousin, Prince Louis Ferdinand, his wife Kira, also a relative, being a daughter of Grand Duke Cyril, and two of their children.

I had known Lu-Lu, as we called him, since I was ten in New York, a time when he was living and working, for the Ford Motor Company, in the U.S. He used to take me for rides in his car, and then complained to my parents that they had brought me up in a very anti-German way, because I kept asking him why his grandfather, the Kaiser, had started the Great War. My parents assured him that I had gotten this idea from my own reading.

He was a handsome man in his late twenties, with a prominent, straight nose, and what I thought was a very Hohenzollern look—something his father the Crown Prince had had, but that the Kaiser had lacked. Four years later, in 1938, he visited us again with his new bride, Kira. I did not see them again for nine years, by which time they were living in Bad Kissingen and had produced six children. On my way back from Paris in my jeep, Yakov Semenovich, I made a detour to pay them a visit, loaded with cigarettes and other useful commodities. They were not home when I drove up, so I took the children for a spin in the jeep. On the main street of the town we encountered Lu-Lu and Kira, who were horrified at the sight, fearing that some American officer was making off with their entire family in a strange blue jeep! To put their mind at rest, I jammed on the brakes, jumped out and kissed Kira's hand, addressing her in Russian.

"You must be Paul and Nina's son," said Lu-Lu, vastly relieved. Later they said, "This was one of the nicest things that could still have happened to us!"

Lu-Lu had become an able composer of *Lieder*, and I learned that a concert of his songs was scheduled to be held at the Titania Palast, a huge theatre in the American Sector of Berlin. I wrote him to be sure to visit us, so he, Kira, and their two eldest sons, Friedrich Wilhelm and Michael, had dinner with us on the night of the concert. I was somewhat skeptical of the monarchist sentiment Lu-Lu insisted still existed in Berlin, but all he said was, "Wait and see!"

We drove to the theatre in my car and were seated in the Royal Box in the center of the balcony. The moment we came into the box, the whole audience stood and cheered. I began to realize that the *Lieder* was a cover for a monarchist rally!

After the performance, Louis Ferdinand took a bow on the stage as the composer, then returned to take another bow from the box as the "emperor." The crowd, composed of ordinary middle-class Germans, again went wild.

With Louis Ferdinand and Kira in another car, we drove through the crowd with their two sons, pelted with flowers and surrounded by dense throngs yelling, "*Kommen Sie zurück und bleiben bei uns!*" (Come back and stay with us!)

After a reception, Lu-lu and I stayed up talking over beers at the Bristol Hotel until six in the morning. I found him to be intelligent, very well informed, with good contacts in all the political parties, including the Social Democrats. He would have made an excellent constitutional monarch had the time been ripe for it.

A few days later Nell and I went off to London for the coronation of Queen Elizabeth II. No, we did not have seats in the Abbey. We had no seats at all! We just decided it would be fun to be there, and we would take our chances. Nell's pregnancy was advancing, and she was not very happy on the channel steamer from the Hook of Holland.

We stayed with Uncle "Vanya" Kleinmichel, he of the Kursk map, and Aunt "Merika," whose name I had once confused with America. Naturally, their house was not heated, and the warmth of their reception did not make up for the fact that it was very cold that year, even if it was almost June. Inured to the temperature, our hosts could not understand why we spent a lot of time under the covers in bed, sipping gin! For the first time I could sympathise with my mother's dislike of England's chilblains and underheated houses.

We went to Hampton Court to see Aunt Xenia, the sister of Emperor Nicholas II, and to Swanage to see Babady, who read us poetry, sang to us with her lute, and presented Nell with a diamond diadem which had belonged to her mother. Her husband, Peter Troubetskoy, kept hunting for Nell's cigarette butts and smoking them, while reading his Bolshevik magazine.

On Coronation Day, June 2, 1953, the Kleinmichels and we got up at five o'clock and took the tube to the center of London. The Kleinmichels were suitably clad for their seats in the royal stalls. Rather sadly Nell and I went to an apartment belonging to friends of the Husteds, who themselves went out to occupy seats along the route.

Actually, we were lucky. The weather outside was frightful, pouring rain most of the time, and we comfortably watched the ceremony on television! After that, studying the papers for exact times, we went out to neighboring Oxford Street and had a close view of the whole procession, including Churchill, Field Marshal

Montgomery, Aunt Marina, the Duchess of Kent, and Prince Philip with the newly crowned queen. She looked as if the weight of the crown was really getting to her. Once in a while there was a blast of rain. The one who stole the show was the tall Queen of Tonga, who stood with the rain in her face, while some Malay sultan in her carriage cowered under the scant shelter the ancient vehicle offered. Somebody remarked that he was probably the Queen of Tonga's lunch!

We went back to the apartment, delighted with the way things had turned out. Our rain-soaked hosts returned from their open air seats, and rather snidely said that somebody in the lobby was asking for me.

"Of course, if you insist that they come up. . . ."

"Oh, yes, that must be dear Count and Countess Kleinmichel from the royal stalls," I should have said, but didn't. Instead we merely thanked our hosts and went downstairs, and there sat the Kleinmichels, absolutely drenched, looking like an overdressed Cockney family.

We went off to a Russian party with my cousins Emmanuel and George Golitsin, where we all sang and so did Theodore Bickel, whom Emmanuel had helped train to sing Russian Gypsy songs. Bickel did not speak a word of Russian, but sang almost perfectly, being a first rate mimic.

We got back to Berlin nine days before the next great episode in the Cold War.

The night of June 16, 1953 we heard radio reports of a strike by German workers in East Berlin, but on the 17th we understood that an actual revolution was going on throughout the Soviet Zone, against the government of the so-called German Democratic Republic and the Soviet occupation.

Nell was already seven months pregnant, but insisted on seeing the action. We went to Potsdamerplatz, on the border of the American and Soviet Sectors. There was a huge crowd, many of them from East Berlin. Tremendous solidarity between East and West Berliners existed. There was no sign of any American military presence.

Then Soviet tanks appeared. I don't know whether they actually crossed the border, but they opened fire into West Berlin. The crowd began to run, except for those with infantry training, who hit the dirt. So did I, bringing Nell down with me, hoping our future child would not be hurt. I landed in a pool of oil, absolutely ruining a green sport coat Ellery had given me. How strange it was to be under fire in anger for the first time, after all those years in World War II and after, and by my family's old nemesis, the Soviets!

The Soviet tanks probably fired in the air, but we didn't know that. I took Nell home and returned to the border, this time at the Brandenburg Gate. I had once been able to scoot through it on Yakov Semenovich without stopping. There had always been a red flag on top; now the flag was gone.

I jammed myself into the crowd of Germans under one of the arches. On the other side, on Unter den Linden, there was a Soviet artillery battery, the troops wearing helmets and blanket rolls. The guns were pointed at us. Off to the left, the Soviet war monument was being guarded by a long line of red-hatted British military police.

An East German Peoples Police, "Vopo," officer came up and threatened to open fire on the crowd. They laughed. Then a British colonel pushed through to the Soviet side, accompanied by an intepreter whom I recognized as one of the old gang at the Allied Control Authority. The Germans jamming the Gate gave this British delegation what can only be described as a Bronx cheer. The colonel had a short and obviously unsuccessful parley with a Soviet colonel near the battery, and returned through the Gate amid more Bronx cheers. The German crowd sensed, quite correctly, that the western powers were doing nothing to help this revolution. The western commandants acted as if there was danger of the Soviets invading West Berlin, while the Soviets pretended they were being invaded by West Berlin. Meanwhile, by evening, Soviet troops had bloodily crushed this first post-war rebellion against them.

Our chief said it best at a meeting we all had that night, "I've been up to my ass in midgets all day!"

Yet there was a counter-intelligence officer at the meeting who still suspected that the whole revolution had been staged by the Soviets to show how liberal they were! "I cannot believe that the Communists would ever stage a labor strike against themselves," I remarked.

"I'll buy that, Dave," the Chief said, adjusting the guns under his jacket.

At the end of June Nell left for Washington, while I had to remain until August.

Our first child made her appearance on August 28, 1953, which I made it back in time for. The sweltering heat had become so unbearable that the Husteds and I had moved to a friend's house which had air-conditioning. Helen and I took Nell to the George Washington University Hospital at 3:30 PM that day, and she was delivered of a healthy girl at 5:02 PM, to the amazement of the doctors. Not only that, but immediatley after giving birth she sat up and lectured them that they were in the right field of medicine, dealing with birth rather than death.

I decided to call the new arrival Maria, solely to please Nell, who was still on her Mexican kick, and could not imagine producing a daughter not named Maria. Maria's nickname was to be Marusya, but of course in English this was soon corrupted into Moosie.

There was a real gathering of the clans in Wellfleet for Marusya's christening on September 12. Officiating were a Greek priest from Hyannis and a Russian from Boston. They eyed each other suspiciously. The Greek could not quite believe the Russian was really Orthodox.

"You khev *hagios miros*?" (holy oil), the Greek asked.

"I khev," said the Russian, and the Greek seemed mollified.

Nyanyushka fussed about the punch bowl that Marusya was to be christened in, making sure the water was not too cold. The Anglo-Saxon element could not quite believe a total emersion was to take place, but it did. According to tradition, Nell and I had to sit upstairs and not watch the ceremony, so as not to upstage the godparents. Ten days later I was back in Berlin, and Nell and Marusya followed a month after that.

The birth of our second daughter took place under vastly different circumstances. It was in Berlin, in deep snow, at four in the morning that I drove Nell to the Army hospital, a race against time, and Nell kept up her record for speedy delivery. The baby was born ot 0525 hours on December 24, 1954. What a terrible birthday to plague a child with!

The new baby we named Alexandra, because both of us liked the name, never suspecting that computers of the future would have nothing to do with anybody who had twenty-two letters, counting the space, in her name! Her nickname was Sasha. With our maid Anneliese as a live-in baby-sitter, the appearance of the children did little to cramp our style, and when I wasn't working at night there was plenty going on.

There were CIA parties but, surprisingly, they were not much fun. The men stood all together whispering about operations, while their wives sat around looking at each other. Perhaps all company parties are like this, but there was a saving grace. All it took was for one uncleared guest to be there and operational talk ceased magically.

At our house there was always a mix of people that precluded these whispered conversations. In fact, with a few exceptions, Nell refused to invite our colleagues at all. The legendary two-gun chief never crossed our threshold. In any other government service, I would probably have been ruined because of this, but to the CIA's credit it did not seem to make much difference.

The mix of guests was usually successful—a few Germans, some State Department people, American correspondents, some CIA colleagues, British officers, and a group of balalaika and mandolin-playing Russians left over from 1946-1947 days, who could get any party going quickly.

We had a number of amusing British friends—three brothers replaced each other at the same British Army post. First there was Captain Robert Wolridge-Gordon of the Grenadier Guards, then Lt. Patrick Wolridge-Gordon of the Argyle and Southerland Highlanders, and lastly, Lt. John McLeod of the Black Watch. John was Patrick's identical twin. The reason for this change of name was that John, the elder twin, had taken the name of his mother and had become heir to his grandmother, Dame Flora McLeod, of the chieftianship of the clan and the lordship of Dunvegan Castle on the Isle of Skye. The castle contained the famous Fairy Flag, which had already won two victories, the last over Harald Hardrada of Norway in 1066, and still had one victory left in it, according to legend. John did a fair amount of practicing with our wine for his investiture ceremony, during which he was expected to empty a huge horn of claret, very much in the style of my Georgian ancestors. John resigned from the army while in Berlin, and we somehow found a civilian job for him on the German economy, not easy, and illegal. When he returned to Skye for his investiture, the whole thing was photographed for *Life* Magazine. The Queen was present. Our maid could not believe what she was seeing. "That's the Englishman whose pants I kept patching!" she exclaimed.

Dinner in the officers' mess of a Highland regiment, pipers and all, is unique, and we had our share of this thanks to the twins. When I visited London in 1956 Robert, the eldest brother, invited me to lunch at the Grenadier Guards mess at Windsor Castle, and I spent the afternoon at the castle listening to the officer of the guard's stories about the Queen's encyclopedic knowledge of guards' uniforms and procedures. I inspected the graffiti of officers in Victorian times, and tried to remember how, at the age of less than three, I used to try to speak to those bearskin giants in Russian.

What energy we had in those days! In Berlin it was a frequent thing, even on weekday nights, to go to a cocktail party, a dinner party, an after dinner party, and end up at the Orient or the Mazurka, where we could sing Russian songs with the orchestra.

In early 1954 there was a foreign ministers' conference in Berlin. John Foster Dulles represented the U.S., and "Iron Pants" Molotov the USSR. Normally I would not have been involved in that at all, but at a party at Spencer and Xenia Barnes', the chief State Department officer in Berlin, Francis Parkman, who had a soft spot for Nell, whisked her off to a reception for the foreign ministers. The old Allied Control Authority Building, tri-lingual latrines and all, had been reopened for the occasion. Somebody at the Barnes' slipped me a pass. By the time I got there, Molotov and my old acquaintance Gromyko were gone, but there were a lot of Soviets left, and at that time contact with them was a rare thing. I almost talked a Pravda correspondent into going back to the Barnes with me. Nell, in her now fluent Russian, not only charmed the Soviets, but put them in their places every time they made a propagandistic statement. The evening ended back at the Barnes, where we sang Russian songs with Ambassador Bohlen. Actually, this happened several times when the ambassador was going to Moscow or returning to Washington. The old songs reminded him of his youthful days in independent Latvia, where he had learned his Russian.

During the June 17, 1953 uprising, some American and German papers concluded that the Soviet commandant of East Berlin must be a woman since proclamations were signed by Major General Dybrova, which sounded like the feminine of Dybrov. We knew better. It was a man with a Ukrainian name. All possible doubts were dispelled when I met the gentleman, standing at an adjoining urinal at the men's room of our officers' club, Harnack House. He smiled at me pleasantly and repeated the old Russian saying for such occasions, "Where the Tsar goes on foot!" It is difficult to go to the bathroom on horseback! I thought this was rather cute, coming from a Soviet general. He was a benign looking gray-haired man with whom I later had several conversations. He seemed to know a great deal about the Bible—perhaps the son of a priest—and not too much about Marixism! I often made myself useful by interpreting between him and our own generals and colonels. Almost always it was fatuous patter about where they would go fishing after they retired. Thanks to my previous experience, I was pretty good at this sort of interpreting, and was welcome at Harnack House receptions and those of various diplomatic missions.

The chief encouraged all this. Almost none of his troops had any opportunity to see the Soviets face to face and obtain first-hand descriptions and impressions. Most of the Soviets who came to these receptions were either KGB or GRU. There was no loss if they tapped me for an intelligence officer; even if I had not been one, they would have assumed I was because of my emigré background and language.

I developed contacts with American officers stationed at the Potsdam Military Mission, and was invited to parties for the Soviets they dealt with. These army officers always encouraged me to sing my repertoire of pre-revolutionary soldiers' songs. I was even invited to social occasions with the Soviets in the Spandau Prison, where a handful of Nazi war criminals were still incarcerated, and the old rotating monthly allied chairmanship was still observed.

Once, for two weeks, I went on active duty with the reserves and did some official interpreting at the top level, in a captain's uniform. This must have confused the Soviets' bookkeeping on me. One KGB man, whom I had met before, had real surprise in his voice when he said, "Do you realize that this is the first time I have ever seen you in uniform?"

At that time most of the KGB could still be picked out by their bullet-headed, jowly secret police faces, and a sort of hooded expression of the eyes, characteristics that appeared to be endemic to the type. I remember meeting one such specimen at the Belgian Mission.

"How do you do. My name is Chavchavadze."

"Mumble."

"What did you say your name was?" I insisted.

"Mumble."

"I'm sorry, I still haven't caught it."

"What's in a name?" he asked.

"Well, I told you mine quite clearly. Chavchavadze. Now tell me yours."

I finally got it out of him. This sort of thing was important to our bookkeeping on the KGB.

Soon a more presentable, younger generation began to appear. Still, there was something about their eyes. Nell was particularly good with them, because they always flirted with her.

"What beautiful brown eyes you have!"

"Yours are extraordinary too," Nell would say.

"Really? Why do you say that?"

"One would expect to see them on a snake."

Nell was not famous for her diplomacy, but this sorft of approach worked. The fellow would then spend considerable time trying to convince her he did not belong to the serpent family.

I was always looking for a chance to convert the Soviets. This was a misapprehension it took me some years to get rid of. Just as my own eyes had been opened, I thought that I could open theirs by proving to them that their government lied about practically everything, and was generally a blight on the real interests of the people. It took me a while to realize that the sort of Soviets that served abroad, particularly the KGB, knew even more than I did about what their government was really like, but it was their closed shop; they were the privileged class, the *apparatchiki* with access to the special stores, medical care, vacation spots, and most of them didn't give a damn about the rest of the population. So it was never a question of converting them, but of looking for the few individuals who for reasons of conscience, hatred of past wrongs, career resentments, or for just plain venality, were ready to turn against their closed shop.

Nell and I met two obvious KGB types at another Barnes party. Spencer Barnes was in charge of a State Department unit and had served in Moscow. His wife, Xenia, a Russian from the old emigration, had been his language teacher, married him, and was with him in Moscow.

The party was a small one. I bantered with the Soviets, making my detestation of their system completely clear, and I also entertained with guitar and Russian songs. Much to my surprise, the evening ended with an invitation from the Soviets to the Barnes and us to have dinner with them a week later in the officers' club of that Soviet holy-of-holies, the Karlshort Compound. I accepted, not thinking for a moment that we would be allowed to go.

"What the hell, Dave," the chief said on Monday morning. "Let's give it a try." He sent a cable and received an enthusiastic approval from the next echelon, and a less sanguine go-ahead from Washington. Headquarters urged me not to be separated for a moment from Spencer Barnes.

I suspect that in reporting the meeting the two KGB officers conveniently left out my anti-Soviet talk and stressed my "Russian soul," and love of Russian music. Moscow approved, but somewhere along the line, some chief added a new wrinkle to the operation. This became apparent soon after our arrival.

I confess to an uneasy feeling when the gates of the compound closed behind us. In 1947 the atmosphere had been quite different. Before leaving home I had lined my stomach with olive oil, expecting to be plied with numerous water glases full of vodka, but there were few toasts and, as a matter of fact, they were tight fisted with their vodka that night. I could have used more. All the olive oil accomplished was to drive me to the bathroom several times, forcing me to leave Spencer's side.

It was Saturday night, but the club was deserted except for members of our party. As I emerged from the bathroom, a third man, a typical bullet-head came up to me and addressed me in Georgian. Some KGB operational genius had thought this up—I had a Georgian last name, hence I had to speak Georgian!

I chuckled inwardly as I realized that their files, at least in this case, were not what they were cracked up to be. They must have had a file on me since at least 1943, and one on my father much earlier. It was totally open information that neither of us spoke Georgian, but evidently it wasn't recorded, and the KGB had gone to the trouble of producing a Georgian-speaking officer for me.

Poor bullet-head! He could not disguise his disappointment when I politely informed him, in Russian, that I couldn't speak the language. But the script had to proceed according to plan. Bullet-head was relegated to the sidelines, but fortunately he was a good pianist and entertained us with music.

After the meal they showed us a movie—about Georgia, an interminable propagandistic color documentary, during which our hosts whispered that he was a consul and would personally issue me a visa if I wanted to spend my next vacation in colorful Tblisi. This was quite funny as there was no tourist travel for Americans at all in those days. When the film announcer said, "The Georgian people respect their great writer, Ilya Chavchavadze," they all shouted, "What a coincidence! You see how your family is respected!" I didn't have the heart to tell them it was not my branch of the family. There were also Georgian posters on the club bulletin board, the approach was total Georgian nostalgia, all directed at me.

The evening ended amicably enough. The two original KGB officers agreed to come to my house the following Saturday. They spoke jokingly of having an ideological duel with me. It was a relief to leave the compound and drive back into the American Sector. I stopped at the first phone and called the chief. He had touchingly wanted to be informed that I had returned safely from the lion's den, no matter how late it might be.

The KGB did not show up the following Saturday. The Soviets often did not arrive at a party, and failed to inform their host; this time one of them called to apologize. They both had to go somewhere on temporary duty. The script was being rewritten.

About ten more days went by, and then one afternoon, when Nell and I were out, they appeared in a Soviet official car, driven by a driver in uniform. This almost resulted in a flap. Our maid let them in the house before she caught sight of the driver's uniform. When she did, she clutched baby Marusya to her and frantically began dialing the American MPs to come quickly. The child was about to be kidnapped! She had lived through the Great Rape of 1945 and was scared to death of Soviets. Nevertheless, they soft-talked her into putting down the phone, and indulged in some developmental chit-chat about how she should come to East Berlin, where they would find her a nice boy friend.

Fortunately we arrived a few minutes later. I could tell that my KGB friends were under pressure to produce, but I could not believe the crudeness of their approach. They were no longer even polite. They brought up the business of an ideological duel again. No serious conversations, they said, could be held in West Berlin because of the constant din of maneuvering American, British and French troops. Therefore, I was to meet them in the Soviet Sector in front of the Friedrichstrasse opera house the next morning. Alone. No wife. No Spencer Barnes, because "he doesn't have a Russian soul." They were acting out a scenario in which they had no belief. From the very beginning I cannot imagine they thought I was susceptabible. Naturally, I did not meet them, and they knew I would not. I had an agent pass by to check, and they were not there. The next time I ran into one of our Karlshorst friends at an official function he turned his back on me.

Since I know that the KGB is capable of doing things right with a long, careful period of development, I can only conclude that this charade was a bureaucratic numbers game—branch so-and-so has a recruitment operation going against an American intelligence officer." This looked good for somebody's norms, and they had to go through some sort of motion before dropping it.

Files can never be complete, and it is easy to overlook a negative fact, such as that I don't speak Georgian, but they should have added this to their files. Yet, several years later, on the other side of the Atlantic, they tried to approach me in Georgian again.

After my return to Berlin in 1952, I went on helping Aunt Sonya, who tried to believe that her son, Yury, would reappear. By the beginning of 1954, she had become quite senile, and spoke only in French, addressing me as *Mon ange*. She died August 13, 1954 at the age of seventy-eight. I arranged a funeral at the little Orthodox chapel in Tegel, in the French Sector, to which Emperor Alexander III had once sent two boxcars of Russian soil so that Russians could be buried in their native soil. I looked for the last time at her very severe Georgian face, inherited from her

Chavchavadze ancestors, in spite of her very Germanic maiden name of Osten-Sacken. I also collected a few family keepsakes.

The irony was that since 1953 Yury had been on the list of the German Red Cross, which had sent packages to him in the GULAG island of Potma. It never occurred to me to check with them, and I blame myself terribly for this. If I had, Aunt Sonya would have at least known that her son was still alive.

In 1955, Chancellor Konrad Adenauer traveled to Moscow where he arranged with Nikita Krushchev for the release of 10,000 German prisoners still being held by the Soviets. Among them were three Russian emigrés, one of whom was Yury, who had always insisted that he was a German citizen. In October Yury was released and came straight to Frankfurt where he immediately made contact with his old friends from NTS. Four days later I went to Frankfurt to visit him. I was particularly excited and anxious to see him, as he had played such a key role in the opening of my eyes about the Soviets.

Yury was thin and gaunt, but much the way I remembered, and he was already in love with a very pretty German-Russian girl, without success as usual! During my visit he told me what had happened. In 1947 he had been flown to Moscow and lodged in the Lubyanka prison, the KGB headquarters building. The Soviets considered him a fairly big catch, and he was personally interviewed by the deputy chief of the KGB, Abakumov, who told him that the Soviet regime destroyed its enemies. Now Yury was safe in Frankfurt while Abakumov and his boss, Beria, were shot in 1953.

In Lubyanka he was interrogated about all of the American officers of Russian origin he had known in Berlin, the Falkenried crowd, and many others, and he observed carefully as their dossiers were lifted off the shelf. The thickest, he said, was Sasha Sogolow's. Mine was the third thickest, about an inch and a half. The interrogator wanted to know whether I was there to organize the Georgian emigration in Berlin!

A few days later Yury came to Berlin and stayed with us. Since the house was full, he slept on the floor in the living room, quite happy after the conditions of Potma. He always wrapped a sheet tightly around his head, and when I passed him on my way to work in the morning, he always came out with some Dostoyevskian phrase like, "conscience is the most important thing!"

Those days resulted in a lot more detail on the eight year imprisonment, which he later published in a book. I drove him to his mother's grave, which he comtemplated in silence, and in silence too, he took the little keepsakes I had rescued from her apartment. He did not want to talk politics, perhaps because I was already converted, but he said one thing that stuck in my mind, "You Americans always overestimate the Soviets. Don't you understand that if you parachuted one platoon of American troops into Red Square, Molotov would be out there on his knees suing for peace!" At that time he may have been right.

Mostly Yury was interested in the parties we took him to, and managed to fall in love with an American girl, again without success. He no longer talked about vampires and werewolves.

My parents arrived in Berlin at this time. They had never seen Sasha, nor Marusya since the age of ten days, so I had sent them $1,000, which covered the whole trip and allowed for a stop over in London, where my mother had not been since 1927. She had not been to Germany since before World War I. I met them at the Frankfurt railroad station, Yury bowing stiffly like a 19th century pedagogue. My mother's anti-German feelings were as strong as ever. The sound of the language and even the uniforms of the railroad men almost made her sick. My father kept saying, "Calm down! Keep repeating to yourself—Brahms, Beethoven, Goethe and so forth!" It did little if any good.

Before going to Berlin we went south to Langenburg so my mother could see two cousins, Margarita of Hohenlohe-Langenburg, and her sister Theodora of Baden, both princesses of Greece by birth, and sisters of Prince Philip. Aunt Margarita ran a small and exclusive hotel in part of her palace, Schloss Langenburg, and took the edge off my mother's Germanophobia by serving us martinis in a little bar in her bedroom. Pleased as she was to see these cousins, Mama could not help noticing that it was not she, the long-lost cousin from the States, who had the place of honor at dinner, but, according to protocol, Theodora, the Grand Duchess of Baden, a frequent visitor. After all those years in New York and Cape Cod, the sight of pre-1918 protocol annoyed her.

On the American military train from Frankfurt to Berlin, my mother saw her first Soviet soldiers. They seemed so short to her, compared to the Imperial Army troops she remembered, but at least they weren't German!

Nell met us at the station and for two weeks my parents got acquainted with their grandchildren and shared our lives, including parties almost every night.

One party was given by Gambarov, now a hugely wealthy East-West trader, the same Armenian who had tried to peddle a 1939 Mercedes Benz for twenty-four cartons of cigarettes on my first night in Berlin. Now, accompanied by a strange staff—a Greek, an Estonian and a Persian, he could frequently be seen in the Mazurka night club, throwing large bills at the musicians. At his house the finest caviar was sculpted into the form of pheasants. Before one of these birds had been fully demolished, somebody mentioned that my mother was a Romanov, and the host and his multi-national staff immediately disappeared. Perhaps he was afraid this would hurt his commercial contacts in the East.

An infinitely more wholesome person was Dr. Wladimir Lindenberg, a Russian whose original name was Chelishchev. He and his wife, a concert pianist and sculptress, lived in a cozy cottage in a rural area of the French Sector. He was a brain surgeon and a latter-day Renaissance man—an artist and a student of all religions. His book, *Mediation and Mankind*, was published in English. Through him Nell and I met many interesting people, including Countess Yorck, the widow of one of the heroes of the July 20, 1944 conspiracy against Hitler. Volodya himself, though neither Jewish nor Communist, had been incarcerated in one of Hitler's camps from 1936 to 1943. Volodya and his wife adored Nell and Marusya, whose head she sculpted, and Volodya was stand-in godfather during Sasha's christening, which took place during my parents' stay.

The Lindenbergs arranged for my father to read from his new book, *Father Vikenty*, based on New York's Father Vasily, at their cottage. It happened that my father arrived first with an American friend of ours, Louise Prince, and was introduced as Prince Chavchavadze and Miss Prince. The audience was thoroughly confused—was Miss Prince his mistress, morganatic wife, daughter, or what? If there was a flaw in Volodya Lindenberg's character, it was over-adulation of titles.

We put my parents on the train on November 14, 1955. I doubt if they understood why I wanted to be in Berlin. They were happy on Cape Cod, with side trips to the south, California or Mexico.

At 11:00 one night a call came from the chief. "Meet me at Tempelhof, Dave!" he rumbled.

Before long I found myself sitting in a bare room, facing a sixteen year old boy called Valery Lysikov, who had walked into this U.S. Air Force installation and asked for political asylum. My first task was to get him to write out an asylum statement in his own words and sign it, which he did with alacrity. Then I questioned him. He was the son of a Soviet air force lieutenant-colonel, stationed in East Berlin. He attended a school for Soviet dependents there, where all the kids were crazy about everything western—music, jeans, gum and even the Pan Am planes which they could see from their classroom. All this western mania became commonplace later on, but this was the first I had seen of it.

We left Tempelhof in the Chief's car, he at the wheel and Valery and I in the back seat. The boss kept talking to me, in English, naturally, prompting Valery to say, "Our chauffeurs never stop talking either!" This rather broke me up, and the two-gun boss chuckled when I translated.

A few days later, after I had spent considerable time with Valery, feeding him all the gum he wanted, but not particularly encouraging him to stay in the West, there was a very painful interview with his parents at OMGUS headquarters in Dahlem. It was conducted by the State Department with me translating. I felt very sorry for his father, facing a ruined career, and equally for his mother, but Valery absolutely refused to go back.

I was the only American this poor couple could talk to, and the mother cursed me, "I hope you'll lose your son some day. Then you'll know how it feels!"

I was not to have a son for another eleven years, but I never forgot Mrs. Lysikov's curse.

Why didn't we force him to go back? Though his stories of how privileged teenagers acted and thought were a revelation to me, he had next to no information of intelligence value. But he was sixteen, the age at which a young Soviet receives his internal passport and is criminally liable as an adult, and he was adamant.

Valery's defection generated considerable publicity in the United States, and he began to receive fan mail, but after about two weeks in West Germany Valery did a 180 degree turn and now wanted to go home! I flew from Berlin to see him. He was totally and completely spouting the Soviet party line, as they all can do when they want to. He insisted that nothing would happen to him. It looked like he was bored with his teenage caper and homesick.

I had in my pocket one last fan letter from the States, which I handed to him and translated. It was from a teenage girl in Baltimore called Marsha Kappelman, who congratulated him on choosing freedom in a very warm, well-phrased way. Valery asked me to translate it again, and then, much to my surprise, sat down to answer it. His letter, devoid of any politics, went something like this: "Dear Marsha. Thank you for your very nice letter. I have decided to go home. Here is my address if you want to write me again." He included a Soviet address, probably his grandparents'.

I put a stamp on the letter and threw it into a mailbox, after taking my leave of Valery for the last time. He went back to the USSR. We put no obstacles in his way. I do not know what happened to him, but I hope that in that early Khrushchev period nothing terrible did happen; he was lucky he did not try his caper two years earlier under Stalin.

In Berlin, Ellery Husted would frequently show up without warning or give warning and then fail to appear. He was always coming back from Tehran on some architectural project, bringing caviar in large quantities, which we polished off with vodka at whatever time of day or night he arrived. He usually departed in disarray, reservations hopelessly garbled, shirts left behind with large sums of money in the pockets. This was always faithfully reported, but I was told to keep shirts and money. It was my good fortune that Ellery's clothes fitted me perfectly.

In the spring of 1954, when Nell was pregnant with Sasha and unable to drive long distances, she flew to Nice, while her mother and I drove out of Paris to meet her. Michelin in hand, Helen and I determined to hit every restaurant with at least one star conveniently located on our itinerary.

As luck would have it, it was lunch time when we got to Vienne, the location of the three-star Pyramides, then perhaps the best restaurant in France and hence the world. As we walked among the outside tables on this beautiful spring day, a gaggle of Berlin case officers greeted me with cheers and jeers.

"I'm his mother-in-law," Helen yelled, "not his mistress!"

We met Nell at Nice, spent an evening at the famous casino in Monte Carlo, and pushed on into Italy. We discovered the beautiful town of Portofino, and found rooms in the Albergo Nazionale, right in the center of things.

Incredibly, as we sat at an outside table admiring the harbor, a couple I knew from Cape Cod walked by, Brooks and Barbara Baekeland, with their young son Tony. We became fast friends, never dreaming that the day would come when this bright, attractive kid, Tony, would murder his mother with a kitchen knife. This murder in 1972 became famous in 1985 with the publication of *Savage Grace*, by Natalie Robins and Steen Aronson.

The following year, 1955, Nell and I went to Athens to stay with her Bennington friend Stella, then married to Peter Moutousis. We had a marvellous time with them, viewing the antiquities, swimming at the beaches, and making a side trip to the islands of Mikonos and Delos.

This was my first trip to Amama's beloved homeland, and on the first evening I went to the royal palace to sign the book, passing a sleepy Evzone and a neon crown. I was told that King Paul was in Corfu. Later, my mother received a rather annoyed letter from him, saying that if he had known I was coming to Greece I could have stayed with him in Corfu. At that point I regretted my custom of not bothering reigning relatives when I visited their countries!

Aunt Marina, the Duchess of Kent, also happened to be in Athens just then. Nell and I were staying in a second rate hotel and were having a drink at the bar, waiting for her to pick us up one evening. There was an Englishman there who was being extremely patronizing to us Americans. Suddenly a car a block long, flying

211

the Greek and British royal standards, drove up with the Duchess of Kent clearly visible in the back seat. I must admit to malicious pleasure as I said to the Englishman, "Nice to have talked to you. Our ride seems to be here."

Aunt Marina took us to a party at the Serpieris, a Greek family who had known my mother well in 1920. Remembering that time in England, Aunt Marina made sure there was a guitar there, and insisted on my singing. All this was most enjoyable until an old gentleman appeared. It was the admiral, Amama's second husband.

I had received instructions from my parents that in the unlikely event that I should meet him in Athens, I should be correct but cold. This was because of the problems regarding Amama's estate, including Apapa's coin collection, and it looked like the admiral was going to keep this. The old man and I could only communicate in French. I tried to be correct but cold, but how can you be cold to a man who, after all, had been married to your grandmother for many years? So our limited conversation was quite warm, though of no significance whatever. Strange, I had been deprived of both grandfathers, but had two step grandfathers—a Russian prince who had become a Communist, and a Greek commoner who was a staunch royalist, and no real communication with either of them.

Before leaving Athens, Nell and I made a call on Aunt Marina's mother, Princess Nicholas of Greece, who had been born a grand duchess of Russia, Helen Vladimirovna, sister of the pretender Grand Duke Cyril. She was then seventy-three years old, a lovely, gracious lady who still retained the beauty, rare among Romanov women, she had had as a young woman. We spoke Russian together—about the family, but mostly she wanted to hear what the Soviets were like. Nell, to whom the Moutousis had given curtsy lessons for this occasion, could only manage a barely perceptible movement of one buttock, which in no way upset the old lady, who was most impressed with Nell's Russian and her beauty.

Back in Berlin after this trip I met George Blake. No, thank God, he was not a friend of mine. In 1955 he was chief of Soviet operations in Berlin for the British MI-6, and already a Soviet spy. He was uncovered by a lead furnished by a defector, and eventually received forty-two years in jail, but escaped to sanctuary in Moscow along with the rest of that traitorous British colony there—Philby, Burgess and McLean.

On one rather typical evening of parties, I was taken to his apartment. It was November 19, 1955. Nell preferred to stay at home, but changed her mind and after I got home she called me from the Mazurka at three in the morning, and I actually joined her there to watch Gambarov and his aides doing their thing. My diary entry of this event was a great help later on in Washington, after Blake had been caught and named me, and my guitar, as one of the Americans he had met. Without it there might have been serious difficulties, because I could not remember him nor recognize his pictures, and yet he had named me.

The German mardis-gras rolled around again while Nell was skiing in Austria. I put on a quasi-Russian costume with a fur hat decorated with an Imperial Army *kokarda*, or cap insigna, and presently found myself in a beer joint where there was a large table occupied by about a dozen students from India. I spent about two hours with these pleasant chaps, speaking with a Russian accent. They showered me with questions about life in the USSR, which at first I answered non-commitally, with a little party line thrown in. They nodded with approbation, but with each new beer I grew drunker, both in real life and within the context of my performance, which I still consider a masterpiece. I began to uncover my disaffection with Soviet life, almost literally crying in my beer. They became more and more silent—thunderstruck. Of course, not one of them suggested that I should defect to the West while I had the chance. I really think, silly costume and all, that I made an impact on this group, who may have thought of me the next time Nehru told them to yell, *Russi-Hindi bhai-bhai.*

Very little has been said here about the Germans in Berlin. We saw a smattering of Prussian aristocrats, including a granddaughter of Bismarck, and a grandson of the double-bearded admiral of World War I, von Tirpitz, but we rarely went to their homes.

The small functionaries, official or non-official, were annoying. Nell complained that all Germans were amateur policemen, always telling you to keep off the grass or obey some sign. Somebody, Lenin perhaps, once said that even revolutionary Germans obeyed signs!

My connection with German officialdom was minimal, but I had to approach minor officials on a couple of occasions—first, to get a dog license, and second, to register Sasha's birth. Both times these characters, sitting behind glass partitions, barked at the public like drill sergeants, and at me too, until they realized that I was an American. This meant that I was part of the occupation and outranked them. Then all was obsequious politeness.

On the other hand, the Berlin workers we encountered—repair men, gardners, taxi drivers and the like, were pleasant, humorous, and seemingly totally without class consciousness. In Nazi times, I have been told, the Berlin proletariat was extremely cynical about the regime, demonstratively saying *Guten Tag* to each other instead of the prescribed Heil Hitler!

We had two moments of great solidarity with the Germans while we were in Berlin. The first time was in honor of the victims of the June 17, 1953 anti-Communist uprising, and the second was when Ernst Reuter, the magnificent Lord Mayor of Berlin, died. He belonged to an extinct breed—a staunchly anti-Communist Social Democrat. He even spoke Russian and used to broadcast to the Soviet troops. At his death all Berliners, ourselves included, put candles in our windows.

As our tour of duty in Berlin grew to an end in 1956, I made a short trip to London. I saw some old friends for what was to be last time. Unfortunately, there was no time to go to Dorset to see Babady, but on a late afternoon at a London pub I called Aunt Marina, Duchess of Kent, at Kensington Palace.

She told me to appear immediately, but not without a guitar! I have no recollection of how I scraped up that guitar, but I took a taxi with it to Kensington Palace. We drove up to the palace where Queen Victoria had lived when she was called to the throne in 1837, and I was sent to the tradesman's entrance because I was carrying a guitar! Taking that route would have been interesting, but I was afraid it might embarrass the servants, so I did what I do only on strategic occasions—dropped my title and last name. This was enough to get me into the front door.

We did a lot of eating, drinking and singing. Princess Alexandra was now an extremely attractive young woman of twenty, and our mutual cousin, Princess Elizabeth of Yugoslavia, equally attractive, was also there.

Princess Elizabeth was the daughter of Princess Olga of Greece—a sister of Princess Marina—and of Prince Paul of Yugoslavia. Prince Paul had served as regent during the minority of his nephew, King Peter II, from 1934 until 1941 when he was overthrown by a coup d'état. Princess Elizabeth later became the mother of the movie actress Catherine Oxenberg.

Alexandra whispered to me, "How exciting to have a cousin in the American secret service!"

This gave me a bit of a pause, but it was easier to explain than old Peter Troubetzkoy's shot in the dark. Somebody must have checked me out with British Intelligence!

Marina went to bed on the early side, and soon put an end to our carousing by banging her feet, or a stick, on the floor of her room, which was just above us. I never saw her again. She died in 1968.

I also went out to Hampton Court for what was to be my last visit to Aunt Xenia, the Emperor's sister, who was then eighty-one. She did not live in the palace, but in a cottage right next to the famous maze. As usual, a rozy-cheeked nun called Mother Marfa tried to control access to the grand duchess, but fortunately she was partial to young men!

"Only ten minutes, not one minute more!" commanded Mother Marfa.

I emerged an hour and a half later. Aunt Xenia, who had numerous grandchildren all of whom called her Amama, told me to call her Aunt Amama, not being used to being addressed as Xenia in any form. She looked a littler shorter and older, but not so different from my previous visits, nor from my memory of her from 1927. She was fascinated to hear my stories about the Soviets I had met, and in general was very interested in the political situation. Every so often she would finish a cigarette and with unerring aim shoot it into a little spittoon on the floor a few feet from her desk. She was so busy debriefing me that there was no time for questions from me! There were so many I would have liked to ask—about her father, Alexander III, her brothers, her husband, Uncle Sandro, and about Apapa and Amama. It would have been fascinating to have her voice on tape. While I was with her I thought, this is almost like talking to the sister of Louis XVI, her brother's reign seemed so remote.

Farewell parties started long before our departure date. Once again, for the third time, I had to leave Berlin, and it wrenched my heart, and I sang that tear-jerking song about a peasant boy about to be drafted—"*Posledniy nyneshnya denyochek; Gulyayu s vami ya druzya. . . .*" (For one last day, my friends, I am partying with you.)

After three and a half years, our house at Sophie Charlotte Strasse 32A was closed, the army asking for $36 in damages. Not bad, after all that wear and tear. I sat on the front steps with tears streaming down my face. It was a real turning point, the end of a wonderful epoch, again the end of Berlin, and, most important, the realization that my marriage to Nell had become extremely shaky.

214

On our last day in Berlin, the British Brigade was good enough, coincidentally, to arrange a Queen's Birthday parade for us. It was fitting to end all my Berlins with a parade, especially by the British, the undisputed world champs in this sort of thing. I mean, who could beat the Brigadier's command—"*For Her Majesty the Queen, Feu de joie!*" and the whole brigade fired its rifles!

On June 1, 1956, exactly five years after my arrival in Germany for the CIA, we took off from Tempelhof. These were still the old propeller days, and the trip from Berlin to New York took a little more than twenty-four hours, but nobody cared because of those blessed Pullman births which allowed us to sleep.

JUDY CLIPPINGER CHAVCHAVADZE with sister SALLY

CHAPTER XIII

From Idewild Airport, now JFK, the Husteds whisked us to Mt. Kisco, where they had acquired a house. Relatives on both sides of the family arrived for their first glimpse of Marusya and Sasha.

A lot had changed in the States in five years. I was particularly staggered by the huge air-conditioned supermarkets. Twenty years later I could still empathize with a new emigration from the Soviet Union as it came face to face with this cornucopia. One lady in Chicago had to be driven all over the city before she was convinced that the supermarket in her new neighborhood was not a Potemkin village specially erected by the U.S. Government to impress the likes of her.

Leaving the family in Mt. Kisco, I took a sleeper to Washington to report for duty in the sweltering heat. As I was shaving in the office washroom an old friend from Camp Ritchie and Berlin dashed in.

"All leaves cancelled," he yelled. "You're going to work for me. I asked for you specially!"

Now this was a real compliment. Nevertheless, to his disgust, I told him that I intended to take the home leave I had coming. This washroom meeting was the start of five years of fascinating, very active and productive work, something that with my Berlin snobbism I could not have imagined existed in Washington.

When the Pennsylvania Railroad sleeper pulled into Union Station, I had had no idea where I was going to sleep that night, but there was no problem. Old friends offered beds, later apartments, and soon I was sitting a house in Georgetown. I scouted out areas where my friends lived, and took an immediate dislike to those early Virginia suburbs, with identical houses and yards stretching out in all directions, and a ghastly commute waiting every morning. No wonder they were all trying to get overseas again.

The action was obviously in Georgetown, within walking distance of so many friends and a short distance from the office. Georgetown was not yet polluted by a notorious M Street strip, nor too expensive for the likes of us. Nell arrived for a visit and within a day found a house on 36th Street, opposite Trinity Church. It was small but attractive, had three floors and three bedrooms, and rented for $150 per month. That was a quarter of my take home pay, but it was worth it.

The summer ended in Wellfleet where, on August 28, Marusya's third birthday was celebrated outdoors around a table built of boards and cinder blocks, with various children of the right age wearing silly hats. This became a tradition, and for several years my father and I would fetch extra cinder blocks as Marusya and the other children grew.

After Labor Day our life in Washington really began. The Husteds settled in, and there were few nights without parties somewhere. It was not Berlin, but we all still had this kind of energy. The children, who could still speak nothing but

German, went to a nursery school run by a German called Miss Keppler, who loved them for it. Nevertheless, it soon disappeared under the influence of their peers, whose favorite phrase seemed to be, "Don't you speak English?" This seemed to be a syndrome among American children, even in an international place like Georgetown.

Aside from the great change it brought us, 1956 was a year of extraordinary political significance. At the XX Congress of the Communist Party, Khrushchev denounced Stalin as one of the bloodiest tyrants of all time. It is impossible to overestimate the effect this had on the while country, and particularly on the younger generation, brought up to believe that Stalin—after Lenin, of course—was the greatest man who ever lived. Khrushchev's speech also set off a period of optimism and some relaxation, now remembered as "The Thaw."

My Yale classmate, John Hanes, had become a special assistant to Secretary of State John Foster Dulles, the architect of our foreign policy at the time. On July 19, I was supposed to meet Johnnie for lunch at the Secretary's office. I walked in a little early. The doors to Dulles' inner office were open, and through them I saw Dulles pacing back and forth the length of the room, his hands clasped behind his back, a very grim and glowering expression on his face. It was a face rarely photographed smiling, but now it looked so worried that my immediate reaction was that something very serious had taken place. Later, Johnnie told me that seconds before my arrival Dulles had concluded a meeting with the Egyptian Ambassador, and had refused him American support for the construction of the Aswan Dam.

This was a very important turning point, because the Soviets immediately offered to build the dam for Nasser, and for years had the upper hand in Egypt as a result. The Soviets were eventually kicked out, and the Aswan Dam itself had unforeseen and very unfortunate ecological results. But that day I could see that Dulles was deeply concerned about a pivotal decision that could no longer be taken back.

On October 23 the Hungarian revolution broke out. My memories of what had happened in Berlin and East Germany were still fresh, and again, as in 1953, Eisenhower and Dulles, who had campaigned for a "roll-back" of communism, not just containment of it, did nothing, not even placing the troops in Germany on alert. I am convinced that a little toughness on the part of the United States could have freed Hungary then, particularly in view of the confusion in the Soviet Union caused by the new leadership and its rejection of Stalin.

After six days all this became academic. The British, French and Israelis invaded Egypt because Nasser had closed the Suez Canal, and dear old Anthony Eden, not one of my heroes, obviously chose the moment because the Soviets were occupied in Hungary. The Hungarians be damned! He was the one who pushed through the forced repatriation of anti-Soviet Russians as early as 1944, as a good will gesture toward Stalin. Eden may have been a great foreign minister in 1938, but to me he personifies whatever truth there is in the old adage, "perfidious Albion!"

The British-French military operation against Suez was a pitiful mess, while the Israelis as usual did well. Eisenhower and Dulles exploded with wrath against their allies, in contrast to their timidity with the Soviets. They had a moral point, perhaps, but meanwhile Hungary went down the drain. On November 3 fresh Soviet troops hit Budapest, violating the promise of smiling, supposedly liberal and cultured Ambassador Yury Andropov, who smiled again as Imre Nagy and General Pal Maleter were led off to their executions. On their bones he built his career as head of the KGB and General Secretary of the Communist Party.

It was all over. On TV I watched my old Berlin friend Spencer Barnes bringing Cardinal Mindzenty into the American Legation, where he was to live for many years. Still, on November 7, in a spasm of idiotic wishful thinking, I wrote in my diary, "39th and last anniversary of the October Revolution."

In the middle of the Hungarian and Suez mess, the election of 1956 was reaching its climax—Eisenhower running for a second term against Adlai Stevenson. I had voted for Stevenson in 1952; now, although his PR men had forced him to be less witty and egghead, I was still for him, despising Eisenhower and Dulles for their lack of action in the rebellions of Berlin in 1953 and Hungary in 1956, and the hypocrisy of their "roll-back" campaign in 1952. They kept quiet about this in 1956. On November 6 Ike won by a landslide. The day before, feeling like Rhett Butler joining the Confederate Army in 1865, I contributed a little money to Stevenson's campaign. It turned out that Helen Husted knew him, and, typically, said to him at a wedding in Ohio, "I can't imagine why, but my daughters and their husbands all voted for you." As a result, I got a scribbled note of thanks for "gallantry in action" on one of Adlai's visiting cards.

Years later a Soviet bloc diplomat, not a Hungarian, was to say to me, "The trouble with your rulers is they play too much golf!"

"What do you mean?"

"I mean we were all ready to rise with Hungary, but Eisenhower was on the golf course."

Or perhaps ruining the floor of the Oval office with his cleats.

In the middle of the Hungarian-Suez drama, Nell started working as a receptionist for the Tunisian Embassy, and we socialized quite a bit with the deputy chief of mission there, Habib Bourguiba, Jr., son of the president and future foreign minister.

Our parties were enriched by a North African presence, including two attractive cousins of Egypt's King Farouk, brought to us by my old Circassian-American friend, Murat Natirboff.

One quite evening in Georgetown was enlivened by the sudden appearance of a Russian friend with a relative of Emperor Haile Selassie of Ethopia in tow. In Russian he whispered to me, "Call him Imperial Highness, and if you have to call him a cousin, don't call him an illegitimate cousin!"

I was surprised at this Russian's knowing this Georgian family joke of ours. Since our ancestors, the Bagration dynasty of Georgia, claimed descent from Solomon, we used to call Haile Selassie our 'illegitimate' cousin since he claimed the same descent, but from a one night stand with the Queen of Sheba. I did not call His Imperial Highness a bastard, but I told him the Bagrations' claim, and he seemed to take it at face value, which nobody else does. He showed us movies of Haile Selassie's 25th Jubilee on the throne.

An appearance was made by an international VIP, Prince Alexander Makinsky, known as Shura in the family. He was married to a distant Georgian relative of mine, and found me by calling Allen Dulles, our director, whom he knew, as he had known Wild Bill Donovan and practically everybody else.

"Of course you know my nephew, David Chavchavadze," he said to Dulles.

"Of course," Dulles replied, wildly waiving to his secretary to find this guy, whoever he was, in the bowels of the organization.

Shura was in charge of the European branch of Coca Cola, and liked to be called "Uncle Coke!" Ironically, another Russian, "Popka" Podlessky, one of our boarders in New York in my childhood, and later an officer at Camp Ritchie, was in charge of Pep;si Cola.

When Uncle Coke was asked what he thought of Pepsi Cola he would always reply, "Pepsi Cola? What's that?"

Eventually these two fought for a Soviet concession and Pepsi Cola won. During this process Shura returned to the Soviet Union to fight for Coke. He was really a Persian, his family having been the Khans of Maku, but, as many Persians were in those days, he was brought up in Imperial Russia and was the first of his family to convert to Christianity. He had been educated in one of the two outstanding civilian schools in Russia, Pravovedeniye, really a law school and one which gave its graduates automatic civil service rank at graduation.

On his first flight back to Leningrad, as it is now called, he was the only passenger in the compartment and he heard the two Aeroflot stewardesses argue over which one was to serve him.

"I guess we have to serve that type there."

"You go."

"No, it's your turn!"

Finally, one of them approached Shura and said in English, "You vant vodka or cognac?" She almost fainted on hearing Shura reply in his fabulous pre-revolutionary accent, "It depends when, and with what."

In Leningrad Shura found that his old house was essentially unchanged, including the apartment in which he had lived with his parents and a brother. They had a bathroom and there was another bathroom for the two servants. The only difference was that now fifty-two people lived there, still using the same two bathrooms with their excellent, but ancient, British plumbing.

In his Leningrad hotel Shura noticed that there was a very gentlemanly looking maitre d'hotel, who spoke several languages. They would bow and exchange a few words. Shura made a point of never reserving a table in advance. On his second trip to Leningrad the man was no longer at the hotel, and Shura inquired about him.

"Oh, you mean so-and-so," was the answer. "He died a few months ago."

Hearing the man's name for the first time, Shura realized that this was an old classmate from the Pravovediniye school. They had not recognized each other.

Since we are back in Imperial Russia again, it is a good time to introduce Washington's Uncle Sergei Sheremetyev, or Cheremetieff, as he spelled it, French style. He was about eighty when I returned from Berlin. He was one of the few people related to both my father and mother, being a grandson of that Stroganov who married Nicholas I's daughter. As a child he spent much time in the family of Alexander III, and thus knew Nicholas II and his brothers and sisters from childhood. Interestingly enough, he frequently complained to me that his relationship with the Imperial Family had been harmful to his career. Nicholas II, who was emperor when Uncle Sergei graduated from the naval academy in 1898, bent over backwards not to show favoritism, while the promotion boards tended to favor people less well-connected and rich than the Sheremetyevs. Thus Uncle Sergei felt that he had been a failure, being stuck at the rank of full colonel in World War I.

The Sheremetyevs were an old and famous Moscow Boyar family. Uncle Sergei belonged to the senior branch which was untitled, and would get very annoyed if anyone called him "count," the title of the junior branch. The junior branch had had thousands of serfs before emancipation in 1861, including a brilliant serf theatre. All the Sheremetyevs I have known were very proud that the head of the family had fallen in love with one of the serf actresses and married her. Her name was Praskovia, a name which they repeated in each generation, and wrote songs about this unusual romance.

This Count Sheremetyev once wanted to go to Vienna, but realized that his wife could not be presented at that snobbish court, which demanded sixteen quarterings of nobility, not peasantry. The emperor came to the rescue—probably Nicholas I, it sounds like him. He ordered the Office of Heraldry to produce a phony family tree for Praskovia. He would be damned, he said, if he would let the Habsburgs snub one of the cream of Russian nobility just because he had married a Russian peasant girl, and such a beautiful and talented one at that.

Uncle Sergei, after six years service in the navy, found himself in Port Arthur when the Japanese attacked in 1904. He transferred to the army and was on the staff of General Kuropatkin, the ground force commander, and leter he commanded a company of the senior guards regiment, the Preobrazhensky, in St. Petersburg. Another transfer brought him into the diplomatic corps and to the Russian Embassy in Constantinople, in charge of looking after the interests of Orthodox Christians in the Ottoman Empire and Mount Athos.

Hearing all this, and being familiar with the workings of the U.S. government, I was amazed at the flexibility of the old Russian government. This was not all. Uncle Sergei switched to civil service and was attached to Prime Minister Stolypin during the latter's dramatic land reforms that would have altered the face of Russia if they had not been interrupted by war and revolution. When Stolypin was assassinated in Kiev in 1911, Uncle Sergei lunged at the assassin with his sword, but missed. In 1914, back in the army, Uncle Sergei became military governor of Galicia, the West Ukraine, just captured from the Austrians. Later he was chief of medical services for one of the field armies. Even given the flexibility of the establishment, I doubt whether any one individual ever had such a varied career. The trouble was that he would not talk about it much. He was much too interested in current affairs, including Washington politics, and he had this complex about not having been a general.

Sergei had kept extensive diaries, but the ones covering the Russian period were lost in the revolution, leaving only the years he had spent as an emigré in France raising rabbits. I was not very interested in the market price of *les lapins* in the 1930s.

Uncle Sergei lived with an elderly American wife, whom he called Kuku. I believe she was a Baltimorean, comfortably off. Kuku stayed home in a wheel chair, but Uncle Sergei could be encountered in some of the best salons in Washington, very much up to date on what was going on. He liked to spend time with me, calling me, "thrice-related David," and insisting that I play chess with him. I am a terrible player, but once or twice I managed to beat the old man, which he recorded in his diary including the precise moves that had led to the checkmate. I valued these evenings for the interesting details he dropped about the old days, which I would type up when I got home. Some of the stories he related were:

King Edward VII had a great deal of finesse. Once in Marienbad he ran into Olga and Michael, the sister and brother of Nicholas II, who were going to Italy by train. The king ordered Lord Fisher to send the battleship *HMS Empress of India* to carry them to Genoa. This was a shrewd move because of the joint German-Italian naval maneuvers then being held. The maneuvers had to stop temporarily while everybody saluted the British ship carrying Russian grand-ducal standards, an early indication of British-Russian solidarity. Uncle Sergei encountered King Edward VII many times, and each time the king would tip his hat and make flattering remarks about Uncle Sergei's father, which convinced Uncle Sergei that the king had an incredible memory.

Uncle Sergei saw the Emperor Franz Josef of Austria in 1896, and was impressed by the cold protocol surrounding him, compared to the much more informal Russian court. Even when approached by an archduke—a Habsburg relative—Franz Josef would address him in the third person.

Archduke, *"Ihrer königlicher, kaiserlicher, apostolicher Majestät gehorsam melden. . . ."*

Franz Josef to court official, *"Sagen Sie diesem Mensch. . . ."*

("Obediently addressing your royal, imperial, apostolic Majesty. . . ."

"Tell this person. . . .")

The Kegsholm Regiment of the Russian Imperial Guard always had an Austrian honorary colonel. Alexander III always wore his Austrian uniform as working clothes, to wear it out quicker.

On his deathbed in 1888, the German Emperor Wilhelm I said the word, "Kaluga," which nobody around him understood. The reason was that in his youth the emperor had commanded a battalion of the Russian Kaluga Regiment during the 1813 campaign against Napoleon and had won the St. George's cross, with which he wanted to be buried.

Life in the Preobrazhensky Regiment, the oldest in the Guards, was a mixture of elegance and simplicity. The waiters, retired soldiers, wore plain Russian shirts, but the officers' mess had a silver service for 120. There was a lot of property to administer, which detracted from soldiering. The Third Company had a large rowboat to commemorate the time when Peter the Great had loaded a company from each of three guard regiments—the Preobrazhensky, Semenovsky and Kegsholm—in the boats to storm a Swedish warship. These companies still wore Peter's initials on their epaulets. The boat was a lot of trouble to maintain, even though it was only used rarely.

Uncle Sergei's company was the one closest to the Winter Palace, hence it was often subject to inspections by important visitors. In peace time a company numbered seventy men, the whole regiment having a strength of 1200-1400. The regiment had a rare collection of 18th century books, and Uncle Sergei was the library officer. During the regimental feast day, August 6th, the regiment was usually on maneuvers, but a beg tent was set up for the officers to celebrate the occasion. Nicholas II, who had served in the regiment, would always attend, sometimes sitting on the right of the commander, sometimes at the head of the table. All the guard regiments had trouble keeping their non-coms, who were offered more lucrative positions such as doormen and janitors.

Uncle Sergei was received by Nicholas II's brother, Michael, while the latter was dressing for the centenary of the 1812 battle of Borodino. Michael talked about Edward VII's funeral when he, though second in line to the Russian throne, was bumped to number fifty-two by the arrival of Wilhelm, II and a whole platoon of reigning German princes and heirs. Michael walked with two other doomed bumpees—Archduke Franz Ferdinand of Austria and the Turkish heir apparent.

My grandfather, Apapa, also attended the Borodino centenary. Some peasants in the area claimed to be old enough to remember the battle, and they were brought to the reviewing stand. "Did you see Napoleon?" asked Nicholas II.

"Yes, Your Imperial Majesty," one old man replied.

"What did he look like?"

"Oh, he was a healthy one, all right—a really tall muzhik with a long beard!"

Said Uncle Sergei, "The Emperor did not like me and hence was ultra-correct and helpful to me. He always discussed serious subjects with me, but only once took me into his confidence, when he told me a certain minister would be relieved three months before the fact. He hardly ever spoke critically of anyone. Once he expressed his anger that Grand Duke Dimtri Constantinovich was indulging in un-grand-ducal horse trading with Jewish merchants. I should have asked Uncle Sergei whether horse trading with non-Jewish merchants would have been all right.

In 1915 the Minister of War, Sazonov, told Uncle Sergei a military secret. The Allies planned to force the Dardanelles, and when this happened, Uncle Sergei would be the Russian representative for civil affairs and military government. All of history would have been changed, said Uncle Sergei, if the Allied fleet had persevered the first day. The Turks were down to sixteen rounds per gun. The supply line to Russia would have been opened and this would probably have prevented the revolution.

"Stolypin discovered me," Uncle Sergei said, "because of my work in the zemstvo local governments. He made me Governor of Volhinia. While I was there, some revolutionaries held a congress there, but I was instructed not to interfere because the police had them so well penetrated."

Uncle Sergei and Kuku moved to Rome in the 1960s. I visited them in 1967, not long before his death. He was amusing himself by doing research on the short-term capture of Rome by Russian marines in 1799, and also by using his pass to the pornographic vault of the Vatican library. The old man had a touch of S&M in his character, though Kuku seemed an unlikely object for this.

He took me to lunch in the Piazza Navona, the site of chariot races and probable horrors, and told me stories while he ate brains and mushrooms, sipping wine and soda. As we drove around in a taxi he pointed out places where Russian authors had lived, and when we passed the American Embassy I realized that to him it was still the palace of Queen Margherita—twice a Savoy, my dear boy—with whom he had taken tea in that familiar building in 1907. To the end, Uncle Sergei refused to write memoirs, regarding himself as a failure.

As 1956 was about to disappear into history, I attended my first office Christmas party in Washington. The old tempo buildings somehow provided a party atmosphere that the new Langley building never did. Our division took pride in throwing the best parties. There was a lot of Russian singing, but our specialty was the *charochka*, the ceremonial drink with its chorus of *pey do dna*! (Bottoms up!) I guess I introduced it that year, and was in demand at the front office, where our chief, John M. Maury, Jr. liked to slug visiting VIPs with musical vodkas. That was how I finally met Allen Dulles. He was at the wrong end of one of my *charochkas*.

Jack Maury ran a very happy shop. In those days a case officer would think nothing of having a casual lunch with the division chief or calling him by his first name. As a marine officer, Jack had been stationed in Murmansk during the war, and he and I had a good natured fight about Russian history, lasting for years. He considered the Soviet regime a continuation of Imperial Russia, and thought the KGB had been founded by Ivan the Terrible. He considered the Bolsheviks a brake against a worse danger—unleashed Russian imperialism, unhindered by Soviet inefficiency. But to his credit, Jack never tried to apply his theory to operations, which would have been disastrous.

I missed Jack's parties when I attended my first one at Langley in 1965. The architecture of the place was just not right for it. The euphoria of the old days was gone. *Charochkas* were encouraged, but it was not the same. Director Richard Helms, who used to knock them down in the old buildings, actually tried to refuse one. He finally took it, obviously not pleased. Let's give him credit—maybe he was on his way to the White House or something.

Beginning with the summer of 1956, Khrushchev opened the Soviet Union to foreign tourism, and thousands of Americans went, including people of my own background. By 1960 practically all of my friends and relatives had been there and I began to feel deprived. There was no way the CIA would let me go. I was too "blown" from the years in Berlin.

Many friends of mine went as guides to the American exhibition at Sokolniki. These Russian-speaking guides were so interesting to the Soviet population that they could have stood on an open field, with no exhibition at all, and still been mobbed by Russians eager for every bit of information they could get about the United States.

Individual tourists who spoke Russian were also surrounded on the street by friendly crowds, who often gave the bum's rush to the inevitable agitators present. Their function was to stick Americans with embarrassing questions.

"What about your Negro problem?"

This was indeed a hard one to deal with on a street corner. One of my friends fixed his agitator with a stare and said, "As is well known, there are no Negroes in the United States!"

There was a moment of silence, and then the whole crowd burst into laughter. They recognized the phrase "as is well known" as the lead-in phrase used by Pravda as a preface to some big lie.

All the Americans were amazed at the warmth and friendship they encountered, in spite of all the years of anti-American propaganda. Or perhaps one should say because of it. The adulation of everything American, which I had first glimpsed when Valery Lysikov defected in Berlin, was in full swing. It was enough for an American to hum or whistle *Lullaby in Birdland* on Gorky Street to attract a crowd of these *stilyagi*, or style boys.

It was terribly frustrating to hear of all this and not be able to experience it. For the first time I had twinges of regret about my career. In the Foreign Service I could have been stationed in Moscow. Anywhere outside the CIA I could have gone as a tourist. Even two of my Romanov cousins went. Vladimir Tolstoy went to the USSR five or six times during this period. He found relatives there and even discovered an obscure suburb of Moscow, colloquially dubbed "Tsarskoye Selo," where a group of overlooked and unslaughtered old titled and noble families lived—people their relatives in the West had given up for dead. These included grandchildren of Leo Tolstoy and Chehkov, and members of the princely families of Volkonsky, Gagarin and Vasilchikov.

Judy Clippinger, my future second wife, went in the fall of 1957, a time of little tourism. With her blond hair and high cheekbones, she easily passed for a Russian if she put a kerchief on her head. Having dealt with Russian refugees in Munich some years earlier, she could communicate quite well in the language. This led to some interesting situations. People pushed and shoved her as if she were one of their own. A simple statement that she was an American would always stop this sort of thing. In spite of all the security, with this light disguise, Judy actually managed to march by Khrushchev and Company, standing on the Lenin mausoleum, on the 40th anniversary of the October Revolution. I have never heard of any other foreigner who succeeded in doing this. The people who march by the leaders in Red Square are all parts of carefully controlled groups.

Judy also went to Georgia. In Tblisi nobody would serve her a drink, she being a woman alone. She also went to Tsinandali where she entertained the locals by playing the piano so late that she had to spend the night there. The Intourist chauffeur refused to drive in the dark, or else had had his fill of Tsinandali wine.

In March of 1957 I took a train to Fort Bragg, North Carolina for two weeks active duty in the reserves to attend a course given by the Green Berets. There were then two battalions of this recently formed elite force, one of them in Germany. The only trouble was some ridiculous general at Fort Bragg would not let the battalion there wear green berets! Can you imagine a British general forbidding the Argyles to wear kilts?

This was the first time I had worn a major's insignia and the new green uniform with scrambled eggs on the hats of field-grade officers. Much to the delight of the regular army captain who checked me in, I had my oak leaves on pointing the wrong way. I should have known better than to accept advice from Sasha Sogolow, also a major, on this subject. Not long before he had turned up in a uniform that was a time warp going back to World War II—brown shoes, the old pinks and greens, a fifty-mission crush in his hat, a tan tie with a gold pin, and of course his oak leaves on backwards, though I didn't notice this. They took one look at him in the Pentagon and sent him back for civilian clothes. Sasha was crushed. He was always very clothes-conscious. Once at Brooks Brothers he tried to buy a preppy sport coat, only to be told, "It's not your style, sir." He was very crestfallen, but felt better when Brooks Brothers sent him a Christmas card.

Even with a proper uniform it was bad enough at Fort Bragg. Anybody without paratroop boots was called a "leg," definitely a second-class citizen. In the Green Beret course an instructor in Class A uniform would sometimes say, "I will meet the class at drop zone so-and-so in twenty minutes, and somehow in that short stretch of time would manage to change, get in a plane and jump out to meet us "legs," who had arrived by bus. Frankly, I have never had the slightest desire to jump out of planes. Master Sergeant Valentin Pavlov felt the same way. I had known him in Germany. Now he was in a psychological warfare company. This was much more to my taste. In that company street one could see a squad of soldiers in Soviet Army uniforms marching by, all of them defectors.

The two week course was interesting, with lots of demonstrations of demolitions and play-acting of Green Beret contact with local partisans. The lesson of separating peoples from regimes was well taught. For instance:

"Our only mission here is to kill Russians!" Green Beret officer.

""What do you mean? I am a Russian," replies Partisan leader.

"Oops, sorry, I mean communists."

But the Green Beret doctrine at that time was strangely a-political. They expected to leave politics to the CIA and the State Department, though it was not clear how this was to be done. Another example:

Roumanian partisan leader, "Before I work with you I want to be sure that you support the restoration of King Peter!"

"We are not here to get involved in local politics."

I raised my hand, "The name of the King of Roumania is Michael," I said.

Loud laughs from my fellow students, most of them from the Agency. Smirks from the Green Berets.

When I got home to Washington my parents were there and I had to tell them there was no hope for my marriage with Nell. Shortly after that we decided on a separation.

From 1956 to 1961 I made frequent short trips within the United States, once all the way to Midway Island. All I can say about the latter is that I was surrounded by "gooney birds," a species of albatross, who sat around looking benevolent on every spare piece of earth on the island. Occasionally one would get up, spread its seven-foot wings, and do some sort of mating dance. The habits of these creatures were the sole topic of conversation among the Navy folk who inhabited the place.

Whenever I complained to the branch chief about his frequent trips to Europe, he would put me down with, "Well, you went to Midway, didn't you?"

I could not complain too much, since my trips to New York and Boston gave me a chance to renew old ties. How different life in New York was from Washington. For instance, at a party given by Francine du Plessix I stumbled across the following notables: Marlene Dietrich, Tennessee Williams, Yale acquaintances

Peter Gimbel of future Andrea Doria diving fame, the publisher Tom Ginsburg, squiring the actress Rita Gam, and of course Francine's stepfather, Alexander Lieberman, himself a celebrity in New York art and publishing circles.

I had known Francine for several years, and had once taken her to a Yale-Harvard football game in New Haven. Bill Coffin's mother was very generous about putting my dates up at her house, and did so with Francine. I warned Francine that she was to meet the world's most perfect young man, namely Bill, which was how I regarded him at that time. At the end of the weekend, Francine said, "I don't think Ned is all that perfect," referring to Bill's older brother. I have to admit a little *Schadenfreude* on this one, because Bill, ever since he had learned Russian had been out-singing me, and out-everything-elsing me, and I was somewhat envious and at times jealous of him.

Francine du Plessix Grey went on to become a well known writer. As for Bill, after leaving the Agency he became a minister and started on his road to fame with the chaplaincy first of Andover and then of Yale. I visited him and his wife Eva in both places, stayed with them, and we remained fast friends and political allies. When he came to Washington, his old CIA colleagues always gave parties for him. To his credit, his cloth did not prevent him from whooping it up with us as in the old days in Germany.

The main advantage of going to Boston was that I could often time them to spend the weekend with my parents in Wellfleet.

My mother's best friend was Elena Wilson. I remember her husband Edmund from childhood, when he was married to Mary McCarthy, whom I recall as very good-looking and pleasant. It was only later I realized how intelligent and talented she was. Edmund, whom almost everyone called "Bunny," had become disillusioned with the Soviets much earlier than most of the American intelligentsia. He had learned Russian well enough to read all the classics in the original, even feeling capable of arguing with Vladimir Nabokov on fine points of translation. The only trouble was that he could not speak it. My mother gave him lessons with little effect. Only once did he speak a Russian phrase to me. I had brought a very pretty girl into his home, and he was always aware of pretty girls. He came out with a phrase praising her looks, grammatically correct, mid-19th century in style, and hideously pronounced.

Wilson's daughter, Rosalind, is one of the brightest and most amusing people I know. We had been friends since we were teenagers. It was my mother who introduced Wilson to his fourth and last wife, Elena Mumm Thornton, a beautiful statuesque blonde, Russian on her mother's side and able to speak fair Russian. On her father's side she was a member of the Mumm Champagne family.

During this 1957-58 period, Elena's uncle, Walter Mumm, was in residence at the Wilson's Wellfleet house. He had fought in the German Army in World War I and had had the bad luck to be captured by the only Russian brigade on the Western Front, dispatched there for the sake of Allied solidarity. He spoke English with a classical German accent. A sense of humor was not his strong point. Edmund took advantage of this.

"Walter," he would say quite often, knowing what the result would be, "what do you think of American champagne?

Uncle Walter always went into a slow, rapidly increasing burn.

"How many times do I have to tell you, Edmund, zere is no American champagne, only shparkling vine!"

Now that I was grown up, Wilson took an interest in me. The break came when I spotted a quotation from the science fiction writer H. P. Lovecraft in Wilson's play, *The Little Blue Light*. Lovecraft had been in the habit of addressing his friends as "Monstro," so this became a form of address between Wilson and me. My father insisted that I say, "Sir Monstro."

Wilson was also interested in my ideas about the Soviet Union. Every time I was in Wellfleet I was invited to his sanctum-sanctorum library to discuss the latest developments. I gave him a copy of *Dr. Zhivago* in Russian, printed in Holland, which excited him greatly.

"Nina," Elena Wilson would call and say, "please send David over. Edmund wants to play Dr. Zhivago with him."

We compared the original with the translation and found a lot of errors. He tried out his theory about Pasternak's intentions on me, such as that the whole thing was an allegory of the legend of St. George. Not knowing much about St. George, I could only listen with somewhat doubtful interest.

Edmund Wilson was very helpful to my father in his writing, although Papa would sometimes get annoyed when Wilson would say, "Volodya would have done it this way."

Volodya—Vladimir Nabokov—always inadvertently turned up to scoop my father. His memoirs of Russia, for instance, were published in the New Yorker at a time when my father's could have been. Eventually, Edmund Wilson and Nabokov became involved in a famous literary quarrel, and Edmund no longer cited Volodya as an example to be followed. It was Wilson who was responsible for my father's getting the contract to translate the second book of Stalin's daughter, *Only One Year*.

Ironically, when Nabokov's novel *Lolita*, so long banned in the States and smuggled in from France, hit the best seller list, it was edged out by Pasternak's *Dr. Zhivago*. Nabokov did not take this lightly. According to his son, who visited me once in Georgetown, Nabokov thought there was something very fishy about *Dr. Zhivago*, perhaps a KGB provocation.

In Washington, or rather McLean, Virginia, I had lunch with my old friend Jackie and her husband Senator John Fitzgerald Kennedy. He was very tired after some sort of campaign swing. I had expected to have no trouble talking to him, but there was no way I could seem to get through, at first. I have never seen such impenetrable eyes. It was as if he was wearing a double set of contact lenses. It was only when somebody told him of my connection with the Romanovs that he got interested. He wanted to know about Anastasia, the youngest daughter of Nicholas II, who had allegedly escaped the massacre of the family in 1918. I told him everything I knew on the subject at that time, and he seemed fascinated. He was later quoted as saying that this was the only part of Russian history worth studying. If he really said that, as president, I hope he was kidding.

I also told him that when he ran for the Senate against Lodge, I had voted for Lodge because although I considered myself usually a Democrat, good Republican senators were such rare birds that they should not be turned out of office.

Kennedy was not amused.

By the time he ran for president in 1960, I was divorced from Nell and married to Judy Clippinger. When the time came for his inauguration there was a huge snowstorm. Judy stayed home with our daughter Katya, born three weeks earlier. I mushed through the snows and as night fell ended up in the stands directly opposite the new president. The people with tickets to these stands had long ago fled. Terrible security! What if I had been Oswald?

I watched the young president smiling and talking to the people around him, while the delegations of the last of the states, in order of admission to the Union, marched past in the snow and dark. I watched the future President Johnson nudge him to take some notice of Arizona, New Mexico, Hawaii and Alaska.

Camelot started that night. Jackie was unwell and retired early. After the balls, the new president dropped in on a party given by the columnist Joseph Alsop. One of the guests was Nell.

Kennedy's church was opposite Nell's house, and he often looked in after the service, greeting Marusya and Sasha, and talking politics with Nell, whom he called *Vox Populi* for her outspoken opinions.

When my parents and Aunt Marina came to town, Nell arranged for them to meet the president at the White House, along with herself and our two daughters.

"Six Chavchavadzes, standing in a row," my mother remarked.

"Oh, I hope Senator Goldwater doesn't hear about it," said the president, or words to that effect, and then he began to question my parents about Anastasia!

229

PRINCE PAUL CHAVCHAVADZE

KATYA and AUTHOR

ZAKHAR MARTYNOV, AUTHOR and date, BARON GEORGE
WRANGEL
At Yar Restaurant, New York

EMPEROR NICHOLAS II's DAUGHTERS:
Standing - Maria, Anastasia, Olga
Seated - Tatiana

CHAPTER XIV

Whoever she was, Anna Anderson was no simple imposter. She claimed to be Anastasia, the youngest daughter of Emperor Nicholas II, but she did everything possible to ruin her own cause.

There were plenty of simple imposters around. In the 1930s there was a character who called himself "Duke Popov." My father was asked by some Americans whether he was a real duke.

"In Russia we had three grades of dukes," my father replied, "dukes, grand dukes, and pizdukes. Popov is a pizduke, the highest type of duke."

Pizduke in Russian means the male sexual organ.

The next time Popov came around these Americans, hoping to please him, called him pizduke, and Popov, thinking the jig was up, disappeared.

Then there was the famous Mike Romanoff. You could tell he was a phony by just reading the names he gave himself—several first names, whereas Russians only have one, and Obolensky thrown in, in case some clod had never heard of the Romanovs. His real name was Harry Gerguson and he spoke no Russian.

My father was introduced to him once at a bar in New York as Prince Chavchavadze.

"Are you for real?" asked Mike.

My parents both took this with great humor, and Mike, appreciating their attitude, would say things like, "Bless you, my subjects," when seeing them at a party. When he became a successful restaurateur in Hollywood, my parents were always welcome to eat there on the house. My mother's cousin, Prince Vasily of Russia, however, was not amused, in spite of his normally outstanding sense of humor. He lived in San Francisco, and when Mike Romanoff moved to California he announced that Uncle Vasily was a fraud. Believe it or not, some Americans stopped talking to Uncle Vasily, a certified nephew of Nicholas II. It is amazing how many people fall for this type of thing.

At a cocktail party on Cape Cod in the 1950s there was a woman who went around saying that her husband was the last of the Romanovs. Naturally she was steered in the direction of my mother, who politely asked for her story.

Here it is. "When the royal family was murdered in 1905, some loyal slaves put my husband on a boat for New York. He is the heir to the throne."

Her husband repeated the same story, tugging at people's elbows. Perhaps he really believed it—some imposters do. This couple's story was so easily blown by the date, 1905, that they probably did believe it, or they would have changed the date.

A lady who wrote my mother from Canada probably believed it. "History says the Imperial Family was murdered in 1918. History is wrong. . .The Tsarevich was my husband." She enclosed some pictures of a man in tails who looked like

Kurt Waldheim.

There was also Eugenia Smith, the Chicago Anastasia. This one, at first, was supported by *Life* magazine, although one could tell just from the material published in *Life* that she was a phony. She had passed a lie-detector test, and everything was based on that. *Life* paid for a trip to New York for my mother, who told me that Eugenia Smith was shorter than Anastasia had been at the age of thirteen and spoke Russian with a Bessarabian accent. It was rather smart of my mother to spot a Bessarabian accent, and it turned out later that the woman had really come from Bessarabia. My mother received mail for years after her appearance in *Life*, even after her death in 1974, and there are still people so eager to be fooled that they write dissertations, convinced that Eugenia Smith was the real Anastasia.

Although *Life* dropped Ms. Smith, she was adopted by still another imposter, a defector from the Polish Communist intelligence service. Undoubtedly a very valuable defector for the U.S., this colonel eventually announced that he was the Tsarevich, although he was ten years younger than that unfortunate lad, had no trace of hemophilia, and spoke Russian with a Polish accent. His story was that the whole Imperial Family had escaped to Poland. Poland, of all places, in 1918! He attracted some support, as usual, because of the supposed Romanov millions in western banks. In the early 1960s, he walked into the Russian cathedral in New York and told the priest that he wanted to be married. He gave his name as Alexei Nikolayevich Romanov. So the priest married the couple and agreed to pose with them for photographs. Like mushrooms, four old bags sprang up behind them—that's right, Olga, Tatiana, Maria and Anastasia, the latter being Eugenia Smith. This picture was widely circulated. I even got one in South America. Ah yes, the colonel was sly, a trained intelligence officer after all, and there was the priest sitting with them, apparently approving of the whole thing.

The priest was a real monarchist, and did not believe any of the imposter stories. But as he pointed out when called on the carpet by the metropolitan, there were a couple of hundred Romanovs or Romanoffs in the New York phone book, a very common name. So how was he to know that this Alexei Nikolayevich Romanov was pretending to be the Tsarevich, particularly since he had a Polish accent?

Yes, there was also Catherine III, Empress of Russia. She was also of the Polish persuasion, but in her version the Imperial Family had fled there without their children. So, to save the dynasty, the emperor and empress had produced her. She lived somewhere in the Washington area, sending out proclamations with titles that anybody could have checked out as being all wrong, and her envelopes bore circular stamps with the words "Catherine III, agent of LBJ"! Johnson was president at the time.

But Anna Anderson was different.

She spent sixty-four years trying to have her identity recognized, from 1920 until her death in 1984. She consistently got into terrible fights with the people trying to help her, and she never showed interest in the alleged material gain which might accrue to her if she were to be recognized as Anastasia, though some of her supporters did.

So much has been written on this woman that I will summarize her basic story in a short paragraph.

She was fished out of a canal in Berlin in 1920, with no identity papers. She did not claim to be Anastasia until some nurses in the hospital she was taken to thought she looked like one of the daughters of Nicholas II, as pictured in an old magazine. Her story, as it gradually came out, was that she had been rescued, half dead, after the slaughter of the rest of the Imperial Family in Ekaterinburg in July 1918. The rescuer was a soldier called Chaikovsky, who took her in a peasant cart through all of Russia from the Urals to Roumania, making her pregnant on the way. A child was born in Bucharest, Chaikovsky died or disappeared, and the woman who was to be called Anna Anderson went to Berlin hoping to contact her German relatives.

I was exposed to this story all of my childhood. My father always thought that the most unlikely part was the trip by cart through Russia in the middle of revolution and civil war. But this part bothers me the least. With a little luck, it was probably the safest way to travel.

In recent years there have been theories that either there was no massacre at Ekaterinburg, or that only the emperor and tsarevich were killed there. I can't believe this. The Whites took Ekaterinburg shortly after the massacre and first on the scene were Babady's brother, Uncle Paul Rodzianko and a British general.

Paul Rodzianko examined the murder room and had the floor removed to study the clotted blood underneath. In addition to numerous bullet holes all over the place, he noticed eighteen traces of bayonet thrusts in the floor at the place where the White Army inspector, Sokolov, later concluded Grand Duchess Anastasia had been killed. Incidentally, Paul Rodzianko also found the tsarevich's spaniel, Joy, alive and well. He took this, presumably, lone survivor of the massacre to England with him. Joy died there a few years alter, and Uncle Paul had him buried at Windsor.

The family conversations I remember always assumed that the Ekaterinburg massacre had taken place, and covered the following points.

How could any of them have escaped? The family thought Inspector Sokolov had done a competent job and had accounted for the right number of stays and clothing for the murdered women in the lime pit into which the bodies had been thrown. However, Sokolov had concluded that Anastasia had fainted when the firing started and had not been hit by bullets but was finished off by bayonets. Anna Anderson had some horrible cuts on her body which some doctors claimed must have been made by the unique Russian triangular shaped bayonet, but how could any doctor tell the shape of a bayonet by looking at a wound many years later?

Second, If she was looking for relatives, why had this woman not tried to contact Queen Marie of Roumania, her mother's first cousin, while she was in Bucharest?

Third, Anna Anderson had turned up in Berlin about a year and a half after the massacre, when Anastasia had just turned seventeen. After such a short period, how could there have been any doubt about her identity on the part of those who had known Anastasia, no matter what horrors she had been through? An answer to this was that most people surviving in the West had last seen Anastasia when she was thirteen, fourteen, or fifteen.

Fourth, Anna Anderson did not speak Russian. This was a hard one to overcome. The emperor's children all spoke beautiful Russian to him and everybody else except their mother, with whom they spoke English. They also knew French and little, if any, German. Still, there was reason to doubt that Russian was entirely gone from Anna Anderson's mind, as I shall point out. Much later I met a Soviet diplomat who had defected in his thirties, and ten years later he could hardly speak Russian, because he deliberately wanted to forget it. Perhaps blows to the head and body and the unspeakable ghastliness of the whole experience could have knocked out her native language.

My mother was always rather silent during these discussions. She had last seen Anastasia when they were both thirteen, and they had disliked each other. My mother's sister, Xenia, had been eleven.

It was Aunt Xenia who, while married to William Leeds, took Anna Anderson into her home in Oyster Bay, Long Island, in 1928, and was the only Romanov who spent any serious amount of time with her, several months.

Three years earlier Anna Anderson had been visited by the emperor's sister, Grand Duchess Olga, who had at first seemed convinced that she was Anastasia, but later retracted, probably under the influence of her mother the Dowager Empress. The old lady could not bring herself to believe that there had been any murder at all, hence in her mind Anna Anderson had to be an imposter. But even Grand Duchess Olga stated that there had been no visual recognition. Why not, after only a few years? Aunt Xenia also said she had no visual recognition, but this was understandable given their ages when they last met. Anna Anderson also received support from Grand Duke Andrei Vladimirovich, and from a collateral member of the Imperial Family, Duke George of Leuchtenberg.

But it was Aunt Xenia who spent all that time with her, looking at albums, listening to the extensive intimate family knowledge that Anna Anderson had. People said that Anna Anderson had been carefully coached by some of the money-hungry people who surrounded her, and did much to damage her cause. I do not believe that this woman, never entirely sane since her appearance in 1920, and always doing willful things against her own cause, could have been coached to do anything. First of all, a coaching job should have included a crash course in Russian.

Aunt Xenia said that she once heard Anna Anderson talking very acceptable St. Petersburg Russian to a couple of birds in a cage. When Aunt Xenia walked in on her, Anna Anderson quickly shut up.

"Why don't you speak Russian, since you know it?" Aunt Xenia asked.

"I hate that language," replied the mystery woman, in English, "because it was the last language I heard before we were killed."

Anna Anderson refused to receive my mother for some time. Finally, Mama did get to see her for about five minutes, trying not to stare or ask questions. She came away without any real impression at all, except that this was a lady, and not some Polish peasant carefully coached, which was one of the stories of the period.

Mama sometimes wondered what other lost St. Petersburg girl of good family Anna Anderson could be from, if not Anastasia. Before receiving my mother, Anna Anderson had asked, "Is Nina still very tall?" This difference in height had been the source of their dislike of one another.

236

Aunt Xenia remained convinced for the rest of her life that Anna Anderson was Anastasia. Unfortunately, she never wrote anything in detail about those months. When I take down books from the extensive Russian library she left me in her will, I keep hoping that something on the subject will fall out of one of them. So far, no luck.

When I was in Germany I was impressed by the vehemence with which members of the Hessen-Darmstadt family, the family of Anastasia's mother, reacted to the question of Anna Anderson—much more than any of the Romanovs. The Hessens practically whipped out pictures of ears and teeth to prove Anna Anderson a phony. The reason for this, I think, is a statement that Anna Anderson made—that she had seen the Grand Duke of Hesse, her (or Anastasia's) uncle, in Russia during World War I. In the 1950s when scarcely a German magazine came out without an article on one of the former German ruling families, the last thing the Hessens wanted was that one of theirs had been treating with the Russians during World War I. Yet, there now seems to be no doubt that the empress's brother, Grand Duke Ernst Ludwig, was actually there trying to make a separate peace, without any success. Whether he did it on his own or with the knowledge of the Kaiser's government is not known.

For years Anna Anderson lived in Germany, under the protection of Prince Frederick of Saxe-Altenburg, who was also involved in other mysteries—what happened to the lost Dauphin, son of Louis XVI—had he become a postman in Bavaria?

There was a series of trials in a German court which did not establish Anna Anderson's identity as Anastasia, but they did not deny it either.

Having quarreled with Prince Frederick, Anna Anderson moved to Charlottesville, Virginia in 1968, where her old-time supporter Gleb Botkin, the son of the doctor who was killed with the Imperial Family, had started a cult of Aphrodite, walking around in robes like an orthodox bishop, but with a sex symbol instead of a cross on his chest. I might add here that all through her long life, there is no indication that Anna Anderson was ever interested in sex.

In Charlottesville, she married John Manahan, a Virginian much younger than herself, and a real expert on genealogy. This at least gave her some financial security for the rest of her life, as well as companionship. John Manahan believed in her absolutely, and was very supportive of her.

What about all of the alleged Romanov money in western banks that attracted support not only to Anna Anderson, but to the obvious imposters I have mentioned? Most if not all of it was supposed to be in the Bank of England. My parents were always convinced that there wasn't any.

For one thing, their great friend, "Uncle Vanya" Kleinmichel spent most of his life working for the Bank of England, and also handling the financial affairs of the emperor's sister, Grand Duchess Xenia. He was absolutely certain there was no money. While he can be accused of being partial to Grand Duchess Xenia, the point is that two undoubted sisters of Nicholas II lived in the West, and they along with, perhaps, relatives of the empress, would have inherited anything that existed. Indeed, the two sisters did inherit a small amount, vastly reduced by inflation, that had been frozen in Germany during World War I.

There had been an account in London, and it was withdrawn during wartime, according to Sir Peter Bark, who had been Russian Minister of Finance during the war and later became a governor of the Bank of England. Quite a career, that. Bark told my father the following: there had been an account in England under the code name OTMA (Olga, Tatiana, Maria, Anastasia). During the war, Nicholas II ordered Bark to withdraw this account and bring it back to Russia as an example to society to do the same thing. Bark tried to talk the emperor out of this, and he said it was the only time he ever saw Nicholas II lose his temper. The withdrawal was accomplished, and most, but not all, of society followed suit. Patriotism was the order of the day. After the war, Grand Duchess Xenia was awarded the proceeds from a Romanov account in a German bank, about $50,000. Reduced by the German runaway inflation, the balance in this account would have been well over five million dollars in 1914.

Many years after my father's death, his contemporary and friend, Baron Constantine ("Steino") Stackelberg told me a similar story. His father, who in 1914 held the court rank of Master of Ceremonies, had told him that a couple of days before the beginning of the 1914 war, the emperor had ordered the duty lord of the bed chamber, Nicholas Yevreinov, to telephone Bark to remove all the imperial accounts from abroad. This incident, Steino said, had been confirmed to him by Sir Peter Bark in London in 1925. I have no way of knowing whether these are two different accounts of the same incident, or whether my father's version specifically about the OTMA account happened later.

While most of the surviving Romanovs did not recognize Anna Anderson as Anastasia, I do not believe that any of them had a financial motive in this, nor a political motive, because under Paul I's law of succession no woman could inherit the throne while a male Romanov was alive. And quite a few of them were and are alive.

Almost exactly fifty-five years after the murder of the Imperial Family, I met Anna Anderson. A very intelligent and knowledgeable young man called Brien Horan came to see me, having already visited my cousin Nancy, Aunt Xenia's daughter. While he was totally convinced that Anna Anderson was Anastasia, and was writing a dissertation on the subject, he retained a degree of objectivity that I respected. He had visited the lady and John Managhan, whom he jokingly dubbed the Grand Duke Jack, many times, and now suggested that I come along, so I did. We drove to Charlottesville with my daughter Marusya.

We were very warmly received. Anna Anderson, always on her feet hovering at the edge of the room, reminisced about Nancy and me fighting over a kiddie car in Oyster Bay in 1928. Whoever she was, she had known me and my close relatives forty-five years ago, and this produced a feeling of warmth. As she hovered she kept part of her face covered with a handkerchief, something she had done since her appearance in 1920, because of a damaged jaw. Her husband showed me his staggering collection of genealogical books, six or seven rooms full downstairs.

My first surpirse was that Anna Anderson spoke such bad English, and with such a Germanic accent, that I soon found I could communicate with her better in German. Her German, as far as I could tell, had no foreign accent at all. Of course, she had lived most of her life there. Still, having had to overlook her lack of Russian, I found it surprising that her English was so bad and so Germanic.

What did she look like? Short, shrivelled, grey-haired, no family resemblance that I could see. But my mother, seeing a picture taken not long before this time, said she saw plenty of family resemblance. This is worth noting, since Mama so rarely made a pro-Anastasia remark. But Anna Anderson had memorable, luminous, blue-gray eyes. Her supporters, who had known Nicholas II, always remarked that she unmistakably had her father's unforgettable eyes. Of course I never saw his eyes, except in black and white photographs.

The things she said seemed un-family to me.

For one thing, she always said "tsar" in both English and German, even though all the Romanovs say "emperor" in English and *gosudar* (sovereign) in Russian. Brien Horan had a rebuttal for this. After fifty years in Germany, where everybody says "Zar" and "Kaiser" means the German emperor, she would have gotten into the habit. To say "*der russische Kaiser*" every time would become a burden.

When we were taken to a club, naturally designed by Thomas Jefferson, for lunch, she introduced me to some people as "a member of the Greek Royal Family." This was totally out of line. It was through a double maternal line. But Brien had a rebuttal for this too. Anna Anderson had made remarks to him to the effect that my mother was the result of an affair between her mother and a Greek admiral. There she got things mixed up. As we know, my grandmother met the Greek admiral when her daughters were grown, and my mother looked strikingly like her father. In this case Brien's rebuttal is not convincing. Even if Anastasia believed the admiral story, and knew that in any case I was more closely related to her through the Greek family than through the Romanovs, the way to handle it would have been simply, "He is my cousin."

At one point Anna Anderson said to me, "You could be Tsar of Russian some day." A very un-Romanov thing to say. All of them are very much aware that I am not a Romanov, am related to them through my mother, and my rights to the throne would have to follow all Romanovs, both male and female, and a few maternal cases like myself. Brien's rebuttal—"She liked you, and has little use for any of the others." Yes, but she didn't like my mother, and circulated that Greek admiral story.

At lunch at that club, John Manahan urged me to speak Russian to his wife. I deliberately chose the story of the birds in the cage at Aunt Xenia's, hoping to jog her memory. I spoke slowly, pronouncing every word with precision.

"Do you remember that time at Aunt Xenia's, when she came across you speaking Russian to those birds, and you said, 'I hate that language because it was the last language I heard before we were killed'?"

She stared at me. I could hear "Grand Duke Jack" behind my shoulder saying, "My God, she doesn't understand a word! Then turning to my daughter, he said, "Are you sure your father speaks the right kind of Russian?"

Marusya said, "It was so clear I could understand it myself."

"Did you understand that?" I asked Anna Anderson in German.

"Everything," she replied, also in German.

239

Did she? I suppose I should have asked her to repeat it in English or in German, but I had heard too many stories about what tantrums such direct interrogation could produce in her.

After lunch, back at the Manahan house, soon to be condemned for an excess of cats, I sang old Russian soldiers' songs. Her first and only request was *Die Schwarze Husaren* (the Black Hussars). This proves nothing. It could have been requested by any German Hausfrau or by a grand duchess. She seemed to enjoy the songs, still hovering at the end of the room, holding that cloth to her jaw.

To sum up—if I had gone there cold, without the background of Aunt Xenia's belief, which I had to respect, my vote would have been negative.

The Manahans often got in their car and drove long distances. Once, when I was away, they turned up at the house where I was living in Washington. John Manahan walked in, looked at a photograph of my future wife Genia's grandfather, who had a Nicholas II-style beard, and said, "My God, you can't miss the family resemblance!"

"Unh-unh," said Genia, "that one's mine."

They drove up once more when I was present. Anna Anderson would not get out of the car. I went out to her and she smiled, presenting me with a little jar of Romanoff Caviar. That was the last time I saw her. She died in 1984, at the age of eighty-three, if she was Anastasia.

She lived long enough to hear about the canonization of Anastasia and the rest of the murdered Romanovs as martyrs by the Russian Orthodox Church in exile.

"They might have waited until after I was dead," she is reported to have said.

In 1984 a friend of mine obtained archival information in the Soviet Union that one of the Romanov women had been posted as missing after the 1918 slaughter. Issac Don Levine had written the same thing years before. Many other pro Anna Anderson items were pulled together in Peter Kurth's book, *Anastasia, the Riddle of Anna Anderson*, published in 1983 by Little, Brown and Co., undoubtedly the best of the many books on the subject. On the other hand it always bothered me that Anna Anderson changed her basic story after various books came out claiming that the Romanov women had not been killed that day in Ekaterinburg. But by that time she was rather senile and easily influenced by others.

It has been impossible here to touch on more than a small part of this mystery, which has lasted for more than seventy years, and will not die with Anna Anderson. I am now half convinced that the wizened woman I saw was the youngest daughter of Nicholas II.

CHAPTER XV

In 1958, after our return from the usual August trip to Wellfleet, Nell and I separated. It was a tearful move. Divorce followed, simply done by Nell in Alabama. We maintained good relations, and even I babysat for her.

I settled into an apartment on top of an old stable with two bachelors, André Stenbock-Fermor and his friend Jim Austin. It was known as the "submarine," because when it rained the water came in from all possible directions. Jim Austin took off for Germany, forcing André and me to bail out of the submarine, and move back to Georgetown, sharing a house with Murat Natirboff and Vladimir Pojidayeff, an old friend from Cape Cod. We referred to this establishment as the "Regiment," and indeed its make-up was reminiscent of an old guards regiment—a Circassian, a Russian with a Swedish name, a Georgian, and one guy with a Russian name, Pojidayeff.

André was a gourmet cook, who spoke English, Russian and French perfectly, stuttering in all three. In honor of living in a house instead of a submarine, he did his cooking in a chef's hat.

I began to see a great deal of Judy Clippinger, the beautiful tall blonde from Cincinnati who had managed to march through Red Square and spend the night at Tsinandali. Our meetings were semi-clandestine until my divorce was final. On the whole, the secret was well-kept. Judy had worked in the refugee business in Munich, and had known Bill Coffin there. She was especially close to Uncle Sergei Sheremetyev, to whom for a while she took care packages, assuming that he was broke like all other Russians. She spoke Russian, Serbo-Croation, German and Spanish, learning them all impressionistically, paying little attention to rules of grammar. She worked in a private organization guiding foreign visitors, which gave her a lot of experience in what people were like the world over.

Another of Judy's old Munich friends was my classmate John Hanes. After a long period as John Foster Dulles's aide, Johnnie had become Assistant Secretary for Security and Consular Affairs in the State Department. Thanks to him, Judy landed a job as a GS-12 in the State Department.

On 15 September 1959 I met her downtown and together we watched Khrushchev drive by the White House. The crowd behaved magnificently, from my point of view. They applauded the American honor guard but maintained silence when Khrushchev was actually in view. That night I watched on TV and heard him make a Freudian slip—"Capitalism will win!" he declared. This was not translated nor noticed by anyone in the media, and it amused me.

Gradually, Judy and I emerged from our sequestered state, which consisted of her house, the Regiment, and on weekends Johnnie and Lucy Hanes's estate in Great Falls, Virginia.

While we were still being semi-clandestine, I sang publicly at one of the great balalaika players, Grisha Titov's, Georgetown boathouse parties, Judy sitting at a different table from me. My rendition of my father's translation of *Stenka Razin*, sung in a Nyanyushka accent, made a tremendous impression on a pretty nineteen-year-old Russian girl from New York called Eugenie de Smitt. She started calling me up and inviting me to parties, and I kept refusing. During one of these calls she said, "You're dating Judy Clippinger, aren't you?" This was downright annoying. Another pushy Russian girl not much more than half my age. She must have called really often, because I finally said something to her I never said before nor since, "Get lost, little girl!"

She got lost all right, but twenty years later she became my wife, and I have never been able to live that phrase down.

In early September I went to Cincinnati with Judy to stay with her family. Her father, John Clippinger, was a prominent lawyer and horseman—Master of the Cincinnati Hunt. He regarded me with some suspicion because of my background, and divorced situation, but he was a very decent and kind man, and after a while we got on quite well. Judy's mother, Jane, was a real sweetheart with whom I had fine rapport from the beginning. I also grew very fond of Judy's younger sister Sallie, married to an Episcopal priest from Northern Ireland, Michael Hamilton, and the baby of the family, John Jr., then fifteen.

A few weeks before I had taken my father to dinner at Judy's. He had met her once before, but told me he had forgotten how good looking she was. He was also impressed with what he called. 'the depth of her spirituality'.

For Thanksgiving we drove to Wellfleet, spending the night with Bill and Eva Coffin in New Haven. In Wellfleet things did not work out so well. For some reason my parents pretended not to know that we were engaged. This, naturally, miffed Judy, who assumed I had not told them. Poor Judy never had a chance with my mother, who, though maintaining a pleasant enough veneer, kept talking about Nell, not just this time, but frequently in the future, until both Papa and I jumped down her throat. My parents were upset with the divorce, but my father looked for and found positive things in Judy, and besides, he had tact. Mama, shall we say, had a straight Russian soul, a.k.a. "tell it like it is."

I had to tell the children that I was getting married, not an easy thing to do. They took it in a remarkably matter-of-fact way.

"Oh, yes, Aunt Judy will be our stepmother, and please order a swing for us in your garden," from Marusya, aged six.

Sasha, almost five, said, "Why do you look so sad, Dad?"

It would be a long time before we had a garden. Judy found a place for us to live practically across the street from the State Department, and an easy walk to work for both of us. The house was small but rather cozy, with two bedrooms. We called it the "Catfish Towers." Judy moved in on December 7. I stayed at the Regiment, which was fast breaking up. Murat Natirboff had married in October.

At that time the Episcopal Church was fully against divorce. I had to line up an Orthodox wedding in Cincinnati. Judy had no objections, she often attended Orthodox services. So I called up the only Russian priest in Cincinnati, Father Ivan Sobolevsky. He was delightful. He explained that our wedding day, December 28, was in the middle of Christmas lent, but he would get a waiver for us from his bishop, on condition that there not be any excessive carousing after the wedding.

In person, Father Ivan turned out to be one of those ideal Orthodox priests like Father Vasily of my childhood, not educated but all heart and, one felt, deeply Christian. He had a long, divided, white beard, like Germany's World War I Admiral Tirpitz. He made his own communion wine for use in a very small church on the second floor of a two-story building.

My parents came to Cincinnati on money borrowed from Edmund and Elena Wilson. They were always living from book to book, and my father was very unlucky. He always had fine reviews, almost made the Book of the Month Club once, but never made much money. My parents and I were the only Russians in the wedding party, but a surprising number of Father Ivan's parishioners turned out on this Monday afternoon, and there was a good choir.

The Orthodox wedding ceremony lasts at least forty-five minutes. The ushers hold crowns over the heads of the bride and groom, spelling each other off, so there should be at least four, preferably six, standing in a column of twos behind the couple. These crowns have nothing to do with titles. They are used at every wedding. After quite a long time, the priest binds the left hand of the groom and the right hand of the bride with a cloth, and, seizing both hands in a tight grip, leads the couple around a stand containing an icon, cross, and Bible, three times. The usher holding the crown over the bride has to do a pirouette to avoid stepping on her skirt or train, and he better know enough to turn the crown over to his replacement for the next trip around. There is religious significance behind every bit of the ritual. I do not mean to be flippant in describing it. It certainly does make you feel thoroughly married.

Afterwards there was a pleasant reception at the Clippingers' house, totally dominated by the figure of Father Ivan, who was an object of great fascination to their friends. Since he could hardly speak English, I spent a large part of the evening interpreting for him. He was obviously reveling in the attention he was receiving, but then he looked at his watch and remembered the bishop's dictum about not too much carousing during lent. So, he got up, made the sign of the cross over the guests, most of whom seemed to be Proctor and Gamble executives, and declaimed through me as interpreter, "God bless you all and continue your fight against Godless Communism!"

They all looked at him with some surprise. They didn't realize that they were fighting Godless Communism by producing and selling soap.

After a three week honeymoon on St. Croix, a present from Judy's father, "El Clip," we returned to a cold winter in the Catfish Tower. Its strategic location had its advantages and disadvantages. It became a haven for my colleagues and Judy's to come to lunch from their offices. But during the deep snows that often hit Washington that winter, when the Pentagon could be reached only by dog sled, I had no excuse whatever to stay home and was actually appointed duty officer during snow emergencies. It was rather fun to mush through the virginal whiteness and then have the office to myself all day.

On snowy days there was always a traffic jam in the evenings on E Street, and Judy and I, as good St. Bernards, would distribute shots of vodka to astonished motorists stuck in front of the Catfish.

Judy was extremely sweet with Marusya and Sasha, and took a real interest in them. There wasn't much for them to do around the Catfish, so on weekends we took them to the Hanes' in Great Falls. They had daughters of the same age.

In February 1960 Yul Brynner was shepherded around the State Department by Judy. He had arrived in support of a project having to do with refugees in which Judy was involved. She enjoyed watching secretaries almost swoon as she led him into various officers, and reveled at their envious glances in her direction. A lot of them assumed that she was his wife or mistress.

We went to a cocktail party in his honor, followed by dinner at the Ghengis Khan Restaurant. We did not eat until very late because the minute the manager saw Yul he refused to show us menus. A real banquet had to be produced from scratch in Mr. Brynner's honor, so we drank and starved while the kitchen staff outdid themselves.

I had not seen Yul since the early 1940s when he was a frequent guest at Uncle George Chavchavadze's. In 1942, with a full head of hair, he had played the guitar and sung in a bar in New York, still totally unknown. By 1960 he had immortalized himself in the leading role of *The King and I* on Broadway.

After the Ghengis Khan manager had reluctantly let us go, Yul invited Judy and me to his hotel suite. He got out a small guitar and serenaded us with Russian Gypsy songs until three in the morning, a truly memorable session. Even then, there were very few people left who could really do these songs justice, and Yul's mother was a real Russian Gypsy. He spoke Russian beautifully as well as Romany. At that time few people knew about Yul's Gypsy blood, nor the fact that he spoke Russian. He preferred to maintain an aura of oriental mystery about his origins, and, indeed, he also had a Mongolian grandmother who had married his Swiss grandfather. Quite a combination. It was only later that he acted in roles calling for Russian, and not until 1966 that he surfaced his Gypsy origins in a magnificent record made with his old friend, the Paris Gypsy star Alyosha Dimitrievich. I still listen to it frequently and remember that night when Judy and I sat on the floor at his feet and heard this magic sung especially for us.

Old Russian Gypsy music lived on precariously, but in that same year, 1960, the last close connection with the Russian monarchy disappeared. In April Grand Duchess Xenia died in England, at the hugely advanced age—for a Romanov—of eighty-five, and a few months later her younger sister, Olga, the last of the real grand duchesses, died in Canada. I had never met Olga, an extremely simple, self-effacing person, who during World War I had married a Russian commoner, Colonel Kulikovsky, but I knew their elder son Tikhon. He was a huge man of grand ducal proportions, looking something like his grandfather, Alexander III, with a sense of humor to match. Once, on a Provincetown street, we heard a Russian conversation coming our way.

"Look at that huge hulk," exclaimed a woman, as usual confident that Russian was a secret language.

Tikhon stopped, bowed, and said, "I may be a hulk, but I don't bite!"

They hurried past, crushed, never dreaming that the huge hulk on Commercial street was a nephew of the last emperor.

In 1960 there were still two ladies in waiting to the empress left in

Washington, Mmes. Mishtowt and Woevodsky. They saw to it that at the te deums for the emperor's sisters, Uncle Sergei Sheremetiev and I, as relatives, were the first to kiss the cross. I wondered what memories must be churning in the old man's mind.

Katya, short for Catherine, was born on the morning of December 29, 1960. She spent her first few months in the Catfish Towers, where she was christened, with my parents present and Uncle Sergei Sheremetiev reading from the apostles.

We were facing a financial crisis. Judy had quit her job at the State Department and my half-pay was not enough. The only solution was an overseas assignment, where, at least, we would have free living quarters. After five and half years in Washington it was time for one anyway. These things take time to work out, and Katya was just over a year old before we left for South America. I had the sad task of parting from Maruysa and Sasha for at least two years. Then we were poured on the plane by a considerable company of Georgetowners.

I had taken a crash course in Spanish, which Judy already spoke quite well. Since this was the sixth language I had studied, not counting Russian and English, I thought I was doing splendidly, but at our destination I found my comprehension left much to be desired, and it was a year before I could hold a real conversation on the phone. Katya's first and only language for two and a half years was Spanish.

Unfortunately, it is against CIA rules to say where we were assigned, so some good stories will have to be omitted. There were Russians in South America—both Soviets and emigrés. The make-up of the latter differed from country to country, but generally speaking there were Whites, post-1917 refugees, who had been driven from places like Yugoslavia after World War II; there were ex-Soviets of the World War II "second wave" emigration, and there were some who had come to South America much earlier, many of them peasants from parts of the Russian Empire that had become Polish between the wars. This group was totally out of it politically. Some of them accepted Soviet passports and went back; others stayed in sort of limbo, holding on to their Soviet passports.

The Whites were mostly out of it politically too. They still conceived of the Soviet Union as being heavily weighted with Jewish officials, although this had not been the case for twenty-five years. But they upheld all their old traditions, passing them and the language on to their children. Like the British and Germans they looked down on the locals as "natives," which their counterparts could not do in Europe and the U.S.

The Whites were also suspicious of the "second wave," ex-Bolsheviks in their eyes, while the latter group made much more political sense, having a first hand knowledge of Soviet life only twenty years before.

These two groups did not mix much, but I remember one touching incident. At a party after church, each of the Whites started singing his own or his father's regimental songs. After all this singing, accompanied by vodka toasts to the defunct old regiments, they turned to a "second wave" character called Ivan, who was indispensible to the church as a janitor.

"I don't have a regimental song," Ivan said. "This is my regimental song, 'Lord save thy People,'" and he sang a church hymn which is one of the themes in

Chaikovsky's *1812 Overture*. There was not a dry eye at the table. They realized that Ivan was the best Christian among them.

The priest of this church had been a young cadet fighting for General Baron Wrangel against the Reds in the Crimea in 1920. Often he would come to our house, where he felt he could be a "hooligan," as he put it. He would dance all over the furniture, long boots under his robe, and a corkscrew hanging under it. He would tell us how these young boys fought and gave their lives for Holy Russian in a hopeless cause, and how they worshiped their general. This priest was from peasant stock. Before fighting in the Crimea, he had concealed himself from the Reds in the cellar of a friendly house for many months. The daughter of the family passed him down food on a string, and removed, as he put it, various waste materials. When it was safe for him to come out he married her. As I listened to his anti-Soviet sermons it occurred to me that I was the only person in the church, or even the country, working against the Soviets full time.

There was another priest there, more like Fathers Vasily and Ivan in his looks, but much stricter. At a christening he blessed us with a strange cross made of wood. Later I learned that this priest had struck British soldiers on the head with this cross, trying to prevent them from dragging his Cossack flock out of church to turn them over to the Soviets in 1945. He too was a peasant, but he had never been a cadet or an officer. His sermons were not sophisticated like those of our "hooligan" ex-cadet. They were super-monarchist and simplistic.

"The Russian people in congress assembled elected the Romanov dyansty in 1613, blessed by the Holy Ghost, and anyone who goes against this is anathema. Anathema!" he would declare.

Still another priest had different opinions. When Uncle George Chavchavadze died in a tragic auto accident in France, we held a Te Deum for him. This priest refused to pray for the traditional "God's servant Prince George," which I asked for because I knew my uncle would have liked it, and substituted "Warrior George" instead. The last label my uncle could have had was warrior, but my father wrote me that perhaps he had been a warrior, spiritually—shades of Babady's, 'But we are very rich, in spirit!'.

Most important from my point of view were the Soviets—diplomats, KGB and GRU. I had hardly seen any for six years. Most of them spoke good Spanish, and were generally more sophisticated than the ones in Berlin had been. They also did not immediately react to my name, as Soviets had since Alaska in 1943. One first secretary actually asked me, "Was your father from the intelligentsia?"

The same diplomat also asked me why I was so anti-Soviet. I thought fast. How to answer this succinctly? So I said, "I don't like to spend my weekends with the people I work with."

Touché. He was silent. No answer. I knew, of course, of the life of Soviet colonies abroad, the obligatory volley ball games and movies on weekends, and if you try to get out of them, just to stay home and read a book by yourself, the KGB man in charge of the colony's security might put you down as insufficiently collective-minded and keep an eye on you. God help any Soviet who gets interested in the local culture, or just goes pub-crawling without an official mission to perform.

It was, surprisingly, weeks before they got their traces on me from Moscow.

Suddenly it was "Prince" Chavchavadze, son of the famous Prince Paul who had helped Russian War Relief during World War II. This was a short episode in Papa's life which could only have come from their files.

It was not hard to distinguish between real Soviet diplomats and the KGB. The diplomats were interested in the local scene. One of them told me he was bored with me because I always wanted to talk about Russia. But his KGB pal was interested, to see whether there was any chance to recruit me, and he kept telling the other one to shut up. "Who cares about the local scene? Let's hear what dear David has to say."

Some of the military intelligence officers (GRU) were easy to spot, because all the military, naval, and air attachés are GRU. Unlike our own service attachés, the Soviets are career intelligence officers involved in clandestine espionage activities. They were not interested in the likes of me, that was the KGB's job. Many of the GRU are under civilian cover, but they are all military officers, picked from line outfits at the grade of more-or-less captain and put through the Military Diplomatic Academy, their spy school.

In every Soviet embassy or mission there are thus two separate espionage stations, or *rezidentury*, one KGB, the other GRU. The two have never gotten along very well. They don't deal with each other much locally, letting Moscow coordinate their activities. A problem between the two services is that the KGB is responsible for the security and political reliability of the armed services, and it has the same function vis-a-vis Soviet colonies abroad. Thus, the KGB has a double charter to spy on the GRU, and it does. A GRU officer once defected because of his anger at the fact that the KGB had tried to recruit him to spy on his buddies.

All this leads to a relationship between the two agencies that is at best uneasy, and at worst downright hostile. Their traditions are very different. GRU officers, though party members, regard themselves as honorable soldiers performing a legitimate G-2 function. The main thrust of their interest is military, and they believe that they would exist under any regime. They look on the KGB as secret police, informers, and finks.

The KGB's tradition, on the other hand, is completely tied to the existing order. They are the "sword and shield" of the revolution, in direct line from "Iron Felix" Dzerzhinsky's Cheka, founded in 1917. They still call themselves "chekists," a word that has a nasty sound to other Russians.

How do CIA officers compare to their KGB counterparts? One heard a lot of nonsense over the years about the KGB being "ten feet tall." Some of this came from within the CIA. One chief had a theory that KGB officers, being versed in the dialectic, could always outsmart ours. Sheer piffle. They are not ten feet tall. They are, on the average, about 5'-6", but there are an awful lot of them. Man for man, in my time at least, I would take our officers over theirs on the whole. They had very good operatives, mediocre ones, and near idiots. We also had a few who were under par, and many very able ones, but we were always outnumbered.

More important is the relative position of the KGB and CIA in their own governments. The KGB holds a position of huge power, while the CIA, no matter what you read in the press, was always controlled and never in a position to dictate to other U.S. agencies.

The Soviet services have thier own disadvantages. They, too, are victims of the Soviet "norms" system—You will recruit x-number of people this year—which causes them to do silly things to meet their quotas and to falsify reports. Also, there have been quite a few defections to us. By the time I retired in 1974, I could count seventeen that I knew about, leaving aside defections-in-place, such as the famous Popov and Penkovsky GRU cases. I am also not counting the numerous defections from the many satellite services. These are not only controlled by KGB "advisors" but also thoroughly penetrated, a wise move from the KGB's point of view. Thus, in 1968, the KGB had no problem purging the Czech service of Dubcek sympathisers when the "Prague Spring" was crushed by Soviet invasion.

We had no defectors to them, at least until Philip Agee came along. What about penetrations, or, as it is now fashionable to say, "moles?" Of course, one can never say for sure. I never agreed with a certain, to me, paranoid school of thought which claimed the Agency was riddled with these animals. Our unfortunate British allies suffered badly from this disease for a long time, but most of the moles uncovered in my time could be traced to the same Communist cell in pre-war Cambridge University. I doubt if they could have passed our routine security procedures. Our security people were anything but impressed by the "old school tie," and we had the polygraph. This controversial machine is not a favorite pastime of mine, and it may be a menace in the hands of poorly trained operators, but the CIA operators I encountered were well trained and very experienced. In their hands the machine, along with the all-important pre-polygraph interview, is a useful tool. Perhaps it can be beaten by special training or drugs, but an experienced operator should be able to spot this.

While my mind recoils at even mentioning the renegade Philip Agee's book, published in 1975, I must say that he gave a good picture of a case officer's life at a CIA station. But how did a case officer like Agee, who had no supervisory functions, learn so much about what other people at the stations he served in were doing? He admits to raiding the chief of station's safe, and he may have done some other snooping, but for the most part he came about his knowledge legitimately.

This lands us squarely into the struggle between those two mutually hostile concepts—security and efficiency. In theory, security always wins. Compartmentation should be practiced at all times. Nobody should know what anyone else is doing, except for the chiefs. In practice a station can suffer serious loss of efficiency by applying compartmentation too literally.

A station must function as a team. If I have no idea what my colleague is doing, I can't look for leads that help him, and he won't be able to help me. People trusted each other, and worked together. Certainly in the past compartmentation was relaxed too far in many places; but equally, very strict compartmentation is irritating and bad for morale..

I shall never forget how offended I felt when I walked into my boss's office at my first overseas post and his secretary demonstratively turned some papers on her desk upside down. Technically, she was right. Paper left lying about at either end threatens security, so every night each station goes through a ritual to make sure that everything is locked up in safes. Not just official stuff, but personal mail, bills, telephone messages. To make sure that there are no slip-ups, every desk top must be clear, the in and out baskets on their sides, the waste baskets checked, the typewriter ribbons removed. Every evening someone is stuck with the duty of checking for loose paper and making sure all the safes are locked. If, in spite of all precautions, something is left out, all the cyptonyms and pseudonyms on the accursed piece of paper have to be changed. I once lost a favorite pseudonym because somebody did not secure a piece of paper at a station hundreds of miles away.

Classified trash, of course, goes into special burn bags, conspicuously marked. In the field we used to store it in safes until the end of the week, and then burn it on the roof. The most junior officer was usually in charge of this detail. In South America we kept him company, helping throw bags into the incinerator as we passed a bottle around, and he, known as the Mad Security Officer, would lead us in a ritual dance around the flames.

In the field, a case officer's work is just about endless. Agent meetings are only part of the story, and even the simplest communication with agents consumes time. While you may be able to receive a phone call safely at your office from an agent, provided that true names, times, and places are not given away, you cannot phone out to the agent. So you trudge out of the building, seeking a phone booth that is reasonably far away and perhaps not monitored by the local police. You can't call an agent from your home, and he can't call you there, unless he knows your true name. You learn to have a pocketful of phone coins or tokens.

After an agent meeting, the case officer writes up a contact report—time and place of meeting, next meeting, what was said, agent morale and family situation, possibilities of access to new information, security difficulties, real and potential, passing of money or operational entertainment, etc. Ideally, any new case officer should be able to pick up the agent by reading the contact reports, but if anything goes sour with the operation, woe to the case officer who has not written complete contact reports, because they will form the basis of a security study on what went wrong.

This is only the beginning of the paper work. Dispatches, cables, orders, analysis and questions are read and answered. It is maddening to the case officer to be second-guessed by some guy at a desk in Virginia, but in most cases a modus vivendi is arrived at, and headquarters is usually careful not to take a dictatorial tone, leaving a lot of discretion to the chief of station, who has to answer not only to headquarters but to the local U.S. Ambassador.

Case officers frequently have a work load from their "cover" organization, so that everything else has to be done outside working hours. All of this can be very rough on family life, but here the case officers' wives can come into their own. There is much they can share in. A bright, attractive wife will not only be a good hostess, but will be able to establish rapport with people of interest. Her evaluations either directly or by getting to know the wives and family, often prove more penetrating than those of her husband. Judy was a tremendous help to me in South America. Her interest in and her kindness toward the people we met were always geniuine and never had to be faked, and this was a priceless asset.

How much are CIA wives told? In the early days of the Agency there actually were officers who told their wives nothing, and even tried to maintain cover with them. This was pretty silly, and they all lived to regret it. The Agency is well aware that a wife will learn a lot, and it therefore puts all wives through a full staff clearance. If she does not pass it, the husband must resign. But wives should not be burdened with information they do not need to know, particularly the identity of their husbands' agents and operational details. A wife should know what her husband is doing in general, and what sort of people he needs to cultivate.

The children? Katya was too young to worry about. She thought I worked in a factory that made whiskey, cigars, cookies and canned food, because I used to bring these things home. But at a certain age the children must be told something, particularly overseas. Inevitably many CIA people become known within the American community, and are talked about in front of children, not realizing the problems caused. The CIA family is faced with a child saying, "Daddy, Johnnie says you're a spy." Beginning with the 1970s this could be tragic. The tears in the child's eyes showed that he thought this meant that Daddy was like a gangster. This is a problem that each family must solve on its own. Anybody who thinks it is dishonorable to serve the United States as an intelligence officer does not belong in the business.

I am often asked about women in the CIA. In my time the Agency employed numerous women in all sorts of capacities, including super-grade jobs. Many also served at field stations, not only as secretaries and intelligence assistants, but as reports and finance officers. There were also women case officers, but not many.

This was not because of any prejudice against them on the part of the Agency. There is nothing about a case officer's job that a woman cannot do as well as a man, except possibly skulking about dangerous parts of a foreign city alone. However, there are limitations having to do with the attitudes toward women in foreign countries. The famous "macho" spirit in Latin America is an example. A lot of such men find it demeaning to work for a woman and take orders from her, feeling that they are undervalued. If they agree to do so, they may try to turn the relationship into a sexual one.

Women agents, in many cases, do not want to work for a woman case officers. All the Mata Hari stories to the contrary, women agents are in a minority. They tend to have less access to interesting targets than men do, although they may have access to a man who does. Of course, women agents sometimes try to turn their male case officers into bed partners. They may succeed at times, but this is frowned on. Sexual relations do not mix with agent handling. Of the three female agents I "handled" in twenty-four years, two of them were obviously interested in sexual relations with me, and their feelings were hurt because I would not comply.

So, a female case officer has natural disadvantages in the business. Nevertheless, there have been a number of successful ones, particularly in the more civilized parts of the world. I remember one young woman who, because of various personnel shortages and home leaves, carried almost the whole case load of a small station quite successfully. I turned a male agent over to her, having explored his attitudes about being run by a woman. He had no objection. His only questions was, "Is she married?" She was not, but no problems resulted from this relationship.

Two and a half fascinating years went by in South America very quickly and it was time for home leave.

During this period we had lived through the Cuban missile crisis. On the evening of October 27, 1962, we went to a party where there were many diplomats present, including some Soviets. It happened to be a costume party, so I wore my *Cherkesska*. There was a strange hush over the room. People really thought that the end of the world was at hand. The guests were treated to an argument in the middle of the dance floor between myself in this *Cherkesska* and a Soviet wife, a very outspoken woman who was a doctor by profession and considered all of us, including her husband, probably GRU, a bunch of parasites. We shouted at each other in Russian. People stared, not understanding a word, but knowing they were watching a Soviet-American confrontation with the American side represented by a man in a "Cossack" costume. She was following the party line, which she may or may not have believed; I was defending the American side, in which I did believe. Nevertheless, I respected her because none of the other Soviets opened their mouths on the subject that was foremost on everyone's mind. When the orchestra started playing and she and I commenced dancing, the relief in the room was palpable. Later I approached her husband and said, "How about saying something interesting?" He giggled nervously.

A little over a year later Kennedy was assassinated. Even the Soviets seemed sincerely upset about this. It was touching that thousands of local people lined up at our embassy to pay tribute to the young president. I could not believe this had happened, and I paced half the night away in our back garden, thinking that he had been alive and happy that very morning.

By the spring of 1964 things were looking up for us. A letter from my father informed me that Nell had married a marine officer, William Lanagan. This meant that henceforth I could keep three quarters of my pay. I was sincerely happy for her, and even happier after I met her husband. I knew he would be a good stepfather for Marusya and Sasha, even though he had five children of his own from a previous marriage to Clark Clifford's daughter.

In those days an American ship plied the east coast of South America. In addition to the real cruise passengers, it filled up with American officials, including us, going on home leave from all parts of South America.

Katya, speaking only Spanish, felt like a second-class citizen. Her only friend was a little girl whose parents had been stationed in Brazil, and who could speak only Portuguese. Still, the two of them got on beautifully. Within two weeks of reaching the States, Katya was speaking a fluent English, though sounding like a Mexican; after a few weeks she never never spoke Spanish again.

Home leave stretched out to a long period of consultation in headquarters, now thoroughly established in the new building in Virginia. Khrushchev was overthrown during this period, but all I could hear on the radios was the World Series.

It was at this time that Judy gave me an ultimatum. She absolutely refused to return to South America for a second tour, even though this was already arranged and I had specifically asked for it without any objections from her. I had thought we were happy there. We had worked together, and lived through exciting times, but she was adamant. The CIA was considerate and easy-going in matters of this kind. There would be no problem, as long as I was willing to return to my station for the length of time it took to find and prepare a replacement. Of course, I had to agree.

Judy had brought this matter up as we had lunch in a Washington sidewalk cafe on October 14, almost three months after we had returned to the United States. I cannot pass the spot without remembering the rage I was in, and yet, all the arrangements were made within two weeks, and I was on my way back to South America alone. The several months became six; it was lonely there but I had plenty of work to do.

The end purpose of this work is to gather information, mostly through the recruitment of agents. Where do agents come from? Some volunteer. Some of these turn out to be valuable, but others could be sent in by the other side, or could be intelligence swindlers—private entrepreneurs of the spy business—or just plain nuts.

One of the most valuable walk-ins we ever had was first judged to be a 'psychotic fabricator" by an overzealous case officer. In this business being overly suspicious can land you in as much trouble as being overly naive.

If agents don't volunteer, they have to be found and recruited. Somebody has to spot a likely prospect and find out enough about him or her to make a file check possible. Then the person must be assessed to see what makes him tick, what his motivations are, what political opinions he holds, what sort of personality he has, whether he has enough stability to work for us. Of course, none of this makes any sense unless it is determined that he has access to something of interest, or some potential utility.

Assuming that everything works out and headquarters grants clearance, the prospect has to be recruited. This is the moment of truth, one of the most dramatic and important moments in a case officer's life, when he is exposed and has to show his greatest talents of persuasion and conviction.

Reactions on the part of the person being recruited range from relief, "I thought you'd never ask!" to a glass of beer in the face, or even a call to the police. In my experience most such scenes, even when there is a turn-down, take place in urbane civility. "Thanks, but no thanks!"

Some reactions are unexpected. I once had a polite turn down from a Communist official who hinted that he might have accepted if he had been asked personally by the American Ambassador. Obviously, status played a huge role in this man's life, and few case officers have much overt status.

Motivation is the key. Why do people let themselves be recruited? Naturally, the resident of a reasonably free country who agrees to perform a support task at little personal risk cannot be mentioned in the same breath as a Colonel Penkovsky, one of the most outstanding successes we ever had. Penkovsky was a Soviet GRU colonel who worked for us in Moscow.

Even with people who are willing to put their lives on the line, motivation varies tremendously, can rarely be simply identified, and moreover changes with time. Some of my colleagues did not believe in ideological motivation at all. Others believed that it was always a cover for some other reason. Colonel Penkovsky obviously thought of himself as a Russian patriot fighting the Soviet regime; some CIA officers said, "Yes, but the real reasons were rage, revenge, disappointment," and so on.

I think ideological factors are often very important, but seldom, if ever, the whole story. Venality is also seldom the complete story, although the least complicated and most easily understood of motives. There are all sorts of other motives—frustration, love of the game for its own sake, a desire for secret prestige, or even to influence history somehow.

Sometimes personal feelings of friendship, trust, and loyalty to the case officer are of extreme importance. This leads to dramas and difficulties when the case officer must be replaced by another.

Motivation has to be studied continually for change. Just as a case officer may start out with patriotic enthusiasm, and twenty years later find himself mostly thinking of the size of his pension, the reason for an agent's collaboration with us can change with the circumstances of his life. He may acquire a family and a stake in his overt life. He may become disillusioned with us, or feel that he has taken enough risks. It is often people in their middle years who are most receptive to a proposition which will dramatically change and give purpose to their lives.

Undoubtedly we have had some simple traitors working for us, simply selling us information. But the word "treason" is a semantic trap. George Washington was a traitor to the supporters of George III. Lenin was a traitor, not only to Nicholas II, but to Russia, because he actively worked for her defeat in World War I and accepted money from the German general staff. Each of them had a purpose, which happened to succeed. Without equating their purposes, each became a national hero having been, by definition, a traitor originally. Why then should a person who is willing to risk his life in fighting an oppressive regime be labeled a traitor?

I suppose this argument could also be used to clear Philby and company. To the extent that they were silly enough to believe that Stalin represented the desirable future of the world, perhaps; although they betrayed a legitimate democracy with a freely elected government. So I, who long ago chose sides, think of them as traitors, but will settle for the term "dangerous enemies."

During those last six months in South America I went to a party, and the hostess told me she had a Russian maid in the kitchen, and would I mind speaking to her? I saw a nice looking old lady by the stove, whose eyes lit up at the sound of her native language. When I told her my name, she almost fainted. I actually had to hold her upright in her chair. She was the wife of an officer of the Circassian Regiment, who had served under my grandfather Chavchavadze in World War I. Considering that the regiment had never numbered more than 600 men, and far fewer officers, this was an incredibly long shot to occur in the middle of South America in 1965. The next day she introduced me to her husband, a Russified Pole who had endless respect for my grandfather and remembered my father, George and Marina visiting the regiment near the front as children. This sort of thing seems to happen to us members of the Russian diaspora.

It brought to life an old story I heard as a child. A former Russian naval officer sailing in some merchant ship after the revolution, was shipwrecked off the coast of South America. He managed to swim ashore and make his way to the nearest town, looking like a total tramp. There, a South American policeman left his post directing traffic when he saw this bum and began to follow him. The officer tried to get away, fearing an arrest for vagrancy, but was too exhausted to run very far. As he collapsed on the sidewalk, he saw the policeman draw himself up to attention, salute, and say in Russian, "Your honor, Petty Officer So-and-so of His Imperial Majesty's Ship Thus-and-such. May I be of service to Your Honor?"

I felt I needed a change of scene, to get away from Russians of every kind and see something more of the continent. A former marine officer whom I had known in Berlin had retired to northern Paraguay. He kept writing to entice me to come visit, promising jaguars, wild Indians, huge red wasps that could knock a man off a horse, and total wilderness, so I flew to Asuncion for a vacation before returning to Washington.

Even here, however, there was a Russian—not Soviet—influence. During its 1934 war with Bolivia, Paraguay had been advised by former Russian general staff officers, who took their revenge for their 1914 defeats over the Germans, who were advising Bolivia. The greatest Russian hero here, then still living, had formerly commanded the Seversky Dragoon Regiment, always brigaded with our family regiment, the Nizhegorodsky Dragoons. No way to get away from it!

This week in Paraguay was a fitting ending to my years in South America. Within three weeks my replacement had arrived and been briefed. I left for Washington, happy to be reunited with Judy and Katya, but regretful that we were not coming back to complete a second tour.

CHAPTER XVI

Judy and little Katya met me at National Airport on a sunny May day in 1965, and whisked me off in a brand-new station wagon to a log cabin in Great Falls, Virginia, very small but cosily furnished. It was located on land belonging to friends of ours.

We were thinking of building a house on two acres we owned, until my classmate John Hanes came up with an irresistable offer. He wanted to sell us a house entirely surrounded by his property, with three acres and a right-of-way to the nearest road. He offered it at a price that was so low the man who came to assess the place for a mortgage could not believe it. Johnnie wanted friends to live there. The house was attractive, built around a pre-Civil War hunting lodge, and looking out on a vista of our feudal overlord's acres, complete with lowing kine and horses. This lasted for twenty years, and only began to disappear in the 1980s as Hanes' land was sold.

While we were "beyond the beltway," as they now say, it was a convenient commute to the new CIA building, except in heavy snow when only a helicopter would have worked, and they never sent one.

We had pleasant and rather eccentric neighbors. One had a cannon, adapted to fire tennis balls, and the other was a mortar expert in the Pentagon. The latter once managed to fire an ice-cream cone out of a mortar and land it in the former's lap. On the Fourth of July all this equipment was hauled to Johnnie Hanes's place and we had sham battles. The motorists on Route 193 were amazed to see a wooden tank, with mortars sticking out, being towed down the road, and the tennis ball cannon was also a surprise.

This was the first house I had ever owned, and, observing Russian custom, we had a priest come out to bless it. Father Arkady Moiseyev did a thorough job, going down into the two basements and dousing the very foundations with holy water. This may sound barbaric to some, but to me it is one of the strengths of the Orthodox Church—this union of the spiritual and material.

At 8:06 AM, August 1, 1966, Judy gave birth to a son. It was a Monday morning and I must admit to a hangover, but this instantaneously disappeared. I forgot all about it and also about the old family custom that a newborn son must be wrapped in his father's shirt. This probably would not have been permitted anyway by the George Washington University Hospital for hygenic reasons.

"Hurrah," said my mother on the phone, "the dynasty is saved!"

Actually, I had been sure it would be another girl. I even had an excuse made up, for Russians, based on a story involving one of those rare birds, a Georgian tightwad. This Prince Orbeliani was asked by Nicholas II to give a ruble to a peasant he had talked to. "If my sovereign doesn't have a ruble," Orbeliani said quickly, "how dare I have a ruble?"

I was going to say, "If my sovereign had four daughters in a row. . . ."
Much to my surprise and delight this was not necessary.

When Judy was pregnant there had been quite a hassle with my father about
what the child would be called if it was a boy. He had never done this before. He
insisted on the boy being called Alexander, after his father, with the nickname
Sandro. I would gladly have reserved this name for a boy if my father had made
similar noises earlier, but I already had a daughter named Alexandra, and it seemed
unimaginative to repeat it in this way. Besides, Sasha was adamant against it.

So my father had to bow to the name of Michael, but then insisted that he
must never be called "Misha," which was exactly what Judy and I wanted to call
him.

"Why, for God's sakes?" I asked.

"Never mind. If I feel so strongly there must be a reason."

I never did find out what it was, so, by way of compromise, I made up a
pseudo-Georgian nickname for my new son—Miko. Pseudo, because in Georgian it
would have been "Mikho," with a hard H, and I knew nobody could pronounce that.
Surprisingly, the nickname has stuck.

Miko's christening in October was the last great family party involving my
parents, and it was a huge success. I was particularly glad that one of Miko's
godparents, Prince Paul Ilyinsky, the son of Grand Duke Dimitri Pavlovich, took the
trouble to come. I had not seen him since childhood, but Judy knew him from
Cincinnati. The other godfather, William Sloane Coffin, could not make it, nor
could one of the godmothers, my cousin Marina Romanov, daughter of Prince Vasili.
They missed a great party, and an unrepeatable occasion. For one thing, it was the
last time my father and I sang together, after the little hero had been put to bed.

I had only just made it to my son's birth. I was on a temporary duty trip
overseas. From late 1965 until I retired in 1974, I made over fifty of these trips,
some for a few days only, some for weeks, most coming up with very little advance
notice. I went to almost every part of the world, except for Communist countries,
and even went around the world twice, each time in a different direction. Some of
this travel was to countries I had been in before, in Europe and South America, but I
must have racked up twenty five new ones in Africa, the Middle East and Far East.

My mother and Aunt Xenia used to have a contest about hom many states
of the union they had visited. Aunt Xenia, who could afford it, finally won by
hitting all the states my mother had missed, and throwing in the provinces of Canada
for good measure. I inherited this urge for counting. I don't know what their totals
were, but I know mine—forty-six states, missing only Maine, Oregon, Mississippi
and Alabama— fifty-seven foreign countries, plus ten more in airport stops.

During this CIA globe-trotting period, I visited many countries where I had
no operational activity, either to confuse the opposition, or as rest stops, or to take a
day or two annual leave to visit friends. I landed in London and Paris on my way to
other places so often that I lost count. On one trip I started off up to my knees in
snow in northern Europe and ended up in the equatorial heat of Africa. This sort of
thing made packing difficult, particularly since I often did not know in advance
where I would go after the first stop. So the vignettes mentioned here did not
necessarily happen in countries where I was involved in operations.

Berlin—after an absence of almost ten years I came back to this city that had played such a key role in my life. Skyscrapers now surrounded the ruins—deliberately left that way—of the church where twenty years before in pitch darkness I had picked up a brick in each hand in case somebody were to attack me. That was Berlin I, the early occupation. Berlin II was when Nell and I had lived there at the height of the Cold War. I say height, because the Cold War never ended, merely changed forms. Here was Berlin III, the main difference being the Wall, erected in 1961. It was shocking to see it, and yet, our old suburbs of Dahlem and Zehlendorf had hardly changed at all.

The was was not the only difference. The Free University of Berlin, once a refuge from Communism, had become radicalized in spite of the Wall. I visited a friend of mine, connected with the university. During Berlin II he had been a social democrat, an enthusiastic supporter of the great Mayor Reuter. Yet now my friend had huge posters of Che Guevara, Ho Chi Minh, and Castro on his walls, with the Big Wall only a few miles away. He praised East Germany for having, at least, introduced "elements of socialism." Mayor Reuter must have been spinning in his grave, as well as all those people who had been killed at the Wall getting away from these "elements of socialism." I guess my friendship with this fellow ended when I threatened to pee on the least favorite of his three posters. He would not tell me which one was his least favorite, but I can still hear his even more radicalized girlfriend screeching like a banshee. Naturally, I had no real intention to irrigate their silly posters.

London: I called on my childhood friend Azamat Guirey, married to the sister of Ivan Obolensky. I arrived just in time, almost literally, to catch Azamat at the bottom of the outside stairs. His marriage, he told me, was over. Never had a friend in need appeared at a more opportune time. He took me to about six cocktail parties, and the next day we recovered at White's Club. This most posh establishment, dating back to the Regency, was still full of young men on weekdays playing backgammon and drinking champagne. The spirit of Wodehouse lived! Azamat went through some hard times before marrying an extremely beautiful and wealthy girl.

Rome, 1966: When Judy and I were married, Uncle Sergei Sheremetyev announced that for a wedding present he was giving us Queen Olga of Greece's hand. Judy and I looked at each other—it could hardly be a mummified hand, or could it? More letters arrived. The hand was in Rome, in the custody of Prince Roman of Russia, and I must arrange to have it shipped out by diplomatic friends, because the Italian government was very strict about works of art leaving the country. So it was a work of art. That, at least, was a relief.

When my mother was told about all this her reaction was, "But my grandmother had such ugly hands, just like mine."

So here I was in Rome, and Uncle Sergei handed me the hand, a life-size piece of marble. There had been a fad at the turn of the century for people to have their hands sculpted, and a whole street in Rome had been involved in this business. I brought the hand out of Italy in my briefcase, and it is still hidden in Judy's house somewhere, an object nobody wants to look at.

London, 1966: Nell and her husband Bill Lanagan had been transfered to

London, so that I was frequently able to visit Marusya and Sasha. They attended a very good school, but had to wear St. Trinian-type uniforms with floppy hats and green underwear, something of a shock after the Potomac School. Otherwise they adjusted well to England.

In London I stayed with my cousin Mysh and her second husband, Dr. Geoffrey Tooth, under an arrangement called B and B (this stood for bed and Bourbon). I got the bed, they got the Bourbon, which was hideously expensive in England, but I could get it through the embassy.

Stockholm: First there was a thaw and my South American boots sprung a leak. This was followed by the coldest night in ninety-five years. I went to the movies, not realizing that frost-bite stations had been set up for the Swedes. I found the captured banners of Peter the Great from the Battle of Narva in the Royal Military Museum, a completely deserted place. The hall with the banners did not even have a guard. I suppressed the urge to liberate one of them.

Stockholm was not a good town for pub-crawling. I finally found a beer joint and got into a conversation with a black Anglophone African who asked me whether I was interested in meeting a deserter from the U.S. Army. Why not?

A handsome blond youngster was brought up to me. I had noticed him before, sitting with two ravishing Swedish blondes. I steeled myself for an anti-Vietnam tirade. Not at all. The boy had been stationed in Frankfurt with almost no chance of shipment to Vietnam. But it had become fashionable to go over the hill. I asked him how he was doing.

"Frankly, Sir," he replied politely, "I'm exhausted. The girls here are really something, but I've just about had all I can take. Besides, I can't get the hang of the language, so I can't find a job. The Swedes give me a few crowns to live off, but it's rough."

He sounded as if he would now prefer a stockade in Frankfurt.

Everywhere in Stockholm where a ray of sunshine hit a wall, there was a lovely girl trying to catch its weak rays. So many beautiful girls, and yet I noticed that most of the Swedes with dates or wives seemed to prefer rather plain young women. The beauties liked foreigners, particularly dark, Mediteranean types.

Accra, Ghana: As I got off the plane I noticed machine-guns pointed at the stairs from two directions. We got into a bus, and two groups of military in different uniforms chased each other all around the bus, pointing guns but not firing. Nkrumah had just been overthrown and things had not settled down to normal, or maybe this was normal.

City transportation was provided by little trucks, people crowded in the roofless rear part. The first one I saw had a sign, "These people, they talk too much!" I was about to assume they were some sort of political prisoners when I noticed that instead of directional signs, all these trucks had some sort of slogan. My favorite, "You show me your love and I'll show you my character."

Lima, Peru: The changing of the presidential guard—a ballet in slow-motion goose step. Inca faces in Napoleonic dragoon helmets.

The Museo de Oro. A skull with a complete set of beautifully made amythist teeth.

"How was it done?" I asked myself out loud.

"Posthumously, I presume," said an Englishman in back of me.

Brussels: I found the battlefield of Waterloo by general knowledge of history and a railroad schedule. I got off at Braine d'Ailleurs and walked, as it turned out, the path of Wellington's army. The main parts of the battlefield were still being farmed and inaccessible; in the middle there were honkey-tonks. Nothing like our Civil War national park battlefields. Also, obviously, Napoleon had won. No Wellingtoniana on sale. I climbed the pyramid and ran into a Soviet delegation with an emigré guide. The emigré was telling them the famous story of *le mot de Chambronne*. This occurred at the end of the battle, which, incidentally, Napoleon did lose, when the British asked the French Imperial Guard to surrender. Chambronne, the commander, replied *merde*, generally rendered in history books as, "The French Guard dies but never surrenders," perhaps the longest mistranslation of one word on record. But when this emigré came to the punchline, he could not bring himself to say the Russian word for "merde," so the whole story fell flat. Of course, I could have saved the day, but keeping ones mouth shut is part of the game.

Madrid, still in Franco's time: All the passport stamping and customs officials seemed to be on siesta, and we walked into the airport with all the formality of going from Washington to New York. This is a fascist state? *Time* magazine on sale everywhere. Spaniards traveling abroad freely.

I went out to look at El Escorial, Philip II's palace, and got into a conversation with an American lady as we wandered through its halls. She asked my name.

"My God," she exclaimed, "I delivered a tricycle to you from your grandmother in 1929. Let me tell you it was no simple matter to get it on the boat!"

I remembered that tricycle in our small apartment in New York, looking huge and welcome, and my parents saying that an American lady had brought it. Poor Babady never got the credit.

Bangui, Central African Republic: From my hotel a view of the Ubangi River with its pencil-thin canoes of hollow logs, curled up on each end, called pirogues. On the other side of the river was Zaire, the ex-Belgian Congo. It was then almost impossible to get a visa to visit Zaire, but I was told that for two francs one could be rowed across the river on a pirogue, no visa necessary. Always eager to acquire another country, I did this.

There was a town on the Zaire side called Zongo, which appears on many world maps but, as I learned, consists of about fifty small houses. Zongo had some powerful loudspeakers which kept Bangui awake half the night with loud music, mostly American. I do not know whether this was some sort of pyschological warfare, or merely the life style of the Zongians.

As my pirogue pushed into the sand on the Zaire side, a barefoot official in a Belgian style cap, sitting in the sand, lifted my passport, promising to give it back when I was ready to return. Somewhat uncomfortable *sans* passport, I began to walk the main street of Zongo, which soon became a jungle road with grass huts, reminiscent of my grade-school geography books featuring Bombo the jungle boy. Very few people were visible. Then, as the grass huts were becoming sparser, I ran into two young men.

"*Vous êtes missionaire, Monsieur?*" one asked.

I assured him that I was not there to preach—just a mere tourist. They looked neither hostile nor friendly. I admit that stories about missionaries being had for lunch unworthily flashed through my mind. So I sort of smiled and waved at them and got the hell back to the man in the Belgian hat, retrieved my precious passport, and fled in a pirogue to the other side of the river.

I shall always regret not being there when Bokassa declared himself emperor and had a Napoleon-style coronation. Silly as it was, it would have been something to see.

Tehran: Speaking of emperors, the Shah was at the height of his glory. The Americans referred to him as HIM (His Imperial Majesty). I never felt any hostility from Iranians. I arrived just in time for their new year in March, for them a new year in the XIV Century. They all left their houses and picknicked in a huge field, sitting on rugs with samovars and lots of vodka, which they offered me whenever I greeted them.

Tokyo: A huge leftist parade of young people yelling, "Yankee go home!" This I had not expected there. A middle aged Japanese standing next to me said, "Young keeds go home!"

India: Fascinating and horrifying. I had never seen such poverty, not in South America, not in Haiti, not in Thailand, where the lowest peasant diving into the klong (canal) seemed middle class compared to the Indians, particularly those in Calcutta.

I passed through India twice without the opportunity to make personal contact with Indians, so I could only judge as a traveler judges—officials, hotel and restaurant personnel, and so on. The officials were surly with very difficult customs checks. The hotel personnel were rude and very stratified. I rode up an old cage-type elevator with a bellboy holding my key, while two turbaned peons ran carrying my luggage up the clearly visible stairs. The bellboy, naturally I suppose, was furious when I tipped him and these peons who had done the work equally.

Then there were the weird liquor laws. One got a liquor ration card with ones visa. These laws differed from state to state, but usually the only Indians allowed to drink in bars were certified alcoholics. This meant that the bars were little hangovers from the Raj—retired British colonels and the occasional tourist. Each time you had a drink it was entered into your visa card, into a ledger at the bar, and into some sort of notebook with three copies. Once in Madras I heard the sound of running bare feet behind me, and this runner begged me to sign the third copy of the notebook, because my signature had not come through the carbon. I have never seen this much red tape before or since.

Frankfurt Airport, 1968: I bumped into a non-agency friend who had just arrived from Moscow. He told me Solzhenitsyn was writing two books, one to be called *GULAG*, the other *Archipelago*. This was six years before Solzhenitsyn was thrown out of the USSR, and it was the first I had heard of what was to become such a seminally important addition to the political literature of the world.

Istanbul: Hagia Sofia, Justinian's magnificent cathedral which had once turned on the emissaries of Vladimir of Kiev to such an extent that they thought they were in heaven, is now a museum. Actually, the Turks had made a concession by neutralizing the building they had used as a mosque for almost 500 years. Still, I furtively crossed myself. Years later a Roman pontiff committed a greater gaffe by prostrating himself there.

Topkapi, the sultan's palace, was open but the harem part closed. What a pity! This city is so full of history for me that all I had to do was stare at the Bosphorous from my hotel to go into a sort of trance. Europa and the bull, not really history, Constantine the Great, the Byzantines, Kievan attacks, the crusader sack and rule, the capture by the Turks; Sultan nutty Ibrahim or whoever it was that threw a harem-load of wives into the Bosphorus, sewn up in sacks; the unrealized ambitions of Catherine the Great and of those 1920 Greeks; the German cruiser *Goeben* escaping to Constantinopel in 1914 and hoisting the Turkish flag; the Allied fleet and its fatal near miss in 1915; the evacuation of Wrangel's White army in 1920 from the Crimea.

There was a live remnant of Wrangel's army right in the hotel—the widow of an officer, now sitting outside the men's room to collect tips. She and her husband had been among the few that had not pushed on further west. How had the Turks treated them? Well, they took us in at least, but they never forgave us for being Russians.

Paris-Orly, 21 August 1968: I noticed that all the flights to Prague had *annulé* signs on them. The Soviets had invaded Czechoslovakia and crushed the "Prague Spring." Big demonstrations in front of the Soviet Embassy in London by the same hippy types who usually demonstrate in front of ours. An amazing amount of indifference in the States, however.

Amsterdam: Loaded with young people of every conceivable nationality. What surprised me was how merry the supposedly dour Dutch were. By about six on weekday evenings there was an explosion of gayety, as middle aged and even elderly women drank, danced and sang.

Hamburg: I went to a strip joint on the Reeperbahn and made friends with an Anglophone black African and his wife. The latter kept agitating for a male strip tease, without success, and they were both eager to see a black girl strip. Finally one came on and was invited to join our table after her very commendable performance. She turned out to be from Martinique, speaking only French, so I ended up interpreting among the three of them.

Fort Lamy, Chad: It was a national holiday. The whole town was full of exotic horsemen from the north, who had temporarily called off their insurgency. They were black, but their accoutrements looked Arab. Their horses were caparisoned with silver, and they wore silver swords and daggers. The chiefs had umbrellas held over their heads by servitors. I was told there were 10,000 of them. There were also a lot of young white men in civilian clothes around, attracting no attention. I realized they were French Foreign Legionnaires after the locals began addressing me as Ajudant, or first sergeant. Perhaps if I had not been on foot they would have called me "colonel."

Frankfurt: I happened to catch Radio Moscow on a shortwave set, which I listen to very rarely. The first program was an interview with the Chairman of Sovkhoz Tsinandali!

Kuwait: It was so hot that one dodged the sun when crossing the street as if it were rifle fire. The Soviet and Chinese embassies were side by side. I noticed that while the Chinese had a brand new red flag, the Soviet one had turned to orange with age and heat. So I posted an anonymous letter to the Soviet Ambassador, expressing patriotic shock at this circumstance. The flag was changed two days later.

Flight from Haiti to New York: The pilot came on in lugubrious tones and announced that the entire East Coast was socked in with snow. Therefore, we would land in Bermuda and spend the night at the Castle Harbor Hotel, courtesy of Pan Am. Loud cheers! Several other jets did the same thing. The whole off-season island trekked to the hotel, guitars, steel bands, the works. It was crowded but all of us, strangers to each other, had a magnificent party, the rum also being courtesy of Pan-Am for those who had the sense to sign for their drinks.

Cyprus: What a delightful place it was before the Turks invaded! There was a "green line" dividing the Greek and Turkish sectors, which passed through the middle of Nicosia, but this was no barrier to foreigners. It was guarded by U.N. troops—Canadians, Irish, Finns, Swedes, Austrians. I had not seen such a collection of uniforms since Berlin I. The Greek part of Famagusta was full of Swedes and Finns in uniform. The Turkish part was frozen in a time warp. There were still cannon balls lying around in that walled city from the siege in 1599, when the Turks had captured the town from the Venetians and flayed their commander alive.

In Nicosia I caught a glimpse of the president, Archbishop Makarios, driving by in his black robes and later addressing a crowd from his residence. The British called him "Black Mac."

At night the tavernas in Nicosia were marvellous. The Greek girls always assumed I was from the Sixth Fleet, which seemed very popular.

I was taken to an archeological dig at an ancient site south of Nicosia. Young volunteers, many of them Americans, dug trenches, marking and sifting everything with infinite care. I later read that these same trenches were used as defensive positions by the Greek Cypriots against the Turks. Nobody can blame soldiers under fire for using a ready-made trench, but what a terrible shame it all was.

These vignettes are a sample of what my eight years of globe-trotting was like. Some of the best parts will have to remain untold.

During most of my globe-trotting the Vietnam War was on, but none of my work for the CIA had anything to do with it. It is often called the war that divided families. This was certainly true in my case.

After a few fights my parents and I completely avoided talking about it. The fights were mostly with my mother, my father agreeing with her, but being more diplomatic.

"Communism is better for the peasants of Vietnam than anything the south has to offer," Mama said.

"Do you think Communism helped the peasants in Russia?"

"Certainly not!" Mama denied.

"Can you think of any place where the peasants have been helped by forced collectivization?"

"Well, perhaps in China.

"It seems to me you are taking a racist attitude on this point," I replied.

Mamma looked at me with great surprise. How could anybody accuse her of being a racist? In fairness, nobody could, except in regard to Germans. This was a ploy on my part.

Another conversation went something like this:

"Isn't it wonderful that the Supreme Court has approved the publication of the Pentagon Papers?"

"No. How can we deal with the USSR, China, or anybody else if any government employee can make public anything classified he disagrees with? There is such a thing as respecting the oath of secrecy you take when you are allowed access to such material," I replied.

"You have taken an oath to a vile organization."

This was rather hurtful. I thought I had taken an oath to the United States, not a particular organization. Still more hurtful was her lack of understanding or sympathy with what I was trying to do within the "vile" organization. Yet, to the end of her life she always said, "There is nothing nasty the Soviets would not do," while she sympathized with other Communist movements. Too many years on Cape Cod!

More amazingly, Judy began to change. She had voted for Goldwater in 1964, though her brother, sister and I had been for Johnson. Now she turned against the war. I attribute this to too much TV and the frequent visits of Bill Coffin. But, like my mother, she remained anti-Soviet, as if there were no connection.

In 1966 and 1967 Bill Coffin still called himself an anti-Communist. Whenever he visited there were great bear hugs, but arguments about the war until three in the morning over drinks.

In a *Playboy* interview he was asked whether he still had good relations with his old CIA friends. He replied that he did. He did not name me, but did mention that he was the godfather of a CIA officer's son, and that we had friendly late night arguments over drinks.

Much to my surprise, in his book published ten years later, these scenes, reduced to one incident, have Judy bringing Coffin back to our house, saying that it would be good for me to see him, though I didn't want to. Actually, I was always delighted to have someone to argue with and never lost my fondness for Bill until his book came out.

Instead of a bear hug, Coffin's book states that I had a "scowl of hatred" on my face and I agreed when he said, "I suppose you are looking at a traitor." He told me he was looking at a murderer. All this is nonsense. If the words were used in some of our sessions, it was done half in jest.

Our late night sessions were always friendly. At least once I thought I understood what was driving him. I brought up the subject of the Vlasov troops forcibly repatriated by the Americans at Plattling, Bavaria, while Coffin was a young lieutenant there. He had not disobeyed orders then, and now that he was again in disagreement with the U.S. Government, he was determined to oppose it actively.

Fine, but as I pointed out to him, he had switched sides. That's what the ghosts of Vlasov's men would have thought, those ghosts that obviously meant a great deal to Coffin. In his book he writes about them movingly. He knew they were not simple Quislings, had committed no crimes against the Jews, and even sheltered many of them, and had merely chosen, in Coffin's words, "between one arch-villain and another," Stalin to them being Enemy Number One. The night before the repatriation by American G.I.'s, when all sorts of atrocities and suicides took place, these Russians had put on a great show, which Coffin describes in his book. He used to tell me, also, that there was a huge sign over the stage—one word: *nadezhda*—hope. Bill had to sit through this knowing what would happen in the morning, but he did not whisper a word of warning to any of them. I have never blamed him for this. I might have acted the same way in his place, remembering my attitudes in 1946.

In his book Coffin admits what I had guessed ten years before its publication. The Plattling experience had motivated him to join the CIA, ". . . . but also made it easier for me in 1967 to commit civil disobedience in opposition to the war in Vietnam." Then he calls the Americans pushing the conflict "war criminals," and equates them with the people who ordered the repatriation of the anti-Soviet Russians into Stalin's hands. A pretty far-fetched analogy. I hope Bill sometimes thinks of the Vietnam boat people, who are analagous to his Plattling ghosts.

In the fall of 1968 Judy announced that our marriage was in serious trouble, which came as a surprise to me. I could not stand thinking of myself as a two-time loser, and I sometimes caught myself hoping the plane would crash so my children would think of me as a hero, but then I would quickly apologize to the Diety for daring to wish harm to my fellow passengers. I was horrified at the thought of leaving Katya and Miko, but this is what happened in the spring of 1969.

I drove away from that lovely place in Virginia with just about everything I owned in the back of my car. With the good luck that I so often have in the middle of bad luck, my cousin Mysh and her husband, now in Washington, took me in on more or less the same bed-Bourbon principle we had enjoyed in London. The next couple of years I led a nomadic life, doing a lot of house-sitting. When there was no house I moved back with Mysh and Geoffrey.

One night we went to a Russian church-sponsored ball. I noticed that the place had been invaded by a half dozen Soviet men from the embassy, who paid their fee and spread out to make contacts. As it happened, Geoffrey Tooth, retired chief psychiatrist of the British Government and looking the part, was bored with the ball and was browsing in the library. One of the Soviets tried to cultivate him.

"Look here," said Geoffrey with great dignity, "I've been to your bloody country and I don't like it a bit. So buzz off, will you?" The crestfallen Soviet did so, and we will never know whether his files told him that the bearded Englishman was married to a Romanov.

Marusya and Sasha had returned from England as wonderfully attractive teenagers, so I saw them frequently; I was also able to see Katya and Miko as often as I liked.

The children came up, in various combinations, to visit my parents in Wellfleet. In 1971 my father looked very robust, but everybody was worried about my mother's health. Over the Fourth of July weekend both my parents derived great pleasure from their five-year-old grandson Miko. A couple of days after I had returned Miko to Judy and stopped off to see friends in Connecticut, my father had a massive heart attack. I took an air taxi to Hyannis where he was hospitalized. I was told he might or might not survive, and it could be a matter of days. I took a room in a motel next to the hospital and sent Mama home. He was dead within a few hours.

The funeral service was in the Greek church in Hyannis. The open coffin at first horrified me, but then, staring at it, I decided the Orthodox Church was right in insisting on it. It forces one to face the facts, and the material body begins to dissolve. My father was buried in Truro, among old American friends of the thirties, near a church on a hill about which he had once written a song.

St. Petersburg, Tblisi, Kishenev, Bucharest, London, New York, Patton's Third Army, Korea, Wellfleet, Truro. A strange but not atypical odyssey for a Russian emigré.

Thus died an extraordinarily charming, deep, and spiritual man who had gambled on becoming a writer. He published five books. The best of them, a novel about the Russian revolution, was turned down by thirty-two American publishers, though it had already had success in England and the Commonwealth and been translated into Spanish. Some of the same American publishers published impossible pot-boilers on the subject. He wrote in English with tremendous self-discipline and perfectionism. He would have been horrified by his obituaries—"Paul Chavchavadze, Svetlana's translator." Yes, he had translated Stalin's daughter's second book, but that was his only translation, and there was hardly a mention of his original writing.

As I sat by the phone in Wellfleet, listening to voices from deep in the past and far off geographically, I realized the extent to which he had been popular and loved.

My mother showed the stuff she was made of and bore up magnificently through all this. But inwardly she was crushed, with little will to live left. She survived him for two and a half years. She felt like hell physically as well, and she, who once thought nothing of driving to California or Mexico, could no longer handle a car, so I had to recruit sitters for her and help with the expenses of the house. Luckily, she received an unexpected sum of money, a partial pay-back of a loan her mother had made in 1919! Nancy generously surrendered her share to Mama. This was the last of the strange little legacies which would appear from time to time, keeping up my parents' faith that God was taking care of them.

Now, during my visits to Wellfleet there were no political fights. She was signing off from the world, convinced that it was going to hell—a good time get off. I spent the last New Year's Eve of her life with her.

On 24 February 1974, Elena Wilson called to say that Mama had been taken to the Hyannis hospital with pneumonia, and it looked bad. Again I flew to Hyannis, which I still associate with death. My mother's lungs were weak from smoking, and she probably had emphysema. That and her general lack of will to live made the pneumonia fatal. She lingered on for three days, unconscious most of the time, and then she died at ten in the evening. She had looked so unexpectedly young and beautiful, Elena said, when the ambulance came for her, that it was a pity she could not have stayed in her own bed and died there.

During our last visit together, after once again telling me how awful old age was, she looked at me strangely and said, "You're approaching old age too." At forty-nine I certainly did not feel this, but there was never any point arguing with my mother.

There was a Greek funeral, this time with a Russian priest present. Hussein, the Tatar groom from Harax was there to mourn the little princess he had taken out riding in antedeluvian 1913. Just before the coffin was closed, Nancy placed a small Russian tri-color we had found in the house on Mama's chest. Again the mournful convoy to Truro, where my mother came to rest beside my father.

She had been beautiful, intelligent, humorous, artistic, strong-willed, rebellious, and interested in practically everything. Not much of this was left at the time of her illness, although she was not quite seventy-three.

It was strange, here in Massachussets, to think that once a Russian guards battery in far-off St. Petersburg had fired a twenty-one gun salute for her birth.

Less than two weeks after the funeral, Nancy called to say that Nyanyushka had terminal cancer. This, after Mama's death, was a bit much to take. It turned out to be a false diagnosis. She merely had her gall bladder removed, "gold bludder," she called it, and she lived for another seven years, dying peacefully at the age of ninety-one. Only then did I feel completely orphaned.

Maybe I was not approaching old age, but I was going to be fifty in May of 1974, the magic age that made retirement possible, and I would have twenty-nine years Federal service, counting the Army and unused sick leave, of which I had a year's worth. I would have enough of a pension to live off comfortably in my single state.

The media attacks on the Agency, and the efforts of some newspapers to dig up and expose every operation they possibly could in the name of "public service," were annoying, but not enough to drive me out. I still loved the work and retained motivation for it. I knew we were not the bad guys, because I had rather extensive experience with the real bad guys. I had survived the various "reductions in force," and had no fear of being forced out. Still, I yearned for the freedom I had given up for almost a quarter century. My best friends were retiring all around me, the World War II generation, of which I was one of the youngest. There were many good younger people left, but I was feeling lonely. My chief seemed upset when I announced my decision, but he offered me a contract, which I accepted. This meant that I could still be useful, paid by the day when actually employed, but free to accept or turn down any assignments. Perfect!

Ten days after returning from my last overseas trip for the Agency, and five days after my birthday, I retired. I waited those five days in order for my retirement to fall on a Friday and a payday. Why challenge the competence of the people or machines who wrote the checks?

A retirement party at the office, and then a magnificent one outside, the invitation to which contained every possible work for freedom in English and Russian the hosts could dream up—manumission, liberation, amnesty, escape, de-collectivization, emancipation, parole, rebirth, commencement, and even coopfly. On Monday I really felt free. I lay in the bathtub listening maliciously to the radio helicopter reports of Washington commuter traffic.

I had no regrets about my twenty-four years in the Agency—the occasional unforgettably magnificent adventures; a first-hand knowledge of so much of the world; and most important, there was the work, always on target for what I wanted to do——working against the Bolsheviks. There had also been pleasant working conditions among first-rate people. Yes, there were also second-rate people, and people I disagreed with, but I was never forced to do anything I though wrong, either tactically or morally.

I knew then, and I know more now, that certain people in the Agency were so obsessed with finding penetrations that they lost all sense of proportion and did damage by assuming that everything we did was tainted. Given the British experience they can be excused for having started this, but I do not excuse them for having left the element of common sense out of their calculations. If the KGB was as all-powerful and omniscient as they thought, there was no point for us to be in business at all.

Several months after retirement I was called back and given a medal. It was the lowest of the several they had, but it was far from routine. I was particularly honored that Director Colby, under daily attack from Congress at the time, and his deputy, General Vernon Walters, both took the trouble to be present. Before the ceremony Mr. Colby chatted with Katya, Miko and me in his office. Katya, aged fifteen was very silent. After it was all over she asked me, "Is Mr. Colby a bad guy?"

This hurt. What did she think of me for having worked for him and been decorated by him? Et tu, Katya? A sign of the times—1975. She has never said anything like this to me again.

I feel no shame. Only pride.

A month before retirement I finally met Stalin's daughter at a party in Northern Virginia.

It is impossible to forget the excitement of that day in 1967 when Svetlana defected to the American Embassy in New Delhi. At first the American government would not let her into the United States. She spent three months in Switzerland. The Washington Post, in a editorial entitled, *Some Other Time, Svetlana*, had the audacity to state that the defection of that bloody-minded dictator's daughter was of little interest to anybody. Its own front pages belied that statement. When she finally arrived in New York, she gave a magnificent plane-side TV interview. When asked whether she wanted to become an American citizen, she compared America with a bridegroom she would have to get to know. Who could have forseen the separation and subsequent reunion?

Within a few months she was involved with my parents. Dissatisfied with the translation of her first book, *Twenty Letters to a Friend*, she accepted my father as the translator of her second book, *Only One Year*, on the recommendation of Edmund Wilson. She came to Wellfleet. My mother, always uneasy about Soviets, was particularly on edge at the thought of receiving the daughter of Stalin, of all people! Even Kerensky she refused to meet, and now Stalin's flesh and blood! But Svetlana was modest and charming and got on very well with my parents. Perhaps what put her over with my mother was this incident. My mother came back from shopping at the supermarket one day to find Stalin's daughter on hands and knees, scrubbing the kitchen floor. Then Stalin's daughter helped the scion of the Romanovs unload the groceries, and they discussed the inner recesses of the

Kremlin, which my mother remembered from one or two childhood visits.

Svetlana's relationship with Papa was very close. Later she told me that she had saved forty-eight letters he had written her. Obviously, problems of translation could have accounted for only a small part of their contents. Most of these were handled on the phone anyway. There was no doubt that Svetlana was deeply religious, but for the most part she did not adhere to the ritualized and organized church. My father felt the same way. Probably this was a topic they discussed. But strangely, since so much else had been saved, I never came across her letters to him after my parents' death. I did discover that Svetlana had been extraordinarily generous to my parents, who were always hard up for money. She sent them a monthly stipend, over and above what was due to my father as her translator.

I wrote her a letter thanking her for her generosity to them. She was then married to William Wesley Peters, an architect who was a member of a commune which divided its time between Wisconsin and Arizona. I congratulated her on her marriage and received something like this for an answer: "The marriage is fine, but the last thing I expected in the United States was to end up in a commune ruled by a dictator. But since I know a great deal about communes and dictators, I suppppose I shall survive."

The dictator in this case was the widow of Frank Lloyd Wright, and Peters' first mother-in-law. He had been married to their daughter, also called Svetlana. Later Svetlana told me about life in the commune. Everybody had to eat in a messhall and obey notices to perform various jobs, posted on the bulletin board. Very much like an army.

From Svetlana's union with Peters came a daughter, Olga, whom Svetlana brought up guarded from the Russian language or any knowledge of her interesting maternal lineage. By the time I met Svetlana she was divorced from Peters and I from Judy.

My CIA friends jokingly egged me on to marry Svetlana. Think of the forms I would have to fill out for the Office of Security! Name of future father-in-law—Joseph Stalin a/k/a Dzhugashvili. Occupation of same—General Secretary of the Communist Party of the Soviet Union, etc. That would really blow Security's collective mind! And what if we produced a child? Chavchavadze-Dzhugashvili-Stalin-Romanov, obviously a candidate for some sort of Ghenghis Khan role in history.

I already had acquired too much respect for Svetlana to think in these terms. She had the same rather beautiful face, crowned with reddish hair that I had admired on TV seven years before. But she was extremely shy and difficult to talk to the night we met. Her English was good, but I knew it would be easier talking Russian with her. Yet she insisted on English.

"Didn't you speak Russian with my parents?" I finally asked.

"Yes," she replied.

"Then why don't you speak it to me?"

After this we spoke Russian together. She started writing me many letters and invited me to visit her in Princeton. She even suggested that we write a book together called *Conversations*, colloquial and not boring, as she put it, to open

American eyes on what the Soviet Union was really like. The last thing she wanted, she said, was to get back into the limelight. She cared nothing for royalties, but because we had "so much in common" this could be a valuable project. It might have been. Ironically, I had started writing a book on General Vlasov, whom her father had had hanged on a meathook. This did not bother Svetlana. Indeed, she grew very close to a Russian priest who had been Vlasov's confessor in Germany during the war.

During the months that I saw her and corresponded with her, Svetlana never had a good word to say about Stalin. Her mother, she said, was the real heroine of *Twenty Letters to a Friend*, which the stupid American critics had not understood. Instead they thought she was defending her father by blaming everything on Beria.

I had always known that Stalin went into a deep depression, unable to function, for a couple of weeks after Hitler's attack in June 1941. Svetlana told me something that I think is significant—all this has been understated, she said. Her father did not recover from his deep funk and take comand until August 1941.

Once she wrote me, "I hate the Soviet regime more than do all your relatives put together, although they may not understand this."

Having retired and being forced to take frequent trips to Cape Cod to put things in order there, I was able to visit Svetlana in Princeton six times, beginning in July 1974, and ending about a year later.

Svetlana fascinated me—to spend hours talking to Stalin's daughter was obviously of supreme interest, but there was more, such as her own intelligence, and her attachment to my family. This was the time when so many giants of Soviet dissidence were pushed out or emigrated—Solzhenitsyn, Rastropovich, Maximov, Sinyavsky, and Svetlana rarely had a good word for any of them, and above all did not want to get involved with them. She dreamed of some far-off sanctuary where not even a newspaper could reach her, but this did not prevent her desk from being covered with emigré publications as well as American ones. Since I was fascinated by these new arrivals, and had met some of them, we argued on this point. I don't think it was the old syndrome of the defector always trying to run down newer ones. It was more complicated than that. She was a deeply troubled woman who could never find a comfortable place in life for herself.

Little Olga was a cute, dark-eyed girl with a very strong personality. Svetlana joked that she had "dictatorial" tendencies, "And you know where that comes from!"

With me, Svetlana, though speaking Russian, was stressing our mutual Georgian background. A fine couple of Georgians we were, she with one half at best, I with a quarter. Between the two of us we probably knew not more than 100 words of this isolated language of our paternal ancestors. Her father though had never eliminated his strong Georgian accent in Russian.

During my second visit to Princeton, Svetlana produced a guitar she had specially bought for the purpose and asked me to sing to her in Russian, but no Soviet songs please! She made me go on and on, almost exhausting my considerable repertoire in all the pre-revolutionary genres. Then she kissed my hand.

No woman had ever kissed my hand before, let alone Stalin's daughter. From some of the things she said that night, I felt that this was Djugashvili's daughter kissing the hand of a prince, at the same time apologizing for what her father and the others had done to us, and Russia.

Was this as sexual pass? All I can say is that several months later she did make an unmistakable pass, which I evaded as politely as I could. I really did respect her too much to toy with her, and any serious relationship of this sort was out of the question for me.

Our friendship continued for another few months. In May 1975 she invited my father's sister, Marina, to visit her in Princeton from England. I went there too. George Kennan and his wife also dined with us. The conversation covered a very broad range—ghosts, the lot of interpreters, Kennedy's assassination, and the mystery of Anna Anderson/Anastasia.

A couple of months later Svetlana broke relations with Aunt Marina over theological matters. Svetlana started a strange life of moving from Princeton to California and back, each time selling and buying houses. She quarreled with so many people who had been helpful to her, George Kennan, for instance, who had been a key figure in getting her started in the United States, and Isaac Don Levine and his wife Ruth, who had aided her in California. As she stated in her letter breaking relations with Aunt Marina, "I am intolerant!" In a letter to me, "It is not given to me to love my enemies." But what enemies? They were friends and well-wishers.

My turn came a year later after my first trip to the USSR. A friend of mine wrote Svetlana in Russian about a Soviet pilot who had defected to Iran. She did write the Shah, asking him not to turn the pilot back (he did anyway), but she answered my friend very coldly in English. His letter, at my request, had included regards from me.

"Please tell Prince Chavchavadze that I do not return his regards. By going to the Soviet Union he dishonored the great name he bears and betrayed his comrades-in-arms." She should have seen the enthusiasm my old comrades-in-arms, some of whom were green with envy.

This put-down seemed even more grotesque after Svetlana redefected. While shocked by the news, I was not entirely surprised. Her last interview in a British newspaper, equating the USSR and US as being both equally under military rule, was so far out of line with what she had said and written before that I decided this very intelligent and deeply sensitive woman was in a mental crisis. It seems that she also quarreled with her son and daughter in Moscow, whom she allegedly wanted to see so much.

By this time I was worried only about Olga, her 100% American daughter whom she had dragged to the USSR with very little warning. I was sure that this spunky girl would someday find her way back to her country. The question was, how long would it take.

Fortunately for Olga, Svetlana re-redefected and is back in the States. I sincerely hope this tortured soul may find peace somewhere!

PRINCESS MARIA CHAVCHAVADZE

PRINCESS CATHERINE CHAVCHAVADZE

AUTHOR, ALEXANDRA (SASHA)
In Winter Palace Square - St. Petersburg

ROBERT MITCHUM and AUTHOR

PAUL (Pusha) OKHOVSKY
(Author's stepson)

DAVID and EUGENIE CHAVCHAVADZE

CHAPTER XVII

It was exhilerating to be free, only fifty, and for the first time in my life having a steady income whether I worked or not. I took off for Europe, visiting Dordogne in the south of France where Mysh and Geoffrey were converting a XV Century hunting lodge into a most attractive residence; I rented a car and drove to Ile de Ré to visit my French relative, Niko Tchavtchavadze and his family—he naturally spelled his name in the French way; and then on to Brittany where my old friend from Porto Fino, Brooks Baekeland, and his charming new French wife, Sylvie, had converted an old farmhouse into an indescribably beautiful place. During my long walks there with Brooks I learned of the horror that had befallen Barbara and their son Tony. Then I flew to Ireland, to stay in a great house in which Azamat Guirey and his gorgeous wife Bo lived, just in time to celebrate his fiftieth birthday.

This self-indulgent castle-hopping had to stop. Back in Washington I was involved in a variety of activities over the next few years. My book on Soviet defections meant research in the National Archives and interviews with veterans; translations—free and for pay; lectures in various schools and colleges; teaching courses in Soviet realities in the George Washington University and George Mason College, and for the 4-H clubs; country surveys of terrorism potential for a private company; contract jobs for the CIA, involving lectures, training exercises, and interviews with people in Russian, but nothing operational—I deliberately wanted to stay away from that. I was also involved in a mail order business selling Russian books printed in Europe and the U.S., and occasionally I sang professionally at the Singers' Studio, owned by Bill Flanders.

Eventually the Singers' Studio closed, not because of my singing, I trust, but because of the high overhead of Georgetown.

In 1971 and 1972, during my house-sitting period, I began to see more and more of Yuri Olkhovsky and his wife Genia. We tended to go to the same parties, and I often spent the night at their house afterwards. Yuri, six years younger than I, had fled the Soviet Union with his family during World War II and had gone through all the "DP" experiences of that emigration. Now he was a professor at the George Washington Unviersity. Genia was none other than that little nineteen-year-old girl to whom I had once said, "Get lost, little girl!" when I was courting Judy so many years before.

By the spring of 1972 I had become a boarder at their house. Russians are strong on boarders, as I have had occasion to state before. The Olkhovskys had had them since they got married, and, indeed, when I moved in there was another one there. He was a young American with a Captain Ahab beard who had been a hopeless alcoholic until he converted to Islam and became an expert on Arabic calligraphy, so good that a few years later he was getting commissions from Arab countries to do the calligraphy that had largely been forgotten there. He had changed his name to Mohammed Zakariya. We called him Urbik.

There was also the Olkhovskys' twelve-year old son Pusha (Paul), very bright and eager to assimilate everything he could from this endless succession of "uncles." As time went by, he and I grew very close.

There were also two large dogs, a mutt called Mishka, the mailman's nemesis, and a very well-bred but stupid English setter officially called "Tref of Windom Hill." Tref used to hang out at a neighborhood bar, Maggie's Gold Posts, a favorite watering hole of the Washington Redskins, where under the name of Waldo he became a favorite mascot. He was given slops of beer at the bar and, once every evening, a bowl of it in the middle of the room to the cheers of the patrons. He became a hopeless alcoholic, red-eyed hangovers and all. On two occasions he hopped into meat trucks at the restaurant, once ending up in western Maryland, and the second time somewhere in Delaware, merrily eating his way. Eventually he disappeared, but not before he was immortalized in the Washington Post by Henry Mitchell in an article about our household.

By 1974 there was really something to write about. The Olkhovsky house became a center, perhaps the center, for the new wave of dissidents from the Soviet Union. We had parties for them, we had TV crews, we had press conferences, and we had them sleeping all over the house. Luckily Urbik had married and moved out, leaving an extra bed, but hardened by Soviet and sometimes GULAG traditions, they had no objection to sleeping on the floor.

We christened the house "Dissident Arms." I can still hear Genia's low, smoky, voice answering the phone, "Dissident Arms, no vacancies!" This pleased an American lady so much that she sent us a set of paper napkins inscribed Dissident Arms.

Poor Genia was at the stove all day. Very often they would make passes at her, as she showed them their quarters, and then, being rebuffed, they would wave her into the kitchen where she, according to them, belonged anyway. Even when invited to banquets later in the evening, they would demand supper before they left. I supplied the booze. Yuri produced the emigrés and made himself useful to them in his energetic way.

The most famous new arrival of all, Solzhenitsyn, did not stay at Dissident Arms when he came to Washington, and just as well too. This super-man, and I do not use the word sarcastically, was the bane of any hostess, because he could or would not ever adapt to the schedule of any house where he stayed.

We all went to hear him speak at a five-course banquet sponsored by the AFL-CIO. I still regard him with the greatest respect, though disagreeing with him at times, but at that time my adulation for him was endless. In this speech he pointed out that whereas President Ford had not received him, the marvelous thing was that the American laboring classes had. He had a good point there, except that he was addressing mink-coated labor union leaders' wives, and there were a few titters in the audience.

When Solzhenitsyn established himself in Vermont, he became totally inaccessible to anybody he did not want to see. At the same time, he was in a position to summon anybody he did wish to see.

When Vladimir Bukovsky stayed at Dissident Arms, having just been released from a Soviet jail, such a summons arrived for him. I tried to book him to the nearest airport, but could only get him as far as Boston. This was no real problem. Yuri got on the phone to some emigré in Boston, told him to pick Bukovsky up at the airport, drive him to Vermont and then return home. Yuri warned him not to expect so much as a cup of tea at the compound, even though it was the middle of winter. The emigré proudly carried out his mission and, Yuri told me, never did get inside the compound. Such, at that time, was the magic of Solzhenitsyn's name. Such people do not appear many times in a century. When they do, they can be forgiven for not wanting to waste time on amenities and small talk. Every minute must be directed at his many-sectioned novel covering the central event of the century, the Russian Revolution.

One Sunday early in 1975, Yuri Olkhovsky and I went to church, leaving Genia thanking God in her own way for a quiet Sunday—no dissidents to feed. After the service we were introduced to the great cellist and conductor-to-be, Slava Rostropovich, and his wife the opera singer Galina Vishnevskaya. Through Vladimir Tolstoy they knew that the newly emigrated, well-known writer, Vladimir Maximov, was driving from New York to Washington that very day, intending to stay with us. The Rostropoviches had not seen him since Moscow, and they had to see him without delay. It was my job to intercept him in Princeton, where he was having lunch with Stalin's daughter, to make sure that he would head straight for the Olkhovsky house and not stop to eat on the way.

Yuri and I headed home, counting heads on our fingers. The trouble was that it was not only Maximov. In addition, there was his wife, Tanya, George Bailey, now associated with Maximov, and his wife, Vladimir Tolstoy and wife, the three of us, and Vera Tolstoy, the great writer's granddaughter. Great God, a total of twelve! We had to break the news to Genia.

She took it surprisingly well, saying that she had some frozen Russian food for such emergencies.

"No," we said. "Rostropovich insists on *bliny*!

Genia shrieked. There was no way she could produce these Russian pancakes, eaten before the beginning of lent with gobs of melted butter, sour cream and various fish, in the five hours remaining. A solution was found. Vladimir Tolstoy had started all this, let him produce the *bliny* somehow. He did, because luckily the ladies at both churches were producing them that day for sale in large quantities.

Meanwhile I called Svetlana, whom I had seen at Princeton the day before. She was delighted to hear from me until she realized that I really wanted to speak to George Bailey. Then icicles dripped from her voice.

The result of this flap was a touching meeting of these two great free-thinking Russian men on our doorstep in northwest Washington, for the first time on foreign soil, and a wonderful dinner followed by singing. With his faultless ear, Rostropovich tuned my guitar, and I didn't want to touch the strings for weeks afterwards for fear the perfect tuning would be lost.

We saw quite a bit of Rostropovich. His charm and humor were overwhelming. We saw him back stage at the National Symphony, sending mothers of violinists into ecstasies with pidgin English phrases like, "Your son—my darling!" We watched him put his tiny dog Puksi on our piano to hammer out a few notes. "Puksi" sounds rather indecent in Russian child language, and it was meant to be indecent in adult langauge, an acronym for *put' k sotsializmu*, the road to socialism.

Galina Vishnevskaya was very beautiful and extremely outpsoken. One night she announced that everybody she knew in Moscow hated Russia.

A murmur arose from the table. "Galya, you mean they hate the Soviet regime," and so forth.

"No," she insisted. "They hate Russia. Of course they hate the Soviet regime, but they have given up all hope for the country itself. The Bolsheviks have ruined it to such an extent that they think there is no hope for it at all."

A very interesting statement from a former member of the high elite.

Vladimir Maximov, who stayed often at Dissident Arms, never made such a statement. Judging from his writings, in his infinite wanderings throughout the country, in the lowest life situations, he was always looking for—and finding—kindness and conscience.

Maximov was very moody, sometimes silent for hours, sometimes extremely amusing. His very pretty wife Tanya found Dissident Arms to be a real vacation and became a great friend of Genia's. When we visited them in Paris and saw her taking care of two little daughters in a small apartment as well as dishing up meals at all hours for their own version of Dissident Arms, we could understand why Washington had been a real rest for her.

Maximov had just started the quarterly magazine *Kontinent*, still published in several languages, and unusual in that it included writers from Eatern European countries and Soviet national minorities. Yuri and I sold subscriptions and mailed it out as part of our mail-order book business. Maximov appointed Yuri *Kontinent's* U.S. representative. I later translated several articles from the magazine, which were published in the all too rare American anthologies that came out. For some reason there was much more interest for this sort of thing in Europe.

While Maximov and other well-known dissidents were staying with us, Dissident Arms operated like a psychological warfare company. I would translate what they wrote. Yuri would reproduce it and see that it got to its destination—the press, AFL-CIO, Congress, or the White House. We even produced instant demonstrations, such as one in front of the Yugoslav Embassy to free the imprisoned Mikhailo Mikhailovich, a Yugolsav dissident of Russian parentage. There were twelve of us, walking in a circle, carrying signs in the pouring rain, with Yugoslavs taking our pictures out of the windows, I suppose. I never could have done these things if I had not retired from the CIA.

At about this time there appeared the famous bard from the USSR, Alexander Galich, who sang at Dissident Arms among other places. He said that at Dissident Arms he felt as much at home as in the Moscow apartments where he used to sing and be recorded for the underground *magnitizdat*. One of his songs was called, *When I Return*, and ended with, "if I return." Not long afterwards he met a tragic death in a freak electrical accident while trying to fix his radio in his Paris apartment. There were those who suspected KGB foul play. I have no way of knowing whether this was so, but my opinion of French electrical wiring is not very high. It could have been a normal accident.

Totally different from Maximov, the brooding man of literature, and from Rostropovich, the ever ebullient musician, was General Petro Grigorenko. This was a military man with a shaven skull, à la Yul Brynner, who came from Ukrainian peasant origins and had served in the Red Army loyally for many years. In 1945 he had commanded a Soviet division, but only with the rank of lieutenant colonel, a clue to the fact he must have been stepping on somebody's toes. He got his general's star after the war. But in this man there arose the conscience that Maximov was always looking for. It was so strong that he was willing to risk all to make his protests; and he lost all, materially speaking—broken to private and deprived of his pension. Furthermore, he championed the cause of the Crimean Tatars, with whom he had no ethnic connection. This Moslem people, the people of Hussein the Harax groom, had been thrown out of the Crimea by Stalin during World War II. Although under Khrushchev they were officially rehabilitated, to this day they have not been allowed back to their ancestral land.

When General Grigorenko arrived in the United States, he was quoted by the press as saying he was still a Communist, in theory. This intrigued me. So, when he appeared at Dissident Arms, I asked him one question each of the three times he was there.

"General, do you believe in God?"

"Absolutely!" Grigorenko replied.

"Can you be a Communist and believe in God?"

"Absolutely not," he answered.

"What do you think of Karl Marx?"

"I am probably the only person in the Soviet Union who has read *Das Kapital* all the way through, and not once but about six times (the full text is not available to the ordinary reader), and I don't think any man was ever born capable of understanding what Marx was talking about."

"What to you think of Lenin?" I asked. Here the general's eyes softened, and I could sense that he still had a positive feeling of sorts for Lenin.

"You know, by 1921 Lenin was totally disillusioned in the theory of Communism, which is why he introduced the New Economic Policy, a form of capitalism. Too bad he died so soon!"

While I had my doubts that Lenin had lost faith in the theory, it was obvious that this truly heroic general was no kind of a Communist.

Totally unlike any of the dissidents so far mentioned was Volodya Dremlyuga, the only real worker among those who managed to get out in those days. He appeared at Dissident Arms the day after Solzhenitsyn's speech to the AFL-CIO, accompanied by Alexander Dolgun, originally an American citizen who had served time in GULAG even though, or especially because, he had worked for the American Embassy. He later published a book on his experiences. As ex-Zeks—GULAG alumni—both had the access to their fellow alumnus Solzhenitsyn that we lacked.

Dremlyuga had been in and out of concentration camps for years. Between these incarcerations he had managed to get around every Soviet law designed to keep people in place. He had real street smarts, Soviet style. And what a raconteur!

He told us how he had gotten his revenge on a GULAG camp commander he hated. Somehow, by listening carefully around the orderly room of the camp, he had figured out the long-distance telephone code to Moscow. He bided his time until the office was empty then he went in to call all his friends in Moscow long-distance, courtesy of the MVD, talking as long as he could. His friends could not believe that he was calling from a GULAG camp. It took about six months for all the paper to come together, and then all hell broke loose. The camp commander and his deptuy were relieved from command, and Dremlyuga got some extension on his sentence for "hooliganism." For him it was worth it.

Dremlyuga wanted to see Stalin's daughter. I don't know whether he ever did, but she told me, "Why do I need Dremlyuga?" My thought was, everybody needs Dremlyuga, you especially. I last saw him at the University of Massachusetts, where Marusya happened to be a student.

By coincidence another recent arrival taught my second daughter Sasha at Middlebury, shortly after he came to the States. This was Anatoly Davydov, an extremely handsome blond young man who had assiduously studied Japanese in the USSR, knowing that sooner or later he would be sent to Japan. He was, and he defected there. His field was the movies, which explains why he turned up at the Dissident Arms such a very short time after his defection. He was of no interest to the intelligence community. The day he arrived coincided with one of my sessions at the Singers' Studio, so I took him along, and presented a *charochka* to him, explaining to the audiencce that this was a brand new arrival in the free world. Anatoly drank his *charochka* down, looking puzzled as all Soviets do, the custom having been lost there. I thought little of this until years later he told me how deeply touched he had been, and how that *charochka* had become the symbol of the beginning of his new life.

Davydov was one of those defectors who had thought it all out in advance and therefore was a successful case of resettlement. And yet, many years later he told me that it took well over ten years before he felt like a normal human being, meaning a normal resident of a normal country.

The appearance of Alexander Nekrich at dinner in Dissident arms was especially interesting to me. This was the historian who had written and published a book called *22 June 1941* in the Soviet Union. In it he showed how Stalin had received every possible warning of Hitler's attack from spies like Victor Sorge, from Roosevelt and Churchill, and even from a German sergeant who defected on the eve of the invasion and gave the exact moment it was to start. No, said Stalin to all of this. It's all a British provocation. Even after the German attack had started he refused to let some of the troops fire back. Implied, but not stated in the book, was that this vicious monster really had begun to trust the only other monster in his class, Hitler, ever since the deal they had made in 1939, and could not believe that Hitler would do this to him.

I remember my mother predicting intuitively that the two monsters would get together a year or two before it happened, much to the disgust of everybody present at that dinner in Truro.

Nekrich's book was attacked in the Soviet press and he was thrown out of the historians' association. Meanwhile, in Washington, I was translating the book, which was published by my old friend, Professor Vladimir Petrov. Although the publisher wanted the translator's name to appear, I refused because I did not want to add to Nekrich's troubles by having him accused of CIA contacts.

Another historian who appeared at Dissident Arms was Andrei Amalrik, accompanied by his extraordinarily beautiful and charming wife Gyusel, a Tatar from the Volga. Both of them, before their emigration, had had considerable publicity in the West as dissidents. Andrei had written a book about his exile to a collective farm in Siberia, and another entitled, *Will the Soviet Union Last until 1984?* The year, of course, should not be taken too literally, obviously being borrowed from Orwell. What bothered me, ten years before the 1984 deadline, was that all of the calamities Amalrik predicted would happen by that time, mostly at the hand of China, the least of all evils seemed to be the continuation of the Soviet regime in its present form.

I took Amalrik over to Averill Harriman's house in Georgetown, acting as interpreter for the talk they had. Amalrik did most of the talking, quite the right anti-Soviet stuff. Mr. Harriman, with every right at his advanced age, appeared to sleep through most of it, though he occasionally told us not to be fooled by his closed eyes. Amalrik thought the whole thing was a waste of time, as did I. Probably Harriman thought so too.

Amalrik, like Galich, was to meet sudden death not long afterwards in a traffic accident on a mountain road in Spain. Again there was speculation of KGB involvement, but I think this less likely than in Galich's case. A truck hit them head on. Fortunately, the lovely Gyusel survived.

It was amazing, or perhaps quite natural, how different these dissidents were from one another. Ernst Neizvestny, the Soviet Union's most famous sculptor, was not only warm but endlessly entertaining. Here was the man who had stood up to Khrushchev during the famous Moscow manège exhiibit of non-conformist art. This had been authorized to take place on the second floor of the old tsarist stables, and all the artists hoped that it was the beginning of freedom for them.

Khrushchev, far from sober, walked in with the sinister ideologist Suslov at his elbow, and already on the first floor, which contained conformist socialist-realist stuff, he was heard to yell, "It's all dog shit!"

Mounting the stairs to the second floor, he began accusing all the artists of being pederasts, anti-Soviets who would be crushed, etc. Ernst stood up to him and actually gained his respect. Nikita was a complex, many-sided character.

Ernst Neizvestny entertained us with imitations of the way the highest Soviet political elite talked, and even those who knew perfectly straight Russian adapted to this dialect. Brezhnev, for instance, pronounced "socialist countries"—*sotsialisticheskiye strany* as *sosisky sranye*, meaning "shitty sausages." A Freudian slip?

Ernst also had a most interesting theory of a layer-cake structure of the Soviet *nomenklatura*, which he called the "red" and the "green" layers. The greens at each level were the very intelligent advisers of the reds, but the greens had very little if any chance to advance to the red level, although they could be promoted to higher green levels. The reds always maintained ultimate control, and they were the ones who spoke the "shitty sausage" dialect. While undereducated and ignorant, they had the brains to know how to place the right people from their own mafia into key positions of power.

Following this scheme years later, I would say that my old acquaintance Gromyko was a green who had reached the top level for this color. Brezhnev and Chernenko were typical reds. And Gorbachev, while following a red career, is better educated and more sophisticated than his fellow reds of the preceding generation.

Ernst Neizvestny took my daughter Sasha, herself an aspiring artist, as an assistant in his New York studio, and I saw more of him with her on Cape Cod.

There were even some monarchists. This was an interesting phenomenon, because during world War II, even among all those ex-Soviets who hated the regime enough to fight against it with German arms, there were practically no monarchists. Now, a generation later, the monarchy had acquired an aura of glamour.

I did not count as a real monarchist a strange, hippy-dressed emigré who came to Dissident Arms, recited some pornographic poems he had written, and then, suddenly spotting a photograph of Emperor Nicholas II, covered it with kisses.

The first and most interesting monarchist I met was Yuri Gendler. Unlike most of the other dissidents who operated in the open, he had belonged to an underground, clandestine anti-Soviet organization with a very complicated name, which I will render here in short as "Social-Christian Union of the People." Naturally, somebody reported on them and they ended up in GULAG.

When I first met Gendler shortly after his emigration, he had no idea of my connection with the Romanovs. I asked him how he became a monarchist.

"It was because of Watergate," he told me.

"Watergate?"

"Yes. In those days that GULAG camp for politicals was probably the freest place in the USSR for frank conversation. We discussed Watergate and decided that it was terrible that the chief of state of a great country, the United States, could be exposed to this sort of thing."

Another example of the Russian thirst to admire the chief of state, I thought. In South America a KGB officer had been shocked when I used bad language to tell him what I thought of Hitler. In the USSR there was a retroactive cult of admiration for Stalin, who had at least been a world figure that one could respect, as opposed to the *muzhiks* Khrushchev and Brezhnev. I encouraged Gendler to go on.

"We decided that while in England it could have happened to the prime minister, the Queen would have remained in place, sacrosanct, a national symbol, a link with the traditions and the entire past of the country." He continued with one of the best arguments for constitutional monarchy I ever heard.

"Remember," he added, "that we are constitutional monarchists. Don't think of us as crazy right-wingers. You should have seen what happened on Hitler's birthday every year at that camp. Some prisoners actually produced leaflets and threw them around, praising Hitler!"

"So who is your candidate to the throne?" I asked.

"We all knew about Grand Duke Vladimir Kirillovich."

"How about electing a new dynasty? It is in the Russian tradition. The Godunovs and Romanovs were elected, after all."

"No, no! Those were other times. Now we need an intimate connection with the past, particularly with the years just before the revolution."

Yuri Gendler became a good friend, unfailingly amusing. It was not long before he acquired a Plymouth fury in New York and was inevitably nicknamed "Yuri the Fury."

Perhaps the most interesting dissident of all, who turned up in December 1976 after being traded for the leading Chilean Communist by the Pinochet regime, was Vladimir Bukovsky.

Young, handsome, and bright, dedicated to the cause and just released under the most dramatic circumstances, Bukovsky became an immediate object of publicity throughout the western world. He was a veteran not only of GULAG, but of those "special psychiatric hospitals" where the inmate is at the mercy of whatever drugs they choose to give him, does not know how long he is going to be there, and is deprived of even the small smidgeon of legal process available for politicals in the USSR.

Our small street filled up with competing TV trucks. When they got inside, it was amazing that they did not blow the wiring with their floodlights. Genia finally demanded reimbursement for the electricity and received it. Yuri also appeared on TV as a "dissident professor."

Bukovsky had taught himself English in prison, and could speak it quite well until something switched off in his mind, then he needed an interpreter. I translated for him at one press conference, a lot of private conversations, as well as doing written translations for him. He was received by Carter, Mondale, Humphrey and "Scoop" Jackson. To Carter's credit he did receive Bukovsky, whereas Ford had refused to see Solzhenitsyn.

Bukovsky also appeared on TV at a Senate committee. One senator, more erudite than the others, managed to ask the most stupid question. He had been reading Dosteyevsky's *House of the Dead*, he said, and hadn't it always been like that in Russia? Dostoyevsky in his book had described convict life in the period before the great reforms of Alexander II. It always amazes me how totally non-Communist Americans, like this senator, and my old division chief Jack Maury, seem to have a compulsion to absolve Communism and the Soviet regime from blame by equating them with what came before. Bukovsky did a magnificent job shooting down this senator.

He had told us that the first book he had read after getting out was Dostoyevsky's *House of the Dead*, and the life described therein, even in the bad old pre-reform days, struck him as almost life in a motel compared to what he had experienced under the Soviets in the 1970s—not even under Stalin, he was too young for that.

We had a reception for Bukovsky for people from Congress and the press, and we took part in fund-raising efforts. That magnificent lady and congresswoman, Millicent Fenwick, was a great help in all this. By coincidence, she had known George and Elizabeth Chavchavadze in the 1940s when they had lived in Bernardsville, part of her New Jersey district.

When we were *en famille*, Bukovsky sang convict songs, fortunately always with tunes simple enough for me to accompany with my guitar. After so few weeks of freedom, drink sometimes got to him and he would begin to talk like a Zek in barely understandable convict slang, laced with perfectly understandable "four letter" words, which in Russian are often two, three, or more letters, but rarely four. One night I objected to his language because Genia had come into the room.

"Come over here and I'll knock your block off!" he said.

It was like a movie. So I upped to him and he upped to me. I was not too sober myself and he was much younger. Just as I thought we were about to slug it out, he looked deep into my eyes and said, "No, I won't hit you. You are a good human being."

In the late 1970s the early dissidents were followed by tens of thousands of emigrés from the Soviet Union, mostly not active dissidents. Collectively they have all received the name "Third Wave." Most of them were Jewish. As the Soviet joke at the time had it, "A Jew is not a nationality but a means of transportation." I suppose most of those who really felt Jewish went to Israel. The ones who came here were practically indistinguishable from other Soviet citizens, except for their last names. Judaism had disappeared among them, and only a handful of old grandmothers remembered any Yiddish. All this was a disappointment to the American Jewish organizations who so generously helped them to get started in their new life. As time went on, it was their children, attending Jewish-American schools, who brought Judaic customs back into their families.

Most of them had emigrated because of the future of these children. In many cases they themselves had good jobs, but felt that the growing anti-Semitic policies of the Soviet government, officially known as anti-Zionism, would make it increasingly difficult for their children to get higher education and good positions.

Though most of them despised the regime, few had done anything overtly against it. They were people of Russian culture to whom the opportunity to emigrate had suddenly presented itself. Many who had disguised their Jewish backgrounds, or in some cases had none at all, discovered a convenient grandparent with a Germanic sounding name. Many fictitious marriages took place. Applying for emigration was a very risky thing to do. There were no guarantees that you would be allowed out, and in most cases you automatically lost your job. This created a large tragic group of "refuseniks," most of whom had to stay, with diminishing chances to get out as the Soviets reduced emigration to a trickle in the 1980s.

The fact that the Jews were being allowed out increased anti-Semitic feelings on the part of others. Why not us? One Jewish emigré told me that a neighbor of his had come to him as he was getting ready to leave and said, "You people brought us this lousy regime and now you are allowed out. What's fair about that?"

Shades of the old White Guards I had heard in my youth! Many blamed the Jews for the revolution. The emigré who told me this story surprised me by not being indignant at his neighbor's accusation. On the contrary, he began to list the early Bolsheviks who had been Jewish.

Another story that stuck in my mind also involved a neighbor of a family about to emigrate. This one was a retired Red Army colonel, covered with medals. He did not blame the Jews for anything. He said, "I shed my blood to defend this damned regime. I wish now that I had defected to Vlasov. How I envy you!" The very mention of General Vlasov—the quintessential traitor in Soviet propaganda, makes this story significant.

Most of this Third Wave of emigration were valued workers in the USSR. If there was any difference between them and the ethnic Russians, it was that they drank less and could be better depended on during working hours. Their emigration was something of a brain drain for the Soviet Union. In the United States most of them also became valued employees in spite of the language difficulties.

The emigrés who visited the Dissident Arms always commented on the Russianness of its ambiance—icons, samovars, engravings and books. So did the Soviets who came there. "You have the real Russia, we don't"

Yes, Soviets came too, although we never mixed them up with the emigrés. For awhile Genia was employed as an interpreter cruising around the country and Canada on buses with a group of Soviet ice-skaters. As usual with such groups, or any Soviets abroad, they were determined to save every bit of hard currency they received to buy stuff to take back, even if it meant semi-starving themselves. Often, they would enter a motel and blow out its electrical system by simultaneously plugging in their hot plates, on which they usually cooked cabbage. The blackouts and the smell of cabbage caused some motel owners to yell, "The Russians are coming!" and refuse to take the group a second time.

On a fine, warm day I sat naked to the waist on the front steps doing research on General Vlasov and his army, with 3 x 5 cards all over the place. Suddenly a bus appeared and stopped in front of the house. The street was not a bus route.

"Oh, no," I thought to myself, "she wouldn't!" But she had, and they all headed for the house.

What should I do? Put on my shirt or push the Vlasov cards and pictures out of the way? There was not time for both, so I opted for the latter. The first of the young skaters said, "I've never seen a naked prince before!"

I wonder how many clothed ones he had seen.

They tramped around the house, many of them making the, "You have the real Russia" remark, and soon departed. Later I acted as interpreter and took them through the FBI building and the White House. The very fact that tourist groups, including Soviets, were allowed through the equivalent of the KGB's Lubyanka and the residence of the Soviet leadership was enough to keep them in a state of amazement.

Then we entertained about ten of their administrative personnel at dinner. One of these, an obvious KGB nursemaid, backed me into a corner of the library for a private talk.

"I am glad to see that you, a descendant of the Romanovs, are not a degenerate!"

Since I had yet to see a degenerate Romanov, I looked at him questioningly.

"I mean," he added, "that I am proud of my ancestors, and they served yours for 300 years. It makes me happy that they did not serve degenerates."

At precisely 10:00 in the evening, as we were all having a great time at the dinner table, it was not my new friend but a woman who announced in firm tones, "Comrades, let's go!"

And they all went, meekly, obediently, though it was obvious all wanted to

285

stay.

I was still in correspondence with Stalin's daughter at the time, and I described these meetings with the skaters to her, hoping to amuse her.

In return came a very stern letter.

"Don't you realize," she wrote, "how you are lowering yourself? You are nothing but a museum exhibit, a fossil to these people!"

She had a point there, but I don't think looking at museum exhibits and live fossils ever hurt anybody. As for "lowering" myself, I had been doing it all my life by her definition, because I was always and still am eager to see and observe as many Soviets as possible.

Three times individual Soviets were brought to the house, all of them interested in recording my singing of pre-revolutionary and White Guard songs. As they departed with these cassettes, I wondered whether I would eventually appear in *magnitizdat* in the Soviet Union, where cassettes and tapes are re-recorded ad infinitum.

Once three Soviet journalists came to one of my concerts at the Singers' Studio. At the end of the concert the journalists, if that's what they really were, were very flattering and addressed me by title. In 1981 one of these journalists was brought to the house. He was a Georgian, Melor Sturua. The first name was not Georgian, but stood for the initials of "Marx, Engels, Lenin, October Revolution." It was a fascinating evening.

We argued politics in a very good-natured manner, Sturua taking the unusual tack that any sort of regime in Russia would act the same way, since Russia would have become the other superpower under any regime. the last part of the statement may be true, but not the first part.

As I argued this point, Sturua suddenly said, "All right, Prince Chavchavadze, Prince Romanov (sic), change places with me and tell me how you would run the country!"

I switched chairs with him, wondering if he thought he ran the country. He was certainly a member of the Mafia that does run it.

I stated that any Russian government truly interested in the welfare of its people could maintain superpower status and get on with the United States quite well. Whatever problems arose could be solved with good will. It was the Soviet regime that caused the trouble, with ambitions that went way beyond the interests of its population, in the name of an ideology that nobody believed in any more, which declared the United States to be the great Enemy No. 1. The people's standard of living paid for a bloated military establishment and aid to Marxist revolutionaries, all justified by false propaganda that the U.S. and NATO had intentions of attacking the Soviet Union.

Melor switched to the subject of Georgia. We were, after all, both Georgians.

"Surely you would not want to separate Georgia from Russia," he asked.

"The important thing," I replied, "is that Georgia's right to secede, as granted in all your constitutions, be respected. My ancestors, King Irakly II and Garsevan Chavchavadze, believed they were saving Georgia from the Persians and Turks by seeking Russian protection. If I were a citizen of Georgia, and Russia had a decent government, I might very well vote for continued association with Russia under some sort of real federal system."

For the first and only time, Melor Sturua lost his cool. It was the word "decent" that did it. By implication it meant that he was serving an indecent government, and that is exactly what I meant.

He simmered down, and we parted, it seemed, most cordially. I was sorry not to be able to argue with him again, but later on he was declared persona non grata and kicked out of the country.

PRINCESS ALEXANDRA CHAVCHAVADZE

CHAPTER XVIII

In 1976 I decided it was time to visit the country that had shaped my entire life. It was rather silly to teach university courses about the Soviet Union without ever having set foot in Russia, when many of my students had been there. Practically everybody I knew had been there, and now that I was retired from the CIA, there was nothing to stop me.

Well, not exactly nothing. I would have no diplomatic immunity, and something could happen, but it was in the middle of detente and I was willing to take the chance. Some of the old Whites were horrified.

Nina Bouroff, then close to ninety, blessed me with a gold cross she had bought for me, which I wore around my neck. She had been married to a general on the general staff, and she had typed his lectures. This military expertise led her to be elected the leader of a group of Cossacks fighting the Reds during the civil war. She was wounded in action, and left for dead. Imprisoned by the Soviets, she had finally made her way out. She rode horses in a Paris circus, became a psychiatrist, an artist, a gourmet cook and, after World War II, she prospected for uranium and painted icons for various churches. After the war she found out that in 1942, when the Germans reached the north Caucasus, the Cossacks were still singing a song about Nina, who had died for the White cause leading them in action. Nina Bouroff tried to dissuade me from going, but she knew it was hopeless. The pull was too strong.

I invited my daughter Sasha to go with me. After two summers at Middlebury, she spoke Russian very well. We booked an eight day trip to Moscow and Leningrad. I decided that the Soviets should have no feeling that I was somehow trying to sneak in, so I decided on what I think was a rather original ploy. I walked into the Soviet Consulate in Washington, and, speaking English, asked to see a consular officer. After some confusion a young man was produced. I asked to see him alone.

"Alone?" he asked. "We don't have any alone offices."

I insisted, and he led me into the kitchen, where we sat at a table.

I suddenly switched to Russian. "I want the following sent to Moscow. 'I am a retired CIA Soviet operations officer. . . .'"

I had to admire the young man's cool. At that point he did not know what he had. Possibly a walk-in!

"My name is Chavchavadze," I continued. "write it down."

He shook his head as if he didn't need to.

I explained that I had applied for a tourist trip to the USSR with my daughter, and I wanted the consulate to know that I was the Chavchavadze on whom the "organs" undoubtedly had extensive files. I had not come to beg for a visa, but I was going in with a clean heart, and if I received a visa, I expected the Soviets not to give us any trouble, provocation, or any other unpleasantness. I did not mention surveillance, knowing this to be hopeless, and I did not give a damn if they wanted to use up some of their goons' time following us around.

The young man took my passport and the information on our tour, disappeared for a while, and then came back to say, "I think it is all normal. You are no longer active."

Our visas arrived at the last minute, which is usual for these trips.

Our adventures started at Kennedy Airport in New York. We were flying Aeroflot, and our fellow passengers, almost all Soviets, were lined up with all the goodies they were taking home, ranging from TV sets to pedigreed dogs in cages. I heard about this phenonemon often enough, but had never see it before.

We took off, but a few minutes later came the voice of a stewardess over the loudspeaker, "Respected passengers, we are returning to New York." No explanation of any kind. I looked at the passengers. Their faces were blank. She might just as well have said, "The captain has just turned off the no smoking sign."

We returned to JFK, deplaned, and sat around for about four hours. Still no explanation. By strolling around and listening to the conversation of airline personnel in both languages, I knew there had been a bomb scare. Finally, we were taken to an airport motel and checked in for the night. This could have been done much earlier, but the Soviet passengers had no complaints, unlike the few Americans. Except for one. He had the nerve to complain to an Aeroflot girl about the long wait, and the lack of information. The rest of them looked at him as if he had done something indecent, really out of line. The Aeroflot girl cut him off with a short, rude phrase.

The next morning we took off successfully, reaching Moscow at about midnight. My feet touched Russian soil for the first time. My first impression—a dozen middle-aged women wearing kerchiefs, fussing around the plane. Inside the terminal—more middle-aged women mopping the floor. If a passenger or his baggage were in the way, they had to remove themselves. These women would allow nothing to impede their straight-line charges with their mops. My God, how Russian their faces looked! And what a thrill to hear that language as dominant, instead of a rare exception. I was too tired to feel much else. One thing was totally missing—fear. For the first time in my life, except for a few instances in east Germany, I was totally under "their" control! Yet I felt no fear.

The young border guard who checked our passports smiled at Sasha.

Our hotel was the Ukraina, one of the seven Stalinesque skyscrapers of Moscow. The elevators didn't work very well, and I was amused to see that there was a missing floor, as I knew there had been twenty years before. That's where all the tape recorders were. Otherwise, our quarters were quite satisfactory.

Taking a walk before breakfast, I realized that my ploy at the Soviet Consulate had left me free to spin like a top if I wanted to, to watch for surveillance. If we had any, it was very discreet, and for the most part unnecessary because of our tight Intourist schedule.

We were fortunate in being a part of a small group of about eight Americans, a bus all to ourselves, commanded by our guide Tamara, a most charming woman in her forties. Some of the other tourist groups were so large they spent most of their time getting in and out of busses.

First we were taken on a drive around Moscow.

"This is Dzerzhinsky Square," Tamara announced in English through her microphone. "Dzerzhinsky loved chidren, and that is why Soviet government has built biggest toy store in Soviet Union here."

On the other side of the square I saw KGB headquarters. For all his alleged love of children, "Iron Felix" Dzerzhinsky had founded that organization under the name of *Cheka*.

"That's Lubyanka, isn't it?" I asked Tamara's assistant in Russian.

"You seem to know a great deal," was that young woman's reply.

A little later Tamara announced, "Today is first meatless day. You may buy only fish." She made it sound like another accomplishment of the Soviet regime. This story used to amuse the new emigrés, who knew there was no fish available on those meatless Thursdays.

One of our fellow Americans discovered that the bus driver could speak English as well as Tamara.

"Why don't you become a guide like Tamara?" he asked.

"Are you crazy?" the driver replied. "I work an eight-hour day, and she has to take you to the theatre every night as well."

I knew quite a bit about the Kremlin, from my reading and seeing movies of it. My mother had rarely been there and only remembered some of the inside rooms in palaces we were not shown.

Babady had danced there after the coronation of 1896. Still, to see the place for myself was worth the trip to Moscow. There was the "Tsar Cannon," a huge piece of 17th century ordnance that had never been fired; the enormous Tsar Bell that had cracked before it ever rang; the Uspensky Cathedral where the coronations had taken place, and the Archangel Cathedral, where the old Muscovite tsars were buried, only the first four Romanovs among them. All of the Kremlin churches had been converted into museums, which did not prevent me from crossing myself as I walked in, and I noticed that a number of Soviet citizens did the same thing. Fortunat. ly, the Hall of Arms was open to view. It contained such interesting items as the double throne of the boy Tsars, Peter the Great, and his brother Ivan V, with a peep-hole through which their sister could whisper instructions to them. Catherine the Great's coach and her wedding dress were there, and the tiny Fabergé model train of Alexis, the last Tsarevich.

It was, however, the people of Moscow who interested me more than the sights. Only about ten percent of those I saw on the street looked like Russians. Moscow, of course, had visitors and residents from all over the country, and I discovered that I spoke better Russian than many of them. Then there was GUM, the great department store on Red Square, where endless lines of grim-faced people of every nationality stood waiting to buy something—and so many uniforms!

On the last day in Moscow I staged a little revolt. "Tamara," I said, "Sasha and I don't want to go to visit the agricultural exhibit. Sasha is an artist and we want to visit the Tretyakov Gallery, which is not on your itinerary. We'll find it for ourselves."

"Well, you know," said Tamara after a pause, "you might get lost. It's on the other side of the river. I will take you myself; my assistant can go with the bus."

Such personalized service!

So the three of us took all kinds of public transportation, fascinating in itself, and Tamara was a great guide for the gallery. She took a real liking to Sasha. I enjoyed all the famous paintings I had seen reproduced since childhood.

Then we flew with Tamara to Leningrad. Internal Aeroflot, I noticed, did not believe in changing its tires just because the tread was gone. At the Leningrad airport we bumped into a large group of American Jews who had been forbidden to go to Odessa, the real object of their trip. They were told to settle for Minsk. No explanations.

Leningrad was what I wanted to see. More than Moscow or the Georgia whose language I had lost, this was what was closest to me—St. Petersburg, the birthplace of both my parents, the city of my father's mother's family and the capital of my mother's ancestors, the Romanovs!

As the Intourist bus swung on to Nevsky Prospekt I spotted one of the great landmarks of the city—the needle-like spire of the admiralty building, for me a really thrilling sight. Then we crossed the Neva to our hotel, the newly built Leningrad, from which there was a breathtaking view of the city. On the surface it looked like the St. Petersburg which I knew from so many old pictures. I could not get enough of this view of what is indeed one of the most beautiful cities in the world.

Standing there, I thought of Peter the Great, who had caused this city to be erected on a swamp as a window to Europe, and I thought of the dynasty so closely linked to this magnificent place—the Romanovs. There was the Winter Palace, where the emperors had lived, and my grandparents had danced. Along the quai of the Neva stood palaces that had once belonged to my family, and closer, on the hotel's side of the river, was the Fortress of St. Peter and Paul, where my ancestors were buried, where they had imprisoned their opponents, and where, when the tables were turned, my mother's father had been shot in 1919. Still closer to us was the cruiser *Avrora* which had fired the signal shot for Lenin's putsch against Kerensky's government in 1917. Sasha grasped my hand, knowing there was no point in trying to say anything.

Later, when Sasha and I were actually wandering around the Fortress of Peter and Paul, I got into a conversation with a Soviet man who knew the place very well.

"My grandfather was shot here," I remarked.

"No executions were carried out here," he said.

"In 1919?"

"Well, that's different. Who was your grandfather?"

"Grand Duke George Mikhailovich."

"Oh, the famous historian."

"No, that was his brother, but they were both shot together."

"Well, they were in good company. Gumilev the poet was shot here too."

"Can you tell me exactly where?"

"Sure, the Alexei Bastion," he answered, pointing.

This was the bastion where Peter the Great had imprisoned his son. There was no time on our tight Intourist schedule to look for it. But I was able to say a

292

prayer at the grave of my great-grandfather Michael, buried among the emperors and grand dukes in the fortress cathedral, because he died in 1909 before all the shooting started.

Our next objective was to find the house where my father had spent a lot of his childhood, the house of his mother's father, Pavel Vladimirovich Rodzianko. All I had to go on was the old address, Furshtadskaya No. 10. The name of the street had been changed, so I sought out the oldest man I could find at the hotel.

"Are you an old Petersburger?" I asked.

"I certainly am," he answered proudly. Because of the wartime siege and postwar population movements, real Petersburgers were hard to find, numbering perhaps twenty-five percent of the population.

"Could you tell me what Furshtadskaya Ulitsa is now called?"

"You have come to the right man, that's my street! It is now called Ulitsa Petra Lavrova. What number are you looking for?"

"No. 10. I'm trying to find my great-grandfather's house."

"I know it well," he beamed. "That was once the house of Pavel Vladimirovich Rodzianko!"

I really felt that I had come home!

Sasha and I took the subway and found Ulitsa Petra Lavrova, née Furshtadskaya, without any trouble. No. 10 turned out to be right across the street from the American Consulate, where I had planned to go anyway to sign the book and give our location, in case anything happened to us, but the old building had been broken up into apartments and changed so thoroughly that it was impossible to imagine what it had been like in the days of Pavel Vladimirovich and Maria Pavlovna.

Our guide, Tamara, had a young assistant in Leningrad too, but she still stuck with us. When I objected to going to the Museum of Nationalities, when the Russian Museum was next door, she left the rest of the group to her assistant and took us on a personal tour of this old palace, the museum of which my grandfather had once been curator.

There were small periods of time to ourselves. One of these, forty minutes, I used to fulfill my promise to Genia to go on Lieutenant Schmidt's Bridge and spit from it into the Neva. I told Tamara this unlikely-sounding story, that I had a friend in Washington who was the grand-niece of the famous 1905 mutineer, naval lieutenant Schmidt. God knows what she thought of it, but I was playing it straight with the KGB. I told the same story to the driver we hired.

I spat once, but the wind on the Neva was strong, and Sasha yelled, "Daddy, you missed!" We couldn't get over to the lee side, but on the second try I made it. I also bent down and picked some pebbles off the bridge, as souveniers for Genia.

I trust the KGB wasted their time afterwards examining the bridge with a geiger counter, or something. So far the KGB had not made itself felt, except in the indirect form of the guides, but at the Hotel Leningrad, Sasha acquired a rather obvious KGB boyfriend.

Volodya looked like a handsome young U.S. Marine. He was dining all alone in one of Leningrad's best hotels, and he spoke English. He said he was a student at the Physical Culture Institute, telling Sasha that he had an apartment in town. "Shall we go?"

All this was so incredibly according to the book that I chuckled inwardly. I could imagine a KGB meeting after I had made my statement at the Soviet Consulate in Washington.

They probably agreed that I was doing nothing clandestine, but considered the possibility that my daughter might go to work for the CIA, or some other place interesting, and wanted an agent assessment of her at least, and if possible, to get her into bed! And so Volodya.

Sasha did not need any kind of briefing to feel his insincerity, and his ineptness. The next day, at a time when I was out of the room, Volodya turned up with three red flowers and handed them to Sasha. I really thought the KGB could have afforded more than three lousy flowers!

"Na!" he said. 'Here you are," and after a pause, "my apartment is still free. Shall we go?" Volodya got nowhere.

It was sad to return to Moscow, where we parted with Tamara at the airport. She had done her duty, and we knew she had, but Sasha and I were sad to part with her.

In addition to being deeply meaningful to me, my trip to the Soviet Union was important to my post-retirement work. I had not really learned anything new, not nearly as much as I had learned from emigrés and from research in preparing for the courses. I felt I knew vastly more about the country than I had when serving actively in the CIA, and I had known quite a bit then.

Retirement was never dull. All sorts of projects kept turning up. One of these was a sort of American *Samizdat*. An old and venerable member of the White Army, George Meyer, who frequently wrote for the New York Russian daily, *Novoye Russkoye Slovo*, offered his readers English translations of his articles. I did the translations for him, and much to our surprise, he got thirty answers the first week, and 300 the following. Almost all of these replies came from the overwhelmingly Jewish Third Wave, often enclosing small amounts of money and letters like, "You are an old White Guard, but you really have the Soviets' number. We have numerous American friends who are charming but totally ignorant about all this."

By the spring of 1978 it was obvious that the marriage of Genia and Yuri was finished. He asked her for a divorce—for the third time, but she was the last to know. First he told their son, Pusha, then me, and lastly Genia. A few months later Yuri changed his mind, got jealous of me, and I moved out. For a long time we had worked as a team through the exciting days of the newly arrived Soviet dissidents, and never a *méage à trois*, as some may have thought.

Luckily, just at this time I was hired by an anti-terrorist firm of CIA alumni to study terrorist potential against Americans in Canada, and later in Germany, Holland, Belgium and France. I talked to the police in these countries, Americans in the various chambers of commerce, and security officers in American embassies.

Meanwhile Genia was visiting old friends stationed in Vienna. After trotting about Berlin, Hamburg, Bonn and Frankfurt, I met her there. I had been there many times before, going back to the days of Soviet occupation, but never in time for *Grinzing*. We had a marvellous time, swilling down the new wine and singing Viennese songs, though we had no idea what would happen when we got back to Washington. The stay in Vienna was made wonderful by our hosts, Eric and Sidsel Anschutz of the U.S. Mission to the International Atomic Energy Agency, and the presence there of a Washington Viennese, Countess Gertrude D'Amécourt.

Through her we met Robert Mitchum and his wife Dorothy, who invited us to a movie set which was a time warp of World War II. The old slaughterhouse area of Vienna had been turned into a 1944 Normandie village. Led by Sherman tanks, most of the Austrian Army, dressed as American G.I.s, charged through the set. A second take had to be shot because one of the Austrians had cursed loudly in German when he dropped his rifle. "Keep your mouths shut, God damn it," yelled an Austrian officer. "You're supposed to be Americans!" Mitchum played the role of an American tank colonel. Curiously, this movie seems never to have been released. We never saw it advertised anywhere.

We had lots of drinks with the Mitchums at the old Bristol Hotel, once American occupation headquarters, and then Dorothy, Genia and I took a one-day trip to Hungary, getting our visas at the border.

It was Genia's first Communist country, and she thought it was terrible, but for me Budapest looked prosperous after the USSR.

I was surprised at the Hungarians' lack of cordiality, perhaps because of our lack of support in 1956, but most seemed too young to remember much of that. People in the street in the Soviet Union had been much nicer, but of course there was no language problem with them.

Genia and I took off for Yugoslavia by train, via Trieste, and by bus to Rijeka and Opatia, those places from which Babady and her children had had to flee from the Austrians in 1914. The Yugoslav border was a joke.

Then to Venice, Paris, where I finished up my terrorist study, and Portugal—Lisbon and Albufeire in the Algarve, where my first mother-in-law, Helen Husted, had offered us a house.

Back to Washington and grim reality while Genia and Yuri thrashed out their affairs. I stayed with our friend, Ruth Uhlmann. This difficult period was made easier by domestic trips under my CIA contract.

In February 1979, much to my surprise, Yuri called me up and asked me to move in with Genia, because he was leaving. I arrived just in time for the two of us to be snowed in by one of Washington's rare snowstorms.

Genia and I were married in June. Unlike my other marriages, my third, and, I trust, the last, was performed by an extremely tall judge, not a priest, at the house of our old friends Colt and Doda de Wolfe. My son Miko acted as best man. Genia's father and stepmother, Vladimir and Lilly de Smitt, were there, and the short ceremony was followed by a great party, numerous old friends participating. Even my old Berlin friend Scherbinine turned up from New York and spent our wedding night in the house with us. He had run the first Dissident Arms.

The most admirable character in this whole drama was my new stepson, Pusha, then eighteen, who showed remarkable strength in the break-up of his parents' marriage, and the scenes that accompanied it. Without ever losing his loyalty to his father, he remained very close to Genia and myself, and lived with us for several years after graduating from college.

A few months after our wedding, Yuri married a very pretty young woman in her twenties and they have had three children.

I made a second trip to Russia in 1977. This time I took my eldest daughter, Marusya. She had not studied Russian intensively, but had graduated from the University of Massachusetts and was spending that summer in Oxford, following in the footsteps of her grandmother, Helen Husted, who had been one of the first American women to attend that distinguished university.

While at Oxford, Marusya had the rare distinction of being cut by the queen. Very few people can make this claim. It happened because she wrote a letter to Prince Philip, the Duke of Edinburgh, explaining that she was the granddaughter of his first cousin, my mother. Much to her surprise, an answer came back with an invitation to a Buckingham Palace garden party, including a ticket to the sanctum-sanctorum, the royal tea tent. So Marusya assembled a suitable outfit-cum-floppy hat and took the tube to Buckingham Palace, her fellow passengers both amused and amazed at the sight. And, indeed, she was very well received by Prince Philip and his uncle, Lord Louis Mountbatten.

Meanwhile the poor queen was standing in the royal tea tent, being gracious to hundreds of people, probably bored and tired, and watching her husband and Lord Louis enjoying a spirited conversation with some pretty young woman.

At long last, Prince Philip brought Marusya over to introduce her to his wife.

"This girl is the granddaughter of one of my first cousins," he explained.

"Oh?" said the queen, "that's very distant indeed!"

Marusya was crushed, until I explained to her that the fact that the queen could relax and let her have it was in itself an admission of relationship, no matter how distant she may have thought it to be.

It was a short distance by air from Buckingham Palace to the Winter Palace in St. Petersburg/Leningrad, where there was no longer any monarch to welcome us or snub us. Marusya and I met in Helsinki and flew into Leningrad with Aeroflot. This time we were right in the center of town, in the Hotel Yevropeyskaya, just off the Nevsky Prospekt and very close to Apapa's old museum. Though still under Intourist, we were free to do what we liked—no groups, buses or guides. We could eat where we liked. One night for twenty-five dollars hard currency at the Sadko, we had a five-course meal with actual, sort-of, Russian music, and the next night for sixty kopeks in a stand-up cellar joint which served nothing but *pirozhki*. Interesting as this real peoples' place was, it was a false economy. Trotsky's revenge struck even my cast-iron stomach, the grease in which the food was cooked having probably not been changed since his day.

I kept the Intourist desk in the hotel informed as to our plans, to make it easier for the KGB. No point in annoying them.

"We want to go to Tsarskoye Selo today."

"It's called Pushkin now."

"Call it what you like. I just want to let you know."

"Well, you speak Russian as well as I do. Simply go to the Vyborg Station and buy a ticket."

I kept waiting for Marusya's "Volodya" to appear, but nothing happened in Leningrad.

It happened on the flight from Leningrad to Tbilisi. I was translating the stewardess' announcements to Marusya when a young man, seated in front of us, stood up and said in English, "You speak such good Russian!"

I had not spoken a word of Russian. This "Volodya" we will call "Ivan." He was head and shoulders above Sasha's Volodya in every way, even though his original approach lacked finesse. But one should not blame him for the "coincidence" of being seated so close to us on the plane. He was in his late twenties, personable, and a native of Leningrad. He said he was on one of his frequent visits to Tbilisi. Hotel space was hard to find, so he stayed with a friend. We made a date to meet him in the lobby of Tbilisi's most renowned hotel the following evening. These Volodyas and Ivans had the run of hotels from which ordinary Soviets are unceremoniously ejected by the doorman. Perhaps Tbilisi was different.

Tbilisi certainly was different. The thrill of being in a place where my name was not an unpronounceable jumble of letters but known and even adulated was wonderful. There was also an atmosphere of greater relaxation, if not greater freedom. Georgians did seem to enter hotels more freely, and there were Georgian restaurants in the upper stories of hotels which were well patronized but were not even listed for tourists.

The fabled Georgian hospitality, which I knew from tradition, was still totally operative. All I had to say, in the few Georgian words I knew, was that I was a Georgian from the U.S., and this was my daughter, and I was immediately asked my name. The effect was magical. Taxi drivers who had been griping about their low incomes refused to take a kopeck from me, restaurants refused to charge us. Even Intourist gave Marusya a free ticket to a show. In their minds descent from somebody was the same as being that person—twice my hand was kissed by women who learned that Alexander Chavchavadze was my ancestor.

Ivan showed up for our appointment, and we walked down a steep hill to a charming outdoor restaurant. Ivan seemed uncomfortable. He wanted to talk English, probably hoping the Georgians would take him for an American. People at the next table sent us bottles of wine, a normal thing to do in Georgia. There were almost no women, a fact which annoyed Marusya's feminist sensibilities.

After a while strange things began to happen. Ivan disappeared to another table, then returned to say that he would not see us again! Then a totally unknown person from that table presented me with a bottle of what I recognized as the best Georgian cognac, announcing that he would see us in Tsinandali. Then a man at another table threw an empty bottle over his shoulder which shattered on the stone floor. Suddenly uniformed militia stationed in the interior of the restaurant appeared and cleared that table. A waitress whispered to me that this crowd had been planning to kidnap Marusya and take her up into the mountains, not, as in the old days, over the pommel of their saddles, but in their Zhiguli cars.

"They are bad people," she said. What fun to make off with a princess over the hood of a Zhiguli!

At this point a young man in civilian clothes came up to us and said, in Georgian-accented Russian, "I will take you back to your hotel now."

"That's very kind of you," I replied, "but may I ask who you are?"

He flashed an MVD identification card—a cop. And he took us back to our hotel in a taxi. He really was a policeman too, because the next day, by sheer chance, I ran into him in the center of Tbilisi in a police junior sergeant's uniform.

So, assuming that the waitress's story was true, the Soviet Georgian police saved Marusya in the nick of time.

The next day we actually went to Tsinandali—not in a carriage, like Princess Anna Chavchavadze in that troubled summer of 1854, but in an Intourist limousine. The place was on limits to tourists because it contained the House-Museum of Alexander Chavchavadze, which was somewhat puzzling, since I knew the great house at Tsinandali had been burned eight years after his death!

We pulled out of Tbilisi, heading east toward Kakhetia. Marusya and I sat in the back seat. In front, next to the Georgian driver, sat a pretty but taciturn Georgian Intourist guide, who had shown us around Tbilisi the day before. Since she was the only non-volatile Georgian I had ever met; I concluded that she was afraid of me, having naturally been briefed on my CIA connection.

The driver chatted away in Georgian and succeeded in getting a laugh out of the guide. I asked to be let in on the joke. After some embarrassment she explained that Kakhetians were called "donkeys" by other Georgians. Georgians are very sectional minded in spite of their small country. So, as a Kakhetian of sorts, I asked her how to say, "I am a Kakhetian donkey," in Georgian.

"*Me Kakheli virre var*," she explained. I repeated it, and the driver laughed so hard he made the car swerve. This rather broke the ice.

As we drove through the grape-growing valley of Kakhetia, I looked at the mountain range to the north and thought how full of menace it must have seemed in 1854—the home of Shamil's warlike Moslems.

The Intourist car came to a fork on the road in a small village. I could have told the driver to take the left fork, but he wasn't sure and the guide asked directions. All I could catch in her Georgian was *Tsinandali-shi* (to Tsinandali). This was thrilling. Tsinandali was as familiar here as Falls Church would be to somebody in Arlington County, Virginia. Had I really live to see this day?

After a two hour drive we entered a driveway decorated with many flowers. The house had two stories but was not very large. It had a porch on two sides, with trellises built in rather oriental looking arches. It was definitely the same house photographed by my second wife Judy, in 1957, which my father had not recognized when I showed him the pictures without identification. He had even speculated that it was one of the Yusupov houses, or a place belonging to Grand Duke Alexander in the Crimea. But this was labeled the House-Museum of Alexander Chavchavadze. Well, whatever it was, there was no doubt that we were in Tsinandali. The chapel where Nina and Gribeyedov had been married was still standing on the grounds. In 1856, David Chavchavadze and his newly liberated wife Anna had built a long, rambling house, according to my father, which hardly described the short and non-rambling museum of today.

Having experienced the hospitality of the Georgians in Tbilisi, I thought that perhaps those in Tsinandali might revive for me the two-quart drill to which my father had been subjected. I had a toothbrush and razor with me in case we had to spend the night.

Perhaps my liver, at least, should be grateful to the KGB. They had obviously spread the word to the locals to treat us correctly and politely, but not to kill the fatted calf according to their Georgian instincts. Half the town was there to gape at us, but the officials never once asked me what I did in the United States. This was the give-away, because it was always one of the first questions that any Georgian we met by chance asked.

We entered the so-called House Museum, of which three or four rooms were on view. People stood around staring at us, and then a woman in her sixties and obviously Russian rather than Georgian timidly approached me and asked me if I was Paul's son.

"Yes," I said, and tears trickled down her cheeks. She told me that she had been a displaced person in an American camp in Germany, run by my father in World War II when he was a Red Cross field director in Patton's Third Army. Her late husband had been a Georgian, and they had settled in Tsinandali after repatriation. I wondered whether they had been forced to endure a typical period of Stalin's "prophylactic" exile, but I obviously could not enquire in public. And I remembered my father's story about a Georgian DP who tried to get an extra pair of underpants on the grounds that he and my father were the only Georgians in the camp. Perhaps this had been her husband. I was touched. The last thing I had expected was someone who knew my father.

I asked where the director was, and was told that he was out picking grapes. That was my last chance of solving the mystery of the house. There was no way the director could not have known about the burning of Alexander's real house in 1854.

I was allowed to sit at Alexander's desk, roped off from visitors. A great honor they said. Well, maybe it had belonged to his son David. There was a large portrait of Garsevan the ambassador in the oriental robes that Georgians then wore, and a family tree of the Chavchavadzes, ending with my father, George and Marina. This was a pleasant surprise, because an earlier visitor had told us that no emigré Chavchavadzes were mentioned. The biggest surprise was a photograph of my father, and copies of two of his books, and then I remembered my father telling me that he had received a letter in Georgian from the Chairman of State Farm Tsinandali, asking for family pictures. He had not sent mine, thinking that this was a KGB trick to get it. The letter had ended with, "We all hope you will someday visit *your* Tsinandali."

If there had been no revolution, my father would have inherited Tsinandali from his childless Uncle Maximilian, who had bought it back from the crown with his rich Moscow wife's money. I could not help feeling a proprietary interest.

We strolled in the beautiful park, leading down to a dry tributary of the Alazan, and looked at the remains of the chapel of the famous marriage. Sitting on a chair in the middle of the park was an obviously Slavic, non-Georgian old lady, like the ones who sit around in all Soviet museums, supplementing their pensions.

"You must be Russian," I said, delighted not to have to be ashamed for my lack of Georgian.

"Oh yes," she replied. "We have noses like this," making a concave gesture, and theirs are like this." Her finger described a nose which could have been Georgian, North Caucasian, Hittite, Jewish, Roman—anything but that up-turned Slavic nose of hers.

"How long have you lived here?"

"About thirty years. It's nice and warm here."

"Have you learned to speak Georgian?"

"Of course not!" she looked at me as if I were an idiot. "But I'll tell you that I worked for so many years in that house that they call me Princess Chavchavadze."

"Well, meet your relative," I said, and we embraced.

After this we met the officials of the State Farm and the wine factory. One of them was old enough to remember the last resident Chavchavadze, Uncle Maximilian. Many were from other parts of Georgia. They were all fascinated in my exact relationship to Alexander, since they did not know he had male descendants. They had not heard of the marriage of Marie and Zakhary.

We were shown how the wine was made and taken down to the old cellars, and then to a conference room where we tasted quite a few bottles of wine, but no food was brought and no lunch offered. Fascinated as they were in us, they were very reserved.

In the house-museum I signed the book in Russian, "This is the most memorable day of my life." An exaggeration, but not much. There was much to think about as our limousine returned to Tbilisi. There, Ivan got back in touch with us.

I had grown rather fond of him, even though I thought he was working for the KGB. We had lunch at one of those hotel upstairs Georgian restaurants.

"Ivan," I said, "it may not be the best thing for you to be hanging around with us. I told you on the plane that I am a retired diplomat, but that was not the whole truth."

"Well, what is the whole truth?"

"I am a retired CIA officer."

At this point Ivan practically had a heart attack. If it was an act, he pulled it off brilliantly. Gradually, he calmed down.

"I am a citizen of a free country," he said in English, "and I have the right to associate with whom I please."

He pretended to ignore my skeptical smile, but my confession did not prevent him from the next part of his scenario. He told me he had no place to sleep that night. His friend's apartment was full, and there was no hotel space for the likes of him. He would have to sleep at the railroad station.

"Come and sleep on the floor of our hotel room," I offered. "The floor woman is often not at her post. I'm sure we can sneak you in."

Ivan was delighted, and indeed, we got him into the room with no trouble. Within twenty minutes, however, the bugs in the room had done their work. He was thrown out with a big fuss.

Does this mean Ivan was clean? Probably not. The hotel was doing its job, and there is no reason to assume that its administration was privy to his operation.

In any case, we took him by taxi to the railroad station and, rather sadly, parted with him forever. The station did not look as if it had changed much since the day my father had parted from his father forever, so many years before.

On our last afternoon in Tbilisi, I felt tired by the emotion of it all—Georgia, Tsinandali, and all the strange events. I encouraged Marusya to take advantage of a free ticket she had been offered by Intourist to see the Georgian dancers, the same ones I had seen in Washington and South America. I relaxed in the lobby of the hotel, mulling over what had happened and what, if anything, would happen next. Obviously, as this second trip to the USSR was drawing to a close, the KGB did not find me worth an attractive woman from their aviary of *lastochki*.

However, a not very attractive middle-aged woman did appear, bearing gifts of Georgian books and records. She explained that she worked for a Georgian gentleman who knew a great deal of history and genealogy and would like to meet me. Right now.

"Would you mind telling me the name of the organization for which you work?" I asked.

"It is called the Society for Contact with Compatriots Abroad," she replied.

Here comes the KGB, I thought.

"Ah, yes, I know all about your organization. It publishes a paper called *The Voice of the Motherland*, trying to lure emigrés back to the USSR."

She was a little taken aback. "Oh, that's the Russian branch," she said, recovering her composure. "We are quite different here in Georgia."

It was stupid of me, but I went with her. My only excuse was this curious lack of fear that enveloped me both times in the Soviet Union, curiosity, and a conviction that they would not do anything to me in Georgia. If they had any such plans, it would happen in Moscow.

She took me in a taxi to an unmarked, new white building, led me through corridors with no signs on the doors and into another unidentified office. There, behind a desk, sat a typical Soviet bureaucrat with stainless steel teeth and a shaven skull. He spoke Russian with a heavy Georgian accent. I shall call him "Gogishvili."

Gogishvili, pacing the floor with me, showed a fairly deep knowledge of Georgian history, and the genealogy of my family, but he was in a hurry. After all, it was about 4:30 PM.

"We are such a small people," he began his pitch, "and every individual is important to us."

I remembered those exact words being used by furiously anti-Soviet Georgian emigrés.

"Do you have a son?" he asked.

"Yes."

"Well, send him to camp here. We will arrange the whole thing. He will learn his native language."

"His mother is American, and I don't think she would agree."

"So, your son is lost to us."

"Yes."

"Well, maybe you're not lost to us," he insisted. "Intourist is all right, but

301

next time we will settle you in with a Georgian family. But now we want you to be the cultural ambassador of the Georgian Republic to Washington. We will send you literature."

"But I can't read Georgian."

"That's all right. There are a lot of pretty pictures, and you can distribute it to all Georgians."

I thought of the ten or so Georgians in Washington, just about all working for the Voice of America, and again had a hard time keeping a straight face.

It was getting very close to five, and Gogishvili and his minions were obviously eager to go home, as was I.

"Sure," I replied, "if you want, send me all the literature you like. Here is my address." Gogishvili seemed very pleased.

He had obviously not done his homework and run a proper trace on me, or had just found out at the last minute that I was in Tbilisi and had decided to show a little initiative. Anyway, if anything happened from now on, I would scream to high heaven that I was the officially appointed Georgian cultural ambassador to Washington!

Gogishvili must have survived; although I never received any literature, I did receive a Christmas card from him, in Georgian, for the next two years.

Marusya and I left Tbilisi the next morning. At the airport a group of Georgians we had not met before, but who knew our last name, made a big touching fuss over us. As I wiped my tears off on the plane, I thought that this unique little nation of my paternal origins was made up of extraordinarily hospitable, volatile human beings.

We landed at Demidedovo Airport in southern Moscow and began to walk out to the street, not realizing that we were supposed to wait for an Intourist car to appear at plane-side.

The loud speaker said, "Citizen of the USA Chavchavadze, report to Intourist."

A group of Georgians standing near us almost went crazy. "Chavchavadze!" So even in Moscow we got a Georgian escort to the place we were supposed to be. This time we were assigned to the Hotel Intourist, very close to Red Square, and with Finnish-made elevators that worked. Then it began to snow. How delightful! How ridiculous it would have been to visit Russia twice without seeing snow!

The next day was Sunday, and we found a working Orthodox church and went. It was not a famous cathedral, but I found the experience very moving. Unlike emigré churches, where people often whisper to each other or go out for a smoke during the sermon, these worshippers were dead serious and the church was packed. There were a lot of young people among them, some of them dressed as hippies, on their knees giving the old Orthodox bow to the ground, rarely now seen in the West. The communion line was very long. Marusya got into it, but she and the others at the end of the line never reached the chalice. The priest had stopped offering communion. These people were actually risking something to go to church, particularly if they had Party membership or big career ideas.

My second departure from Sheremetyevo Airport turned out to be more complicated than the first. While still not feeling any fear, I realized that something could happen at this point, and I got a little worried when the border guard soldier checking passports held us up and called out, "Comrade Lieutenant!"

An officer appeared, but it seemed the soldier had merely run out of the forms he needed. We got through that stage and took our place at the island where our Aeroflot flight to East Berlin was about to board. Then we, and only we, were approached by a sergeant, who asked for our passports. He made three-digit numerical notations in them in pencil, and gave them back. After we were already seated in the plane, an officer walked through it, again checking passports, but this one was interested only in Soviets, waving our American passports aside. This was only the beginning of a day of border checks such as I have never seen in all my travels. We flew first to East Berlin.

This was the first time I had arrived in East Berlin from the East. At the airport we received temporary East German visas and boarded a bus headed for West Berlin. The bus was thoroughly checked by a Vopo, who made sure that our photographs matched our faces. It was not far to West Berlin.

The driver zigzagged through the concrete barriers between the two parts of the Wall with skill, and then we were at the American Sector. What a relief it was to see the old familiar West Berlin police board the bus! This check turned out to be more thorough than any of the previous ones. The West Berliners were looking for terrorists and narcotic smugglers. Two Turks were taken off the bus.

After this check, the East German bus took us to Reichskanzlerplatz in the British Sector, not far from the apartment of my old friends, George and Beate Bailey, with whom we were to stay. I did not realize how tense I had been until we saw their smiling faces.

The Baileys had not seen Marusya since she was a baby, and she had not been in Berlin since the age of almost three. The next day I took her to the house we had lived in. It was still occupied by an American family, and we were graciously allowed in. For me it was a sentimental visit, but Marusya, naturally enough, had no memories.

Marusya and I parted company at this point, and I met Genia in Munich, where we drank up the bottle of good Georgian cognac presented to me by that strange man in Tbilisi, sharing it with the Georgians who worked for Radio Liberty, some of them recent emigrés and defectors. Eat your heart out, Comrade Gogishvili, I thought. I hereby resign from your little army!

PRINCESS XENIA ANDREYEVNA

PRINCE NICHOLAS ROMANOV
PRINCESS VERA CONSTANTINOVNA

CHAPTER XIX

In August of 1983 there was a tremendous party at the Urbana, Maryland seat of the Stancioff family, to celebraate the eightieth birthday of their matriarch, "Aunt" Marian Stancioff. More than 200 people attended in black tie. We were all seated at innumerable tables in back of the Stanicoffs' pre-Civil War mansion, with the old Georgetown crowd in force.

I called Marian Stancioff "aunt" because she and my mother had been girlhood friends in London during World War I. She was then Marian Mitchell, a wealthy American girl of radical politics, which, of course, never turned off Mama unless one were specifically pro-Soviet. Marian became engaged to a young Bulgarian diplomat named Ivan Stancioff. His mother was French, and he was therefore a Catholic. Marian converted enthusiastically to Catholicism. The Stanicoffs were definitely the first family of Bulgaria, other than the royal family, which had no Bulgarian blood.

The status of the Stancioffs in Bulgaria cut no ice with my Greek-chauvinist grandmother. When she spotted Ivan Stancioff's name on my parents' wedding list, she made a scene and insisted that the "Bulgarian pig" be removed. He was, in spite of his native English and French.

Ivan and Marian produced four boys and three girls, all of whom were present; Ivan, however, had died. He had pursued his Bulgarian diplomatic career until the end of the monarchy in 1944, when the Stancioffs joined the rest of us emigrés.

I first met them in 1950, although I was vaguely aware of their existance before that, because when I was a child in the late 1920s, Mrs. Mitchell, Marian's mother, used to come around and bestow the still legal five dollar gold pieces on me. These were promptly confiscated by my parents.

The Stancioffs were famous for their hospitality. Lunch on Sunday for twenty people was routine. There were also frequent evening parties. When I first started going there I became good friends with "Uncle" Ivan Stancioff. He and I would sit up with drinks after everyone else had gone to bed. He would tell me about his ingloriously short career in the Bulgarian Army in World War I, on the Dobrudja front.

Thanks to the machinations of King "Foxy" Ferdinand, Bulgaria had been on the German side in that war. Commissioned just as it was ending, because of his languages, Ivan was attached to the Bulgarian commanding general, just in time to surrender to the British. So his first and last military action was to cross the lines under a white flag, boiling with shame. He never forgot the kindness of the British general who received this delegation. "Have some breakfast, dear boy!" he said to the Bulgarian lieutenant.

Later in London, Ivan attended some sort of affair wearing a striped tie. A

British brigadier came up to him and said, "Are you Tenth Hussars, young man?"

"No, Sir. Bulgarian howitzers."

The brigadier turned red in the face and went off to the hostess to complain, "That young man is pulling my leg!"

At one party of the Stancioffs' that I attended, the King of Bulgaria was present. King Simeon had actually been on the throne as a child after the death of his father, Boris III, during World War II. I presented the king with a Russian *charochka*. The Bulgarian kings called themselves "tsars," so the *charochka* was presented to "Tsar Simeon Borisovich," which made me feel I was back in Muscovite Russia. Has anyone else living presented a *charochka* to a tsar?

Simeon had been to an American school, and on one occasion he and the future King Constantine XII of Greece, who evidently did not share Amama's prejudice against "Bulgarian Pigs," had been stopped for speeding in Virginia. Constantine told the cop, "I am the Crown Prince of Greece, and this is the King of Bulgaria." Predictably, the policeman replied, "Yeah, and I am Napoleon Bonaparte. You'd better follow me to the station."

The King of Bulgaria was not able to attend the party for Aunt Marian, but his most attractive sister, Marie Louise was there. She is married to Bronislav Chrobok, a Canadian Pole, and lives in New Jersey.

The high point of the evening was when Aunt Marian's cake was brought to her, without candles. Then, in a procession which must have been rehearsed, two by two came her descendants, beginning with the young great-grandchildren, each one carrying a candle which he or she would put in the cake, saying, "I love you, Baba!" There were over forty of them, ending with her seven children. It was a truly moving scene.

The eldest Stancioff daughter, Anne, I had last seen as a girl about to be a bride in 1950 or 1951. Now she was a grandmother. Not that she had changed much. It made me realize the terrible, ceaseless pasage of the years.

In the Orwellian year of 1984, "time's winged chariot" deposited me into my sixties. How ridiculous! How obscene! How unfair! I felt fine; I could still put in a good day's work. But there was compensation. I was still a kid to a number of active people who were twenty, even thirty years older than I was.

On the other hand, so many were gone—Falkenried 9, our billet in the first Berlin, was wiped out; both Onoshko brothers, Duncan and his Klara, were dead. Sasha Sogolow, who had cleaned latrines in Camp Ritchie, received a lieutenant colonel's funeral at Arlington National Cemetery. How he would have loved it! A whole platoon of troops, firing squad, horses and caissons, taps.

Ilya Wolston, of Camp Ritchie, Alaska, Berlin and Washington, concluded a life of incredibly bad luck. Cursed with two uncles who had been convicted as Soviet spies, and always in bad health, his raison d'être for years had been his suit against a book in which he too had been listed as a Soviet agent, without the word "alleged" attached. The case made legal history as *Wolston v. Readers Digest*. It dragged on for years and poor Ilya never got the day in court that he so passionately desired to clear his name.

When one is sixty, it is depressing to read the obituaries and note the ages—but to hell with all that! My sixtieth birthday turned out to be a magnificent occasion.

My daughter Sasha, working for the Tolstoy Foundation in New York, organized the first fund-raising lunch at the Tolstoy Farm in Nyack, New York. It happened to fall on my birthday, May 20th.

The Tolstoy Foundation was founded by Leo Tolstoy's youngest daughter, Alexandra, before World War II. My father had worked there for a while in 1940. It had always done good work with Russian refugees, as well as those of other nationalities. By this time old Countess Tolstoy was dead and my cousin Teymuraz Bagration was in charge. The farm at Nyack was maintained as an old people's home, complete with an onion-domed Orthodox church.

We arrived there considerably hung over from a dinner the night before at a Caucasian restaurant in Manhattan, run by new emigrés. Actually, it had had to change its name to *Kavkazian*, the word "Caucasian" having racial overtones for some people in English. In addition to relatives and friends, some from Washington, one of the participants in this feast was Vakhtang Jordania, a Georgian orchestra conductor who had defected via Finland and Sweden a few months before, with a young violinist called Victoria Mullova. They had been handled in their first days in the U.S. by Sasha, for the Tolstoy Foundation.

The great tents put up at the farm were unnecessary on this beautiful day. The important thing was that I was surrounded by people who went back to my earliest childhood—my cousin Nancy Leeds Wynkoop, Ivan Obolensky, Nikita Romanov—and so many others from later periods of life that there is no point trying to name them all. I had never been much interested in celebrating my birthday, but what could have been better than this?

At a moment which seemed convenient, I picked up a guitar and sang two very traditional songs. Without any advance practice, the youthful choir came in perfectly on the choruses. So many dear faces surrounded me, it was the most magical moment of a perfect day, made even more magical when I was told that these two songs were broadcast to Russia over VOA!

* * *

To skip back in time for a moment, in 1981, the Russian Orthodox Church in Exile, with headquarters in New York, decided to beatify, or canonize all those who had been done to death by the Soviet regime whose names it could gather. These numbered into the tens of thousands. They were to be known as the "new martyrs," and they were led by the Imperial Family, not only the last emperor and his family, but all the other Romanovs who had been killed, including Apapa. They were all to be saints, their earthly sins forgiven automatically for having been martyred by the Bolsheviks.

I was uneasy about the whole idea. I thought it would hand the Soviets a propaganda opportunity, to ridicule the Romanovs and others. If ever done at all, I thought, it should occur on Russian soil after the eventual fall of the Soviet regime, not in the emigration.

By this time there were only two Romanovs in the U.S. who had been born before the revolution—Prince Vasily Alexandrovich[1] in San Francisco, and Princess Vera Constantinovna in New York. Aunt Vera, who was very religious, went along with the idea, but Uncle Vasily was very much against it, for reasons similar to my own. I knew my parents would have agreed with him. Yet, since the ceremony was to take place no matter what we thought, what harm was there in attending? How often is ones grandfather declared a saint?

I wanted to explain this to Uncle Vasily, whom I remembered from childhood when he and his wife were boarders, and from later times as having a wonderfully eccentric sense of humor.

I called him up, and he did not disappoint me. "*Schweinhund*," he said, answering the phone. This broke me up. Was he describing himself or the caller? We spoke for an hour, and I think he understood why I was going. There was another reason. I had been in correspondence with my cousin Nicholas Romanov who lived in Italy and whom I had never met. He asked me specially to come to New York that weekend so we could meet in person.

In order to explain the significance of this, I will have to delve into the position of the dynasty in regard to the succession to the throne, no matter how pointless it may seem. Who knows? It might yet acquire importance some day.

After the murders of Nicholas II, his son Alexis, and brother Michael, the descendents of the emperor's senior uncle, Grand Duke Vladimir Alexandrovich, became the senior line by primogeniture. His eldest son, Grand Duke Cyril, therefore became head of the family, and in 1924 Grand Duke Cyril issued a manifesto declaring himself Emperor of Russia, while residing in France.

This declaration was not received with universal applause. Some monarchists, and some members of the Romanov Family, including the Dowager Empress Marie, did not recognize that Cyril had a right to the throne, believing that he was barred from the succession by provisions of the Romanov succession law, known as the Pauline Law, enacted by Emperor Paul I, and still in effect at the fall of the monarchy.

The Pauline Law was not the only strike against Grand Duke Cyril. Many monarchists resented the fact that he was the only grand duke who, donning a red arm band, came over to the Provisional Government in March 1917, leading a detachment of marines before the abdication of Nicholas II. This broke a double oath to his Emperor, and was an act of treason.

By declaring himself Emperor, Cyril also violated a family agreement that nobody would do this while the Dowager Empress was alive. As "emperor" he handed out titles and military promotions, which rubbed a lot of people the wrong way. It was said that some of this was done for money, but I know of one case when it wasn't.

When Cyril announced his accession, a friend of my parents, in his cups, sent him a telegram congratulating "His Imperial Majesty," and signing it Ensign So-and-So. Back came a telegram from France, "We thank Admiral So-and-So for his loyal sentiments."

Cyril died in 1938, leaving a son, Prince Vladimir, to whom he had 'given'

---

1. Prince Vasily died at Woodside, California 24 June 1989.

the title of 'grand duke.' Born in 1917, Vladimir did not call himself "emperor," and did not give out titles—except for promoting the senior surviving Romanov prince, Gabriel Constantinovich, to grand duke. Vladimir, however, left no doubt that he considered himself the pretender to the throne.

For a long time nobody in the family worried much about this. But in 1948, Vladimir married Princess Leonida Bagration-Mukhransky, and they had only one child, a daughter called Maria, born in 1953.

Here is where Vladimir and the rest of the dynasty parted company seriously. Since under Pauline Law, Maria would lag behind all the males, Vladimir thought up a scheme that would disinherit all the surviving males. He announced that all of them had married morganatically, hence their children were out of the running, whereas he had married a royal princess of Georgia! So, their daughter was the only possible heiress to the throne.

There were two things seriously wrong with this scheme. First, it ignored Nicholas II's 1911 ukase under which princes and princesses of the imperial house, but not grand dukes and grand duchesses, were allowed to marry non-royal women of good family, including Russian subjects. All of them had done this. Secondly, Vladimir's own marriage to a Bagration-Mukhransky was in no way considered dynastically superior to the marriages of all the other Romanov males of the older generation. The Bagration-Mukhranskys, though descended from Georgian royalty, were not the Georgian royal family, which had died out. There was a telling precedent to this. The first marriage of an imperial princess to a Russian subject before the revolution was that of Princess Tatiana Constantinovna, to a Bagration-Mukhransky. The second was that of Irina Alexandrovna, to Prince Felix Yusupov. Both marriages were considered equally right, and proper. Both Princess Tatiana and Irene were required to "renounce their right to the throne for themselves and their descendents," by Nicholas II.

Vladimir's move turned all the rest of the Romanovs against him. Then his daughter, Maria, married a Hohenzollern, Prince Franz Wilhelm of Prussia. Vladimir created him a grand duke of Russia, giving him the name of Michael. This was also a highly questionable procedure, even had Vladimir been a reigning emperor, and was without precedent. Maria and the Prussian prince produced a son, George, who was called Grand Duke George Mikhailovich by Vladimir—by coincidence, Apapa's exact name. As far as Vladimir was concerned, this baby assured the succession. In the eyes of the rest of the family, the baby was simply Prince George of Prussia. In any case, the baby's father separated from Maria and resumed his "maiden" name of Prince of Prussia.

For those who know all this, who would be next in line today? By primogenture, the same Nicholas Romanov from Italy, who made a point of asking me to come to New York so we could meet. In his case there were no violations of Pauline Law. He is the son of Prince Roman and the grandson of Grand Duke Peter Nikolayevich, whose brother had been the Russian commander-in-chief at the start of World War I. The only problem with Prince Nicholas is that he has only three daughters, all of them Roman Catholic, having married a Florentine countess, which does not affect his own claim, but would raise the question of 'who' after him. This would be his brother Dmitry, who is childless. And then? Then the line of primogeniture switches to the descendants of Apapa's brother, Uncle Sandro—Grand Duke Alexander Mikhailovich, and his wife, Xenia, the eldest sister of Nicholas II. Four of their sons had male issue, and some of them have had male children in turn. The point is, there is no shortage of Romanov males in this, once the junior, branch of the dynasty, unlike the three senior branches.

Nicholas Romanov, whom I had come to New York to meet, turned out to be a handsome man of grand ducal height, two years older than myself, and just as intelligent and amusing as his letters had led me to expect. What a pity to meet so late in life!

The very solemn service of the canonization of the New Martyrs commenced in the early evening of October 31, 1981, at the cathedral on 93rd Street and Park Avenue, the old Baker mansion where as a child I had once attended a Christmas party and received the princely present of a radio. The service was led by the metropolitan and fourteen ancient, gray-bearded bishops from all over the world, except the Soviet Union.

The cathedral was jammed with worshippers. Genia and I, who lack the self-discipline to stand through a normal two-hour Orthodox liturgy, knew that we could not make it for six hours. Hence we were at the back of the cathedral, making no effort to join my relatives, including Vladimir, at the front.

On our knees we heard the names of the emperor and his murdered family intoned, and all the others, including Apapa. This was a moving moment.

Then I suddenly realized that they had left one name out—Apapa's brother, Grand Duke Nicholas Mikhailovich, shot with him—Uncle Bimbo, as he was known in the family. Why?

The next day I made inquiries from the clergy. Well, they said, Uncle Bimbo had been a socialist, a Mason, and probably an atheist. My mother had always said he was a socialist. It was news to me that he had been a Mason, and how did they know that he was an atheist? And so what? The church's own rules stated that the fact of martyrdom at the hands of the Bolsheviks wiped out earthly sins. I thought this was frightfully unfair to Uncle Bimbo, an eminent historian, and probably the most intellectual member of the dynasty.

The service resumed in the morning; all night the names of the New Martyrs in their thousands had been chanted. The service finished at noon, to allow people to attend the banquet at the Hilton, called by the monastic name *trapeza*.

I had hoped to meet Vladimir, to see for myself what he was like, but he had demanded to sit with the bishops on a raised dais, and the bishops, this time making some sense, had refused because it would have been a total endorsement of him as the pretender. There was a table for the Romanovs and their relatives, centrally located at the foot of the bishops' dais, but Vladimir refused to sit there and boycotted the trapeza entirely.

There were only seven of us at the table—Prince Nicholas, Princess Vera, Prince Nikita Romanov, a year older then myself whom I had known since toddler days near Windsor Castle; and on the distaff side, two Georgians—Prince Teymouraz Bagration-Mukhransky, Princess Vera's nephew, and chairman of the Tolstoy foundation, and myself with our wives Irina and Genia.

The fourteen ancient bishops' faces, bearded and icon-like, stared down at us severely. I wondered how many volumes these lives of secular and spiritual experience would fill.

So ended the canonization of the New Martyrs. A huge icon had been painted for the occasion, now available in postcard size. The members of the Imperial Family were clearly recognizable, including Apapa.

I turned out to be wrong about my main misgiving. The Soviets passed over the whole affair in silence. No propaganda. It was not because they thought it unimportant. It was better for them not to publicize the murders. The church received many enthusiastic letters from believing Christians in the USSR, and those icons became a hot item, proving that monarchist sentiments are not entirely gone even in the USSR.

PRINCE MICHAEL CHAVCHAVADZE
("Miko") Author's son

EPILOGUE

The cause to which I have devoted what talents I possess has not done very well—at first glance. Soviet influence, bases, advisers, and arms have spread to areas undreamed of forty years ago. On the other hand the rot at the core of the Soviet system—economic, moral and ideological, has never been so evident. It has existed for a long time and has led to victories for us in the spy world, not as well publicized as our defeats. The fact that the cream of Soviet literature, art and music fled to the West in the Brezhnev years should not be forgotten. The official ideology is dead within the country, or close to it.

Organizations working for the overthrow of Communism exist today throughout the Soviet satellites from Bulgaria to East Germany to Poland. Even within the Soviet Union itself, movements are underway to at least modify the regime, and in some instances to overthrow it. The legal government bodies of Estonia and Latvia recently enacted legislation which if permitted, would ultimately mean their separation from the USSR. Rebellion has broken out in Armenia, requiring the use of Soviet troops to put it down; and in my Georgia, there exist organizations which have staged riots and demonstrations calling for independence, also bloodily suppressed. In Russian cities the national tricolor flag is seen frequently, waved by crowds.

And what of the Romanovs?

Monarchies long lost on the dustbins of history have been restored in the past, and sentiment for the lost dynasty is not dead, even within the Soviet Union. One recently formed "new political party" within the USSR included among its member groups "monarchists." For me, though, the form of government is of secondary importance. Russia must be free, for its own sake and that of the world.

In 1983, before the era of Gorbachev, an open letter arrived from the Soviet Union addressed to whatever "White Guards" were still left alive. It was addressed to my parents' generation, to those then teenagers who fought with Kolchak, Yudenich, Denikin and Wrangel. To some extent I have tried to carry on their battle, and this letter, no matter how few it may have represented, was remarkable in that it was written at all.

This young man's letter is, perhaps, the best way to close this story—the story of Imperial Russia, exile, emigration, and the continuing struggle—which is also my life—the life of a Russian Prince in exile, who spent twenty-five years in the CIA working to the best of my ability against the Bolsheviks who destroyed Russia and my family.

"Open letter to the participants of the White movement.

313

I am not sure this letter will reach you in time. Less and less of you are still alive. But I am sending it, maybe against common sense, in the hope somebody is left to read it.

I am twenty-two and I live in Moscow, where I was born. Like all my contemporaries, I heard from childhood about how the heroic Red Army smashed the White Guards and gave the people freedom. Like everyone else I believed this. That's the way they educate us here, on the heroism of the Reds and the baseness of the Whites.

However, recently strange things are happening in the world. Among my friends the usual values have shifted. In our conversations, in the songs we sing, it is not the Reds who look like heroes. Our hearts and sympathies are on the side of the Whites.

The Red Army guaranteed freedom, but where is it? (Not the Army, of course, it's there, but freedom!)

Those of us who have not become hopeless drunks are beginning to think deeply. You read the papers: everything is great—happiness, equality, enthusiasm, freedom. You look around you, and it's all different: drunkenness, unfairness, lies, and slavery. Of course, few of us are ready to state this out loud, and it is hard sometimes to admit it to ourselves. But, if only subconsciously, almost everybody thinks this way.

Even our parents' generation has turned the hero of the civil war, the Red division commander Vasily Ivanovich Chapayev, into a joke—the hero of dirty jokes. There it is, the judgement of the people.

And for us, the officers of the White Army have increasingly become an example of honor. Of course, we know very little about you. The books of M. Bulgakov are very hard to get. The newspapers of those years are not available in libraries. History text books, without a doubt, lie. But in spite of this lack of information, or thanks to it, a romantic picture of the White officer has formed in the folklore of city youth—a man who, knowing that he is doomed, meets death manfully for the right cause.

You would probably have a hard time imagining such a scene: the 80s of the Twentieth Century. Evening. A crowded Moscow apartment. A group of young people. Somebody picks up a guitar and sings quietly. The rest sing with him. It might be a new underground song, or even a legally permitted song from an old movie, but understood in a new way.

> 'We don't have enough men to fill our ranks,
> And the last autumn is embroidering crosses on
> The worn gold of our shoulder boards.'

And each of us in his thoughts sees himself in the place of this officer and is lost in thought. Your ranks and names sound exciting and sublime. Here are the heroes of a new song, one of the most popular ones now at our parties:

> 'Don't lose heart, Lieutenant Golitsin,
> Cornet Obolensky, pour us some wine.'

We even have a new fad: to sign our names in the old orthography.

I decided to write this letter because maybe, in the sunset of your days, you will be pleased to know that YOU ARE NOT FORGOTTEN, that the long decades of Soviet propaganda have not been able to strike you from the people's memory, that the youth of Russia see you as knights without fear and reproach and thinks that you did not fight in vain.

We are the grandsons of Red Army men and commissars (personally, I am the great-grandson of a Red regimental commander). Looking around us and thinking, we are beginning to realize with horror the abyss into which the Bolsheviks have led the people. Looking back into a time that is misty for us and full of lies, we come to the following conclusion:

Time, history, and possibly the majority of the Russian people were on the side of the Communists.

Truth, honor, and Russia were on your side.

We are sorry that you did not win. We don't reproach you. You probably did everything you could. We thank you for that!

If you believe in God, pray for us."

# # #

INDEX